WHAT IF CHINA DOESN'T DEMOCRATIZE?

Asia
and
the
Pacific

WHAT IF CHINA DOESN'T DEMOCRATIZE?

IMPLICATIONS FOR WAR AND PEACE

EDWARD FRIEDMAN

AND

BARRETT L. MCCORMICK

EDITORS

AN EAST GATE BOOK

M.E. Sharpe

Armonk, New York
London, England

An East Gate Book

Library of Congress Cataloging-in-Publication Data

What if China doesn't democratize : implications for war and peace / edited by Edward
Friedman and Barrett L. McCormick.
    p. cm. — (Asia and the Pacific)
"An East gate book."
Includes bibliographical references and index.
ISBN 0-7656-0567-8 (cloth : alk. paper) — ISBN 0-7656-0568-6 (pbk. : alk. paper)
    1. Democratization—China. 2. China—Politics and government—1976- 3. China—
Foreign relations—1976- I. Friedman, Edward, 1937- II. McCormick, Barrett L.
III. Asia and the Pacific (Armonk, N.Y.)

JQ1516 . W47 2000
320.951—dc21
                                              00-020162

Printed in the United States of America

The paper used in this publication meets the minimum requirements of
American National Standard for Information Sciences
Permanence of Paper for Printed Library Materials,
ANSI Z 39.48-1984.

BM (c) 10   9   8   7   6   5   4   3   2   1
BM (p) 10   9   8   7   6   5   4   3   2   1

For
Leslie Spencer-Herrera
and
Susan Stanford Friedman

Contents

Preface
    Andrew J. Nathan   ix

Introduction
    Barrett L. McCormick   3

Part I: Whither China?

Section One: Little to Worry About

1. "We are Patriots First and Democrats Second":
    The Rise of Chinese Nationalism in the 1990s
        Suisheng Zhao   21

2. Democratization and China's Nation Building
        Jianwei Wang   49

3. China's Evolution Toward Soft Authoritarianism
        Minxin Pei   74

Section Two: Much to Worry About

4. Preventing War Between China and Japan
        Edward Friedman   99

5. Human Rights in China's International Relations
        Samuel S. Kim   129

6. China and Its Neighbors
   June Teufel Dreyer   163

Part II: A Democratic Peace?

7. China's Democratization: What Difference
   Would It Make for U.S.–China Relations?
   David Bachman   195

8. Immanuel Kant's Relevance to an Enduring
   Asia-Pacific Peace
   Edward Friedman   224

Part III: Concluding Overviews

9. Caution: Rough Road Ahead
   Harvey Nelsen   259

10. Aggressive Engagement, Not Containment:
    Political Repression's Role in Sino-American Relations
    Su Shaozhi and Michael J. Sullivan   284

11. U.S.-PRC Relations and the "Democratic Peace"
    Barrett L. McCormick   305

Conclusion: Points of Agreement and Disagreement
   and Thoughts on U.S.–China Relations
   Barrett L. McCormick   329

Editors and Contributors   343

Index   347

Preface

Andrew J. Nathan

If debate over major national issues is a good thing, then this has been a good couple of years for U.S.-China policy. In 1997, while the Clinton administration was struggling to define a way of dealing with China that could command broad public support, Richard Bernstein and Ross H. Munro energized the debate with their book *The Coming Conflict with China*. This became the classic statement of "China threat" theory and elicited several responses, now including this volume.

The context of the debate was the public's distaste for business as usual with China after the Tiananmen Incident of 1989. The Beijing massacre of June 3-4 destroyed the favorable image Deng Xiaoping's regime enjoyed among the American people and raised the question whether virtually any form of normal state-to-state relations with China might help nurture an enemy instead of a friend. China's economy continued to flourish, especially after Deng's "southern tour" of 1992 accelerated the open-door policies seeking foreign investment and foreign markets.

Worry grew around the edges of post–Cold War American triumphalism that the "rise of China" meant trouble for the American-centered world order in the twenty-first century. The Bernstein and Munro volume envisioned U.S.-China conflict possibly breaking out over Taiwan, or a Chinese challenge to the American-guaranteed stability of the region surrounding the South China Sea. Some contributors to the present volume see special danger in a possible conflict between China and

Japan. My own 1997 book coauthored with Robert S. Ross, *The Great Wall and the Empty Fortress: China's Search for Security,* suggested that the vulnerability of China's geopolitical position and its limited military and political means would prevent China from threatening American interests in the foreseeable future, unless the two sides pushed one another into hostile postures by unwise policies.

The issue has usually been construed as whether the United States should "engage with" China or "contain" it. The contributors to the present symposium offer a more complicated sense of the alternatives. Two premises underlie their approach. First, the future is not foreordained by mechanistic forces of history, but is open to be made by Americans and Chinese—and by Japanese and others—for this volume sees a greater role for Japan in the regional security equation than many others do. And second, foreign policy is not just a matter of national interests which objectively clash or overlap, or of a chessboard of global strategies which can be clever or flawed. Rather, peace and war are also the outcome of political processes within nations, which determine both how national interests are defined (and hence, what they actually are) and by what means they are to be pursued.

Thus arises the question asked by this volume: what if China does not democratize? Much American thinking assumes that if Chinese authoritarianism persists it will produce policies antagonistic to American interests, but that a democratically transformed China will think more like we do, and will adopt a relatively congenial foreign policy. This rationale underlies many of the efforts to establish closer relations with China: by engaging China, the argument goes, we can change it, and by making it more democratic we can reduce its disruptive potential.

Not only policy is at stake, but also one of the treasured theories of contemporary political science, that of the "democratic peace." Proceeding from an essay by Immanuel Kant, this theory argues that democracies do not go to war with one another. The argument suggests that democratic mainlanders would not use force to gain control over their compatriots in Taiwan, which would remove the major concern of those who fear a China threat. In addition, a democratic China would cease to impose its will by force on Tibet, although it would be unlikely to grant independence; would negotiate settlements with rival territorial claimants in the South China Sea instead of arming itself for a future conflict there; would adopt human rights policies acceptable to the United States; would more readily accommodate U.S. concerns about proliferation of weapons of mass destruction; and would join more actively with other nations to control environmental pollution, drug trafficking, and other so-called global concerns. Anti-Japanese sentiment might continue, but a free press, an open legislature, and political parties competing for the vote would not allow the kind of hysteria that could lead to war.

The distinguished group of contributors to this book express skepticism about this argument. Their skepticism is founded not on reluctance to accept the importance of domestic determinants of foreign policy—indeed, this is one of the few volumes that takes that linkage seriously—but rather on unusually careful thinking about the possible shape of a future democratic China. Many authors discuss the scenarios by which a democratic transition might occur in China and the diverse versions of democracy which might result. In most forms of Chinese democracy, they find, government is likely to be weak and nationalism strong. The product of this combination is not necessarily going to be a less assertive foreign policy. As the steps of the argument unfold we are offered a comprehensive, authoritative briefing on the latest trends in Chinese thinking about China's place in history and in the world.

Not only might a democratic China driven by nationalism insist on all its territorial prerogatives even more firmly than does the present regime—which pursues its ambitions with considerable discipline and long-term tactical restraint—but it might resent the very American prodding from the sidelines that helped loosen up the authoritarian regime in the first place. And there is danger that a democratic system would not alleviate but exacerbate the anti-Japanese passions that the present regime suppresses. In the view of some of the contributors, there may be more to fear in the long run, even for Americans, from the dangers of Japan-China confrontation than from problems directly between the United States and China.

The present volume agrees with Bernstein and Munro and with Nathan and Ross in arguing that conflict over the rise of China is not inevitable. But it offers a different emphasis on how to avoid it. Bernstein and Munro stress preparedness by the United States for containment in case that should become necessary; Nathan and Ross argue for accommodating China's legitimate security needs. The contributors to the present volume look to the leaders on all sides, and especially within China, for the wisdom to avoid conflict. If nationalism is the driving force of Chinese behavior in the world, the prospects for managing this force constructively depend mostly on the wisdom of Chinese leaders and opinion makers. One hopes that they too—as the rest of us should—will pay attention to this book.

WHAT IF CHINA DOESN'T DEMOCRATIZE?

Introduction

Barrett L. McCormick

This book grew out of the editors' related concerns over the growing animosity between the People's Republic of China (PRC) and the United States and the limited prospects for democracy in the PRC. In 1997, when we organized the conference that led to this book, we were concerned about the increasingly nationalistic tone of Chinese foreign policy and popular culture and equally concerned by Americans arguing that the United States and China were inevitably headed toward conflict. Nationalist Chinese books such as *The China That Can Say No* were matched by American books like *The Coming Conflict With China*.[1] Similarly, we were concerned by both the slow pace of political reform in China and by American writers who argued that China is incapable of democracy. In 1997 it was already long clear that the suppression of political dissent following the 1989 demonstrations "worked," at least in the sense that the authorities restored the semblance of stability. But we do not believe that this substantiates Samuel Huntington's argument that democracy is only relevant to Western values.[2]

As this book goes to press, the situation has deteriorated. Chinese nationalism is more intense and Americans are more prone to perceive China as a threat. Most Chinese believe that the May 7, 1999, bombing of the Chinese embassy in Belgrade was deliberate and intentional and that the subsequent apology was insincere and implausible.[3] Large crowds stoned the American embassy in Beijing. The Chinese government endorsed and facilitated those demonstrations, but many Chinese were still critical of their government for not responding more militantly. Only a short time later, on May 25, the U.S. Senate issued the Cox Report[4] which, despite a paucity of evidence, proclaimed that twenty years of aggressive Chinese espionage has netted the plans for all American nuclear weapons, and the American press was filled with lurid headlines proclaiming China's "total penetration" and speculating on China's "mushrooming" nuclear capability.[5] Only a few weeks later, on July 9, Taiwan President Lee Teng-hui's statement that China's and Taiwan's relations were a special case of state-to-state relations stimulated vitriolic language in Beijing, including not very veiled threats that China would use neutron bombs against Taiwan, and should the United States intervene, could use nuclear weapons against the United States as well. President Clinton was subsequently criticized by the leading Republican presidential candidate, George W. Bush, for being too soft on China. Forty-four percent of Americans believe that the U.S. government has not been "tough enough" in its dealings with China.[6]

Nor do we believe that there has been any decisive move toward democracy in China. There have been signs of progress, such as the much-discussed village elections,[7] the people's congresses' continuing campaign to create laws, signing two recent United Nations' human rights covenants, and the development of an increasingly affluent, diverse, and educated society. China's leaders, at least intermittently, have encouraged the press to investigate and report abuses of power, and are at least rhetorically committed to holding government officials accountable to legal standards.

But these signs of progress have taken place within a state that remains overwhelmingly hostile to the public expression of independent opinion, autonomous political organizations, and dissent. In late 1998 and in 1999 the leadership undertook yet another crackdown. Facing a series of politically significant anniversaries, workers displaced by layoffs at money-losing state-owned enterprises, peasants upset by corrupt local government, and a massive demonstration organized in Beijing on April 25 by the religious exercise organization, Falun Gong, the government has continued to harass, arrest, and exile "dissidents." Those who have attempted to organize themselves into independent organizations such as labor unions or Falun Gong have received especially harsh treatment.

The space for legitimate politics and public discourse remains tightly restricted. Throughout the summer of 1999, the Chinese media was dominated by denunciations of the two Lis, namely Taiwan's Lee Teng-hui and Falun Gong's Li Hongzhi. Many Chinese intellectuals found the language of these diatribes reminiscent of the early stages of the Cultural Revolution. It is possible, even probable, that China will someday enjoy democracy. But this cannot be taken for granted, and will not be the automatic or inevitable result of economic growth.

The prospects for democracy in China and U.S.-China relations are each an important concern in itself. If China were to decisively reject democracy, it would be important first because China itself represents a large portion of humanity, but since China is an increasingly important and influential country in world affairs, China's continuous antidemocracy diplomacy would have a significant impact on the diffusion of human rights and democracy throughout the world. China already has a significant impact on the diffusion of democracy, both through its active participation in multilateral forums (as described in Samuel Kim's contribution to this volume) and through bilateral support for dictatorships like Burma's present government. If antidemocratic tendencies remain entrenched in Beijing, this kind of diplomacy will doubtless intensify.

Openly hostile relations between China and the United States could have a decisive impact on the evolution of the entire world system. Francis Fukuyama's vision of a "liberal end of history" proved overly optimistic, but what about his claim that nationalistic alternatives to liberalism lack broad or universalistic appeal? In 1995, for example, referring to a country particularly at odds with the liberal international vision of the world, he wrote: "It is not particularly surprising that Serbia has failed to become a model society for anyone in Europe, East or West."[8] In 1999 in China, however, Slobodan Milosevic was hailed as the heroic leader of a small socialist country courageously resisting the unprovoked and unjustified aggression of the world's richest and most powerful countries. China's government, in other words, is striving to construe the enemies of liberal internationalism as morally heroic underdogs. One must ask if working together with other countries such as Russia, China could become the focus of a powerful antiliberal coalition?

Considering China's prospects for democracy and U.S.-China relations jointly enables us to better understand each issue and raises important theoretical concerns. Namely, U.S.-China relations are a critical case for democratic peace theory. This theory, as Edward Friedman's essay in this volume elaborates, draws its inspiration from Immanuel Kant.[9] In 1982 Michael Doyle called attention to Kant's argument, and in the late 1980s and 1990s, scholars such as Bruce Russett and John M.

Owen led the development of a large literature on democratic peace theory.[10] Their central claim is that democracies seldom go to war with each other. These authors justify this claim with various statistical analyses which suggest that in fact democracies have very seldom, or in some versions of the argument, never fought wars with each other. This has been explained in various ways, including that when the citizens who will actually pay the cost of war in blood and treasure have authority, they will seldom fight, that the habits of compromise and negotiation taught by pluralist institutions lead away from war, and that liberal ideology itself leads away from war.

If true, democratic peace theory has enormous implications for American foreign policy in general and for U.S.-China relations in particular. Most important, democratic peace theory challenges realpolitik. The latter claims that all states are equally constrained by the violent and anarchic nature of international politics to act in terms of their national interests and that Machiavellian strategies should be expected from all sides. Democratic peace theory instead suggests that democracy could be the foundation of mutual trust leading toward a more peaceful international system. If this is true, then the United States truly does have an interest in democracy in China, and conversely, an authoritarian China is a potential threat to American security. If democratic peace theory works, then American concern for human rights in China is not just idealism, but is a matter of practical politics.

Other scholars, however, emphatically reject democratic peace theory.[11] They reject the democratic peace theorists' empirical claims. Their statistical analyses indicate that the appearance of peace among democracies is an artifact of the relative rarity of democracy and the infrequent incidence of war rather than any proclivity toward peace. This argument is strengthened by the observation that democracies are no less likely to go to war than other states, albeit, usually with states that are not democracies. Critics also note that democratic peace theorists disagree over the reasons why democracies seldom go to war with each other, that is, that the reasons why democracies do not fight each other remain unclear. The critics conclude that if democratic peace theory is based on appearances that have no statistical foundation, then rejecting realpolitik is a dangerous indulgence in romantic idealism.

If these criticisms of democratic peace theory analyses are accepted, then the United States should devise China policy along traditional realpolitik lines. In that case, there would be little reason to expect that democracy in China would change these or lessen the chance of conflict. Given China's potential to become a great power, this argument has the potential to suggest that relations between China and the world's presently most influential power will be increasingly difficult for the foreseeable future.

The debate between realism and idealism in U.S.-China policy is nothing new. The initial breakthrough in U.S.-China relations owed much, of course, to Richard Nixon's realism. China, he and Henry Kissinger believed, could help the United States not only to extricate itself from the war in Vietnam, but could also provide critical leverage against the Soviet Union. Such realism, however, raised difficult questions. What was America fighting in the Cold War? Was it communism's threat to democracy? If so, why was Chinese communism less of a threat than Soviet communism? Or did the Cold War, despite all pretensions to the contrary, simply pit American national interests against Soviet national interests?

In the aftermath of 1989, the debate shifted to pit economic instead of strategic interests against human rights diplomacy. This debate focused on whether offering China normal trade status should be contingent on improving human rights in China. Human rights advocates argued that trading with dictators would be unethical, while others argued that cutting China off from the wider world would slow domestic reforms.

Democratic peace theory recasts this argument yet again. The Polish Solidarity activist Adam Michnik was among the first to suggest that the alternatives in the post-communist world were either to build civic identities based on inclusive and participatory democratic politics or to build exclusive and authoritarian politics based on ethnic identities.[12] In other words, a short time after the collapse of communism in Eastern Europe, Michnik predicted that the range of alternatives ran from Vaclav Havel to Slobodan Milosevic. As the initial triumphalist reaction to the collapse of East European communism crumbled in the face of an increasing number of violent ethnic conflicts, Michnik's alternatives gained currency in both academic and policy debates.

One of the most striking responses to Michnik's distinction came from the prominent American political scientist, Samuel Huntington, who argued that the civic virtues that Michnik and other East European liberals struggled for are actually only relevant to European civilization. Huntington argues that attempts to "construct" democracy in non-European civilizations are unrealistic romantic ventures that will very probably be counterproductive.[13] This means that the "democratic peace" is and can only ever be peace among Europeans. He concludes that it is more "realistic" to accept that conflict between civilizations is endemic than to attempt to remake others in our own image.

Nonetheless, democratic peace theory has gained increasing weight in American foreign policy. In President Clinton's 1994 State of the Union address, he succinctly said "Democracies don't attack each other," a statement that echoed the previous administration's secretary of state, James Baker, who stated:

> The Cold War has ended, and we now have a chance to forge a democratic peace, an enduring peace built on shared values—democracy and political and economic freedom. The strength of these values in Russia and the other new independent states will be the surest foundation for peace—and the strongest guarantee of our national security—for decades to come.[14]

Of course, as critics have pointed out, U.S. concern for democracy and human rights has always been tempered with the concerns of political realism. Countries that are economically or strategically important to the United States or to Western Europeans are judged by different standards. Consequently, more distant groups such as Tibetans or Turkish Kurds are unlikely to win the same sort of support granted to European Albanian Kosovars.

It is, however, unreasonable to pit realism and idealism as absolute opposites. Kissinger's realism did facilitate China's transition from Mao's ideological tyranny to Deng's more open and less inhumane reforms. Alternatively, proponents of lowering trade barriers between China and the United States argue that economic exchanges promote exchanging information, ideas, and even values that will facilitate eventual democratization far more than high-handed moral criticism.

The late 1990s war in Yugoslavia has been an important test of the application of democratic peace theory, and it bears consideration because the interests and passions it activated will very likely be a part of future incidents as well. Some argue to the contrary that NATO's war in Yugoslavia refuted the central claims of democratic peace theory. Milosevic, after all, is an elected leader who was attacked by a league of democracies. But if Yugoslavia is to be considered a democracy—a debatable proposition—it is certainly a nonliberal democracy, far more beholden to exclusive ethnic identities than inclusive civic identities. As such, it clearly falls on the far side of Michnik's divide. In John Owen's version of democratic peace theory, it is indeed liberalism which matters more than democracy.[15]

The Yugoslav case presents an additional difficulty in that NATO's attack was not authorized by the United Nations. Kant's version of democratic peace theory, as Edward Friedman points out in this volume, argues that democratic republics can build peace by building international organizations. From the perspective of China's leaders, or for that matter, from the perspective of democracies like India and Russia, NATO's policy amounted to an unauthorized unilateral armed intervention and a flagrant violation of fundamental international law. The Chinese leaders, in particular, proclaim that the war in Yugoslavia demonstrates the fundamentally aggressive "hegemonic" intentions of America's leaders.

By the logic of democratic peace theory, Milosevic's violently aggressive ethnic nationalism is a threat to the peace and stability of democracies in Europe and elsewhere. Milosevic's personal success offers an inspiration to those who would imitate his politics elsewhere. The refugees that his regime creates destabilize neighboring regimes. And there is the perpetual threat that Yugoslavia's internal violence will lead—as it in fact did—to a war involving more states. By the logic of democratic peace theory, Europe has better prospects for peace and stability when all its states are constrained to accept certain fundamental values.

It is too soon to judge the success of NATO's war against Milosevic's regime, even in terms of Europe. Perhaps new precedents have been set that will lead to increasing respect for human rights. However, this is by no means certain. Ethnic tensions are still strong and people are still being chased from their homes. Kosovo may yet be partitioned. Serbia has suffered economic and ecological catastrophes. The Serbian people have been severely punished by the unjust standard of collective responsibility. Milosevic remains in power.

Some of the most serious consequences of the war will be the damage done to relations between the NATO countries, especially the United States, and countries such as China. From Beijing's perspective, NATO's war in Yugoslavia most regrettably elevated human rights above national sovereignty, thus threatening the Chinese people's best hope to secure fundamental rights such as the rights to live in peace and develop their economy. In Beijing's realist view of world politics, no other country, and certainly no wealthy capitalist country, can be trusted to respect the best interests of the Chinese people.

Yugoslavia is linked to China by far more than the embassy bombing. The Chinese government and many Chinese citizens were outraged by the war in Yugoslavia long before their embassy was bombed. In part this stems from a lack of awareness of and appreciation for the suffering that Milosevic's regime inflicted upon the Albanian Kosovars. Indeed, the Albanian embassy in Beijing, which is adjacent to the American embassy, was stoned along with the U.S. embassy.[16] The more critical point, though, is that the Chinese government and many Chinese citizens identify with the Yugoslav government and people. Yugoslavia, like China, is criticized in NATO capitals for human rights violations. Yugoslavia probably seems more socialist to Chinese than to Yugoslavs, but in Chinese eyes, Yugoslavia and China are both threatened because they dare to resist the dominant powers of a cutthroat capitalist world. Chinese, like Serbs, have constructed a national identity that draws heavily on the belief that for much of their history they have been singled out for special persecution by rapacious dominant powers. Both Chinese and Serbs see themselves as still resisting Nazi aggressors.

The war in Yugoslavia provided a convenient catalyst for Chinese already critical of U.S. policy toward China. Chinese critics of the United States had a wide range of incidents and issues to discuss before that war started. Purported American hectoring over human rights issues; the annual congressional debate over China's trade status; attempts to get various UN agencies and meetings to investigate China's human rights record; the supposedly stiff terms demanded for admission to the World Trade Organization; complaints about China's alleged unfair trade practices and inflated charges regarding China's trade surplus with the United States; penalties for violations of regimes for controlling missiles and weapons of mass destruction; the deployment of American aircraft carriers in waters off Taiwan to counter the PRC's military exercises; the attempt to deepen and expand U.S.-Japan security cooperation; not least talk of deploying a theater missile defense that might include Taiwan; and the evident U.S. intent to give the Japanese military a more active role in East Asian regional affairs, all seem like a rather long list of charges and complaints. There can be little wonder that the Beijing government has an anti-American faction.

This foundation made the portrayal of the United States as arrogant, lawless, and violent eminently plausible to the majority of Chinese citizens. While there were some who approved of NATO's war in Yugoslavia, probably more were concerned that their government had failed to maintain China's dignity in the face of America's supposedly calculated aggression and were shamed by the country's inability to offer meaningful military assistance to the Serbs.

The popularity of nationalist anti-American sentiment poses another challenge to democratic peace theory. There can be little doubt that in the immediate aftermath of the embassy bombing an appeal to radical nationalism along the lines of Milosevic or Russia's Zhirinovsky would have won many votes in a democratic China. As Mansfield and Snyder have pointed out, new democracies are significantly more likely to be involved in wars.[17] On the other hand, it is unfair to judge what public opinion might be in a Chinese democracy based on what it is in present-day authoritarian China. With freedom of the press, patterns of public discourse would be substantially altered and might well reach different conclusions. Russian democracy has its problems, but in contrast to Milosevic in less democratic Yugoslavia, Zhirinovsky has not been elected president.

Moreover, the spirit in which Washington has conducted its China policy cannot offer Beijing much comfort, and indeed, challenges any claim that democracies produce superior foreign policy. Quite regularly Washington's complaints and criticisms are driven by the exigencies of American domestic politics. Criticizing China and attacking the president for being "soft on China" have become regular features of American presidential campaigns since Nixon's time, regardless of which party is in the opposition and who the incumbent is. Candidate Reagan was critical of President Carter, candidate Clinton was critical of President Bush, and the Republican Congress and the leading Republican candidate (the son of the same president whom candidate Clinton criticized for being "soft on China") are now critical of President Clinton for being "soft on China." The 1999 Cox Report on alleged Chinese espionage typifies this sort of politics. Representative Cox produced hundreds of pages of text (which actually contained very little new information) but still made charges—such as that the secrets allegedly stolen will result in a new generation of more threatening nuclear weapons—that are not clearly supported by the evidence. Indeed, the allegations against Wen Ho Lee, the Chinese-American scientist said to have perpetrated the most serious espionage, are badly tainted by the appearance of racism.[18]

In sum, a U.S. foreign policy based on democratic peace theory is little to Beijing's liking. Those Chinese leaders who already feared "peaceful evolution" found NATO's unauthorized intervention against a sovereign state a fearful turn of events. Where some see an idealistic commitment to human values, they see an immoral, racist, and powerful country hypocritically trying to impose its values on others. Moreover, if the United States really does prefer a world of democracies, the current Chinese regime is clearly in an awkward position. Simply put, many Chinese wonder if they will be next on NATO's list. Unfortunately, Washington's sometimes irresponsible, ill-considered, and partisan politics lend credence to these fears.

Despite these pressures and concerns, there is still reason to believe that Beijing can cooperate with Washington even while the latter pursues a democratic peace. Zhu Rongji has been criticized in Beijing for offering too many concessions and putting up with too much criticism during his April 1999 trip to the United States, but he nonetheless arrived surprisingly offering to make important concessions related to China's admission to the World Trade Organization. Throughout the embassy crisis, Chinese officials were concerned about guaranteeing the safety of foreigners in China and assuring the world that China still welcomed international investment. Even Jiang Zemin's eventual attempt to bend the energies stimulated by the embassy bombing to modernizing China should be considered an attempt to moderate patriotic passions. Despite the anger and violence of preceding months, Washington and Beijing were able to negotiate terms for China's entry into the World Trade Organization. While it would be reckless to conclude that China's diplomacy will inevitably give way to the demands of economic rationality, there are important Chinese interests with much to gain from their economic ties to Europe, Japan, and the United States. Foreign trade and investment have played a major role in China's economic expansion, and no Chinese leadership can easily forego the benefits of more trade and investment.

In addition, not all of the problems in the relationship stem from Washington's pursuit of a democratic peace. If the troubles in the relationship could be explained as simply the result of Washington's arrogant paternalism or unprincipled partisan wrangling, there would be little need for a book of this sort. Unfortunately, many of Washington's complaints have substance. Beijing's limited respect for international norms ranging from missile control regimes to accounting practices; the threat to use violence to "reunify" Taiwan; the prickly relationships with Japan, India, Vietnam, and the Philippines; and the aggressive pursuit of Westphalian sovereignty—all coupled with secrecy—would present problems for even the most gifted and broadminded leaders in Washington.

But despite all that China challenges, leaders in Washington face enormous pressures to negotiate a working relationship with Beijing. As noted above, presidents who have criticized their predecessors for being "soft on China" have themselves been persuaded to work for a better relationship. This includes both Reagan and Clinton. The pressures to promote a better relationship were apparent again recently when Clinton, under fire from his congressional critics as noted above, rejected Zhu Rongji's concessions regarding WTO, only to be so sternly criticized by business leaders that he concluded a similar agreement a few months later.

This book considers questions such as the following: How serious are the disputes between Beijing and Washington? Are these disputes based on fundamentally different national interests, conflicting cultures, or divergent histories? Or do they result from more malleable factors such as misperceptions, the irresponsible pursuit of domestic politics, and the impact of impermanent institutions? Is China as presently constituted a threat to the existing international status quo? Or are some Americans' fears more a reflection of American partisan politics than China's intentions and capabilities? How much political reform has China had since Mao died? Can American attempts to promote human rights in China succeed? Or is the hope that China will democratize a reflection of America's own nationalism? If China were to democratize, would the tensions between the United States and China actually evaporate? Or would the relationship remain much the same?

While the preceding outlines the thinking that led to this book, as befits any serious collaborative effort, our contributors have challenged our assumptions and understandings on many issues. To cite just one critical example, while the contributions written by the editors generally accept the arguments of democratic peace theory, several other contributors are skeptical that democracy in China would have much impact on U.S.-China relations. In general, readers will find that this volume presents debates on these questions rather than consensual answers. It is a complex debate with authors who agree on some points vigorously contesting others rather than a simple division into one or two camps. Those who would like a more detailed account of the debate before proceeding might read the conclusion first. Otherwise, the contributors to this volume approach the above questions as follows.

Part one of the book consists of six articles debating "Whither China?" in two sections. The first section consists of three articles by Suisheng Zhao, Jianwei Wang, and Minxin Pei whose primary focus is on the implications of Chinese nationalism and the prospects for democracy. They argue that there is little to worry about from today's authoritarian China.

Suisheng Zhao explores the development of nationalism in China in the 1990s. He argues that nationalism has been promoted by the regime, but also has autonomous roots among intellectuals. Zhao argues that since the roots of nationalism are largely internal, it need not have a decisive impact on Chinese foreign policy. Zhao agrees that leaders in

Beijing promote and manipulate nationalism for their own narrow purposes. Yet he is relatively confident that their purposes have more to do with maintaining their regime than provoking war.

Jianwei Wang asks whether authoritarianism in China is likely to make China more aggressive, and forcefully asserts that it is not. Wang argues that Beijing is no longer beholden to a revolutionary ideology that might drive it to aggression. He asserts that contemporary Chinese nationalism is part of a process of "nation building" which Western nations have already completed, but which remains necessary in China. He examines a series of issues where others have found the Chinese leadership guilty of aggression, and finds instead that Beijing has been patient and reactive. Wang finds that democracy might have some long-term benefits for Chinese foreign policy, such as improving American perceptions of China, but that for the near term, "nation building" will be the central issue, regardless of whether China is democratic or authoritarian.

Minxin Pei considers the prospects for democracy in China. He finds China to have enjoyed far more political reform than other observers. He argues that China now has a "soft authoritarian" regime with increasing institutionalization; younger, better educated leaders; and a significant and increasing degree of pluralism. He discusses four trends to demonstrate China's gradual democratization: the strengthening of the National People's Congress, continuing legal reforms, the spread of village elections, and the emergence of civil society. Pei concludes that China's insecure leaders still maintain a high level of repression, but that the above trends will help to insulate the regime from social turmoil, and will thus continue, gradually leading China to democracy.

The second section of part one consists of three articles by Friedman, Kim, and Dreyer. They focus on China's relationship with the wider world and reach more alarming conclusions than the previous three chapters. Edward Friedman traces the evolution of anti-Japanese attitudes in the People's Republic of China. He finds that Chinese leaders have unfairly demonized Japan for most of the history of the People's Republic. He regrets that despite Japan's "peace constitution" many Chinese believe that Japan presents a grave military threat, and further, that the Chinese are woefully blind to others' perceptions of how they were threatened by the Chinese empire in the past and to how present-day Chinese policies appear similarly threatening. Friedman argues that this insensitivity will persist for some time under any circumstances, including in a fledgling democracy, but can only be overcome by open debate and discussion such as can only be found in a democracy.

Samuel Kim explores China's international human rights diplomacy. He first explains and criticizes Beijing's relativist perspective. He argues that despite recently signing UN conventions with contrary implications, Beijing still claims that rights are relative to time, place, culture, and economic condition and are inherent in states, not citizens. Kim rejects Beijing's version of the Asian values argument, noting that Asia is far too diverse to support any single theory of rights. He then presents the history of Chinese rights diplomacy since 1989. He finds that Beijing has enjoyed considerable success in its attempts to deflect criticism and some success in its attempts to limit the strength of the international human rights regime. However, he concludes that in general, as demonstrated by the war in Yugoslavia, that the international human rights regime has been gaining strength at the cost of state sovereignty, and in addition, Chinese law has been slowly adapting to this trend.

June Teufel Dreyer examines Beijing's relations with China's Asian neighbors. Carefully examining issues such as territorial disputes over islands, she finds a pattern of aggressive claims followed by placatory statements that do not withdraw the initial claims, followed by more aggressive claims. Dreyer finds most of China's neighbors to be deeply troubled by this pattern, but mostly lacking effective responses. Some, she explains, accept that China is the "natural" regional hegemon and prepare to make do as best as may be, others turn to the United States, and others have attempted to coordinate their response with like-minded neighbors. Noting the Chinese people's support for expansive nationalist claims, Dreyer concludes that democracy might not make much difference.

Part Two of *What If China Doesn't Democratize?* consists of a debate between David Bachman and Edward Friedman over whether democratization advances peace. Bachman begins with a careful catalogue of six areas of disputes between the United States and China, namely, human rights, trade and economic issues, Taiwan, the People's Republic of China's rising power, outlaw international behavior, and new world order issues such as environmental protection. He concludes that in some of these areas, such as human rights, democracy might make an immediate difference, but that in most, democracy would not have much of a positive impact. Bachman concludes with a study of several different scenarios by which China might democratize and considers how each of these might affect relations with the United States.

In contrast, Friedman finds great wisdom in the Kantian idea of preventing war by building a confederation of law-abiding nations which benefit from expanded economic interactions. He explains that Kant's argument is not that democracies are incapable of fighting each other, rather that they are more, but not exclusively, capable of building peaceful confederations with other states. Friedman argues that the critical point is to accept the possibility that China is capable of democratization and of playing a responsible role in international politics regardless of the status quo. Those who understand otherwise, whether they are in Beijing or Washington, drive the world toward war. Thus, while Friedman is pessimistic about the U.S.'s ability to build democracy in China, he argues that peace lies in working to include China in peaceful confederations.

The final three essays presented in section three offer concluding overviews on the issues of democratization and authoritarianism, of war and peace. Nelsen considers the prospects for democracy in China and finds that China will democratize, but probably gradually, no time soon, and under the aegis of the existing state. While he sees some of the political reforms that Minxin Pei cites, he also finds obstacles to democratization, including nationalism. He finds that democracy is not a panacea, and indeed, cites U.S. paternalism as a significant problem. He takes some solace in China's integration into the world economy and concludes that nationalism is not an insurmountable obstacle to U.S.-China relations.

Like other authors in this volume, Su Shaozhi and Michael Sullivan assert that there are important forces favoring democracy in China. But unlike some others, they argue that the primary forces for democracy come from Chinese society, not from the state. They find the current leadership to be the primary obstacle to democracy. Specifically, they argue that Deng Xiaoping and Jiang Zemin incorrectly regard maintaining the stability of the undemocratic "partyocracy" as essential to reform. As regards Chinese foreign policy, they find that Jiang Zemin has both manipulated nationalism and taken steps to contain it. In both cases his purpose has been to maintain the stability of the "partyocracy." This leads to the conclusion that a U.S. policy of "containing" China would confirm and exacerbate the worst aspects of Jiang Zemin's dictatorship.

My chapter contrasts democratic peace theory with cultural determinism and realpolitik. I reject cultural determinism, finding that while there are cultural continuities, perceptions and values do change. I similarly find that realpolitik does not have an adequate grasp of how cultures and countries define their interests. I argue that many of the disputes between China and the United States are indeed rooted in perceptions and institutional commitments and vulnerabilities rather than immutable cultural values or national interests. The two states are not locked into a zero-sum game, but instead could work to expand many existing complementary interests and mutually beneficial exchanges. This leads to the argument that democracy is possible in China, and a more hopeful assessment of the impact of democracy in China. Democracy, however, is no panacea, as can be readily discerned from the all too frequent appearance of narrow nationalism in American foreign policy.

In sum, those who read the following chapters will find a diverse range of views on important issues such as the prospects for democracy in China, the prospects for U.S.-China relations, and the relationship between the two. Readers will not find a general consensus, although they will find carefully reasoned arguments based on extensive data, and a general belief in the potential for democracy in China and the possibility of better relations between China and the United States. Perhaps, in a world where violence and polemics are all too common, this is itself an achievement.

Notes

1. Song Qiang, Zhang Zangzang, and Qiao Bian, eds., *Da Zhongguo keyi shuo bu* (The China that can say no) (Beijing: Zhonghua gongshang lianhe chubanshe, 1996). Richard Bernstein and Ross H. Munro, *The Coming Conflict with China* (New York: Alfred A. Knopf, 1997).

2. Samuel P. Huntington, *The Clash of Civilizations: The Remaking of World Order* (New York: Simon and Schuster, 1996).

3. One poll reported that 9 out of 10 respondents in Beijing, Shanghai, and Guangzhou believed that the attack was planned. See "Attack Intentional, Claims Poll In Main Cities," *South China Morning Post*, May 13, 1999 [www.scmp.com].

4. For the text of the Cox Report, see http://hillsource.house.gov/Cox-Report/ -report-welcome2.html.

5. John Barry and Gregory L. Vistica, "The Penetration Is Total," *Newsweek,* March 25, 1999 [http://newsweek.com/nw-srv/issue/13_99a/printed/us/na/ na0813_1.htm] and David E. Sanger and Erik Eckholm "Will Beijing's Nuclear Arsenal Stay Small Or Will It Mushroom?" *New York Times*, March 15, 1999.

6. This poll was conducted in March of 1999 by the Pew Research Center. In contrast to the 44 percent of people who said that the United States has not been tough enough in its dealings with China, 43 percent said it has been just about right, but only 2 percent said it had been too tough [http://www.people-press.org/ china99rpt.htm].

7. See for example, Tianjian Shi, "Village Committee Elections in China: Institutionalist Tactics for Democracy," *World Politics* 51, 3 (April 1999): 385-412.

8. Francis Fukuyama, "The Primacy of Culture," *Journal of Democracy* 6 (January 1995): 10.

9. "Eternal Peace" in Immanuel Kant, *The Philosophy of Immanuel Kant* (New York: Modern Library, 1949), pp. 430-476.

10. Michael W. Doyle, *Ways of War and Peace* (New York: W.W. Norton & Company, 1997); Bruce Russett, with W. Antholis, C. Ember, M. Ember, and Z. Maoz, *Grasping the Democratic Peace: Principles for a Post-Cold War World* (Princeton, NJ: Princeton University Press, 1993); and John M. Owen IV, *Liberal Peace Liberal War: American Politics and International Security* (Ithaca, NY: Cornell University Press, 1997). Portions of these books and earlier articles are collected in Michael E. Brown, Sean M. Lynn-Jones, and Steven E. Miller (eds.), *Debating the Democratic Peace* (Cambridge: MIT Press, 1997).

11. Ibid. See, for example, the articles by Christopher Layne, David E. Spiro, Farber and Gowa, and Ido Oren in Brown, et al. (eds.), *Debating the Democratic Peace.*

12. See, for example, Adam Michnik, "After the Revolution," *New Republic*, July 2, 1990; and "The Two Faces of Eastern Europe," *New Republic*, November 12, 1990.

13. Huntington, *The Clash of Civilizations.*

14. Both cited in John M. Owen IV, *Liberal Peace Liberal War*, p.7.

15. Ibid.

16. See Renee Schoof, "Day Two of Protests," *ABC News* (May 9, 1999), which can be found at http://www.abcnews.go.com/sections/world/DailyNews/kosovo_chinareax_990509.html.

17. Edward D. Mansfield and Jack Snyder, "Democratization and War," *Foreign Affairs*, 74, 3 (May 1995): 79-97.

18. William J. Broad, "Official Asserts Spy Case Suspect Was a Bias Victim," *New York Times*, August 18, 1999 [http://www.nytimes.com/library/world/asia/081899china-nuke.html].

PART I
WHITHER CHINA?

Chapter 1

"We are Patriots First and Democrats Second": The Rise of Chinese Nationalism in the 1990s

Suisheng Zhao

Liberal democracy is rejected by some East Asian leaders on the basis that "democracies can . . . prevent rapid economic development."[1] Nationalism, instead, is on the ascendancy in many East Asian countries. China is not exceptional. When communism's appeal ended in the post–Cold War era, nationalism moved quickly to fill the vacuum. The 1996 National Day editorial in the *People's Daily* portrays patriotism (a benign term for nationalism) as part of "*guohun*" (the national soul) that "reflects state interests and national will." It continues to say that nationalism "is the most effective way . . . to create great undertakings that will shake heaven and earth."[2]

Comments on an earlier draft of this paper by participants at the conference, "What If China Does Not Democratize," held at Marquette University on July 11–12, 1997, are gratefully acknowledged. In particular, the author would like to thank Edward Friedman and Barrett McCormick for their efficient work in organizing the conference and for very constructive comments on several drafts of this paper. Two anonymous referees' comments are also greatly appreciated.

Partially spontaneous and partially state-led, nationalism has become a driving force in China's political life and economic modernization. Observing the rally of Chinese from all over the world behind the Union to Protect the Diaoyu Islands in the fall of 1996, after a right-wing Japanese group erected a lighthouse on the Diaoyu/Senkaku Islands over which China claims sovereignty, an exiled Chinese democratic activist in the United States warns that "a mighty wave of Chinese patriotism is sweeping across the globe, uniting Chinese people of all different political stands. The scale of the movement well exceeded the protest movement after the 1989 Tiananmen massacre."[3] Indeed, while thousands of Chinese students demonstrated in Tiananmen Square urging democracy in confrontation with the People's Liberation Army (PLA) in May 1989, many Chinese showed enthusiastic support to their armed forces when the PLA launched missiles just off the shores of Taiwan to defend China's territorial integrity and sovereignty in 1995–96. Nationalistic books, such as *The China That Can Say No*,[4] became instant bestsellers in the summer of 1996. The accidental bombing of the Chinese embassy in Yugoslavia by the NATO force on May 7, 1999, caused the largest Chinese patriotic and anti-imperialist demonstrations in major Chinese cities since the May Fourth Movement of 1919. One Chinese scholar finds that although most Chinese intellectuals would not say that democracy is less appealing to them in the 1990s, many of them would emphasize that "they are patriots first and democrats second."[5] Talking about democracy has almost become verboten among many Chinese students. Such talk may be regarded as unpatriotic as nationalism has come to be dominant in the thought of Chinese intellectuals, if not the whole nation, making it hard for democracy to take root. As one *New York Times* reporter in Beijing found, "NATO's bombing of Yugoslavia and the deadly attack on China's embassy in Belgrade have caused some Chinese to question the sincerity of American ideals." This reporter quoted a liberal Beijing University graduate student saying, "Many people will feel disillusioned about Western values, and that will make it more difficult for people like myself who lean toward them."[6]

This development has drawn extensive attention and alarm in the West because few aspects of China as a rising power trouble Washington as much as the emergence of an assertive nationalism under an authoritarian regime. Bernstein and Munro, two prominent Western journalists once based in Beijing, warn that "driven by nationalist sentiment, a yearning to redeem the humiliations of the past, and the simple urge for international power, China is seeking to replace the United States as the dominant power in Asia."[7] Samuel P. Huntington, one of the West's most eminent political scientists, finds that Chinese now increasingly assert their intention to resume the historic role of "the preeminent power in East Asia" and "to bring to an end the overlong century of humiliation and subordination to the West and Japan that began with British imposition of the Treaty of Nanking [Nanjing] in 1842."[8] James Lilley, the former U.S. ambassador to China and Taiwan, states that "there is a rallying cry for Chinese everywhere . . . that after a century of humiliation and Mao's social and economic experiments China's time has come . . . it [China] will rise in the world to the place it deserves."[9] Such views fuel fears of a rising Chinese threat. Are these concerns justified? What are the causes for the rise of Chinese nationalism in the post–Cold War world? Is Chinese nationalism a source of international aggression? These are important questions yet to be answered.

The current rise of nationalism began to emerge after the Tiananmen crackdown of the democratic movement in the spring of 1989. Because the democratic movement was developed under the influence of Western liberal ideas, the communist government took nationalism as an instrument to block Western influences and shore up its waning legitimacy in the post-Tiananmen era. These nationalistic sentiments and anti-Western rhetoric gained wide currency among Chinese intellectuals in spite of the fact that popular nationalism emerged largely independent of official propaganda. Intellectuals advocate nationalism out of their concern that China faces a crisis of national disintegration comparable to the one faced by the former Soviet Union and Yugoslavia after the sudden collapse of communism. Under these circumstances, Chinese intellectuals who once snatched ideas from the West and totally negated their own traditions have rediscovered the value of their own past and rejected a Western mind-set.

A shared objective of holding a nation together during the turbulent transitional period has brought the government and intellectuals together under the banner of nationalism. Chinese nationalism is thus a result of a volatile mix of rising pride and lingering insecurity in response to profound domestic crises after the decline of communist ideology and the disintegration of the Soviet Union. This Chinese nationalism is characterized by pragmatic concerns of both the Chinese government and intellectual elite about overriding domestic problems and represents an aggregation of varied political forces.

It also has a strong moral and ethical appeal. Chinese perceive it as largely defensive and internal in orientation. This nationalism is invoked in at least partial explanation of a remarkable range of phenomena such as aversion to foreign ideas and celebration of national traditions. It also explains why China is particularly sensitive to any infringements on its territorial integrity or national sovereignty. This foreign policy implication is very important. It helps answer the question whether China will become a potential threat.

A State-Led Nationalism

Nationalism is a modern concept consisting of doctrines or a set of ideas that dictate political action or movement. Hans Kohn sees nationalism as a "political creed" that "centers the supreme loyalty of the overwhelming majority of the people upon the nation-state, either existing or desired."[10] Relying on documentary and behavioral referents of Qing diplomacy, Immanuel C. Y. Hsu states that "doubtless, imperial China was not a nation-state."[11] Therefore, Chinese people were not imbued with an abiding sense of nationalism before the nineteenth century. James Harrison observed that the traditional Chinese self-image was generally "defined as culturalism, based on a common historical heritage and acceptance of shared beliefs, not as nationalism, based on the modern concept of nation-state."[12] Joseph Levenson's influential writings also indicate that, because of "Chinese culture as the focus of loyalty," nationalism did not exist in traditional China and culturalism permeated traditional Chinese thought.[13]

The concept of the Chinese nation was a relatively recent creation influenced by foreign intellectual discourses. There was not even a serviceable word for the historical and ethical community of "China" before the nineteenth century. As John Fitzgerald points out, "the Chinese custom of referring to their historical community by dynasty (*chaodai*) rather than by country (*guojia*) implied that there was in fact no Chinese nation at all."[14] According to the study of two Chinese scholars, *Zhonghua minzu,* an inadequate English translation would be "the Chinese race" or "the Chinese nation," is a rather modern concept that emerged only at the turn of the twentieth century. By 1895 *minzu* began to appear in Chinese revolutionary journals, adopted from the writings of the Japanese Meiji period. But it did not become popular among intellectuals until 1909. The term, *Zhonghua minzu,* was first used by intellectuals during the early Republican period and was often associated with nationalistic

[handwritten margin notes: "not defined by nationalism" and "Class discussion."]

writings warning the Chinese people of the danger of annihilation under Western invasion.[15]

Unlike the formation of nationalism in Europe as an indigenous process driven by a combined force of mercantilism and liberalism, nationalist consciousness in China was triggered from the outside. Andy Nathan and Robert Ross state that "while European ideologies had their roots in European culture, China's ferment was reactive in motives as well as in content."[16] Most Chinese scholars hold the view that modern Chinese nationalism has arisen largely in response to threats from foreign imperialism. Xiao Gongqin calls it a *yingji-zhiwei xing* (reactive-defensive type of) nationalism which is "derived from the reaction to the challenges from the West."[17] A reactive sentiment to foreign incursions was a starting point of Chinese nationalism. The vast, powerful, and wealthy Chinese empire stagnated and was ruthlessly humiliated by Western powers in the long century starting from its defeat in the Opium War of 1840–42. During the century of humiliation, foreign imperialists carved out spheres of influence, sold opium to the Chinese masses, and enjoyed the protection of extraterritoriality in their enclaves on Chinese soil. Nationalism held a powerful appeal in China's struggle to rid itself of foreign imperial powers. In the early days of the People's Republic of China (PRC), its leaders brought with them traumatic memories of China's inability to determine its own fate in the preceding hundred years. China viewed itself as the victim of Western and Japanese imperialism. Nationalism as much as Marxism-Leninism drove China's vision of its role in the world in the years following 1949.

However, there were no major military threats to China's security after the end of the Cold War. Instead, the internal legitimacy crisis became a grave concern of the Chinese communist regime. During the reform years of the 1980s, the regime was deeply troubled by "*sanxin weiji*" (three spiritual crises, namely, a "crisis of faith" in socialism, a crisis of confidence in the future of the country, and a crisis of trust in the party). When communist official ideology lost credibility, the communist regime became incapable of enlisting popular support for a vision of the future. Under these circumstances, some intellectuals turned to Western liberal ideas and called for democratic reform. "*Sanxin weiji*" led to a prodemocracy movement and the large-scale Tiananmen demonstrations in spring 1989. How to restore legitimacy and build broadly based national support became the most serious challenge to the post-Tiananmen leadership.

At first, the government concentrated all its efforts on stabilizing the nation. Order was established through the persecution of those who were involved in the democratic movement and through the administration of draconian penalties for the agitators. After the government forcefully reasserted its authority and democratic voices were virtually silenced, extremely conservative leaders tried to turn the clock back by initiating repeated attacks on market-oriented reform policies and by attempting to resuscitate Maoist ideology.[18] The conservatives, however, were not successful. They encountered strong resistance from Deng and other reform leaders who were not willing to abandon lucrative economic reforms. The nation endured a period of political and intellectual stagnation while the party searched for a means of reversing the decline of faith and confidence among the Chinese people. One lesson that the party leaders, reformers and conservatives alike, learned from the Tiananmen Incident was that political indoctrination of the younger generation was an urgent need. They all saw the Tiananmen Incident as a fatal consequence of the loss of "spiritual pillars" (*jingshen zhizhu*) which had been incarnated as Marxism-Leninism and Mao Zedong Thought and had guided the Chinese people to support and even sacrifice for the regime under Mao. For the reformist leaders, an added lesson was that nothing in the communist arsenal now could garner mass support, that resorting to old communist ideology was ineffective for indoctrination. They rejected efforts made by conservatives to restore Maoist ideology and looked for something else that could replace Marxism-Leninism dogma as a cohesive ideology.

Nationalism was thus rediscovered. Deng Xiaoping and his successor, Jiang Zemin, began to wrap themselves in the banner of nationalism, which, they found, remained the one bedrock of political belief shared by most Chinese people in spite of the rapid decay of communist ideology. In fact, the prodemocracy demonstrators in Tiananmen Square, even while confronting the government, claimed that patriotism drove them to take to the streets in the spring of 1989. Most people who were involved in the demonstration, both the students and their supporters, also equated promoting democracy with patriotism. Urging the government to start political reform was considered a most patriotic action. With the renewed discovery of the power of nationalism, Chinese communist leaders began to place emphasis on the party's role as the paramount patriotic force and guardian of national pride.

The power of nationalism in the modern world comes from the fact that it "locates the source of individual identity within a 'people,' which is seen as the bearer of sovereignty, the central object of loyalty, and the basis of collective solidarity."[19] In modern world history, "nationalism proved to be stronger than socialism when it came to bonding working classes together, and stronger than capitalism that bound bankers together."[20] This is also true in modern Chinese history. After Chinese political elites embraced modern nationalist doctrines in the late nineteenth century, while other movements and ideologies waxed and waned, nationalism permeated them all.

Although nationalism has in much of this century been expressed in Chinese as *minzuzhuyi*, a nationalism with a strong racial dimension, the CCP has preferred to use *aiguozhuyi* (patriotism) to refer to nationalism. The PRC government has never officially endorsed nationalism. The sentiments of the Chinese people were not described as nationalistic but as *aiguo* or patriotic, which in Chinese literally means "loving the state." CCP General Secretary Jiang Zemin emphasized in 1990 that "the patriotism we advocate is by no means a parochial nationalism."[21] In the PRC official discourse, the terms, "nationalism" and "chauvinism," referred to parochial and reactionary attachments to nationalities, whereas "patriotism" was love and support for China, always indistinguishable from the Chinese state and the Communist Party. From this perspective Chinese patriotism can be understood as a state-centric conception of nationalism or, in Charles Tilly's term, a "state-led nationalism." With state-led nationalism, "rulers who spoke in a nation's name successfully demanded that citizens identify themselves with that nation and subordinate other interests to those of the state."[22] This was exactly what patriotism demanded in China. Michael Hunt has observed that "by professing *aiguo*, Chinese usually expressed loyalty to and a desire to serve the state, either as it was or as it would be in its renovated form."[23] As a conception of state-led nationalism in the PRC, patriotism portrays the communist state as the embodiment of the nation's will. A *People's Daily* editorial on the 1996 National Day stated: "Patriotism is specific . . . Patriotism requires us to love the socialist system and road chosen by all nationalities in China under the leadership of the Communist Party."[24] By identifying the party with the nation, the regime would make criticism of the party line an unpatriotic act.

The CCP launched a patriotic education campaign in the early 1990s. At the beginning of the campaign, the conservative and reform-minded leaders (or in Chinese terminology: leftists and rightists) of the party had different emphases. The conservatives, such as Ding Guan'gen (director of the CCP Central Propaganda Department) and Deng Liqun, regarded the West as an enemy and tried to turn the patriotic education into an anti-Western liberalization campaign. The reform-minded leaders, led by Deng Xiaoping, worried about the potential damage that a campaign against bourgeois liberalization could bring to China's economic reform and, therefore, focused on patriotism and traditional culture.

After Deng Xiaoping made his famous southern China tour to garner support for continuing economic reform in early 1992, patriotic education unfolded as a youth education campaign. In January 1993, the State Education Commission issued a document, "Program for China's Education Reform and Development," which laid out patriotism as a guiding principle for China's educational reform. In November of the same year, the CCP Central Propaganda Department, the State Education Commission, the Ministry of Radio, Film, and Television, and the Ministry of Culture jointly issued a "Circular on Carrying Out Education in Patriotism in Primary and Secondary Schools Throughout the Country by Films and Television." In implementing the document, more than 95 percent of primary and middle school students in Beijing were organized to watch patriotic films recommended by the State Education Commission by May 1994. Beijing cinemas and television stations aired the films and some projection teams were sent to the mountainous areas to show the films. Television stations copied videotapes for schools in the suburban areas. Beijing's students wrote more than 1.5 million articles about what they learned from the heroes or heroines in the films.[25]

A national on-the-spot meeting (*xianchanghui*) on patriotic education in primary and middle schools was held in Shanghai on May 18–21, 1994. The Central Propaganda Department, the State Education Commission, the Radio, Film, and Television Ministry, the Cultural Ministry, and the Communist Youth League of the CCP Central Committee jointly hosted the meeting.[26] In June 1994, a national conference on education adopted a document, "Guidelines for Patriotic Education," which embraced the patriotic themes of the 1993 program and was passed down to all educational institutions from kindergartens to universities. For the first time since the university entrance examinations were reinstated in the late 1970s, students applying for science subjects at colleges were exempted from the examination of the Marxist course, which had been widely resented by students. Instead, patriotic education courses were added to the curriculum of high schools and colleges. By getting rid of the Marxist examination the government removed one more source of tension between the students and the authorities. Students claimed that the State Education Commission forced students to study Marxist doctrine and Communist Party propaganda and gave students something to rebel against. A Beijing University student revealed that "several officials in the Commission believe the 1986 and 1989 student protests were in some part a revolt against the political dogma of the time."[27] However, in abolishing the examination, the authorities were not easing up on the student population. The authorities switched to the softer approach of patriotic education. At the time of abolishing the political dogma examination, the authorities launched an "I am Chinese" program in universities, which taught students to be proud of being Chinese by concentrating on the "great achievements" of the Chinese people and especially the Communist Party. The aim was to win more respect for the party by demonstrating what it had done for the people of China. By appealing to the students' sense of patriotism rather than trying to convert them to Marxism, the communist regime hoped to reassert the legitimacy of the party.

The patriotic education campaign reached a climax when the CCP Central Committee published a central document, "The Outline for Conducting Patriotic Education," drafted by the Central Propaganda Department and carried in *Renmin Ribao* on September 6, 1994. The goal of education in patriotism was "to boost the nation's spirit, enhance its cohesion, foster its self-esteem and sense of pride, consolidate and develop a patriotic united front to the broadest extent, and direct and rally the masses' patriotic passions to the great cause of building socialism with Chinese characteristics." The outline particularly singled out youth as a targeted group and called for incorporating education in patriotism into teaching at kindergartens all the way through to universities.[28]

The long history of China and of Chinese cultural achievements held a prominent place in education. Special emphasis was given to efforts to improve China's position in the world and to struggle against foreign aggression and oppression after repeated setbacks. The CCP tried to discover a noncommunist past of the PRC and define patriotism in terms that had everything to do with Chinese history and culture and almost nothing to do with Marxist doctrine. After the outline was published in 1994, Li Ruihuan, the chairman of China's People's Political Consultative Conference, broke a long-standing communist taboo against ancestor worship by laying flowers and planting a pine tree by the mausoleum of China's Yellow Emperor, the legendary ancestor of the Chinese people. That legend was spun by nobles in 450 BC who transformed a local agrarian god into a common ancestor to legitimize their claim to power. As a historical site, the mausoleum drew many visitors during the patriotic education campaign.[29] The Great Wall also was celebrated as a patriotic symbol of Chinese history.[30] The celebration of Chinese tradition was accompanied by the revival of Confucianism and other Chinese cultural activities. Icons in Tiananmen Square, itself symbolic of the mandate of heaven in imperial times, were reshuffled. National Day celebrations no longer include large portraits of the communist philosophers Marx and Engels. Instead, a giant portrait of the noncommunist Chinese nationalist Sun Yat-sen stands alone in the square. In the official statement on the patriotic education campaign, "Chinese people's patriotism and brave patriotic deeds" rather than the CCP's socialist experiments became "the greatest epics ever written in the Chinese history, and they represent a glorious page in world history."[31] The leadership of the CCP was legitimated by its patriotism in China's long struggle for national independence and prosperity, not because of its communist ideals. Patriotism rather than communism thus became the basis of the CCP's legitimacy.[32]

Another emphasis of the patriotic education campaign was on China's national essence (*guoqing*). The purpose was to help the Chinese people understand where China was strong, where it lagged behind, and what its favorable and unfavorable conditions were so as to enhance their sense of historical mission and responsibility. Patriotism was used as a national call, while the peculiarity of the "national essence" offered a rationale for that call. A communist government that otherwise would be hardly acceptable to the Chinese people after the end of the Cold War was justified by its national essence. As a result, some intellectuals, including those who had sharply criticized the government during the spring of 1989, changed their attitudes. They accepted the themes of the patriotic education campaign about China's special conditions, that is, the argument that sudden democratization in China would result in rapid social disintegration, as witnessed in the former Soviet Union and Eastern European countries. The fear of total disintegration in China was thus used as a lever to boost nationalism and to alleviate the crisis of legitimacy faced by the regime.[33]

Intellectual Discourse on Nationalism

While the communist regime was the driving force of nationalist sentiment from above, Chinese intellectuals developed a nationalistic discourse in the 1990s. Although this intellectual discourse overlaps, to a certain extent, with the patriotic rhetoric of the Chinese government, its emergence was largely independent of official propaganda. Those who contributed to the intellectual discourse on nationalism are from various political backgrounds. Some were liberal intellectuals who supported the 1989 democratic movement. Early advocates of Chinese national-ism in the 1990s include such liberal intellectuals as Yuan Hongbin, who participated in the Tiananmen demonstrations and was later pun-ished for his role in the movement by the government. Established schol-ars of neoauthoritarianism, such as Xiao Gongqin, were the leading articulators for the intellectual discourse on nationalism. Extremely con-servative intellectuals, such as He Xin, who are against any kind of West-ernization, also had a voice in this discourse.

What brought together intellectuals with such different political views under the banner of nationalism? The important common denominator among them is concern over the threat of social disorder and even disin-tegration following the course of the former Soviet Union and Eastern European nations. These intellectuals deemed it necessary to promote nationalism as a new force of unity in order to achieve their shared *qiangguo meng* (the dream of a strong China). National greatness is an agreed upon objective and historical mission of Chinese intellectuals, notwithstanding their other differences. Far from being detached schol-ars observing the rapid sociopolitical changes from the sidelines, Chi-nese intellectuals are active participants in the process and their embrace of nationalism is a result of soul-searching for their nation's destiny.

In the nineteenth century, China fell prey to an imperialist world be-cause political decay, technological backwardness, and economic weak-ness had eliminated any capacity for China to defend itself. The Middle Kingdom had been a major world power built on a superior culture ex-tending back for millennia. Many Chinese intellectuals pointed to the lack of modernization as the reason China became an easy target for aggressive Western imperialism. Recollections of ancient grandeur, com-bined with outrage at China's humiliation, provided the starting point for modern Chinese nationalism. To revive China, many had adopted a hostile view toward their own past, calling for the complete rejection of Chinese tradition and boundless adoption of Western culture. From the May Fourth Movement through the Maoist years to Deng's reform era, there have been repeated attacks on China's cultural heritage. During the early reform years of the 1980s, there was a rise of "cultural fever" (*wenhua re*) among Chinese intellectuals.[34] There were two basic themes in the cultural fever: "criticism of traditional Chinese culture and criticism of Chinese national character."[35] Many Chinese intellectuals blamed China's "feudal culture" for the country's absolutism, narrow mindedness, and love of orthodoxy, even calling Chinese people the ugly Chinese. In this cultural fever, antitraditionalism (*fanchuantong zhuyi*) dominated Chinese intellectual discourse. Modernization was confused with Westernization. In the minds of many Chinese intellectuals, the West represented material wealth, rationality, freedom and democracy, and modernity.

After the 1989 Tiananmen tragedy and the end of the Cold War, however, antitraditionalism quickly vanished. Many Chinese intellectuals decided that the post–Cold War transformation in Eastern Europe and the former Soviet Union was not as positive as expected. The West, its values and systems, did not make much difference to postcommunist countries. Although Russia took a big-bang approach to adopt a democratic system, the Western countries, as Chinese saw it, still tried to weaken Russia's standing in international affairs by expanding NATO to Eastern Europe as it struggled internally with its reform program. Even those who supported the 1989 student movement concluded that if China were to initiate the dramatic democratic reform promoted by the West, the nation could well suffer a similar disorder as Russia.

In contrast to the former Soviet Union, China's incremental economic reform brought about rapid economic growth in the 1990s. Economic success transformed the nation's intellectual discourse and built up Chinese intellectuals' self-confidence in their tradition and awakened national pride and cultural identities. Many social scientists and humanities scholars called for a "paradigm shift." A conservative, nationalistic intellectual discourse emerged. This discourse supported neoauthoritarianism by arguing that a centralized power structure must be strengthened in order to maintain social stability and economic development. It also vocally promoted cultural nationalism or an "anti-Westernism" movement (*fan xifangzhuyi yundong*) by advocating a nativist value system.

Neoauthoritarianism is a less-Marxist-colored but nondemocratic intellectual discourse that emerged in the late 1980s. It supported a strong and authoritarian state to enforce modernization programs and an "enlightened autocracy" for economic development.[36] Neoauthoritarianism argued that the economic miracle of the four "little dragons" in East

Asia was created because they all shared Confucian collectivism, family loyalty, and frugality as well as a patriarchal power structure. Before the Tiananmen Incident, neoauthoritarianism was only a heatedly debated topic.[37] It was advocated mainly by some personal aides to Zhao Ziyang, then the CCP general secretary, and by a few scholars, including Shanghai-based Xiao Gongqin and Wang Huning. Many liberal scholars, especially antitraditionalist scholars, argued strongly against neoauthoritarianism by questioning the validity of the alleged causal relationship between Confucianist authoritarianism and economic success.[38]

After the Tiananmen Incident, when the government enforced official ideological control, non-Marxist voices, even neoauthoritarianism, were silenced. Deng Xiaoping's southern China tour in 1992 undermined the extreme rigidity of the conservative ideological control, setting the stage for some less-communist ideas, including some neoauthoritarian arguments under a new name, neoconservatism, to reemerge. Neoconservatism emphasizes political and economic stability and control while restoring moral values based on the conservative elements of Confucianism.[39]

Immediately after the Tiananmen Incident, He Xin, a conservative scholar at the Chinese Academy of Social Sciences, was the most visible symbol of neoconservatism. He vigorously supported official slogans such as "stability above everything" to defend government action suppressing student demonstrations.[40] But He Xin was quickly rejected by most intellectuals because he was seen as merely saying what the most conservative authorities wanted him to say. In 1992, a group of politically ambitious intellectuals published a widely circulated article, "Sulian jubian zhihou Zhongguo de xianshi yingdui yu zhanlüe yuanze" (Realistic responses and strategic choices for China after the disintegration of the Soviet Union), which became a banner of neoconservatism.[41] The group argued that Marxism-Leninism was no longer effective in mobilizing loyalty and legitimating the state. It was necessary to develop a new ideological vision that drew selectively from China's culture. The CCP should base itself firmly on Chinese nationalism.

Some prominent scholars also joined the orchestra of neoconservatism in arguing for strong state power to ward off the possible break-up of the country and economy. In 1994, Xiao Gongqin issued warnings about the dangers of weakening ideological control. Xiao saw no solutions in Western nostrums or in communist ideology but only in nationalism. Xiao's view was elucidated in two articles, "Nationalism and Ideology in China in the Transitional Era," and "History and the Prospect for Nationalism in China."[42] Xiao worried about the possible disintegration of Chinese society resulting from the decline of the official ideology and argued that "the central political task of modernization is to prevent the problems of de-substantiation (*kongdonghua*) and povertization (*pinkunhua*) of the ideology due to the lack of ideological resources. Therefore, the overriding issue of China's modernization is how, under new historical circumstances, to find new resources of legitimacy so as to achieve social and moral integration in the process of social transition."[43] According to Xiao, nationalism could play "the function of political integration (*zhengzhi zhenghe*) and cohesion (*ningju*)" in the post–Cold War era.[44] Commenting on South Korean experiences, another scholar, Yi Baoyun, states that "For nations lagging behind, the appropriate choice is not a renunciation of nationalism, but a revitalization of it so as to integrate and elevate people's loyalty on the national level. . . . Nationalism insures national integration so that through a change of the system, the nation can be led to the road of self-strengthening and peaceful competition."[45]

How to understand the changing nature of international conflict in the post–Cold War world is a central concern of the discourse on nationalism. Chinese intellectuals especially noted two views from the West. Fukuyama portrays the end of the Cold War as a triumph of capitalism and Western liberalism and believes that the end of the Cold War is not just "the passing of a particular period of postwar history, but the end of history: that is, the end point of mankind's ideological evolution and the universalization of Western liberal democracy as the final form of human government."[46] Samuel P. Huntington, on the other hand, foresees "the clash of civilizations" and argues that geopolitical struggles in the post–Cold War world are not ideologically motivated but defined by different civilizations.[47] More and more Chinese intellectuals were convinced that after the end of the Cold War, nations and countries that used to be confined by ideology have come to realize their own national identity, interests, and values. As a result, a confrontation between different nation-states, understood as cultures, but under the banner of nationalism, is going to replace the opposition between communism and capitalism. The vacuum left by the end of political-ideological confrontation has been filled by nationalism.

Chinese intellectuals paid special attention to Huntington's argument that the biggest threat to Western civilization is Islamic and Confucian culture, thus the West should be alert to a Confucian and Islamic alliance. This argument faced vociferous attacks from Chinese intellectuals. Wang Jisi, director of the American Studies Institute in the Chinese Academy of Social Sciences, put together a group of Chinese scholars' articles on Huntington's *Clash of Civilizations* into a book, titled *Civilization and International Politics*.[48] Wang Xiaodong (using a pen name, Shi Zhong), one of the editors of *Zhanlue yu Guanli*, published an article in the first issue of the journal to rebuff Huntington. He argued that there was no desire on the part of the Chinese to Confucianize the rest of the world and that useful Western values were generally welcomed by the Chinese, apart from the instances where their transmission involved economic and other forms of imperialism. According to Wang, any future conflicts would depend on economic interests; the thesis of a clash of civilizations was little more than a guise for a clash of national interests. China could come into conflict with other powers because of its growing economic strength.[49] In another article, Wang criticized the overly optimistic view of globalization on the grounds that the real power of this globalization process is singularly beneficial to the West. That is, interdependence and liberal internationalism were seen as myths hiding the continuing reality of neomercantilist nationalism. Under these circumstances, nationalism is indispensable and a rational choice to advance the interests of China.[50]

Chinese intellectuals took more critical attitudes toward Western mainstream scholarship. In the 1980s, Chinese intellectuals became familiar with the West mostly by reading a large number of Western scholarly works, which were translated into Chinese. Many of these books were printed in hundreds of thousands of copies, outnumbering the printing in their native languages. Frequent and wide international exchanges, especially with the United States, allowed many Chinese intellectuals to take a closer look at Western societies and their academic world, which helped remove the myth of Western modernization models and gave Chinese the courage and ammunition to criticize Western theories.

Previously the West was a remote object of admiration and imitation, convincing Chinese scholars that all nations would converge on the model of modernization found in Western industrialized countries. When Chinese scholars traveled to the West and obtained a deeper understanding, they saw the inherent problems in the West and came to believe that the so-called universal theories and principles of modernization were only unique products of Western history and culture. There was a huge gap between the Western model and Chinese reality. This led these intellectuals to doubt the worth of modern Western values for Chinese society and the utility of mainstream Western theories for building a strong China. Therefore, some Chinese intellectuals turned to critical theories of the West, such as postcolonialism and post-Marxism, in an attempt to find intellectual inspiration for a new path of modernization that would fit the Chinese essence (*guoqing*). Some other scholars looked toward non-Western civilizations, including Chinese, to discover a new path that can resolve the problems that arose in the process of China's modernization.

As a result, Chinese intellectuals rediscovered the value of the Chinese cultural legacy, which the party had so relentlessly attacked for so long. Aware of the incompatibility of the orthodox official doctrines with the needs of modernization, many intellectuals argued that old-styled communist indoctrination would not be effective. A new way of thinking must be found. This new way is an embrace of Chinese culture and a negating of the so-called Western value system. A new awareness arose of a need to articulate a more vivid sense of Chinese collective identity. The authors of *The China That Can Say No* confessed that back in college they craved Western culture and things, but they began to think differently after Beijing's 1993 defeat in the Olympic site competition and after the U.S. aircraft carriers were sent to defend Taiwan in March 1996. Before Chinese could say no to the Americans, they had to say no first to their own lack of nationalistic spirit and to their blind worship of the United States.[51] This feeling gave rise to cultural nationalism, which took Chinese culture as a symbol against Western cultural hegemony (or cultural colonialism). Only Chinese culture could serve the positive function of maintaining political order. Opposition to Western cultural hegemony and cultural colonialism is a central concern of cultural nationalism. As a result of the upsurge of cultural nationalism, the "Western learning fever" (*xixue re*) was replaced by a "Chinese/Confucius learning fever" (*guoxue re*) among intellectuals, especially humanities scholars. Intellectual debates were redefined in terms of "Chineseness." Some scholars called for an academic nativism (*xueshu bentuhua*), namely, extracting a brand new set of concepts and theories from ancient Chinese thoughts and experiences. Liu Kang and Li Xiguang, two leading advocates of cultural nationalism, stated that "in the 1990s, Chinese intellectuals ought to . . . liberate themselves from 'modern' Western speech and thought patterns, and acquire a new understanding of modern nationalism and nativism, to form a genuinely humane spirit (*renwen jingshen*) and rebuild their 'academic lineage' and 'ethical traditions' with Chinese culture."[52] In this intellectual discourse, Chinese culture not only counteracted the invasion of Western culture, but also replaced the unwelcome official ideological doctrines. *Fayang chuantong* (getting back to tradition) became a call of cultural nationalism. In this way, Chinese intellectual discourse concurred with the central theme of state-led nationalism advocated in patriotic education by the communist government. But it arrived at this point largely independent of government indoctrination. Because it discarded official ideological rhetoric, its arguments seemed more influential and persuasive to many Chinese. [53]

The Dynamics of Chinese Nationalism

A prominent Western scholar finds that "the 1990s are the decade of nationalism."[54] There indeed exists a growing global trend of nationalism in the post–Cold War world. Thus the rise of Chinese nationalism is not unique. But Chinese nationalism has some unique dynamics.

First, the recent revival of nationalism represents a great aggregation of various political and intellectual forces with different motivations and agendas. Besides the government propaganda campaign in fanning nationalistic flames, the intellectual undercurrent moved almost simultaneously in the same direction. The rallying under the banner of nationalism occurred after the Tiananmen Incident in 1989, which presented a harsh challenge to the basis of the regime's legitimacy. Promoting nationalism is a measure taken by the Communist Party leadership to redefine its legitimacy. While some extreme conservative leaders wanted to make nationalism a weapon against any kind of Western liberalization, reform-minded leaders understood the potential damage a campaign against bourgeois liberalization could bring to China's economic reform. The campaign was thus limited to youth education programs on patriotism and traditional culture.

The intellectual discourse on nationalism does not stem from one group with an identifiable political view. As observed by Wang Xiaodong, one of the leading contributors to the intellectual discourse on nationalism in China, "Among those under the banner of nationalism, there is a full array of people: some of whom advocate authoritarianism, others who support expansionism; while some people believe in more state controls, and others uphold the total freedom of a market economy. There are also those who propose a return to tradition and others opposing this restoration."[55]

Reasons Nationalism
succeeded.

Second, the rise of Chinese nationalism in the 1990s is characterized by pragmatic concerns of both the Chinese government and intellectual elite about vital domestic issues. Nationalism helped the communist regime to create a sense of commonalty among citizens when the regime faced a threat to its legitimacy. The leading advocate of Chinese nationalism, the communist state, stressed the pragmatic or instrumental aspect of nationalism, not the intrinsic value of nationalism. To the Chinese government, promoting nationalist sentiment would hold the nation together during a period of rapid and turbulent transition and reduce the threat of liberalism and democracy to communist authoritarian legitimacy. Nationalism also helped Chinese intellectuals to participate in the modernization process by identifying with the Chinese nation. When patriotic intellectuals say that China has been bullied and humiliated frequently by foreign powers, they also indicate that "backward is apt to be beaten" and China's backwardness in economic development should share some blame for China's past humiliations. Thus, Chinese nationalism calls upon the Chinese people to work hard and to build a prosperous and strong China so that China's international status would be improved and nobody would dare to bully China anymore.

In this case, Chinese nationalism is still far from its complete formation because it does not have independent political, economic, cultural value or ethical values. Many Chinese intellectuals who advocated cultural nationalism were trained in the West. They used the critical knowledge they learned in the West, such as postcolonialism, postmodernism, post-Marxism, and Orientalism, to attack Western culture. Chinese intellectual advocates for cultural nationalism have chosen as their weapons the language, concepts, and style of Western discourses. Chinese intellectual discourse on nationalism is so full of Western jargon that anyone unfamiliar with Western intellectual discourse would hardly understand these erudite exponents of Chinese nationalistic writings.

Third, Chinese nationalism has a strong moral and ethical appeal. It is closely related to a popular conservative political and intellectual tendency. The resurgence of the Chinese intellectual discourse on nationalism is based largely on the fate of Chinese culture, as well as on how Chinese culture can contribute to the solution of many problems of modernity. Some Chinese scholars argue that Asians in general and Chinese in particular have their own set of values different from those of the West. Some even suggest that Asian values are superior and should therefore be the criteria of the values of the world in the next century.

Sheng Hong, a controversial economist in Beijing, launched a fierce attack on Western civilization in an article published in a 1994 issue of *Zhanlüe yu Guanli*. According to Sheng, Western civilizations developed out of monotheistic religion. Because each religion worshiped only one god, war and competition were inevitable. In the context of religious conflict and competition, social Darwinism developed. Sheng claimed that Western culture thus would neither be able to save China nor the world but would lead humanity to catastrophe. He also criticized Western culture's double standard. While the West demanded a certain degree of liberty, democracy, and human rights for its own people, it imposed a law of the jungle, social Darwinism, on the outside world. China could not develop on the basis of social Darwinism. Only Chinese civilization could save China and eventually help save the world because it was not developed from a monotheistic religious form. Confucian respect for universal harmony and collectivism in Chinese culture are instrumental for world peace and development.[56] Following the lead of Prime Minister Mahathir of Malaysia and Shintaro Ishihara of Japan in their books, *The Voice of Asia* and *The Japan That Can Say No*, Chinese authors published a series of "Say No" books. [57]

Chinese nationalism is hostile toward the United States because the United States represents an opposing value system, that is, liberalism and individualism. Deep-rooted nationalist sentiments among Chinese people are also directed against Japan, due mainly to the humiliation and injustices suffered by the Chinese people at the hands of Japanese imperialists during World War II. The animosity toward Japan does not have a cultural value dimension. Thus, the United States is treated in a very different way in nationalistic sentiments. The 1996 bestseller, *The China That Can Say No*, states that "The moral decay[58] inside the United States for the past several centuries has formed evil results" and the United States will "inevitably face a *fin-de-siècle* type general squaring of accounts." The United States is "annoying yet futile, despicable yet pitiful, and has lost its future directions." As a comparison, the book writes that "the liberalization movements of the world all have bathed in the sunshine of Chinese thoughts. The peace and progress of the world all have benefited from Chinese merits and virtues." It asserts that "the power of Chinese thoughts and Chinese managerial ability will deeply affect the world, and become the only force leading the future human ideological trend."[59]

Conclusion

Nationalism has played two different roles in the modern world. It could be inward-directed sentiments and hold a nation together or outward-directed sentiments and aim hostility toward others. At times, nationalism functioned to free nations from alien rule, created a state of its own, and contributed to modernization.[60] However, nationalism, especially its extreme versions that are associated with racist arrogance and ignorance, is also responsible for many human tragedies. A new nationalism, or "a nationalistic universalism" as Hans J. Morgenthau called it, has been seen as a bad thing when one state is strong enough to impose its will on others and hence become a source of international aggression and confrontation.[61]

Is Chinese nationalism a source of international aggression? Allen Whiting has tried to explore this issue by asking the following question: Is Chinese nationalism affirmative, assertive, or aggressive?[62] In his 1983 study, Whiting discovered that China had experienced a transition from an affirmative nationalism, which emphasizes an exclusive but positive "us," to an assertive nationalism by adding a negative "them." However, Whiting did not find in 1983 any imputation of belligerence or aggression attached to his concept of assertive nationalism. In a 1987 study, Michael Oksenberg agreed that "the leaders of modern China have not exhibited the ultra or expansionist nationalism that so many rising powers have manifested."[63] He used "confident nationalism" to explain the nonaggressive nature of Chinese nationalism. According to Oksenberg, confident nationalism is a "patient and moderate nationalism rooted in confidence that over time China can regain its former greatness through economic growth, based on the import of foreign technology and ideas."[64] After China rose to be one of the world economic powerhouses in the 1990s, however, Whiting has become cautious and is not sure if Chinese nationalism will not become aggressive.[65] His study of ASEAN's concern over Beijing's military behavior in 1995–96 reveals a "growing Chinese challenge to stability in East Asia." Although he does not anticipate "an expansionist China seeking to take over any country by attack, subversion, or economic domination," he indicates a well-grounded fear by ASEAN countries that "territorial disputes can prompt forceful assertiveness by Beijing that will threaten individual claims and disrupt the regional environment for economic growth dependent on trade and investment."[66]

This study shows that the current rise of Chinese nationalism is primarily a result of internal crises rather than immediate threats from the outside world. Preoccupied with complex internal issues, it is difficult for the communist regime to mobilize popular support of nationalist xenophobia. Although nationalism could work as a unifying force to hold the country together under the leadership of the Communist Party and have the function of turning the past humiliation and current weakness into a driving force for China's modernization, it is a double-edged sword and the cost of ultranationalism could become disproportionately high. Once unleashed, nationalistic xenophobia can cause a serious backlash and place the government in a hot spot facing challenges from both domestic and international sources.

Domestically, Chinese nationalism in essence is an assertion of the Chinese nation-state. However, nation and state are not the same. A nation is an ethnic or cultural group and a state is a sovereign political community.[67] Most states today include more than one nation or potential nation, with complex overlapping or competing national claims on their citizens. The conflict between nations and states has given rise to two types of nationalism. One is state nationalism, which defines the nation as a territorial-political unit and sees nationalism as a sense of essential political identity. Another is ethnic nationalism, which sees the nation as a large, politicized ethnic group defined by common culture and alleged descent.[68] China is a multinational state. The rising nationalism, however, appeals largely to the Han history and nation. This could be dangerous because ethnic divisions have always been a source of tension in the PRC. In spite of the dominance of state nationalism, ethnic nationalism, particularly among Tibetans, Uighurs, other Muslims, and Mongols, has never been suppressed. They are still bitter about the personal and collective (ethnic) suffering they have experienced under Han Chinese rule, particularly during the period of the Cultural Revolution. Although the Chinese government has granted minorities various kinds of special representation and autonomy and has been relatively effective in resisting open espousal of Han Chinese ethnic nationalism, anti-Han ethnic identity endures. They see themselves "engaged in a struggle to keep culture and national identity afloat in a world of one billion Han."[69] In Tibet, for example, ethnic nationalism has triumphed over the state's version of Han-Tibetan relations. Ethnic nationalism among minorities makes it clear that some may choose greater differentiation and autonomy over integration into the PRC nation, a trend that on all sides can only strengthen awareness of the distinctiveness and dominance of the core Han Chinese nation.

Internationally, the rise of Chinese nationalism has been seen as "a potent force in a country that is striving to shake off its image as the sick man of Asia and regain ancient glory."[70] Although the absence of nationalism in imperial China was a fatal weakness, the new tide of Chinese nationalism has caused anxiety in Asia and America in the 1990s. Many analysts, sobered by two centuries of imperialism, revolution, and war, have taken a negative view of nationalism. Chinese military exercises in March 1996 may have fired a shot across the bow of Taiwanese independence, but it also set off alarms all over East Asia, causing a series of moves, detailed in June Dreyer's essay in this volume, that were against China's national interests. The Japan-U.S. relationship was strengthened. The American military withdrawal from Okinawa was shelved temporarily. Indonesia was drawn closer to Australia and protested China's claim to a gas field in the South China Sea. The Philippines strengthened its military and improved relations with Taiwan.

Yet, Chinese nationalism has largely been defensive and internal in orientation so far. To be sure, China's decision makers and strategists have displayed a consistently realpolitik worldview in the post–Cold War world. Nevertheless, their preferred ends have predominantly remained the preservation of territorial integrity and the defense of their own political power. Admittedly, the Chinese communist regime plays up a history of painful Chinese weakness in the face of Western imperialism, territorial division, unequal treaties, invasion, anti-Chinese racism, and social chaos. Eliminating "the century of shame and humiliation" is at the heart of a principal claim to CCP legitimacy today. But this does not necessarily result in an aggressive anti-Western policy. While appealing to patriotism and criticizing the West for its "peaceful evolution" attempt, CCP General Secretary Jiang Zemin stated that "The development and progress of China is inseparable from the achievements in civilization achieved by every country in the world. China needs to learn and assimilate the excellent achievements in the creation of civilization achieved by the people of every country in the world, including those who live under the capitalist system."[71] A *Renmin Ribao* editorial in commemoration of the 150th anniversary of the Opium War echoed Jiang's point, "While we must hold high the banner of patriotism, we should not indiscriminately reject anything foreign and close our doors to the outside world. Yet while we must open to the outside world, we should not yield to any pressure and to advocates of total Westernization."[72]

Nationalism has not made China's international behavior particularly aggressive. In a study in 1996, David Shambaugh characterizes current Chinese posturing as "defensive nationalism" which is "assertive in form, but reactive in essence."[73] Bernstein and Munro are right that "China is quick to take offense and to view disagreements that other countries might take more easily in stride as assaults on national dignity, requiring uncompromising response."[74] China is sensitive to infringements of national sovereignty. One Western report found that "Even though it [China] is reestablished as an important power, China still acts like a country with something to prove, and it collects what it sees as new slights to its pride."[75] President Jiang Zemin refused to go to Washington to meet President Clinton for a "working visit" in 1995 because he wanted the 21–gun salute that goes with a state visit.

If nationalism continues to rise, China may remain nondemocratic but not necessarily be a threat to the West. The danger is, however, that if an ideologically based America begins to treat China as an enemy, China could be turned into a threat. Experientially defensive and inward-directed nationalism does not exclude its potential threat of prejudice and hostility toward other nations because the memory of "national humiliation" engenders an urge for China to be strong, capable of contending with any challenges throughout the world. Chinese nationalism generates anxieties about why China still is weak and how it can become strong, about lost territory, and about reclaiming a leading position in the world. Chinese nationalism has often been uncompromising with foreign (particularly American) demands and extremely reactive to any foreign criticism. As a result, the revival of Chinese nationalism has raised the question of how to incorporate China into the world civilizations infused by liberal international norms. If the United States and the international community cannot find an effective way to accomplish this, Chinese nationalism may become irrational and produce a regime that is insular, paranoid, and reactive. This is a development that the United States and the international community should work hard to avoid.

Notes

1. Kishore Mahbubani, "The Pacific Way," *Foreign Affairs*, vol. 74, no. 1, January/February 1995, p. 103.

2. *Renmin Ribao*, October 1, 1996, p. 1.

3. Liu Binyan, "Big Drama about Small Islands," *China Focus*, vol. 4, no. 10, October 1, 1996, p. 1.

4. Song Qiang, Zhang Zangzang, Qiao Bian, eds., *Zhongguo keyi shuo bu* (The China that can say no). Beijing: Zhonghua gongshang lianhe chubanshe, 1996.

5. Samuel Wang, "Teaching Patriotism in China," *China Strategic Review*, vol. 1, no. 4, July 5, 1996, p. 13.

6. Erik Eckholm, "China's Liberals Look for Silver Lining," *New York Times*, May 17, 1999 (electronic version).

7. Richard Bernstein and Ross H. Munro, "The Coming Conflict with America," *Foreign Affairs*, vol. 76, no. 2, March/April 1997, p. 19.

8. Samuel P. Huntington, *The Clash of Civilizations and the Remaking of World Order*. New York: Simon & Schuster, 1996, p. 229.

9. James R. Lilley, "Nationalism Bites Back," *New York Times*, October 24, 1996.

10. Hans Kohn, "Nationalism," *International Encyclopedia of the Social Sciences*, vol. 11, 1968, p. 63.

11. Immanuel C. Y. Hsu, *China's Entrance into the Family of Nations: The Diplomatic Phase, 1858–1880*. Cambridge: Harvard University Press, 1960, p. 13.

12. James Harrison, *Modern Chinese Nationalism*. New York: Hunter College, Research Institute on Modern Asia, 1969, p. 2.

13. Joseph Levenson, *Liang Ch'i-ch'ao and the Mind of Modern China*. Berkeley: University of California Press, 1967, p. 108.

14. John Fitzgerald, "The Nationless State: The Search for a Nation in Modern Chinese Nationalism," in Jonathan Unger, ed., *Chinese Nationalism*. Armonk, NY: M. E. Sharpe, 1996, p. 67.

15. Han Jinchun and Li Yifu, "Hanwen 'minzu' yi ci de chuxian jiqi chuqi shiyong qingkuang" (The emergence of the term 'minzu' in Chinese language and usage). *Minzu Yanjiu*, no. 2, 1984, pp. 36–43.

16. Andrew J. Nathan and Robert S. Ross, *The Great Wall and the Empty Fortress: China's Search for Security*. New York: W. W. Norton, 1997, pp. 32–33.

17. Xiao Gongqin, "Zhongguo minzu zhuyi de lishi yu qianjing" (The history and prospects of Chinese nationalism), *Zhanlüe yu Guanli*, no. 2, 1996, p. 59.

18. For one study of the struggle between the conservatives and reformers in the ideological arena after the Tiananmen Incident, see Suisheng Zhao, "Deng Xiaoping's Southern Tour: Elite Politics in Post-Tiananmen China," *Asian Survey*, vol. 33, no. 8, August 1993, pp. 739–756.

19. Liah Greenfeld, *Nationalism: Five Roads to Modernity*. Cambridge, MA: Harvard University Press, 1992, p. 3.

20. Joseph S. Nye, Jr., *Understanding International Conflicts*. New York: Harper Collins, 1993, p. 61.

21. Jiang Zemin, "Patriotism and the Mission of the Chinese Intellectuals," Xinhua, May 3, 1990.

22. Charles Tilly, "States and Nationalism in Europe, 1492–1992," in John L. Comaroff and Paul C. Stern, eds., *Perspectives on Nationalism and War*. Luxembourg: Gordon and Breach, 1995, p. 190.

23. Because of its state-centric nature, Michael Hunt argues against reducing Chinese patriotism to the Western term nationalism. Hunt, "Chinese National Identity and the Strong State: The Late Qing-Republican Crisis," in Lowell Dittmer and

Samuel S. Kim, eds., *China's Quest for National Identity.* Ithaca, NY: Cornell University Press, 1994, p. 63.

24. "To Construct the Motherland More Beautiful and Better," *Renmin Ribao*, October 1, 1996, p. 1.

25. "Beijing Students Watch Patriotic Films," Xinhua, May 16, 1994.

26. "Ding Guangen, Li Lanqing Commend Patriotic Education Meeting," Beijing Central Television Program, May 21, FBIS-CHI-94–102, May 26, 1994, p. 18.

27. Geoffrey Crothall, "China: Patriotic Patter Winning Students," *South China Morning Post*, July 10, 1994, p. 8.

28. "The Outline for Conducting Patriotic Education," *Renmin Ribao*, September 6, 1994, p. 1.

29. Steven Mufson, "Maoism, Confucianism Blur Into Nationalism," *The Washington Post*, March 19, 1996, p. A1.

30. For one excellent description of how the CCP used the Great Wall for patriotic education purposes, see Arthur Waldron, "Scholarship and Patriotic Education: The Great Wall Conference, 1994," *The China Quarterly*, no. 143, September 1995, pp. 844–850.

31. "Beijing Radio Commentator on Party's Patriotic Education Document," *Reuters Textline*, September 7, 1994.

32. "Gaoju aiguozhuyi qizhi" (Hold high the banner of patriotism), *Renmin Ribao*, November 28, 1993.

33. Some parts of the discussion in this section are adapted from my article "A State-Led Nationalism: The Patriotic Education Campaign in Post-Tiananmen China," *Communist and Post-Communist Studies*, vol. 31, no. 3, September 1998.

34. For one systematic description of the cultural fever, see Wu Xiuyi, *Zhongguo wenhua re* (China's cultural fever). Shanghai: Shanghai renmin chubanshe, 1988. Chen Kuide, the former chief-editor of *Shixiangjia* (Thinker) in Shanghai and one of the active participants in the cultural fever wrote an excellent article to reflect the cultural fever, "Wenhua re: Beijing, shichao ji liangzhong qingxiang" (The cultural fever: Background, ideology, and two tendencies), in Chen Kuide, ed., *Zhongguo dalu dangdai wenhua bianqian* (Contemporary cultural changes in mainland China). Taipei: Guigan chubanshe, 1991, pp. 37–61.

35. Merle Goldman, Perry Link, and Su Wei, "China's Intellectuals in the Deng Era: Loss of Identity with the State," in Lowell Dittmer and Samuel S. Kim, eds., *China's Quest for National Identity*, p. 143.

36. Liu Zaiping, "Summary of a Seminar on New Authoritarianism," *Guangming Ribao*, March 24, 1996.

37. For a collection of debate articles, see Qi Mo, ed., *Xin quanwei zhuyi: Dui Zhongguo dalu weilai mingyun de lunzheng* (New authoritarianism: A debate for the future of mainland China). Taipei: Tangshan chubanshe, 1991. For a collection of English translation articles on this debate, see Stanley Rosen and Gary Zou, eds., "The Chinese Debate on the New Authoritarianism," *Chinese Sociology and Anthropology*, vol. 23, no. 2, winter 1990–91.

38. See, for example, Huang Wansheng, "Questions and Answers on the Criticism of New Authoritarianism," *Wenhui Bao*, February 22, 1989; Bao Zunxin, "Confucian Ethics and the Four Little Dragons of Asia," *Wenhui Bao*, May 12, 1988.

39. For one systematic analysis of neoconservatism, see Joseph Fewsmith, "Neoconservatism and the End of the Dengist Era," *Asian Survey*, vol. 35, no. 7, July 1995, pp. 635–651.

40. He Xin's articles are collected in *Zhonghua fuxing yu shijie weilai* (Renovation of China and the future of the world) (two volumes). Chengdu: Sichuan renmin chubanshe, 1996, and *Wei Zhongguo shengbian* (Defending China). Jinan: Shandong youyi chubanshe, 1996.

41. This article was first published in the name of the Ideology and Theory Department of the *Zhongguo Qingnian Bao* (China Youth Daily) as an internal-circulated article in September 1991. It quickly leaked abroad and was reprinted in *Zhongguo Zhichun* (China Spring) in New York City. I interviewed one of the authors of this article in Beijing during the summer of 1994. He confirmed the above speculation that it was written based on the proceedings of a meeting held at *Zhongguo Qingnian Bao* and the participants were a group of party and government officials active in policy analysis and consultants for the post-Tiananmen leadership.

42. Xiao Gongqin, "Minzuzhuyi yu Zhongguo zhuangxing shiqide yishi xingtai" (Nationalism and ideology in China in the transitional era), *Zhanlüe yu Guanli*, no. 4, 1994, pp. 21–25, and "Zhongguo minzuzhuyi de lishi yu qianjing (History and the prospect for nationalism in China), *Zhanlüe yu Guanli*, no. 2, 1996, pp. 58–62.

43. Xiao Gongqin, "Minzuzhuyi yu Zhongguo zhuangxing shiqide yishi xingtai," p. 23.

44. Xiao Gongqin, "Zhongguo minzuzhuyi de lishi yu qianjing," p. 62.

45. Yi Baoyun, "Minzuzhuyi yu xiandai jingji fazhan (Nationalism and modern economic development), *Zhanlüe yu Guanli*, no. 3, 1994.

46. Ibid., p. 4.

47. Samuel Huntington, "The Clash of Civilizations," *Foreign Affairs*, vol. 72, no. 3 (Summer 1993); *The Clash of Civilizations and the Remaking of World Order*.

48. Wang Jisi, ed., *Wenming yu guoji zhengzhi: Zhongguo xuezhe ping Huntington de wenming chongtulun* (Civilization and international politics: Chinese scholars on Huntington's *Clash of Civilizations*). Shanghai: Shanghai renmin chubanshe, 1995.

49. Shi Zhong (Wang Xiaodong), "Weilai de chongtu" (Future conflicts), *Zhanlüe yu Guanli*, no. 1, 1993, pp. 46–50.

50. Shi Zhong (Wang Xiaodong), "Zhongguo xiandaihua mianlin de tiaozhan" (The challenges to China's modernization), *Zhanlüe yu Guanli*, no. 1, 1994.

51. Song Qiang, Zhang Zangzang, Qiao Bian, eds., *Zhongguo keyi shuo bu*, pp. 3–15.

52. Li Xiguang and Liu Kang, "A Look at the Coverage of China by the Mainstream US Media," *Zhongguo Jizhe* (The Chinese journalist), May 15, 1996, p, 19. For an English translation of this article, see FBIS-CHI-96–147, July 30, 1996, pp. 4–8.

53. Some parts of the discussion in this section are adapted from my article, "Chinese Intellectuals' Quest for National Greatness and Nationalistic Writing in the 1990s," *The China Quarterly*, no. 152, December 1997, pp. 725–745.

54. Ernst B. Haas, *Nationalism, Liberalism, and Progress: The Rise and Decline of Nationalism*. Ithaca: Cornell University Press, 1997, p. vii.

55. Shi Zhong (Wang Xiaodong), "Zhongguo de minzuzhuyi yu Zhongguo de weilai" (Chinese nationalism and China's future), *Huaxia Wenzhai* (China digest) (an Internet electronic magazine), 1996.

56. Sheng Hong, "Shenme shi wenming" (What is civilization?), *Zhanlue yu Guanli*, no. 5, 1995; "Cong minzuzhuyi dao tianxiazhuyi" (From nationalism to cosmopolitanism), *Zhanlüe yu Guanli*, no. 1, 1996; and "Jingjixue tiaozhan xifang" (Economics challenges the West), *Dongfang*, no. 1, 1996.

57. Shintaro Ishihara, *The Japan That Can Say No*. New York: Simon and Schuster, 1991; and Mahatir Mohamad and Shintaro Ishihara, *The Voice of Asia: Two Leaders Discuss the Coming Century*. New York: Kodansha International, 1995.

58. Some parts of the discussion in this section are adapted from my article, "Chinese Intellectuals' Quest for National Greatness and Nationalistic Writing in the 1990s."

59. Song Qiang, Zhang Zangzang, Qiao Bian, eds., *Zhongguo keyi shuo bu*, pp. 50, 230, 49, and 51.

60. For a recent discussion on nationalism and its historical role in the West, see Liah Greenfield, *Nationalism: Five Roads to Modernity*.

61. Hans J. Morgenthau, *Politics Among Nations: The Struggle for Power and Peace*. New York: McGraw-Hill, 1993, pp. 272–273.

62. According to Whiting, affirmative nationalism fosters patriotism and its implications for foreign policy are minimal. Aggressive nationalism arouses anger and mobilizes behavior targeted against foreign enemies. Assertive nationalism lies between the two, sharing attributes of each and tending toward either depending on its intensity. See Allen Whiting, "Assertive Nationalism in Chinese Foreign Policy," *Asian Survey*, vol. 23, no. 8, August 1983, pp. 913–933.

63. Michel Oksenberg, "China's Confident Nationalism," *Foreign Affairs*, vol. 65, no. 3, 1986–87, p. 504.

64. Ibid., p. 505.

65. Allen S. Whiting, "Chinese Nationalism and Foreign Policy After Deng," *The China Quarterly*, no. 142, June 1995, pp. 295–316.

66. Allen S. Whiting, "ASEAN Eyes China: The Security Dimension," *Asian Survey*, vol. 37, no. 4, April 1997, p. 300.

67. Hugh Seton-Watson, *Nations and States: An Inquiry into the Origins of Nations and the Politics of Nationalism*. Boulder, CO: Westview, 1977; and Louis L. Snyder, *The Meaning of Nationalism*. New Brunswick, NJ: Rutgers University Press, 1954.

68. To make a distinction, some scholars use ethnonationalism to refer to ethnic nationalism. See, for example, Walker Connor, "Ethnonationalism," in Myron Weiner and Samuel Huntington, eds., *Understanding Political Development*. Boston: Little, Brown, 1987, pp. 196–220.

69. Melvyn C. Goldstein, "Outside Instigation and the Disturbances in Tibet," *The Journal of Contemporary China*, no. 4, Fall 1993, pp. 94–95.

70. Steven Mufson, "China's New Nationalism: Mix of Mao and Confucius," *International Herald Tribune*, March 20, 1996.

71. Jiang Zemin, "Patriotism and the Mission of the Chinese Intellectuals," Xinhua, May 3, 1990.

72. *Renmin Ribao*, June 3, 1990, p. 1.

73. David Shambaugh, "Containment or Engagement of China," *International Security*, vol. 21, no. 12, Fall 1996, p. 205.

74. Richard Bernstein and Ross H. Munro, *The Coming Conflict with China*. New York: Alfred A. Knopf, 1997, p. 42.

75. Steven Mufson, "Maoism, Confucianism Blur into Nationalism," *Washington Post*, March 19, 1996, p. A1.

Chapter 2

Democratization and China's Nation Building

Jianwei Wang

3 aspects of Chinese system.

The U.S. National Security Adviser Samuel R. Berger in his speech at the Council on Foreign Relations on June 6, 1997, appealed for rebuilding a broad national consensus on China policy. The lack of such a consensus prevented the formation of a consistent and constructive U.S.-China policy since the end of the Cold War. Such a consensus, however, can only be established on a realistic and nondogmatic understanding of the essence of China as a nation-state in the international system, the stage of its nation-building process, and its current foreign policy concerns imprinted with historical conditions. To make a bold generalization of a wide range of existing views of China in the United States in recent years, the debate has focused on the following three aspects about China: the nature of China's political system and its implications for foreign policy; the state of China's military and economic power and its influence on foreign policy; and the foreign policy objectives and intentions of Chinese leaders based on the combination of the first two factors. It is the main argument of this chapter that given China's preoccupation with its nation building and increasing economic interdependence with the outside world, Chinese authoritarianism is not necessarily threatening and Chinese democratization will not necessarily be benign. *aurg. current system not a threat, democracy may not = peace.*

A U.S. consensus on China more or less existed at different stages of the Cold War depending on how these three dimensions were perceived by U.S. policymakers and the general public. Before the 1970s, the U.S. foreign policy consensus was cast in the framework of global anticommunism, with China policy an integral part of the broad strategy of containment. The communist victory in China fundamentally changed the U.S. parameters of observing China's international behavior. A deterministic linkage was drawn between China's domestic system and its foreign policy: a totalitarian regime with an agenda of external aggression and expansion. China was seen as no different from the Soviet Union and consequently a regime that subordinated its national interest to the Soviet strategy of global dominance. China actually pursued an even more radical communist ideology than the Soviet Union. Thus domestic tyranny and external expansion were considered inseparable twins. The perception of China as a clear and present danger to U.S. security was exacerbated with the perceived increase of Chinese power. For a while after China exploded its first atomic bomb in 1964, China replaced the Soviet Union as the archenemy of the United States, and was seen as more irrational and unpredictable than Soviet Union. Taking China's communist ideology and system as determinative, the United States formed a consensus on China.

During the 1970s and early 1980s, this domestically determined consensus was gradually replaced by a more internationally determined consensus on China. This time, China's domestic communist system was basically left out of the equation of the U.S. perception of China. Indeed Soviet communism and Chinese communism were perceived as quite different, not just in their foreign policy, but also to some extent in their domestic configurations. On balance Chinese communism was perceived as much less threatening than Soviet communism. Again this perception was tied up with the perception of China's capability. While China at one point was considered by Nixon and Kissinger as one of the five economic power centers in the world, clearly it was not of the same caliber as the two superpowers. As a matter of fact, China was bullied by its more powerful northern neighbor.

Another reason for Americans to ignore China's domestic system was that post-Mao China was among the first group of communist countries to embark on economic reforms. Such reform rekindled a hope of eventual convergence of the Chinese system with American democracy. But during this period, China's position in a strategic triangle rather than its domestic ideology and political system provided the foundation of U.S. policy toward China. *Chinese relations was based*

Thus the American consensus on China in the past was established either on a deterministic understanding of the impact of China's domestic political system on its international behavior or a conscious and unconscious discounting of this factor in evaluating China's foreign policy. In the case of the former, an increase of Chinese power was automatically considered ominous, while in the case of the latter, an increase of Chinese power could be harmless or even beneficial to the U.S. foreign policy interest.

The problem with consensus building in the post–Cold War period is that neither of these two approaches can work easily. With China becoming the largest leftover polity of world communism, it is almost unthinkable for Americans to ignore the fact that China is still an authoritarian regime which stubbornly sticks to an unpopular course against the world trend of democratization. On the other hand, communist China has changed so much during the last two decades that another anticommunist crusade against China seems irrelevant in face of a more complicated reality, thus leading to a policy dead end. In the midst of all these ambiguities, for better or worse, China has become the world's fastest growing economy since 1979. Thus the big question turns out to be: What is the short- and long-term impact of China's increasing economic and military clout on its foreign policy objectives when China has yet to join the family of democracies?

A Modified Internal-External Linkage

The debate on the linkage between China's internal system and its external behavior is not new. The question is, if we agree with Bernstein and Munro that China will not democratize in the foreseeable future,[1] is a domestically authoritarian China bound to be externally aggressive? According to the logic underlying the U.S. consensus in the 1950s and 1960s, the answer is definitely yes. The conventional wisdom suggests that domestic tyranny and international expansion are often correlated. Germany and Japan in World War II and the Soviet Union in the Cold War can all be cited in this regard. China's own history in the 1950s and 1960s could also arguably prove this point. However, whether an authoritarian political system will inevitably pursue a foreign policy of domination needs careful examination. To declare that "governments behave internationally as they behave toward their own citizens"[2] is simplistic.

Several arguments are proffered as to why authoritarian regimes tend to be more aggressive in their foreign policies. First, modern authoritarian regimes are often characterized by radical ideologies such as fascism and communism, which are all-encompassing and take world domination as an ultimate foreign policy goal. According to Marxist communist theory, the proletariat cannot liberate itself until it liberates the whole of mankind. Individual socialist countries would never feel safe until the entire world has become communist. Therefore it is a duty of socialist countries to spread their political system abroad by both peaceful and coercive means.

Second, political power in an authoritarian system is highly concentrated in the hands of a dictator or political oligarchy with no checks and balances. In such a system, paramount leaders such as Stalin and Mao Zedong could make decisions about war and peace without consultations with domestic constituencies. Consequently authoritarian regimes can more easily mobilize the resources at their disposal and plunge the whole nation into bloody conflict with other countries. If the leader happens to be paranoid and does not care too much about the people's life and welfare, then the probability for such a country to engage in foreign adventure is even greater.

Third, there must be a close connection between a regime's domestic and international behavior. "Regimes that tend to engage in [domestic] physical suppression . . . are more likely to engage in foreign policy activity that seeks to justify this behavior."[3] If a government tends to use repression to keep a tight rein on domestic dissent in order to maintain its power, then it is only natural that it will use the same instrument, force, to realize foreign policy objectives. In other words, if the ruler believes that coercion can work domestically, there is no reason why the same cannot be applied to interstate relations so long as the regime has enough power.

These internal-external linkages hold true in many historical cases. They are also applicable to China to various degrees. Nevertheless, some modifications are needed for today's China.

To be sure, China used to be a very ideological country. Mao took "the emancipation of the whole mankind" as China's historical mission. The first generation of Chinese leaders believed that socialism could save not only China, but also the whole world from the exploitation and oppression of the evils of imperialism and capitalism. For a long time, China's foreign policy was characterized as "revolutionary diplomacy." "Countries want independence, nations want liberation, and the people want revolution" was China's standard slogan to describe the world situation. Motivated by the communist ideology, China did provide significant military, economic, and moral assistance and support to revolutionary movements in other countries.

On the other hand, partially resulting from its own bitter experience with the Soviet Union and the Comintern, promoting revolution abroad through direct and coercive means has seldom been a main thrust in the CCP's foreign policy unless radical leftist leaders such as Lin Biao and the Gang of Four temporarily took control of foreign affairs, for instance, during the early years of the Cultural Revolution. As early as the 1950s, Chinese leaders like Mao Zedong and Zhou Enlai strongly opposed the idea of exporting revolution.[4] Mao firmly believed that it was impossible to win a domestic revolution by importing it from abroad.[5] Although China was often militant in rhetoric, it rarely attempted to install overseas revolutionary or communist regimes through direct military intervention. Revolutionary zeal never led China to pursue a regional or global communist crusade. China did send its troops across borders occasionally to fight limited wars but usually only after a perceived foreign intervention or potential encroachment threatened its national security. Without exception, the Chinese troops withdrew immediately after the fighting was over. Establishing a puppet regime in neighboring countries for ideological reasons was not an objective of Chinese policy.

While communist ideology still served as an important yardstick for China's international behavior before the 1980s, in the last two decades, this ideology gradually lost most of its relevance to China's foreign policy. Although theoretically the Chinese leaders still declare that they believe communism will eventually prevail throughout the world, promoting socialism abroad has no place at all in China's diplomatic practice. The word "revolution" has been eliminated from the dictionary of China's diplomacy.[6] While one can often hear Chinese leaders talk about the danger of the Western conspiracy of "peaceful evolution" to undermine China's socialism, such ideological jargon is mainly aimed at domestic audiences and does not have much impact on China's foreign policy. The main purpose of the campaign is to forestall "peaceful evolution" in China, not to project communist influence abroad. It is true that China holds different views on human rights and democracy from most democratic countries. But that has little to do with the communist ideology. China tends to interpret these differences in cultural and economic terms.

Instead, the so-called Five Principles of Peaceful Coexistence have became the cornerstone of China's diplomacy. Zhou Enlai elaborated these five principles in 1954 to indicate the defensive nature of Chinese communism. Initially China considered these principles only applicable to countries with different social systems. Since the late 1980s, however, China extended the five principles to the relationship between all countries, including countries with similar social systems. Chinese leaders told foreign visitors that what China follows internationally are the five principles rather than ideology.[7] The essence of the five principles is that the domestic system and ideology should not affect interstate relations whatsoever. This deliberate effort to separate domestic politics from international relations, of course, also protects the Chinese regime from international scrutiny and is self-serving. It still indicates the diminishing role of ideology in China's diplomacy. Such a tendency is at odds with the behavioral pattern of traditional hegemonic powers which tend to be eager to sell their ideology abroad. Deng Xiaoping even extended the principle of peaceful coexistence and non-interference to China's "internal affairs" by articulating the "one country, two system" formula to solve the Taiwan and Hong Kong issue.[8]

In short, China is different from Germany, Japan, and the Soviet Union in history because it lacks a powerful, offensive, and all-encompassing ideology to guide a foreign policy for world domination. Historically such an ideology usually has been a necessary condition for a rising power to become a hegemon.[9] A related issue is whether domestic repression will automatically lead to external assertiveness. Again empirical evidence does not establish such a causal relationship in the case of China. There, of course, have been instances in the PRC's history when internal turmoil and repression led to assertiveness and paranoia in foreign policy. During the early years of the Cultural Revolution, the radicalization of Chinese domestic politics spilled over to China's foreign relations. "Chairman Mao's revolutionary line of diplomacy" led the country into self-inflicted diplomatic isolation. The power struggle in domestic politics also contributed to China's militancy toward the Soviet Union that eventually led to a border clash in 1969. In turn, the perceived hostile external environment also propelled Chinese leaders to pursue more repressive and intrusive domestic policies. While there have been discernible interactions between China's internal politics and external behavior, the open question is whether the Mao era pattern of linkage holds under today's very different circumstances.

In the light of conventional wisdom, domestic repression after the Tiananmen democracy movement in 1989 should have led to external belligerence. The Chinese response to outside pressure in the 1950s and 1960s was "tit-for-tat" that often paved the way for major confrontations between China and its targeted enemies. However, post-Tiananmen Chinese diplomacy apparently broke this pattern. While domestically the screws were tightened immediately after the crackdown, externally China took a more flexible and conciliatory posture. In dealing with pressure from the United States, the Maoist blow-for-blow strategy was largely discarded, apart from some rhetoric and symbolic gestures. Instead, China took pains to stick with an approach known as "reducing troubles and avoiding confrontation." China also took more accommodating policies in resolving regional conflict such as the Cambodia issue and in improving its relations with neighboring countries. In other words, rhetoric notwithstanding, the Tiananmen incident did not radicalize or dogmatize China's foreign policy.

The emergence of this new pattern resulted from some new internal and external conditions. First, the Chinese regime became much less repressive than it was before the 1980s.[10] Maoist totalitarianism changed into a softer Dengist authoritarianism. Even in light of an unprecedented crisis of legitimacy, the domestic crackdown was limited in both scale and intensity. The limited scope of domestic repression explains its limited influence on foreign policy.

Second, after more than ten years of integration with the international system, China has developed a high degree of economic and other functional exchanges with the outside world. This is drastically different from the 1950s and 1960s when China was largely isolated from the international community. China has developed such high stakes in the existing international system that foreign policy regression is just too costly.

Finally, the objective of China's foreign policy has significantly changed in the process of reform and modernization. As one Chinese scholar pointed out, after the establishment of the PRC, China's foreign policy objective was "survival security," but now it has become "economic security."[11] During the period of survival security, the Chinese people could bear a minimal standard of living without challenging the legitimacy of the Chinese government. No more; the economic reform and openness toward the outside world have reduced the people's willingness to bear hardship. People demand a decent economic life and well-being. This huge change constrains China's freedom of action in the international arena.

Domestic authoritarian rule need not always go together with a benign and defensive foreign policy in China. After Tiananmen, some hardliners did advocate much harsher policies. When its survival is in danger, the communist regime may well use all means at its disposal including external adventures to secure its hold on power. But post-Tiananmen diplomacy indicates the possibility of delinking China's domestic suppression from external belligerence due to new factors that shape China's foreign policy options.

Power and the Status Quo

Despite a peaceful foreign policy in the 1990s, is China increasing its military and economic power? What is the impact on Chinese foreign policy? The American perception of China has undergone dramatic change since the end of the Cold War, from a collapsing China to a rising China, from China as a non-issue to China as a potential threat. While China's capability has not changed as drastically as the American projections, the perceptual swing reflects an increasing American sensitivity toward the rise of China's economic and military strength in the post–Cold War period. It is not the purpose of this chapter to check the inventory of Chinese power. Some analysts have already pointed out that the "Chinese threat" in military terms has been greatly exaggerated.[12] What we are more interested in is the implication of China's undoubted rise for its international behavior. For the Chinese, the growth of national power offers hope of restoring China's historic glory among nations, which they consider is long overdue. For many Americans, China's enhanced capacity is a source of great concern.

It is said that any rising power is bound to bring conflict and disruption to the existing international order. This is said to be a law attested to by the rise and fall of countless powers throughout history. Analysts declare China is not an exception.[13] The fact that China is an authoritarian dictatorship makes the impact more worrisome.[14] In short, a rising power tends to demand a new international order commensurate with its new power status. So even if communist ideology and the authoritarian nature of China's political system have little impact on its foreign policy,

why a concern?

that China has been rising, these critics conclude, justifies concern regarding its long-term intentions. Not Fair.

This has been a concern even in China. No one can predict for sure how China will behave after it reaches a par with the United States. Even Chinese leaders themselves sometimes were not so confident about it. In the 1950s, Zhou Enlai cautioned his foreign guests: "China is a big country. Because of historic tradition, big countries tend to ignore and disrespect the interest of small countries. So we have to examine ourselves very often."[15] In 1974, Deng Xiaoping declared publicly to the United Nations: "If one day China should change her color and turn into a superpower, if she too should play the tyrant in the world, and everywhere subject others to her bullying, aggression and exploitation, the people of the world should identify her as social-imperialism, expose it, oppose it and work together with the Chinese people to overthrow it."[16] China was a regional hegemon in East Asia before the nineteenth century. There is no guarantee that China will not resume this position when it once again becomes the most powerful country in the region. In this respect, Samuel Huntington, Richard Bernstein, and Ross Munro's warnings make sense, except that realpolitik projections about an amoral international system do not change whether China is democratic or authoritarian. Indeed, in case China becomes expansionist, the Chinese should welcome the U.S. policy of containment if they really follow what their beloved late leaders said.

However, it is one thing to say that in the long term China may reassert its hegemonic position in East Asia, and quite another to say that the current leadership already has a grand strategy to become the dominant power in Asia and has already started a process of systematic expansion.

First, the historic conditions are different such that China will not follow in the expansionist footsteps of rising powers such as Great Britain, Germany, Japan, or even the United States. In contrast to the eighteenth and nineteenth centuries when nations gloried in imperial expansion, territorial expansion is no longer a viable means to maximize influence. Iraq's invasion of Kuwait was condemned. The Soviet Union withdrew its troops from Afghanistan. The Vietnamese had to leave Cambodia under constant pressure from the United Nations. Britain, no matter how reluctant, handed its last sizable colony, Hong Kong, back to China after 150 years. Chinese leaders are fully aware of these historical lessons. For them, the practical question is internal: how to maintain Beijing's domestic "empire," including Tibet and Xinjiang, rather than expanding further.

Second, no major rising power has faced the daunting domestic problems that China confronts today. Most rising powers, such as Germany
and Japan, first consolidated their domestic order before they embarked
on external expansion. For them internal unification and domestic legitimacy were not serious problems. But China is still in a primitive
stage of nation building in which both issues remain unresolved. The
transition from a command economy to a market economy gives China's
rise a unique character. The growth of China's economic power has been
accompanied by a decrease of domestic cohesion and legitimacy. Just a
few years ago, people were talking about a possible system collapse in
China. While internationally China probably is in its strongest position
since 1949, domestically the communist regime is much weaker compared to its "golden age" in the 1950s and 1960s. This domestic weakness constrains China's foreign policy options. Most resources and
capacity generated by economic development have to be devoted to solving internal problems, not to external expansion. An ill-fated foreign
expedition could even bring down the regime.[17] In addition, China is
still struggling to fulfill its nation-building aspiration: reunification with
an increasingly breaking away Taiwan.

Third, China has a huge stake in the existing international system.
Since 1979, China's economic growth has been sustained largely by
foreign capital and foreign trade. China became the largest recipient of
the economic and financial assistance from mainstream international
financial institutions. Whereas expansionist Germany and Japan cut their
ties with the prevailing international regimes as a prelude to aggression,
China is seeking to be further integrated into various international regimes.[18] After China becomes a member of the World Trade Organization, its economy will be even more intertwined with the world economic
system, and the degree of foreign economic penetration in China will
further increase. While politically China may still seem alien to the international system, economically and functionally China is already an
insider. For China to seek systematically to change the status quo of the
international system would be economically suicidal and hence politically a very risky business.[19] Therefore China's foreign policy tasks in
the short-to-medium term are to maximize its benefits from the existing
international system rather than creating one of its own.

Since China started its comeback to the international community in
the early 1970s, it has benefited tremendously from the existing international system, not just in economic but also in political terms. China's

resumption of its position as a permanent member of the UN Security Council gives it veto power in international affairs. With China's ties to the international system ever thickening, its foreign policy has become more and more conservative. To some extent, China did not want to see the end of the Cold War because it could maximize benefits from the international system while minimizing domestic and normative costs. Although the end of the Cold War eliminated the most imminent security threat to China, the Soviet Union, the side effect is that China has to pay a higher price to enjoy the same or even less benefit from the international system. For instance, China enjoyed late–Cold War ties with the United States, a pure strategic relationship without many normative and domestic connotations. The subsequent vicious cycle of action and reaction between the two countries since 1989 was hardly a product merely of "fundamental change in the Chinese attitude toward the United States."[20] It is the United States that has wanted to change China rather than the other way around. Nothing the United States has accused the Chinese of doing now: crackdowns on political dissidents, weapons proliferation, unfair trade practices, and so on, had not been done before. If China is an international "villain," it was more so in the era of warm Washington-Beijing relations. As a matter of fact, one can argue it has become less so compared to its past record. In sum, it is not China that has become more revisionist with an increase of its power, but the United States and others that have become less tolerant of much better Chinese behavior at home and abroad.[21]

There has been no conclusive evidence to indicate that China's international behavior in recent years has a strong correlation with the growth of its economic and military power. Indeed China was more aggressive and assertive when it was weaker. The Chinese fought Americans when the PRC did not even have a modern army. China was prepared for a confrontation with all "imperialists, revisionists, and reactionaries" in the 1960s when its economy was in shambles. From 1949 to 1989, China was involved in military conflicts almost every ten years (the Korean War in 1950, the Sino-Indian War in 1962, the Sino-Soviet conflict in 1969, the Sino-Vietnamese War in 1979, the Sino-Vietnamese conflict in the South China Sea in 1988). But since America reversed itself on the PRC in 1989, China has not been involved in any direct military conflict with other countries although its economic and military power has been growing. There are no overwhelming signs to indicate that China will repeat this ten-year cycle of military conflict in the next few years except under extreme circumstances.[22]

What about China's policies toward Taiwan, Hong Kong, the South China Sea and other territorial disputes? Has the PRC become more assertive? Does it have something to do with its growing military and economic power? Actually China has been reactive too on these issues. On the Taiwan issue, while Beijing wants eventually to integrate Taiwan into the PRC, Chinese leaders realize that that is not attainable in the near future. Therefore, in the short run, China would like to see Taiwan's political status remain unchanged. That is, Taiwan continues to be a de facto separate political and economic entity with no statehood, which is how most countries treat it. Beijing would be satisfied with the status quo of "neither independence nor unification" at least for the time being. China made it clear that there is no timetable for the reunification with Taiwan and that it has enough patience so long as Taiwan does not go independent. It was Taiwan's "pragmatic diplomacy" to raise its international profile and to fight for equal footing with the mainland in the international system that raised Beijing's eyebrows.[23] The United States also changed the status quo by upgrading its relations with Taiwan to the point of issuing Lee Teng-hui a visa to visit the United States. These changes imposed by others forced Chinese rulers to worry about how long the status quo can be maintained.[24]

China's handling of the Hong Kong issue shows the same tendency. Beijing maintained the status quo with Hong Kong for almost forty years without taking it back by military means. In the early 1980s, China was not very eager to take Hong Kong back. It was the British side that pushed Beijing to make a decision. China then had no choice but to take Hong Kong back.[25] After the signing of a joint declaration in 1984, Beijing thought it had a deal. Irrespective of whether what the British governor Chris Patten did was good or bad for the Hong Kong people, it was the British side that unilaterally changed the rules of game. Developments since the handover of July 1, 1997 demonstrated again that Beijing indeed means to continue business as usual. Alarmist predictions that "the unhappy fate of Hong Kong promises to reshape the course of U.S.-China relations"[26] did not materialize. Hong Kong became a facilitator rather than an obstacle in Sino-U.S. relations.

On less important territorial issues such as the South China Sea and Diaoyu (Senkaku) Islands, no sufficient evidence shows that China is determined to systematically change the status quo. With regard to the Spratly Islands, although China has long claimed sovereignty, it did not physically occupy any islands until 1988, more than ten years after some southeast Asian countries had taken a total of some twenty islands and reefs in the region. The Mischief Reef incident was widely cited as a sign of China's "creeping expansionism." But in 1998 China offered to let the Philippine fishermen share the facilities China had built on the Mischief Reef.[27] The Vietnamese subsequently seized another two reefs in the area. China's reaction was moderate. On the Diaoyu Island, China and Japan made a deal in the early 1970s that the dispute on sovereignty should be left for the next generation to solve. Incidents in 1996 were largely provoked by Japanese rightist groups landing on the island. China had to react because of popular resentment both at home and among Chinese overseas. In the meantime, China has worked hard to reach border agreements with Russia, central Asian countries, India, and Vietnam. In April 1996 China signed an agreement on military confidence building in the border region between China and Russia and with three central Asian republics to create a stable and peaceful border of 7,000 kilometers. The five countries signed another agreement in 1997 to cut their military forces along the border. So far the long disputed borders between China and Russia and between China and Kazakhstan have been settled peacefully. The border negotiation with Vietnam has also made some important progress. After difficult negotiations, the leaders of the two countries were able to keep their promise by signing a land border agreement on December 30, 1999. They are now aimed at resolving the maritime dispute in the Tonkin Gulf in the year 2000.[28] Overall, while China's record is not perfect, the evidence of Beijing's actual behavior argues against the false claim that China has a grand irredentist design of expansion.

Yet, China's "missile diplomacy" in the Taiwan Strait in 1996 is often cited as proof that China's external behavior is out of line with the international mainstream and that China has become more assertive in its foreign policy. However, the policy objective behind China's coercive diplomacy is national unification rather than regional hegemony. The Chinese feel frustrated by the fact that as a rising power China is still unable to unify its own country. Needless to say, the Chinese leaders accept the premises of the Westphalian state system. They stick with the traditional concept of national sovereignty and territorial integrity. Sovereign nation-states have an exclusive monopoly over the use of force internally. While Chinese elites, including the Chinese military, now can accept the idea that the use of military force is no longer a legitimate instrument of foreign policy for solving international disputes, they need not accept the same idea regarding internal disputes. Chinese leaders believe that internal disputes and external disputes should be handled with different approaches. For the former, using military force is legitimate. Since the Taiwan issue is considered "internal," Chinese leaders do not see anything wrong with the use of force as a final resort to deter Taiwan from moving further toward independence. That is, China can be very rational when talking about the peaceful resolution of China's disputes with other countries but very irrational when talking about the Taiwan issue. The irrationality in the latter case does not necessarily negate the rationality in the former. The Chinese see a clear conceptual boundary between the two. Different logics apply. Whether China will use force against Taiwan will not be decided by an international relations analysis of the military balance between the two sides and the related rational calculation of cost-benefit. For the Chinese, such a calculation would not be decisive. If Taiwan seeks de jure independence, China has no choice but to fight.[29]

The Taiwan issue further reflects the distinct nature of China as a rising power. As a country still in its early stage of nation building, China cares most about national sovereignty and territorial integrity, not hegemony or domination. While some analysts of international relations claim that the concept of national sovereignty is out of date and that the world is entering a post-Westphalian era, that is beyond the comprehension of the Chinese.[30] China has not completely entered this system yet. As a late riser, there is a time lag in China's nation building. It took China almost a century to accept the concepts of sovereignty and nation-state. It might take another century for China to modify these concepts and understand them in a less absolute fashion. That is why the Chinese leader Li Ruihuan declared, "We would rather lose thousands of lives than an inch of territory. . . . The territory our ancestors left to us should never become smaller and less in the hands of our generation."[31] Here Huntington's theory of a clash of cultures cannot fully explain this conceptual conflict since the idea of national sovereignty that impassions Chinese patriots originally came from "the West." China, as many other Asian countries, is in a particular stage of national development.

To sum up, in the foreseeable future, China's foreign policy objective is national unification rather than regional dominance. Chinese leaders clearly distinguish territories under China's indisputable sovereignty and those whose sovereignty is also claimed by other parties. While China may have hardened its position on Taiwan and Hong Kong, China has been cautious and restrained on other territorial disputes. There is no reason to conclude that what China has done regarding Taiwan and Hong Kong signals a reorientation of its foreign policy in general.

Does Democratization Matter?

The "China problem" surfaced in the 1990s from a combination of disgust over its nondemocratic political system and anxiety over its increasing power. It seems that the lack of either of these would ease the strong sentiment. If China were a democracy or at least a democracy in transition like Russia, would its rapid economic development be less alarming? Or would a China that is still an authoritarian power but weak give peace of mind to Americans who feel that a strong China will disrupt the existing international order and cost America its leverage? Let us generously assume that for most Americans, whether China is a democracy is more crucial.[32] In addition to Americans' natural inclination for democracy and human rights, the international logic of stressing democratization also comes from the prevailing theme of "democratic peace."[33] That is, democracies do not fight each other. So the deduction is that if China democratizes, there is not much to be worried about, even if its economy is booming and its military is modernizing.

But, are democracies more peaceful than nondemocracies? Some empirical studies show that democracies are not necessarily more peaceful than nondemocracies. In the last two centuries democracies have been at war about as often as nondemocracies have. The Correlates of War Project, conducted at the University of Michigan, identified 118 large-scale international wars from 1816–1980; the top three states most often involved in war were France, Britain, and Russia.[34] Therefore one may argue that no political system, either democratic or authoritarian, is inherently warlike or peaceful.

As for the claim that democracies seldom fight each other, that refers to "stable" democracies. Unstable democracies early in nation building are not necessarily safer for the world. Actually peoples building a new nation-state during the transition period from nondemocracies to democracies could become more aggressive and war-prone, not less. The empirical evidence shows that formerly authoritarian states where democratic participation is on the rise are more likely to fight a war than are stable democracies or autocracies.[35] A transition period could be very long. In the case of some Western European countries, it took several centuries to consolidate democracy. On the other hand, nondemocracies do not necessarily fight each other either. For instance, most ASEAN countries are not full-fledged democracies. However, just like the European Community, a mechanism of peaceful resolution of conflict has also been in existence among ASEAN member states.

Most important, the relationship between democracy and small military conflicts may have little to do with the alleged peacefulness of democracies. Most stable democracies have had the longest history as modern nation-states. They long passed the early stage of nation building in which they fought their wars to solve various territorial disputes and ethnic conflicts.[36] One reason most military conflicts took place in poor and authoritarian third world countries in the postwar period is because these countries were still in their early stage of nation building with many territorial and ethnic problems to be settled. That is also the major difference between states in Western Europe and East Asia. Democratizing governments in Seoul or Taipei do not effect this decisive reality about nationalism. That is why, even if Samuel Huntington is right that Europe's past might be Asia's future,[37] such a difference cannot be changed simply by democratization.

As mentioned earlier, China is in an early stage of nation building. In the modern history of China, internal turmoil and external invasions have repeatedly interrupted this process. Chinese intellectuals and politicians, at least from the time of Sun Yat-sen, have endeavored to turn an ancient civilization into a modern state, and to turn "a heap of loose sand" into a unified and strong nation. In the 1930s, Chiang Kai-shek might have had a good chance to accomplish this process, but his dream was shattered by the Japanese invasion. After the communist takeover, Mao did not have the patience to gradually build up the nation. He attempted to move China by radical political and economic campaigns and failed badly. One bitter lesson the current Chinese leaders learned is that China is still in the "primary stage of socialism." China also has yet to achieve its national unification or to solve territorial disputes with many of its neighbors. In such a stage, China is ultrasensitive about national sovereignty and territorial integrity. China's frequent involvement in military conflicts during 1949–89 is mostly a symptom of this nation-building process.

It is not clear that democratization will make a telling difference to China's international behavior on issues related to this process. Taiwan is a good point of reference. If we regard Taiwan as a separate political entity, it is also in an early stage of nation building. Democratization made many Taiwanese feel different from the Chinese in the mainland and further stimulated their seeking of a separate national identity.[38] While President Lee Teng-hui often criticized the mainland government for its stubborn adherence to the "out-of-date" concept of national sovereignty, he himself tirelessly reminds people that Taiwan is a sovereign state. Taiwan is vigorously seeking international recognition, spending millions of dollars to establish diplomatic relations with even tiny countries that only have symbolic significance. Actually, democratization further agitated Taiwan's desire to expand its "international space," namely its status as an independent nation. It did not make it easier for the authorities to modify territorial claims similar to the mainland's over the South China Sea and Diaoyu Islands. Taiwan has yet to recognize officially the political independence of a democratic Mongolia, whereas the mainland recognized Mongolia long ago.

Democratization tends to polarize and sometimes even radicalize Taiwanese society along the line of proindependence versus prounification as well as Taiwanese natives versus mainlanders. Rather than making compromises easier, it is making the relationship with Beijing more complicated and volatile. An isolated incident, such as the "Lake of Thousand Islands" incident a few years ago and the murder of a DPP legislator in the mainland more recently, could well create a crisis due to the emotional reaction of media and public opinion in Taiwan. Democratization brought little moderation to Taiwan's policy on issues such as the "three direct links" of post, trade, and communications. Democratization further radicalized Taiwan's attitudes toward reunification. While the mainland advocates a formula of "one country, two systems" by which no change of status quo on either side is required, the Taiwan authorities are now asking for a change of China's social system, namely democratization, as a prerequisite for unification. Moreover, Lee Teng-hui publicly abandoned the well-recognized framework of "one China" by declaring that Taiwan was a separate state. His provocative remarks created new tension across the Taiwan Strait.

In other Asian democracies where nation-building issues remain salient, such as India, foreign policy can hardly be said to be peaceful and moderate. Democratic India has been frequently involved in military conflicts with its neighbors. It has sought hegemonic influence over smaller neighbors such as Nepal, Bhutan, and Sikkim. It has strongly opposed the Nuclear Nonproliferation Treaty and the Comprehensive Test Ban Treaty rather than blocking nuclear proliferation. The nuclear blasts by India in May 1998 seem to support the argument made by the Chinese leaders that a country's foreign policy has little to do with its domestic political system. India's international behavior shows very little substantial difference from its more authoritarian neighbor Pakistan.

Among Southeast Asian countries, the Philippines is the most democratic so far as the domestic political system is concerned. Does this make the Philippines' foreign policy different from more authoritarian ASEAN countries such as Singapore and Indonesia? Not at all. Its foreign policy turns out to be no less nationalistic. In the South China Sea dispute, the Philippines appear to be more assertive than other concerned ASEAN countries.

In short, democratization may not have a quick soothing impact on countries that are still in an early stage of nation building. To the contrary, democratization may even aggravate sensitive nationalism and make a country's foreign policy more assertive.[39] To apply the same logic, democratization is unlikely to change China's foreign policy on key issues. Even if China democratizes tomorrow, the government would still want to take Hong Kong, Macao, and Taiwan back; would still want to keep Tibet and Xinjiang within the Chinese "empire," and would not easily give up its claim of sovereignty over the South China Sea and the Diaoyu Islands. Rather, the situation could become worse. Yet critics see rising Chinese nationalism as a result of the manipulation and agitation of the communist government for its ambitious foreign policy agenda. At a minimum, this is an incomplete argument.

Needless to say the government in Beijing does attempt to utilize nationalism to serve its own interest. But the surge of nationalism is largely a spontaneous phenomenon reflecting the change of China's international position. To a large extent, it is transgenerational and transnational, as well as transideological. It is shared by Chinese overseas, including many who are strongly antiregime and anticommunist. The vehement reaction in Taiwan, Hong Kong, and North America to the Japanese landing on the Diaoyu Islands cannot easily be explained by government manipulation. Actually many Chinese democratic dissidents criticized the Chinese government as too soft rather than too assertive on territorial disputes with other countries.

Might it be that an authoritarian regime could be more successful at effectively reining in the rising Chinese nationalism? Beijing understands that excessive nationalism can endanger its domestic rule and disrupt China's paramount foreign policy objective of creating a long-term peaceful environment for its modernization program. In other words, nationalism is a double-edged sword and has to be handled very carefully. So while Chinese leaders like Jiang Zemin advocate patriotism, they never forget to point out that what they seek is not narrow and militant nationalism. Rather what they would like to see is a kind of nationalism that can be transformed into domestic support for government policies and programs.[40] That is why the radical school of nationalism, as represented by individuals such as He Xin and the authors of *The China That Can Say No*, have never received official endorsement. Strong anti-Japanese sentiment among the Chinese first emerged in the student demonstration in 1985. It might be let loose under a democratic government. If one compares the reaction to the Japanese provocation over the Diaoyu Islands in 1996 in the mainland, Taiwan, and Hong Kong, the mainland reaction was the most muted.[41] The authorities in Beijing have discouraged an autonomous anti-Japanese movement. The Chinese government's response to the reported massive looting, killing, and raping of ethnic Chinese in Indonesia in the Asian financial crisis again paled by comparison to the outrage of the overseas Chinese. The most recent example to show the Chinese regime's cautious dealing with nationalism was the NATO bombing of the Chinese embassy in Yugoslavia. The pouring out of anti-American sentiment among the Chinese could hardly be said to be a result of government mobilization. To the contrary, the government itself was caught off guard by the strong reaction triggered by the tragedy. Indeed the government was accused of being "too weak" in dealing with the United States. Every Chinese could tell you that if the government had not taken measures early enough to dredge the emotions among the masses, the American embassy and consulates could have been burned to the ground and diplomats killed. Actual behavior establishes that for a country like China, which is still in its early stage of nation building, an enlightened authoritarian regime can temper the destructive power of excessive nationalism more effectively.

Democratization may not bring a dramatic improvement in China's foreign policy because Beijing's current foreign policy is not warlike and the foreign policy of a democratic China would not necessarily be peaceful. Critics tend to make sweeping judgments about authoritarianism and do not bother to differentiate China's authoritarianism from Franco's or Mussolini's totalitarianism.[42] They are repeating the same mistake as when they equated Soviet communism and Chinese communism in the 1950s and 1960s.

Nonetheless, democratization, as a gradual process for the long term, may bring positive changes to China's foreign policy, particularly when China moves into a higher stage of nation building in terms of economic modernization, political and legal institutionalization, national reconciliation, and less absolute understanding of national sovereignty. A process of democratization would increase the transparency and accountability of China's foreign policy, particularly its defense and military policy. Foreign policy remains the least open domain in China and is little subject to public scrutiny. China is still more comfortable with the secretive and elitist diplomacy of the 1970s, which was not much constrained by domestic constituencies. Such a diplomacy would be more difficult under a more democratic system. A more transparent diplomacy will reduce unnecessary suspicions over China's foreign policy on issues such as its military expenditure and arms transfer. While China has legitimate reasons to protect itself, excessive secrecy hurts rather than helps China.[43] Transparency is largely a systemic problem that can be more effectively addressed by further democratization.

Another possible positive effect of democratization might be the reduction of the role of the Chinese military in foreign policymaking. The Chinese military's role in foreign policymaking as an institution used to be minimal. Even today its influence on China's international behavior is not as big as people speculate. However, with political strongmen like Mao and Deng gone, the military could be more proactive on foreign policy issues directly related to its vested interests in arms transfers and military spending. Some unauthorized arms sales and provocative remarks that alarmed its neighbors and the United States in recent years indicate that the Chinese military needs stronger civilian control and oversight. Institutionalization of civilian control of the military under a democratic system would effectively check military intervention in both domestic politics and foreign policy.[44]

Furthermore, democratization may reduce misperceptions. One serious problem between the United States and China is the conflict of concept rather than the conflict of interest. Because both sides have deeply-rooted suspicions and predispositions about the other side's social and value system, fruitful communication is difficult. Common interests are obscured for lack of a common language. Democratization in

China certainly can alleviate this problem, as both sides would then share a more common discourse on such issues as human rights. Both sides can more readily take what the other side says at face value rather than constantly speculating what lies behind an alleged smoke screen.

Finally, democratization may actually help China's nation building by depriving Taiwan of an excuse not to be integrated with the mainland. The Taiwanese leaders now emphasize that the squabble between Beijing and Taipei is about the social system and the way of life. Taiwan skillfully plays the card of "democratization" to enhance its international image and to win the sympathy of the international community. This strategy is a threat to the mainland leadership. Further democratization would help Beijing win back the diplomatic initiative and the moral high ground. Although it still remains to be seen whether Taiwan is genuinely willing to become part of a democratic China,[45] democratization definitely would increase Beijing's leverage on Taiwan. In a sense, a more effective strategy to prevent Taiwan from slipping away is to speed up the pace of political reform in the mainland.

All in all, the soothing effects of democratization on China's foreign policy are for the long term. Democratization will not end China's dynamism as a rising power and is not the cure-all to avoid a conflict between China and other major powers such as the United States and Japan. The key for peace is a successful nation-building process that can continue without major interruptions both at home and abroad.[46] In the short term, an enlightened authoritarian regime can more effectively limit the overflow of nationalism during the process of nation building. With swift and chaotic democratization, things could get out of control before democratic norms and values take root in China.

Conclusion

Nation Building

The American consensus on China should be based on an understanding of the unique historic conditions under which China has been rising as a major power. On balance, China is becoming a "non-ideological, pragmatic, materialistic, and progressively freer" society.[47] It may remain an authoritarian regime for many years to come. However, any negative influence of this authoritarianism on China's international behavior is quite limited. Contrary to the conventional wisdom, under post–Cold War circumstances, a domestic hard line should not necessarily be followed by external aggressiveness.

Therefore if China does not democratize in the near future, it will not be a disaster for the world. As a nation-state still in its early stage of nation building, China's main foreign policy objective is to realize national unification rather than regional domination.[48] Democratization will not bring much change to this foreign policy orientation, although it could make China's international relations unstable in the short run.

Understandably an increase of economic and military power will make a country more confident and sometimes more assertive on international issues. In the process of rising, no existing major powers, including the United States, can claim a better record than China. But China's toughness on Hong Kong, Taiwan, and Tibet is not evidence of a grand design of expansionism in the Asia-Pacific region. China has drawn a clear line between "internal affairs" and territorial disputes involving third parties. For the latter, a cool and hard rationality prevails.

China wants to restore its position as one of the major powers in East Asia as well as in the world. But that does not necessarily mean it has to become another "evil empire." While Chinese leaders' assertions that China will never seek hegemony sound empty, the accusation that China is already seeking world domination similar to Nazi Germany and fascist Italy is baseless.[49] China's decent performance in the South Asian nuclear crisis and East Asian financial crisis has demonstrated that an authoritarian and rising China could also be a responsible member of the international community. Gradual democratization will further increase the chance for peace and cooperation by increasing the transparency, accountability, and moderateness of Chinese foreign policy. In the protracted and difficult era of nation building and political transition, however, how the major powers treat China will be as important as political change within China in determining its orientation toward the outside world.

Notes

1. Richard Bernstein and Ross H. Munro, *The Coming Conflict with China.* New York: Alfred A. Knopf, 1997, pp. 15–17.

2. Jim Hoagland, "Simply China," *Washington Post National Weekly Edition*, June 12–18, 1995, p. 8.

3. Charles Hermann, "Political Opposition as Potential Agents of Foreign Policy Change: Developing a Theory." Paper presented to the Annual Meeting of the International Studies Association, Washington DC, 1987, p. 12.

4. *Selected Works of Mao Zedong on Foreign Affairs.* Beijing: CCP Documentary Press, 1994, p. 189; *Selected Works of Zhou Enlai on Foreign Affairs.* Beijing: CCP Documentary Press, 1990, p. 197.

5. *Selected Works of Mao Zedong on Foreign Affairs*, p. 189.

6. China's characterization of the world situation has been changed to "the world wants peace, countries want stability, economies want development, and mankind wants progress." Tieying Li, "China Marching Toward the Twenty-first Century and the Develoment of the World Economy,"*People's Daily*, November 15, 1996.

7. They observed that history since World War II has demonstrated that even countries with the same social systems and ideologies, if they do not follow the principle of peaceful coexistence, could have tensions in the relationship, even fighting each other. On the other hand, countries with different ideologies can live together peacefully if they follow the five principles. "Central Leaders Talk about International Issues and Foreign Relations," *Shanghai Foreign Affairs*, no. 5, March 20, 1988, p. 2.

8. Deng Xiaoping, "The Principles of Peaceful Coexistence Have a Potentially Wide Application," October 31, 1984, in *Selected Works of Deng Xiaoping, Volume III (1982–1992)*. Beijing: Foreign Languages Press, 1994, p. 102.

9. Even Bernstein and Munro recognize that because communist ideology is dead in China, the country has none of the messianic impulses that made the Soviet Union more threatening. China does not seek to spread its way of life to other countries. Richard Bernstein and Ross H. Munro, *The Coming Conflict with China*, p. 18.

10. See Minxin Pei's chapter in this volume.

11. Yan Xiutong, "China's External Security Strategy in the Post-Cold War Period," *Study of Modern International Relations*, no. 8, 1995, p. 24.

12. See Robert Ross, "Beijing as a Conservative Power," *Foreign Affairs*, vol. 76, no. 2, March/April 1997, pp. 33–44; Michael D. Swaine, "Myth about China's Military," *Washington Post National Weekly Edition*, May 27, 1997, p. 22.

13. Ross H. Munro, PBS Online Newshour, "U.S.-China Relations," April 6, 1997.

14. Richard Bernstein and Ross H. Munro, "The Coming Conflict with America," *Foreign Affairs*, March/April 1997, p. 26.

15. *Selected Works of Zhou Enlai on Foreign Affairs*, pp. 132, 180.

16. "Speech by Teng Hsiao-ping, Chairman of Delegation of People's Republic of China at Special Session of U.N. General Assembly, April 10, 1974," *Peking Review*, p. V. According to Zhou Enlai, this was what Mao asked him to say. *Selected Works of Zhou Enlai on Foreign Affairs*, p. 503.

17. One might argue that just like Bismarck's and Hitler's Germany and Meiji Japan, Chinese rulers could turn to external expansion to solve domestic problems. The domestic popular support for such a policy, enjoyed by both Germany and Japan, is simply not there in today's China.

18. For China's growing integration with the web of international organization, see Samuel Kim, "Thinking Globally in Post-Mao China," *Journal of Peace Research*, vol. 27, no. 2, May 1990, pp. 192–193, 196.

19. As a Chinese commentator points out, "It is hard to imagine that China would harm the existing peaceful international environment at the risk of its own development program." Ren Xin, "'China Threat' Theory Untenable," *Beijing Review*, vol. 39, February 5–11, 1996, p. 11.

20. Bernstein and Munro, *The Coming Conflict with China*, p. 28.

21. Both Huntington and Zuckerman pointed out that the Chinese have some reasons to believe that the United States has tried to prevent China from rising. Samuel Huntington, *The Clash of Civilizations and the Remaking of World Order*. New York:

Simon & Schuster, 1997, p. 223; Mortimer B. Zuckerman, "Realism about China," *US News and World Report*, June 9, 1997, p. 104.

22. For example, if Taiwan declares formal independence or its equivalent. Lee Teng-hui's attempt in July 1999 to redefine the cross-strait relations as "state-to-state relations" was a dangerous first step toward this direction.

23. James Shinn, "Playing the China Cards, the Clinton Administration Will Be Facing Three Crises in the Next Few Weeks," *Washington Post National Weekly Edition*, February 26–March 3, 1996, p. 21.

24. A senior PLA officer remarked at a seminar in Washington, DC in November 1996 that China would not mind seeing the continuation of the status quo across the Taiwan Strait. The question is how long it will last. Unfortunately, China's worry proved to be somewhat true. Lee Teng-hui's repeated attempts to challenge the status quo in cross-strait relations increased Beijing's sense of urgency to settle the Taiwan issue. That is why the Chinese leaders have emphasized since late 1998 that the Taiwan issue cannot remain unsettled indefinitely. Lianwei Wang, "All Walks of Life in Beijing Held a Forum to Commemorate the Fourth Anniversary of Jiang Zemin's 'Eight Points,'" *People's Daily*, January 29, 1999.

25. Frank Ching, "Misreading Hong Kong," *Foreign Affairs*, vol. 76, no. 3, May/June 1997, p. 65.

26. "China the Issue," *The Weekly Standard*, February 24, 1997, p. 11.

27. Reuters, "China Says Spratlys Sovereignty 'Indisputable,'" August 5, 1998.

28. Reuters, "Vietnam China Sign Land Border Agreement," December 30, 1999; *Chinesenewsnet*, "China and Vietnam Strive to Resolve Maritime Dispute Next Year," December 30, 1999; Dequan Ling, "China and Vietnam Held the Sixth Round of Border Negotiations," *People's Daily*, September 29, 1998.

29. A senior Chinese military officer remarked at a seminar in Washington, D.C. in November 1996 that if that happens, China does not care whether they can win and whether the United States will intervene. Victory is not an issue here. Why are the Chinese very rational on one hand, and so irrational on the other? The answer is: this is the difference between internal and international affairs.

30. The president of China's Academy of Social Sciences Hu Sheng said, "Nowadays some people talk about how the concept of sovereignty is out of date. It belongs to the nineteenth century. I strongly oppose this opinion." "For World Peace and Development," *The World Economy and Politics*, no. 10, 1990, p. 4.

31. "Li Ruihuan Met Cambodian Prime Ministers," *People's Daily*, December 8, 1995.

32. Some analysts again took a deterministic approach in the 1950s and 1960s, arguing that so long as China remains a communist dictatorship, conflict with the United States is inevitable. See Michael A. Ledeen, "No Tyrants Allowed," *The Weekly Standard*, February 24, 1997, p. 28.

33. According to Jack Levy, "This absence of war between democratic states comes as close as anything we have to an empirical law in international relations." "The Causes of War: A Review of Theories and Evidence," in Philip E. Tetlock, Jo L. Husbands, Robert Jervis, and Paul C. Stern, eds., *Behavior, Society, and Nuclear War, Vol. 1*. New York: Oxford University Press, 1989, p. 270. Also see David Lake, "Powerful Pacifists: Democratic States and War," *American Political Science Review*, vol. 86, March 1992, pp. 24–37; Bruce Russett, *Grasping the Democratic Peace: Principles for a Post-Cold War World*. Princeton: Princeton University Press,

1993; William J. Dixon, "Democracy and the Peaceful Settlement of International Conflict," *American Political Science Review*, vol. 88, March 1994, pp. 14–32; Zeev Maoz and Bruce Russett, "Normative and Structural Causes of Democratic Peace, 1946–1986," *American Political Science Review*, vol. 87, September 1993, pp. 624–638.

34. Melvin Small and David J. Singer, *Resort to Arms: International and Civil Wars, 1816–1980*. Beverly Hills: Sage, 1982.

35. Edward D. Mansfield and Jack Snyder, "Democratization and War," *Foreign Affairs*, vol. 74, no. 3, May/June 1995, pp. 79–97.

36. Of course, there still exist some outstanding territorial disputes among democracies. Military conflict is still a possibility in some cases (e.g., the complex maritime, air, and territorial disputes between Greece and Turkey).

37. Samuel Huntington noticed this difference although he did not explain why. *The Clash of Civilizations*, p. 220.

38. Qingguo Jia, "Toward the Center: Implications of Integration and Democratization for Taiwan's Mainland Policy," *Journal of Northeast Asian Studies*, vol. 13, no. 1, Spring 1994, p. 57.

39. Aaron Friedberg, "Broken Engagement," *The Weekly Standard*, February 24, 1997, p. 12.

40. Jiang Zemin, "On Education of Patriotism," *People's Daily*, May 12, 1997.

41. Song Qiang, Zhang Zangzang, and Qiao Bian, eds., *Zhongguo Keyi Shuo Bu* (The China that can say no). Beijing: Zhonghua gongshang lianhe chubanshe, 1996; Mure Dickie, "China Keeps Nationalism Leashed in Islands Dispute," Reuters, May 11, 1997.

42. Bernstein and Munro, "The Coming Conflict with America," p. 29.

43. Edward Friedman rightly emphasizes the importance of transparency in reducing the possibility of war in the region. See his chapter in this volume.

44. It has to be pointed out, however, that an enlightened authoritarian regime is also able to address these issues to a certain extent. China has made some progress recently by publishing its defense white paper and prohibiting the PLA from conducting commercial activities. But further democratization will provide a more solid institutional basis for such policies.

45. If only democratization matters, one wonders why Quebec and Northern Ireland still seek political independence.

46. In this regard, Bernstein and Munro are right to point out that the area mostly likely to trigger U.S.-China military conflict is the Taiwan Strait if the United States decides to intervene. *The Coming Conflict with China*, p. 18. Chinese foreign minister Qian Qichen also clearly pointed out that there is no possibility of conflict between China and the United States unless the United States encroaches on China's sovereignty and territorial integrity, *People's Daily*, March 8, 1997.

47. Bernstein and Munro, *The Coming Conflict with China*, p. 18.

48. As Chinese President Jiang Zemin made clear, "The supreme interest of China is peace and nation-building." "Jiang: 'The Supreme Interest of China is Peace and Nation-Building,'" *Washington Post*, October 19, 1997.

49. Bernstein and Munro, *The Coming Conflict with China*, p. 19.

Chapter 3

China's Evolution Toward Soft Authoritarianism

Minxin Pei

There is a consensus that China's economic system has undergone dramatic transformation since the end of the Cultural Revolution, but there is widespread disagreement about the extent of change in the political system. Many China watchers have detected signs of "creeping democratization" in China, citing the examples of an increasingly assertive National People's Congress, legal reforms, village elections, and growth of civil society.[1] However, the influential mainstream Western media are dominated by a very different view of China—one which insists that China's political system has experienced remarkably little change despite revolutionary economic progress, questioning the positive relationship between market-led economic development and political liberalization that has been observed elsewhere in the world, especially in East Asia. Skepticism about the prospects of democratization in China has even legitimated a harder line in dealing with Beijing.[2]

Actually, the empirical data provide substantial evidence on considerable political change in China since 1976. The one-party regime has undergone important, albeit slow-paced, institutional changes that have laid a basis for future political pluralism. Since the late 1970s, the political system has been evolving into soft authoritarianism with real potential for democratic transition, perhaps in the second decade of the twenty-first century. Therefore, policies toward China that further enhance and accelerate this process of political evolution will most likely succeed in peacefully facilitating China's rise as a world power in the next century. The real challenge to foreign policymakers is not just to engage China but to defend such a policy from increasingly strong domestic opposition. To do so, policymakers must understand both China's declining level of political repression and increasing level of political pluralism, as well as the causes and implications of China's slow political evolution.

China's Political Evolution: Transition to Soft Authoritarianism

Despite the absence of dramatic political liberalization, China's political system has made a decisive break with its totalitarian past and begun to move, however slowly, toward a form of soft authoritarianism. This transition is most evident in, first, the steady decline of the level of political repression and, second, the emergence of rudimentary institutions of separation of power, rule of law, popular participation, and civil society.

Declining Political Repression

A hallmark of the transition from totalitarianism or hard authoritarianism to soft authoritarianism is the steady decline of political repression. Regimes undergoing this transition typically adopt a strategy of focusing their limited resources on a small number of committed political dissidents while granting a high level of personal freedom to those who do not openly challenge the ruling elite. Although this policy has allowed the expansion of public space and individual freedoms in these soft authoritarian systems, it ironically receives little credit from the international community because of the regimes' selective repression of high-profile dissidents, which is widely publicized by the international media and creates a false impression of unrestrained political repression. In China, the level of political repression can be reasonably measured by two statistics: (1) the percentage of political prisoners (classified as "counter-revolutionaries") in Chinese jails since 1978, and (2) the number of counter-revolutionaries arrested and tried annually in the same period.[3]

The Deng era saw several brief waves of conservative backlash against reform. In the fall of 1983, the conservatives launched an "antispiritual pollution" campaign in an attempt to roll back the then-fragile reform movement. This campaign cracked down especially hard on the arts, literature, and popular culture. In early 1987, in a direct response to the student-led pro-democracy movement that sparked street demonstrations in several major cities and caused the resignation of Hu Yaobang, then the general secretary of the Chinese Communist Party (CCP), the government carried out a campaign against bourgeois liberalization aimed at stemming liberal influence in Chinese society. The post-Tiananmen democracy movement crackdown of 1989–90 represented the strongest backlash against the forces of reform, resulting in the imprisonment of perhaps several thousand political dissidents and two years of suspension of economic reform. The mid-1990s saw another round of repression against political dissent. The government rearrested dozens of dissidents, including the country's two most famous pro-democracy advocates, Wei Jingsheng and Wang Dan. Both were sentenced to lengthy prison terms despite strong international protest. But the crackdown in the mid-1990s was a narrowly focused operation and did not have any negative impact on economic reform or lead to an overall reduction of personal freedom for the majority of the people.

Despite these episodes of conservative counterattacks, the post-Mao government in Beijing has not opted for a return to totalitarian rule. Unlike the Maoist regime that attempted to rely on mass terror for a radical social transformation, the Deng regime treated state-controlled means of violence mainly as defensive instruments against those who dared to challenge the government publicly. This essentially reactive strategy resulted in a decline in the overall level of political repression. The regime's use of brute force became more selective, as the state's security apparatus directed most of its resources to the suppression of a small group of vocal dissidents. The implicit social and political contract between the regime and the Chinese people is that the regime will permit a high degree of personal and economic freedoms in exchange for a tacit acceptance of its rule. In this regard, the ruling elite in Beijing today is perhaps no different from its counterparts in Seoul and Taipei in the late 1970s and early 1980s, a period in which little open opposition was tolerated by the soft authoritarian regimes while most personal and economic liberties were permitted.

The falling level of political repression during the Deng era is especially dramatic when compared with the totalitarian Mao era. Although a lack of data makes it impossible to measure precisely political repression in either the Deng era or the Mao era, three sets of figures provide clues as to the differences between these two periods. Table 3.1 contains

Table 3.1

Percentage of Counter-revolutionaries in the Prison Population in Shaanxi Province, 1953–83

Year	Percentage	Year	Percentage
1953	39.1	1968	34.3
1955	37.9	1975	26.1
1957	34.5	1979	11.5
1959	32.5	1980	6.8
1961	34.8	1981	5.2
1963	30.5	1982	3.0
1965	31.7	1983	1.9

Source: Lu Xueyi and Li Peilin, eds. *Zhongguo shehui fazhan baogao* (China's social development report) (Shenyang: Liaoning renmin chubanshe, 1991), p. 379.

data on the percentage of counter-revolutionaries in the prison population in Shaanxi province during a thirty-year period (1953–83) that spanned the Mao and Deng eras. Since many political offenses were prosecuted as "counter-revolutionary" crimes, a large percentage of counter-revolutionaries could be political prisoners.[4] Their share of the prison population could be a proxy of political repression. It indicates that the overall level of political repression—if the Shaanxi sample is representative—was extremely high in the Mao era, with nearly one out of three prison inmates a political prisoner. The level of repression began to fall toward the end of the Cultural Revolution. But the real dramatic plunge occurred in 1979, a year marking Deng's rise to political supremacy. Throughout the early 1980s, the level of repression continued to fall.

Table 3.2 provides some data on the percentage of political prisoners in the entire country in the 1980s. The national data are roughly in line with the provincial data from Shaanxi and indicate a steady downward trend in political repression during the Deng era. For instance, in 1980, about 13 percent of all prisoners were counter-revolutionaries, but ten years later, only 0.5 percent of all prisoners were counter-revolutionaries. The data in Table 3.3 show that the current level of repression, measured by the number of counter-revolutionaries prosecuted each year during the late 1980s and early 1990s, displays an inverted-U curve. Although government statistics do not provide information on the number of counter-revolutionaries prosecuted each year before 1987, Table 3.3 suggests that fewer counter-revolutionary cases were being pros-

Table 3.2

Percentage of Counter-revolutionaries in the Prison Population in China, 1980–1989

Year	Percentage
1980	13.35
1981	4.3
1984	1.19
1985	1.13
1989	0.51

Source: Lu Xueyi and Li Peilin, eds. *Zhongguo shehui fazhan baogao* (China's social development report) (Shenyang: Liaoning renmin chubanshe, 1991), p. 379.

Table 3.3

Counter-revolutionary Cases Prosecuted in China, 1987–1997

Year	Cases accepted by the court	Cases prosecuted by the court
1987	372	358
1988	214	208
1989	572	448
1990	716	728
1991	354	413
1992	231	253
1993	192	187
1994	180	180
1995	208	208
1997	280	271
Total	3,111	3,046

Source: Zhongguo falu nianjian (Law yearbook of China) (Beijing: Zhongguo falu nianjian chubanshe, various years).

ecuted in the late 1980s. The rise in the number of prosecutions in 1989 was the result of the post-Tiananmen Square movement crackdown. The increase of political repression was temporary. In 1992, the number of counter-revolutionary cases prosecuted fell significantly. By 1995, it fell to the same level as in 1988, generally considered a year of relative political openness.

If the overall level of repression in China has declined significantly since the late 1970s, why has China been routinely singled out as one of the most repressive countries in the post–Cold War world? Has the bar been raised in ways that hide China's similarity to Taiwan and South Korea in the 1970s? In the early 1990s, there was a general improvement in human rights as despotic regimes made a transition to democratic rule (especially in the former Soviet bloc and parts of Latin America and East Asia). Compared to these, the improvement in China did not seem all that impressive.

Building Internal Norms of the Regime

A second characteristic of a soft authoritarian regime—again based on the experience of other East Asian newly industrializing countries (NICs)—is a high degree of institutionalization of the rules and norms governing intra-elite competition for power and distribution of rewards. In post-Mao China norms and rules have gained increasing constraining power. In the two most critical power struggles in the Deng era, the removal of Hu Yaobang and the dismissal of Zhao Ziyang, the ruling elite consciously avoided a massive purge. Although Hu and Zhao lost power, their followers were gradually incorporated by reformist elements among the ruling elite.[5] A recent study of the mobility of the Chinese provincial leadership shows that while massive purges of provincial leaders routinely accompanied power struggles at the top prior to the 1980s, the provincial leadership has remained very stable during the Deng era, indicating greater security of China's ruling elite.[6] Moreover, the exit of disgraced leaders (both hardliners and reformers) has been made less painful. Instead of public humiliation and physical abuse, they were given sufficient material amenities to ensure their physical comfort. Under Deng, not a single top leader (a member of the Politburo or the Central Committee Secretariat) was stripped of his or her party membership and publicly denounced.[7]

Three institutional mechanisms installed by Deng have contributed to the relative stability and cohesion of China's ruling elite: (1) elections, some *pro forma* and some semicompetitive, for many leadership positions in the party and the government; (2) mandatory retirement of all officials; (3) promotion based on educational qualifications. Elections were initially instituted to give some substance to the notion of "democratic centralism." While such elections may not fully create a limited "democracy," they have a homogenizing effect on elite cohesion because these elections prevent the rise of radical conservatives and liberals alike. The arch conservative Deng Liqun, for example, did not receive enough votes to become a member of the Central Committee because he was viewed as too conservative. Even in situations where such elections are not competitive, the CCP leadership is constrained by this procedure. If nominees do not have a credible record of administration and cannot demonstrate leadership, they may not get an overwhelming endorsement or receive half of the vote (for delegates can spoil their tickets or refuse to vote). This procedure forces the CCP leadership to exercise caution in selecting candidates for major offices, thus insuring the promotion of relatively competent administrators while screening out less capable careerists.

The mandatory retirement system has increased the circulation of elite within the regime and opened the door for ambitious Young Turks.[8] One official figure shows that about 5.5 million government officials had been retired by the end of 1989. In 1989, of all the government officials, only 1 percent were older than 60 while 80 percent were younger than 50.[9] An important lesson the post-Mao regime learned from the Cultural Revolution was that introducing mandatory retirement would increase the stability of the political system. Previously, many ambitious and capable officials saw their paths to higher positions blocked by the first-generation revolutionaries occupying those offices.[10] Mao mobilized these frustrated young and middle-aged elements in the lower echelons of the CCP in making the Cultural Revolution. As mandatory retirement reduces the uncertainty of upward mobility (everything else being equal), this lessens the incentive for resorting to political intrigue in seeking personal advancement. Another unanticipated benefit of the mandatory retirement system is the strengthening of the People's Congress and the Political Consultative Conference (PCC). Most officials who are forced to retire from the CCP and government positions are eased into positions in the People's Congress and the PCC. Their prestige and connections have strengthened these institutions as counterweights to the CCP's monopoly of power and laid rudimentary foundations for institutional pluralism.

The emphasis on educational qualifications as a key criterion for promotion has brought about a fundamental transformation within China's ruling elite.[11] This change is reflected in the increasing share of government officials who have received higher education. According to official sources, of the 4.55 million government officials in 1989, 23 percent had received a higher education and 25 percent had been educated in vocational schools. The educational requirements seem to be higher for the upper echelons. The same official sources show that nearly 60 percent of government officials in the State Council and its ministries have received a higher education, mostly in natural science and engineering.[12] The effect of this system of merit-based promotion has been similar to that of limited intraparty elections and mandatory retirement: it serves to homogenize the ruling elite. Although these new institutional features put into place in the Deng era cannot eliminate personal rivalries and policy differences, they seem to have greatly reduced ideological conflicts. Indeed, it is hard to identify a hardline ideologue among the younger generation of leaders who has been promoted through this process.[13]

Emerging Institutional Pluralism

A third characteristic of soft authoritarianism is institutional pluralism. The dominant political force in control of the state—whether a one-party or dominant party regime or a military regime—faces limited political competition from the legislative and judiciary branches of the government. Although the independence of these institutions may not be fully guaranteed and protected, they exert a moderating influence on the government, especially concerning routine, secondary matters of governance. The current Chinese regime's progress in this direction is more limited than its progress toward internal cohesion and stability. Nevertheless, evidence suggests a trend toward institutional pluralism. This trend is noticeable in four areas: (1) the emergence of the National People's Congress and provincial People's Congress; (2) progress in legal reforms; (3) grassroots democratic experiments, such as village elections; and (4) the growing strength of civil society.

The National People's Congress. The Deng era saw a gradual emergence of the National People's Congress (NPC), the country's constitutionally supreme lawmaking body, as a potential source of rivalry to the monopoly of power by the Chinese Communist Party. The strengthening of the NPC is especially visible in such areas as the drafting of legislation, negotiation with the CCP and the bureaucracy over proposed laws, debate on national policy, and expression of popular discontent with regard to certain government policies.[14]

Several factors were responsible for the rise of the NPC. First, the general decentralization of power allowed this revived political institution to assume some functions formerly completely under the purview

Table 3.4

Composition of Deputies of the National People's Congress, 1978–88[a]
(sociopolitical background of deputies; in percentages)

	1978 (5th Congress)	1983 (6th Congress)	1993 (8th Congress)
Workers & Peasants	47.3	26.6	20.55
Cadres	13.38	21.4	28.27
PLA	14.38	8.97	8.96
Intellectuals	14.96	23.5	21.8
Returned overseas Chinese	1	1.3	1.21
Ethnic minorities	10.9	13.6	14.75

Source: *Zhongguo falu nianjian* (Law yearbook of China) 1992, (Beijing: Zhongguo falu nianjian chubanshe, 1992), p. 851.
[a]Figures do not add up to 100 percent.

of the CCP. An American researcher explicitly attributed the relocation of the day-to-day control of lawmaking from the CCP to the NPC as the most important cause of the rise of the NPC.[15] Second, the increasing autonomy of the NPC flowed from the appointment of several CCP heavyweights as its chairmen: Ye Jianying, Peng Zhen, Wan Li, and Qiao Shi. Their presence in the NPC gave the body considerable bargaining power. Third, the NPC has a higher degree of representation from the intelligentsia, government officials, and ethnic minorities. Correspondingly, there has been a decline in the presence of workers, peasants, and the People's Liberation Army (PLA). Table 3.4 provides some information on the social background of NPC deputies in the 1980s. The data show that the representation of intellectuals in the NPC increased by 56 percent from 1978 to 1993 while that of workers and peasants fell by more than half. The gains in the representation of the intellectuals allowed this more liberal social group a stronger voice in the NPC.

Although the NPC has not openly challenged the CCP's monopoly of power, it has begun to assert its influence subtly.[16] NPC deputies propose new legislation, debate and amend proposed legislation, and, on occasion, openly vote against some top-priority laws the passage of which was eagerly sought by the government.[17] The Enterprise Bankruptcy Law was held up in the NPC in the early 1980s because many deputies were skeptical about its efficacy in solving the problems of the state-owned enterprises (although the law was eventually passed in 1986). At the NPC annual session in 1995, deputies heatedly debated the proposed Central Banking Law and the Education Law. More than a third of the deputies in the end voted against the banking law and a quarter voted against the education law.

A second area where the NPC has begun to act on its constitutional prerogatives is the process of confirmation of senior government officials. In a few provinces, deputies in local people's congresses rejected the nominations of senior provincial officials and selected candidates not originally endorsed by the local CCP leadership. At the national level, such open display of dissatisfaction with the top CCP leadership has become more frequent. At the March 1995 session of the NPC, a third of the deputies voted against the nomination of a CCP Politburo member to be a vice premier. Twenty percent of the deputies voted against the nomination of another Politburo member to be a vice premier. Moreover, the NPC deputies symbolically expressed their discontent with the government's policy performance by voting against the annual reports of key government institutions. At the 1996 session, 30 percent of the NPC deputies publicly refused to endorse the report given by China's top prosecutor on law enforcement and anticorruption. Twenty percent of the deputies voted against the report given by the chief judge of the Supreme Court. At the March 1997 session of the NPC, to demonstrate their dissatisfaction with the government's ineffectiveness in combating official corruption and rising crime, 848 deputies (32 percent of all deputies) voted against or refused to support the annual report of the Supreme Court, and 1,065 (about 40 percent) of the deputies voted against the annual report of the Supreme Procurator.

Finally, the NPC is slowly gaining visibility as a public forum for expressing popular sentiment and redressing grievances. A poll conducted in late 1994 showed that an increasing proportion of the public views the NPC and the media as important channels to voice their views and seek justice. While the same poll showed that about 43 percent of the respondents said that they would go to the "relevant authorities" (i.e., party and state officials) to lodge complaints in 1988, that fell to 38 percent in 1994. In contrast, the media and the People's Congress gained influence as forums to air private grievances, with nearly a quarter of the respondents saying that they would choose the media to voice their complaints (compared with only 9 percent in 1988). Twenty-two percent said that they would lodge their complaints with the deputies of the

People's Congress (compared with 13 percent in 1988).[18] The image of the NPC as an institution that can provide solutions to problems prompts more than 100,000 private citizens to write requesting assistance each year. Influential NPC members have sometimes intervened in cases of miscarriages of justice by government officials.

Legal Reforms. China's legal reforms since the end of the Cultural Revolution have received intensive coverage.[19] These limited reforms may have laid some foundations for the rule of law. Recognizing the connections between a market economy and a sound legal system, the CCP identified the building of such a system as a top priority. Consequently, the NPC received a CCP mandate to push through a comprehensive program of legal reforms. Between 1979 and 1992, the NPC enacted more than 600 laws; provincial and local people's congresses passed 2,300 laws during the same period.[20] Given China's lack of legal expertise, Western legal doctrines, concepts, frameworks, and technical terms have exerted enormous influence in the drafting of Chinese laws. Enforcement, however, remains difficult and haphazard. The office of research of the Supreme Court disclosed that, of the 302,497 commercial cases adjudicated by the courts in 1993, 146,801 (about 50 percent) had not been enforced at the end of the year.[21]

However, even the poor rate of enforcement of laws and court decisions has not discouraged the Chinese public from using the law to protect its interests, especially commercial interests. Indeed, China's legal reforms have had a most visible impact on the country's commercial activities. As China gradually moved toward a market economy, the demand for legal enforcement of contracts increased rapidly despite the difficulties in enforcing contracts and lack of autonomy of the court. Table 3.5 shows the rapid increase in the number of commercial litigation cases tried in China's courts of first instance between 1986 and 1997. The 480 percent increase in the ten-year period (from 308,000 in 1986 to 1.48 million in 1997) indicates that the legal system is providing some real benefits to litigants who seek protection of their property and contract rights.

Two decades of legal reform seem to have raised the public's awareness of rights. This is evident in the increase in the number of cases filed against the government. The government promoted the development of an administrative litigation system that provides a limited form of judicial relief to citizens and "legal persons." The centerpiece of this system is the Administrative Litigation Law (ALL), which was passed by the

Table 3.5

Number of Commercial Litigation Cases Tried in Chinese Courts of First Instance, 1986–97

Year	Number of Cases	Change
1986	308,393	—
1987	365,848	18.6
1988	486,483	33.0
1989	669,443	37.6
1990	598,314	−10.6
1991	583,771	−2.4
1992	648,018	11.0
1993	883,681	36.4
1994	1,045,440	18.3
1995	1,271,434	21.6
1996	1,504,494	18.3
1997	1,483,356	−1.4

Source: Zhongguo falu nianjian (Law yearbook of China) (Beijing: Zhongguo falu nianjian chubanshe, various years).

NPC in 1989 and fully implemented in October 1990. Before the passage of the ALL, victims of abusive government agencies and officials had no recourse to judicial relief. Occasionally, a handful had tried to take the government to court for violations of their constitutional rights. Official figures show that about 44,000 such lawsuits had been filed by ordinary citizens and "legal persons" between 1983 and 1990 (averaging about 10,000 a year at the end of the 1980s). After the ALL was implemented, lawsuits against the government exploded, reaching 25,600 in 1991. Official figures indicate that between 1991 and 1995, citizens won about 20 percent of such suits and, in addition, obtained favorable out-of-court settlements in about 17 percent to 22 percent of the suits.[22] That the new system of administrative litigation could allow plaintiffs judicial relief in about 40 percent of the cases filed encouraged more citizens to rely on the ALL to protect their rights. As a result, the number of suits against the government rose to 90,000 at the end of 1997 (Table 3.6).

Another powerful force promoting China's legal reform is the emerging professional legal community. Table 3.7 provides a glimpse into its rapid growth. Lawyers rose from 31,000 in 1988 to nearly 100,000 in 1997, and should have exceeded 150,000 by the end of this century. Moreover, as shown by the rapid growth of nonstate (mostly private) law firms, China's legal community may be acquiring some measure of autonomy

Table 3.6

Number of Administrative Litigation Cases Accepted (*shouli*) and Tried (*shenli*) by the Court, 1986–97

Year	Accepted	Change (%)	Tried	Change (%)
1986	632	—	—	—
1987	5,240	729	4,677	—
1988	9,273	77	8,751	88
1989	9,934	7	9,742	11
1990	13,006	31	12,040	24
1991	25,667	97	25,202	109
1992	27,125	6	27,116	8
1993	27,911	3	27,958	3
1994	35,083	26	34,567	24
1995	52,596	50	51,370	49
1996	79,966	52	79,537	55
1997	90,557	13	88,542	11

Source: Zhongguo falu nianjian (Law yearbook of China), various years; figure for 1986 was obtained from *Falu yu shenghuo* (Law and life), no. 82 (October 1990), p. 19. Figure for 1996 was obtained from *Renmin Ribao*, March 21, 1997, p. 2.

Table 3.7

The Growth of the Legal Profession in China: The Number of Law Firms and Lawyers at Year-end, 1988–97

Year	Law firms	Non-state law firms[a]	Lawyers
1988	3,473	—	31,410
1989	3,653	—	43,533
1990	3,653	—	38,769
1991	3,706	73	46,850
1992	4,176	198	45,666
1993	5,129	505	68,834
1994	6,619	1,193	83,619
1995	7,247	1,625	90,602
1996	8,265	2,655	100,198
1997	8,441	2,957	98,902

Source: Zhongguo falu nianjian (Law yearbook of China), various years.
[a]These are predominantly private partnerships; the total number of law firms includes these partnerships.

from the state. Such autonomy was first demonstrated in 1995, when members of the All-China Lawyers Association voted out the officials of the association who had been appointed by the Ministry of Justice, and elected a new slate chosen by the members.[23] There have also been reports of Chinese lawyers' support for various social causes. The Law School of Wuhan University, for instance, is known for its Center for the Protection of the Rights of the Weak, which has more than 40 volunteers from the school's faculty and student body. They perform pro bono legal work for citizens who cannot afford professional legal representation.

Before the launch of a full-scale democratization transition, the emerging economic interests and political forces will most likely wage their battles against the monopoly of power by the CCP in the legal system. It will thus be the "backdoor" through which the process of democratic transition can be quietly initiated. Compared with other forms of political reform that directly challenge the CCP's rule (such as open elections and a multiparty system), gradual legal reforms present no imminent threat to the one-party dictatorship and, in the short term, may even serve some of the interests of the ruling elite. However, in the long run, as legal norms become consolidated and acquire constraining power on the government, China's current experiment with the establishment of a *system of law* may evolve into a *rule of law*.

Village Elections. Village elections in China began as the part of the regime's efforts to forestall the rapid erosion of its authority and organizational integrity in rural areas following the dismantling of the communes in the early years of the reform. According to the Organization Department of the CCP, there were 730,000 party branches in villages in the mid-1990s. In terms of their effectiveness and organizational cohesion, the department considered about a quarter of these branches "good," 60 percent "so-so," 7 percent "backward," and 8 percent "paralyzed."[24] A power vacuum alarmed top CCP leaders, who opted for limited experiments in rural self-government. Some senior CCP leaders (chiefly Peng Zhen, the head of the NPC in the early 1980s), later became strong supporters. In 1982, the amended Chinese Constitution granted legal recognition to village committees as a form of local civic organization. Peng was the driving force behind the 1987 passage of The Organic Law of the Village Committees of the PRC, which solidified the legal status and administrative functions of village committees. Initially, villagers elected only a village committee with five to seven members; later, they also elected a villagers' representative assembly (with about 30 members). These two elections are held concurrently. By 1994, the government reported that about half of Chinese villages had elected such assemblies.[25]

The elected village committee manages the day-to-day affairs of the village. When these committees, which function like executive councils, are confronted with difficult decisions that they lack the necessary authority to make, such decisions are turned over to the villagers' representative assembly. These assemblies decide issues such as the budget and major public works expenditures, and also monitor and evaluate the work and performance of the village committees.

With official encouragement, village self-government spread nationwide. Between the second half of 1988 and 1989, fourteen provinces held a first round of village elections. Although the Tiananmen crackdown temporarily halted this reform, village elections were resumed in 1992 after Deng's famous southern tour reignited economic reform. By the end of 1995, twenty-four provinces (out of thirty) had passed local legislation on village committees. According to Wang Zhenyao, an official in the Ministry of Civil Affairs who oversaw village elections until 1997, between 1988 and the beginning of 1997, three rounds of village elections had been held in eighteen provinces; in addition, Heilongjiang and Fujian had held four rounds of village elections; other provinces had held two rounds of village elections.[26] To gain technical expertise in conducting elections and developing models for the entire country, the central government had selected sixty-three counties (comprising 3,917 towns and 82,266 villages) between 1990–95 as "demonstration sites." These villages—about 8 percent of the total number of villages—were given more technical help and supervision from the Ministry of Civil Affairs.[27]

Given the brief history of village elections and the huge regional variations in the openness and fairness of such elections, it is premature to draw conclusions as to their impact.[28] However, there are indications that the experiment is consequential. Two surveys report a high degree of villagers' interest in these elections. A 1990 survey of 4,418 villagers showed that 88 percent of the respondents said they were "concerned" with the election of the head of the village committee. A 1996 survey of 5,000 villagers reported that 80 percent were "concerned" with the election of the members of the village committee, and 91 percent were concerned with the management of village affairs, especially its budget.[29]

In villages where experimental self-government has been successful, voter turnout was high. One official study reported a turnout rate of 90 percent in seven provinces.[30] The degree of competition differed. Elections were highly competitive in only some villages. One survey showed that non-CCP candidates won about 30 percent of the elections for chair

Table 3.8

The Number of Registered Civic Organizations at Year-end, 1991–96

Year	Total	Provincial	Prefecture	County
1991	115,738	9,518	36,306	69,914
1992	154,502	13,652	45,791	93,789
1993	167,506	16,314	53,085	97,725
1994	174,060	17,792	56,555	99,605
1995	180,538	19,001	59,309	102,215
1996	186,666	20,058	61,239	103,524

Source: Zhongguo falu nianjian (Law yearbook of China), various years.

of village committees in demonstration jurisdictions in three provinces.[31] Many CCP incumbents have failed to be reelected. In the 1991 elections in Fujian, 51 percent of the 11,930 chairmen of village committees were members of the CCP.[32] Surprisingly, the Chinese government was also receptive to Western technical assistance in conducting experimental rural self-government and in monitoring these elections. Both the European Union and the United States provided financial and technical help. According to an assessment by an American organization with close ties to the Republican Party, Chinese elections officials had implemented, fully or partially, most of the suggestions made by the organization aimed at making village elections fairer.[33]

To be sure, village elections represent only a small and tentative step toward democratization. Progress has been slow and difficult. However, this experiment may have started an important process of political participation. If this experiment continues and gains full legitimacy, it could replace the monopoly of power by the CCP in rural China, where three-quarters of the population live.

Emerging Civil Society. The nascent trend of institutional pluralism described and analyzed above has been accompanied by the emergence of an embryonic civil society.[34] Table 3.8 shows that there were 180,000 registered civic organizations in 1995. The growth rate was about 4 percent in the early 1990s. The data in Table 3.9, based on the changes in the number and structure of civic organizations in Shanghai, show that the number of civic organizations in the five urban districts and five suburban counties in Shanghai rose by more than 1,300 percent in 15 years—from only 57 in 1978 to 745 in 1992. These grassroots civic organizations also became more diverse. In 1978, three categories ac-

Table 3.9

Distribution of County and District Social Organizations in Shanghai, 1978 and 1992[a]

Type	Number in 1978	%	Number in 1992	%
Arts, health, and education	23	41	149	20
Natural science, technology, and engineering	20	35	161	22
Charitable, religious, and public affairs groups	11	19	41	5
Recreational and friendship groups	3	5	195	26
Business and trade	0	0	86	12
Social science, humanities, and management studies assoc.	0	0	75	10
Professional and managerial	0	0	38	5
Total	57	100	745	100

Source: Based on the original data in Ma Yili and Liu Hanbang, eds., *Shanghai shehui tuanti gailan* (A look at Shanghai's social organizations) (Shanghai: Shanghai renmin chubnshe, 1993).

[a]Five urban districts and five suburban counties are included here.

counted for 95 percent of the registered civic groups. In 1992, the top three categories accounted for 68 percent.

Several factors facilitated the rapid growth of civic organizations. China's economic reform has led to a revolutionary transformation of its economic institutions and structure, as well as a considerable decline of the state's role in the economy. The diminishing presence of the state has eroded the system that had stifled local initiatives and prevented the accumulation of social capital. The most striking example has been the decline of the so-called *danwei* (unit) system that used to severely limit social and physical mobility of Chinese citizens. In China's transition to a market economy, two forces hasten the decline of the *danwei* system. First, as the state's share of national wealth began to fall, it had fewer resources to maintain the *danwei* system. Second, the rise of market forces, especially in the housing, health care, and labor markets, has considerably reduced the *danwei*'s control over its employees (even though in the state-controlled sector, the *danwei* remains most important).

The slow evolution of China's political system from totalitarianism to soft authoritarianism has provided momentum for the growth of a nascent civil society. The Deng era was marked by a gradual and voluntary withdrawal by the state from areas of social control. Firm boundaries between the state and society began to emerge. This is evident in the amount of leisure time available. Scholars of civic organizations have identified the amount of leisure time as an important factor in the accumulation of social capital, because less leisure time (or leisure time devoted to activities not directly contributing to the accumulation of social capital) has a negative impact on the growth and health of civic organizations. The state had a near-total claim on a citizen's leisure time in the Mao era. The Deng era saw a significant expansion of leisure time, from 2 hours and 21 minutes in 1980 to 4 hours and 48 minutes in 1991.[35]

The emergence of civic groups has also been driven by rapid economic development. The accumulation of material resources is crucial to the construction of a civil society. One study comparing the density of civic groups in various regions shows that it is positively correlated with the level of wealth: provinces with higher per capita income have more civic associations.[36] Clearly, rising wealth enables Chinese citizens to pursue civic activities that would have been otherwise impossible. Finally, China's new civic organizations have benefited from the country's increasing openness to the international community. Foreign foundations, universities, and civic groups have created many exchange programs with China and contributed to the growth of many nongovernment organizations. American foundations alone provide millions of U.S. dollars in grants to fund their programs in China each year. Most of the financial support goes to Chinese civic organizations and academic institutions.

The rise of a nascent civil society, if it continues, may have profound implications for the evolution of the Chinese political system. In the not-too-distant future, one may expect to see relatively autonomous civic organizations play a more visible role in public affairs and defend ordinary citizens from the intrusive state. Eventually, these organizations will help determine whether China can make the transition to democratic rule.

Causes and Implications of China's Slow Evolution

The Chinese political system has undergone considerable change since the end of the Mao era. Although the pace of this transformation is slow, the impact is real. The Chinese political system has acquired many of the characteristics associated with the soft authoritarian regimes that dominated East Asia in the late 1980s (South Korea, Taiwan, Indonesia,

Thailand, Malaysia, and Singapore). However, the Chinese political system in the late 1990s lacked strong institutional foundations (such as relatively developed legal systems, electoral systems, and representative bodies) and organizational support (especially corporatist organizations), and relied more on political repression and less on other indirect and more subtle means of political control to maintain power. The level of political repression, although much reduced since the totalitarian era of Mao, remains relatively high in China.

The regime has strongly resisted semifree elections at all levels but the village. By contrast, such elections were a hallmark of soft authoritarian regimes in East and Southeast Asia in the 1980s. In these regimes, semicompetitive elections were held for many practical reasons, such as obtaining a level of political legitimacy, institutionalizing local political autonomy, gauging public mood and policy preferences, and channeling political opposition into a controlled arena. Moreover, state corporatist arrangements prevalent in many soft authoritarian regimes also helped the ruling elite win elections, thus obviating the need to rely on a more naked use of force to stay in power.

The failure by the CCP to institutionalize a semiopen process of political participation has made it difficult for Beijing to govern state-society relations, manage new social conflicts generated by fast-paced socioeconomic changes, and deal with China's small but active political opposition. Nonetheless, the political system has changed. In the Mao era, most major political catastrophes originated from intraregime conflicts as Mao's dictatorial rule precluded the functioning of the norms of regulating intra-elite struggles.[37] In the post-Deng era, the emergence and strengthening of such norms will make similar political eruptions less likely. However, the weakness in the institutions governing state-society relations means that future political instability will originate from social discontent and conflicts between the state and social groups.

Why, then, has the ruling elite in Beijing not opted for semifree elections as an alternative, given the apparent attractiveness and effectiveness of this institution in many East and Southeast Asian countries? Beijing's strong resistance seems to have stemmed from the regime's insecurity, which is deep despite an impressive economic performance. Beijing is anxious about new regional and social tensions because the economic gains have been unevenly distributed among different social groups and regions. Some sectors have gained, but others have not, at least in relative terms. There has been a considerable reduction in the state's effectiveness in maintaining law and order, raising questions about its competence. Also, rapid economic progress has reduced the influence of the communist ideology as an instrument of mobilizing political support. At the same time, the regime has not fully confronted the legacies of Maoism, such as the Anti-Rightist Movement in 1957–58, the Great Leap Forward famine, and the tragedies of the Cultural Revolution, creating the danger that a small political opening may trigger a Soviet-style *glasnost* which could devastate the legitimacy of the CCP. Finally, integration into the international system has increased the regime's sensitivity and vulnerability to outside influence and pressure.

The Chinese leadership's fear of loss of control is a direct consequence of its lagging efforts in constructing the three key institutions of soft authoritarianism—semicompetitive elections, limited institutional pluralism, and state-corporatist organizations.[38] Such institutions, when well established, can insulate the regime from uncontrolled social discontent. While the regime may be forced to cede considerable autonomy and power to these institutions and processes, it will also gain significant benefits. Robust soft authoritarian institutions can insure the regime's stability through nonviolent means. In their stead, Beijing's ruling elite has no alternative other than reliance on its repressive apparatus to ward off challenges from new political and social forces.

Why, then, has Beijing not been able to establish such soft authoritarian institutions? There are many answers to this difficult question. Deng was not committed to the limited political reforms that would move the political system further along the soft authoritarian path. The Chinese leadership, which was deeply scarred by the Cultural Revolution and then shocked by the turmoil in Eastern Europe and the former Soviet Union, is leery of initiatives that might unleash powerful social forces threatening its rule.

In addition, in the more effective soft authoritarian regimes in East Asia, each had a strong central institution—either a dominant party (the PAP in Singapore, the KMT in Taiwan, and the UMNO in Malaysia) or a strong military (South Korea and Indonesia). In China, however, the Cultural Revolution severely weakened the CCP as the central ruling institution. Its internal norms were nearly totally destroyed under Mao's rule; its members were demoralized; its elites were divided on ideological and personal grounds; its organizations were in disarray; its ties to the population were strained; its reputation was in tatters. It lacked the self-confidence to institute limited political reforms. It was afraid that it would not be able to control the new political process if it did not renew itself first. Therefore, the first priority of the post-Mao leadership was the restrengthening of the CCP. Although it has made some progress in this respect (such as reimposing some internal norms), the process of restrengthening faced new challenges created by economic reform. Society became less dependent on the state and the party. The influx of new values competed with the values of communism and further reduced the ideological appeal of the CCP. More economic opportunities attracted the talented away from careers in the party, especially in the countryside. Economic reform also produced more temptations and opportunities for CCP members to engage in corrupt practices, thus further sullying the party's reputation. Greater personal liberties promoted by a market economy allowed more direct criticisms of the CCP and increased the reach and impact of such criticisms. The CCP's withdrawal from economic management has also led to its organizational decline in villages and factory workshops.

These changes severely eroded the CCP's organizational capabilities. It has gained no new function or mission that might reinvigorate the party. Like firms, political parties must be subject to constant challenges and competitive pressures to maintain a minimal degree of organizational capacity and effectiveness. A dominant party atrophies its organizational muscles if it does not constantly engage in electoral campaigns and mobilization of political support. Without the challenges of electoral campaigns, a dominant party degenerates into a huge patronage machine, as the CCP is today.

The initial weakness of the CCP left it unable to maintain credible control of a semiopen political system. This led the CCP leadership to postpone major political reforms in order to build up the CCP first. However, without competitive pressures and activities from a semiopen political system, the CCP is unlikely to renew itself and enhance its capacity, which further increases the risks of a political opening for the CCP.

The post-Deng leadership faces different choices. The status quo is not sustainable indefinitely. Only limited political reforms will help maintain China's stability. To reduce the risks of runaway reforms, the post-Deng leadership could heed the lessons of other East Asian countries. Despite its numerous flaws, the CCP remains the most powerful political force in China and enjoys strong competitive advantages vis-à-vis other political forces. If the CCP can complement its own strength with the growth of state-corporatist institutions to back up the CCP in future electoral and political competitions, its political dominance will be nearly unassailable in the near and medium term, without frequent resort to repression. Such a change would move the Chinese political system a step closer to mature soft authoritarianism and help insure political stability into the next century.

It remains unclear whether the post-Deng leadership under Jiang Zemin will be up to this monumental task. A major foreign policy implication of this study is that economic reform and integration with the international community can indirectly promote political liberalization, as shown by the extent of political change, however slow and partial, documented in this chapter. For those seeking to advance human rights and democracy in China, the most workable policy is to encourage the growth and development of the internal forces of political change in China while avoiding confrontational tactics aimed at pleasing disparate domestic pressure groups. Experience during two decades of economic reform has vindicated such a strategy. The combination of domestic reformist forces and international support has significantly opened up Chinese society and the economy and reduced the influence of the CCP. Indeed, the foes of reform inside the CCP have repeatedly warned against the danger of the trends of political evolution discussed in this chapter. A hardline policy toward China will only serve the interests of the conservative forces in the regime and effectively halt the slow but steady process of political evolution in China.

The challenge to America is thus twofold. On the one hand, Americans should work hard to foster a new domestic consensus on China and prevent the hijacking of its China policy by various interest groups. Such a consensus may be achieved, in part, by more educational efforts aimed at better informing the public about the enormous social and economic progress in China since 1978 and the real potential for democratization. On the other hand, the United States and its allies in East Asia must devote more resources to the acceleration of the trends of political opening in China. More specifically, they should encourage and support China's program of legal reform, provide technical assistance to China's national and provincial legislature and village elections, and forge ties with nongovernmental organizations (NGOs). Such a program of comprehensive engagement is more likely to prevent the rise of ultra-nationalism while giving a considerable impetus to the continuation of the political opening in China.

Notes

1. See Kevin O'Brien, "Implementing Political Reform in China's Villages," *Australian Journal of Chinese Affairs*, no. 32 (July 1994), pp. 33–67; O'Brien, "Agents and Remonstrators: Role Accumulation by Chinese People's Congress Deputies," *The China Quarterly*, no. 138 (June 1994), pp. 359–80; M. Kent Jennings, "Political Participation in the Chinese Countryside," *American Political Science Review*, vol. 91, no. 2 (June 1997), pp. 361–72; Minxin Pei, "Creeping Democratization in China," *Journal of Democracy*, vol. 6, no. 4 (October 1995), pp. 64–79; Murray Scot Tanner, "The Erosion of Communist Party Control over Law-making in China," *The China Quarterly*, no. 138 (June 1994), pp. 381–403; Pitman Potter, ed. *Domestic Law Reforms in Post-Mao China* (Armonk, NY: M.E. Sharpe, 1994); Stanley Lubman, ed., *China's Legal Reforms* (New York: Oxford University Press, 1996); Gordon White, Jude Howell, and Xiaoyuan Shang, *In Search of Civil Society: Market Reform and Social Change in Contemporary China* (Oxford: Clarendon Press, 1996).

2. See Richard Bernstein and Ross Munro, *The Coming Conflict with China* (New York: Knopf, 1997); Special Issue on China of *The Weekly Standard*, February 3, 1997; Robert Kagan, "What China Knows That We Don't: The Case for a New Strategy of Containment," *The Weekly Standard*, January 20, 1997, pp. 22–27; "Dancing with the Dragon," *The New Republic*, March 10, 1997, pp. 9, 15–26.

3. There is some concern about the reliability of official Chinese data. Some skeptics argue that dissidents may be tried under categories other than "counter-revolutionary" crimes, thus reducing the number of political dissidents charged with counter-revolutionary crimes. Although such practices may exist in China, Western human rights watch groups have not reported or documented cases in which political dissidents were charged with ordinary crimes.

4. Espionage and sabotage were also prosecuted as counter-revolutionary crimes.

5. The only exception in the Deng era was the case of Bao Tong, a close aide to Zhao Ziyang. After the Tiananmen crackdown, Bao was imprisoned for seven years, reportedly at the insistence of Deng Xiaoping himself.

6. Zhiyue Bo, "Economic Performance and Political Mobility: Chinese Provincial Leaders," *Journal of Contemporary China*, vol. 5, no. 12 (July 1996), pp. 135–54. However, the stability of the ruling elite did not result in ossification of the leadership in post-Mao China because of the mandatory retirement system established under Deng (to be discussed later).

7. Chen Xitong's case was special. A former Politburo member and party chief of Beijing, Chen was involved in a massive corruption scandal and dismissed from the Politburo in 1996. On the eve of the fifteenth party congress in September 1997, Chen was formally expelled from the party and placed under criminal investigation.

8. For a study of the implementation of this system, see Melanie Manion, *Retirement of Revolutionaries in China: Public Policies, Social Norms, Private Interests* (Princeton: Princeton University Press, 1993).

9. These included 1.13 million officials in the government's administrative agencies, 2.56 million in state-owned enterprises, and 1.81 million in nonprofit government institutions. The figure also included about 500,000 officials retired in 1989. To put this number in perspective, the total number of officials in various government agencies at all levels in 1989 was 4.55 million. *Zhongguo renshi nianjian*

(China's personnel almanac) *1988–89* (Beijing: Zhongguo Renshi Chubanshe, 1991), pp. 738, 742.

10. This was caused largely by a historic accident. The Communist revolution in China succeeded in a relatively short period of time (less than 30 years). As a result, most of the leaders and their followers came to power in the 1940s and 1950s. The relative "youth" of China's "founding fathers" later became a major factor in the low mobility of the aspiring elite of the post-revolutionary generation.

11. See Li Cheng and Lynn White III, "Elite Transformation and Modern Change in Mainland China and Taiwan: Empirical Data and the Theory of Technocracy," *The China Quarterly*, no. 121 (March 1990), pp. 1–35.

12. *Zhongguo renshi nianjian 1988–89*, p. 738.

13. In theory, level of education should not have a definitive impact on the formation of ideological views. However, it has often been observed that those trained in engineering are pragmatic "problem solvers" and less ideological. This appears to be the case in China since no newly elevated ministers and provincial leaders were identified as hardliners. Of course, there were a few exceptions, such as Premier Li Peng, an engineer by training. But Li's rapid rise was mainly due to his close connection to the conservatives in the CCP and his status as "adopted child" of the late Premier Zhou Enlai.

14. See Murray Scot Tanner, *The Politics of Lawmaking in China* (Oxford: Oxford University Press, 1998).

15. Tanner, "The Erosion of Communist Party Control over Lawmaking in China," p. 387.

16. For an account of the NPC's increasing political assertiveness, see Michael Dowdle, "Realizing Constitutional Potential," *The China Business Review* (November–December 1996), pp. 30–37.

17. In 1993, after the NPC rejected five drafts of a company law written by the ministries under the State Council, it then wrote its own version and approved it in December 1993. This marked a milestone in the NPC history because this was the first law exclusively written by the NPC, and not by the CCP or the State Council.

18. *Far Eastern Economic Review*, December 7, 1995, p. 35.

19. See Pitman B. Potter, ed., *Domestic Law Reforms in Post-Mao China* and Stanley Lubman, ed., *China's Legal Reforms*.

20. *Liaowang*, no. 10, March 8, 1993, p. 13.

21. *Liaowang*, no. 5, February 2, 1994, p. 20.

22. *Zhongguo falu nianjian* (Law yearbook of China), various years.

23. *Far Eastern Economic Review*, March 7, 1996, p. 28.

24. Yu Yongyao, "Jiaqiang nongcun jiceng dangzuzhi jianshe" (Strengthening the building of grassroots party organizations in rural areas), *Zhongyang dangxiao baogaoxuan* (Selected reports to the Central Party School), no. 19, 1995, pp. 26–27.

25. Research Group on the System of Village Self-Government in Rural China, *The Report on Villagers' Representative Assemblies in China* (Beijing: 1994), pp. 9–13.

26. *World Journal*, April 12, 1997, p. A12; Wang himself was transferred to a different division within the ministry in 1997, a move some interpreted as a negative signal, but others saw it as a routine bureaucratic reshuffling.

27. *Beijing Review*, vol. 39, no. 1, March 11–17, 1996, p. 14.

28. Several scholars have studied village elections, see Kevin O'Brien, "Implementing Political Reform in China's Villages" and M. Kent Jennings, "Political

Participation in the Chinese Countryside"; Melanie Manion, "The Electoral Connection in the Chinese Countryside," *American Political Science Review*, vol. 90, no. 4, December 1996, pp. 741–65; Daniel Kelliher, "The Chinese Debate over Village Self-Government," *The China Journal*, no. 37, January 1997, pp. 63–86.

29. Mi Youlu, "Cunmin dui zizhi de canyu ji pingjia" (Villagers' participation in and evaluation of self-government), paper presented at Duke University, April 1997, p. 3.

30. China Rural Villagers' Self-Government Research Group and the Chinese Research Society of Grassroots Government, *Study on the Election of Villagers' Committees in Rural China: Main Report* (Beijing: Chinese Social Science Publishing, 1993), pp. 88–90.

31. *Democracy and Law*, November 1992, p. 40; *Main Report*, p. 76.

32. International Republican Institute, *People's Republic of China: Election Observation Report* (Washington, DC: International Republican Institute, 1995), p. 9.

33. International Republican Institute, *Village Committee Elections in the People's Republic of China* (Washington, DC: International Republican Institute, January 1997).

34. For a fine study of Chinese civil society, see Gordon White, Jude Howell, and Xiaoyuan Shang, *In Search of Civil Society*.

35. Shaoguang Wang, "Siren shijian yu zhengzhi" (Private free time and politics), *Chinese Social Sciences Quarterly (HK)*, no. 11 (Summer 1995), p. 113.

36. Minxin Pei, "The Growth of China's Civil Society," paper presented to the Cato Conference, China as a Global Economic Power, Shanghai, June 16–19, 1997.

37. The Anti-Rightist Movement was different, however. In this case, the absence of an institutional mechanism mediating state-society conflicts contributed to the event's tragic outcome.

38. Although the trends of institutional pluralism are visible in China, progress has been very limited, as discussed in this chapter.

Chapter 4

Preventing War
Between China and Japan[1]

Edward Friedman

If China does not democratize, Beijing's hostility to Tokyo could facilitate a war in the twenty-first century. In the section on "Sino-Japanese Relations" in his 1997 study of *Asia's Deadly Triangle*, Kent Calder, a senior adviser to the U.S. State Department for East Asian and Pacific Affairs, foresees arms races, tensions, and flashpoints for war.[2] The dynamics of these dangerous forces lie deep inside China's authoritarian nationalism.

Even during the May 1999 Chinese riots sparked by the murderous NATO bombing of China's embassy in Belgrade, many angry Chinese still focused on Japan. Web postings included, "The Americans are the enemy of the Chinese Communist Party. The Japanese are the enemy of the Chinese people. Which is more dangerous?" "Let me predict that in thirty years the U.S. embassy in Japan will be attacked by ten Chinese guided missiles." "China should take care of Japan first." "Right! China should take care of the Japanese devils first. It should start with a boycott of Japanese goods!" "Some say don't forget June 4 [the crushing of the 1989 democracy movement]. If you can't remember September 18 [1931 Japanese invasion], then you are not a true Chinese." "Where will the Chinese people find their living space in the future? In the ocean! We need to move toward the east, toward the east, toward the east!"

Except for the era from 1972 to 1982, a special moment when Mao Zedong's policy line of allying with any nation possible against a threatening Soviet Union dominated Chinese politics, making for a momentary Tokyo-Beijing entente, Japan has been treated by the People's Republic of China as a real or potential enemy. In the original Valentine's Day 1950 military treaty with Stalin, Mao took as China's adversary "aggression on the part of Japan or any other state that may collaborate in any way with Japan."[3] As Moscow worried after World War II about German revanchism, so Beijing naturally worried about Japanese revanchism. There should be no doubt that what the two Axis powers did to people they conquered was evil, absolute evil. China's foreign minister, however, declared on August 15, 1951, "The United States Government and the Yoshida government are conspiring to rearm Japan, to enslave the Japanese people, and to drive Japan once again onto the path of aggression."[4] Leninist ideology had imperialism as expansionist and impoverishing. But obviously China's first getting it wrong and then later abandoning Leninism have changed little in Beijing's attitude toward Tokyo. Throughout, China views Japan as tomorrow's military threat. Entering the twenty-first century, even cosmopolitan Chinese intellectuals tend to see Japan as dynamized by right-wing super patriots, as a government and people which are unrepentant for World War II atrocities in China. Chinese patriotism is dangerously out of touch with core Japanese political realities.

When Kishi Nobuske became Japan's prime minister, China's foreign minister in 1958 denounced the U.S.-Japan security treaty, claiming, "Under the name of 'mutual defense,' the United States could despatch Japanese troops to China's Taiwan and to any place in the West Pacific."[5] Obviously the charges were untrue. No such thing, or anything close, ever occurred. But China kept drumming up fear of and hate toward Japan. That deadly anger pervades Chinese society. On December 7, 1958 the New China News Agency announced that Japan's arms expansion plans took "nuclear armament as the core" and made Japan the "arsenal for Southeast Asia."[6] Actually, there were no such plans. Nonetheless, the security treaty that Prime Minister Kishi renegotiated in 1960 was again erroneously denounced by China in 1960: "This treaty not only provides for Japan's unlimited arms expansion and accelerated nuclear armament but also its dispatch of troops to foreign lands."[7] Obviously, this is a lie. Ruling groups in China, for the first twenty years of the People's Republic, continually revved up indignation toward an alleged revival of Japanese militarism, not informing the Chinese people about the actual attitudes of Japan's people in Japan's antiwar constitutional democracy in opposing nuclear weapons or resisting military involvement in the Cold War. Beijing has successfully kept burning and fomenting in China hate for Japan.

A 1984 book noted that, "The political relationship between Beijing and Tokyo reached an all-time low during 1969 and 1970 when the Chinese assailed the revival of Japanese militarism."[8] Just prior to a brief and transient 1972–82 era of good relations, Beijing again launched massive campaigns against Japan, claiming that the result of President Nixon's Guam doctrine of no longer having America fighting ground wars on the continent of Asia would be that Japan would replace America in Asia, that is, Japan would go nuclear and have its military take over for the American military in Southeast Asia. Early in 1972, when Nixon and Kissinger discussed removing the American military from Taiwan, Chinese Premier Zhou Enlai asked, "Can the U.S. control the 'wild horse' of Japan?"[9] China was especially worried that the United States, while withdrawing its own troops from Taiwan, might encourage its Japanese allies to station their forces on the island." Hanoi leader Pham Van Dong told Mao in November 1968 that Vietnamese "were very much afraid that Japan would . . . participate in the Vietnam war."[10] During a visit to North Korea in spring 1970, "Zhou [Enlai] argued vigorously that 'Japanese militarism has revived and has become a dangerous force of aggression in Asia.'"[11] Vietnam's Communist Party Chief Le Duan agreed with Zhou in 1971 that "Japan has a plan for Southeast Asia. It wants to control the region."[12]

Beijing further stoked up baseless anti-Japanese rage just prior to normalizing relations with Tokyo in 1972 by falsely asserting that America's return of the Senkaku Islands, along with the Ryukyus, to Japan was an illegal support of Japanese imperialism's taking of Taiwan and the Senkakus from China in 1895. Actually, Japan's incorporation of the Senkakus and the Shimoneseki Treaty's ceding of Taiwan were two separate events. Beijing associated them for the first time at the very end of 1971.[13] Linked to the American reversion of the Ryukyus to Japan, the Senkakus and Taiwan were reinterpreted as an entity in China's new nationalism. No longer was Taiwan merely an unfinished issue of Mao's revolutionary civil war, the site to which Chiang Kai-shek's defeated force had retreated. Increasingly since 1970–72, Taiwan has been treated by Beijing as an unresolved humiliation of the imperialist era, a Japanese crime against national sovereignty and dignity, similar to Britain's seizure of Hong Kong in the wake of the Opium War, a shameful humiliation to China that would one day soon be ended by a strong China, with force if necessary. China's rhetoric has grown ever more war-prone.

By 1982, at the outset of the post-Mao era of independent maneuver, when Deng Xiaoping ended Mao's policy of leaning toward America to stave off a revisionist Soviet Russia, China once again began to attack Japan as a nation bent on militaristic expansionism in Asia. It also dropped its backing for Japan's claim that Russia return four stolen northern islands to Japan. "In 1982 and 1985–86 large anti-Japanese demonstrations took place in Beijing and other major cities. These demonstrations were led by university students who were inspired by Beijing's sharp criticism of the Japanese."[14] "On 18 September [1985], the anniversary of . . . Japan's invasion of Manchuria in 1931, nearly one thousand Chinese students . . . marched . . . shouting 'Down with Japanese militarism.'"[15]

The view grew that even Mao had not stood up for China when he normalized relations with Japan without demanding reparations. Some Japanese believe rather that, in fact, Japan offered China generous so-called commercial terms in lieu of reparations. But Japan cannot mention its aid in lieu of reparations because no matter how large the amount, Chinese will naturally feel that no amount of money can ever recompense for the cruelty of the invading army and the loss of Chinese life. Therefore Deng Xiaoping won popularity in the 1980s for his view that Japan, "has the biggest debt to China. In 1972 China did not ask for reparations. Frankly speaking, we harbor dissatisfaction over this point."[16] Anti-Japanese nationalism intensified in China. Increasingly, the Japanese could feel that they were being picked on unfairly. No matter what democratic Japan did, China intensified propaganda about Japanese as monsters. No matter how sternly Beijing stood against Japan, Chinese people increasingly saw their government as soft on Japan. Chinese nationalism had turned into a metastasizing cancer. It was out of control.

One of the victims of anti-Japan passions was Communist Party general secretary Hu Yaobang, a political reformer. As has been the case since the 1930s in China, nationalism defeated democratization, making freedom seem at best a luxury, and at worst an obstacle to unity, strength, wealth, dignity, and power. Hu's efforts at genuine reconciliation with Japan, an analyst found, "aroused widespread indignation particularly among younger Chinese, and antagonized his party cohorts."[17] Hu's commitment to reconciliation with Japan was one of the causes of his ouster. Reconciliation with Japan is a casualty of the defeat of political reform in China.[18] There is no way for Chinese to comprehend that Japanese governments must commemorate the brave Japanese war dead, must embrace the heirs of soldiers who died in an unjust cause. In the United States, the same is true with the brave soldiers of the pro-slavery confederacy and their bereaved heirs.

Meanwhile, as China moved from Mao's policy of class war to a politics of nationalist legitimation, ever more attention was given to Chinese suffering in the era of Japan's invasion, 1931–45. In fact, the era of aggression was expanded to begin in 1874. China was eternally angelic innocence, a pure victim. The evil was not the Showa-era Imperial Army atrocities but Japanese. Japan was demonic evil, militaristic cruelty inherent in a barbaric culture. There was no mention of a very different Japanese understanding, that, as one Japanese scholar put it, "the Fifteen Year War . . . was an unfortunate deviation in Japan's modern history, whose keynote was gradual democratization."[19] China's understanding of Japan has almost nothing to do with Japan's self-understanding. The Chinese misunderstanding is getting nastier.

In the Mao era, the Communists basically celebrated only themselves. Holidays were May 1, July 1, August 1, and October 1, the days of the proletariat, the Communist Party's founding, the Red Army's founding, and the inauguration of their new People's Republic. That changed with the rise of post-Mao nationalism.

Little had been said in the Mao era about the Nanjing massacre. It occurred, after all, in the capital of Mao's anti-Communist enemy, Chiang Kai-shek. One of the heroes of the massacre who saved Chinese lives, John Rabe, was actually a Nazi who was kept in food after the war by the Communists' hated adversary Madame Chiang Kai-shek.[20] There were no Communist heroes or martyrs in Nanjing. So it had been with Showa-era Japanese Imperial Army aggression during the Manchurian incident of September 18, 1931 and the Marco Polo Bridge incident of July 7, 1937. Now all of these, plus the end of the war, as well as Japanese Imperial Army atrocities—such as medical experiments leading to death at ten times the rate of the Nazis—became commemorated, highlighted, institutionalized in museums, monuments, and markers, in books and visits by school children, central to a new patriotism in which a once-victimized China was rising so that an evil Japan could never again predominate in Asia. Chinese youth insisted on standing up against Japan as their elders had not.

No attention was paid to the difference between Japan in 1935 and in 1985. Anti-Japanese passions, perhaps greater than those of the Mao era, drive Mao's heirs entering the twenty-first century.[21] The major differences are that in the post-Mao era of rapid economic growth, China increasingly has the wherewithal to act on its anti-Japan agenda and that the hateful energies that Mao aimed violently against invented domestic enemies, so-called revisionists, are increasingly aimed against invented foreign enemies, alleged to be denying China its rightful territorial demands and its rightful place as the predominant power in Asia in the twenty-first century. In contrast to Cultural Revolution–era domestic purifiers, Chinese patriots entering the twenty-first century want China's international environment purified of forces that supposedly keep China from its true global greatness.

As Benito Lim put it in September 1996 in Beijing at the Twenty-First Century Forum, "China may become a superpower . . . with a proud 5,000 year history. China currently is already more than a nation; it is a civilization, a cultural force that has influenced her neighbors throughout history. . . . It can shape regional politics."[22]

That shaping influence includes the use of force. A former top U.S. official, Charles W. Freeman Jr., after talking with leaders in Beijing, reported that "China's leaders have always said they would go to war to prevent the permanent division of China. They now believe that they are likely to have to do so. China's armed forces have begun a decade-long effort to acquire the capabilities and do the planning required to have a serious chance of overwhelming Taiwan's formidable defenses."[23]

Aware of China's vision of its future and its willingness to use force, former Japanese Prime Minister Morihiro Hosokawa told the U.S.-Japan Society in Seattle on March 12, 1996[24] that "the most serious issues Japan may confront in the future may well be those related to China." In China, "nationalistic impulses haven't been entirely fulfilled. . . . Neighboring countries are aware of a 'big China' and must inevitably have strong concerns." Indeed, "the other newly industrializing countries of Asia along with Japan would not feel comfortable being influenced heavily by China. This is why a continued American presence in the Pacific is necessary."

Most directly worrisome as a cause of war, the Japanese prime minister found, were China's military actions aimed against Taiwan. "The issue of Taiwan for Japan is similar to that of Calais in relations between France and England, or Gibraltar during the Napoleonic wars, or the issue of Iceland or the Azores during World War II. . . . For maritime nations, they are vital lifelines of support."

Actually, the problem has been intensified by post-Mao reform. As Soviet Russian reformer Khrushchev's government was legitimated by the Great Patriotic War against Nazi Germany and made opposition to purported military revanchism in an actually democratic and antiwar Germany central to Moscow's expansionism in East Europe,[25] so unfounded concerns about and against a democratic Japan inflame nationalist passions and war potential even for reformers in post-Mao China.[26] The Chinese people continually remind themselves of their suffering at the hands of Japanese aggressors, supposedly from 1874–1945, that is, the entire modern era, and swear that it shall never be allowed to happen again, interpreting virtually every Japanese gesture as if Japanese militarism might soon be on the march all over Asia. Japan is treated as inherently evil. Actions premised on such worst case readings readily create security dilemmas because defensive efforts by Tokyo are taken in Beijing to be threats that must be met in a tit-for-tat way. A vicious spiral has been unleashed.

Consequently, peace and prosperity in the Asia-Pacific region in the twenty-first century require a major change in Beijing-Tokyo relations, a move toward genuine reconciliation. This large change may be impossible unless China democratizes. Analogous transitions which illuminate what is at stake include initial efforts at democratization in Russia allowing, at least momentarily, an end to Cold War tensions, and, more clearly, post–World War II German-French reconciliation after Germany democratized. Prior to Germany's democratization, from Napoleon's invasion of Germany to Hitler's invasion of France, France and Germany were regularly at war with each other. Mistrust, hate, and desires for vengeance suffused the relationship. Only the trust, transparency, and cooperation facilitated by democratization could, over time, reduce the hates and angers that provided the tinder that could be ignited into war by unfortunate incidents and domestically needed maneuvers. So I believe it is with China and Japan. Democratization, and getting past the passions of early democratization, are required for genuine China-Japan reconciliation. As French and Poles both decided to treat the post-Nazi German democracy as not responsible for Nazi crimes, so Chinese will have to change their view of democratic Japan if peace is to prevail.

To understand where China may be heading, one should not, as many do, focus in isolation on the impact of economic modernization or on Washington-Beijing relations. The Tokyo-Beijing relationship is central.

There already are popular, patriotic, entrenched, conservative, and hardline military forces in China dynamizing a chain reaction toward war. What is most worrisome is the inability—in fact, the unwillingness—of ruling groups in China to face up to their political crises. Instead they compound their problems by holding on to power in ways that make far more likely disintegration and violence internally and antagonism and war externally. Ruling groups have failed to resolve both the crisis of faith in China accompanying the discrediting of Marxism-Leninism and the center's budget crisis which comes with the reform process which decenters money accumulation. Instead of an open debate to build a democratic consensus on behalf of a national agenda to share the pain of reform in China, chauvinism is used to hold the loyalty of local people and to keep locales paying taxes. Because Beijing is unwilling to promote a popularly-informed, participatory federalism, a corrupt and self-serving center is seen by Chinese as plundering the regions that people increasingly identify with. Consequently, the center overproduces superpatriots who, to hold power, stress a foreign threat as a reason for internal unity and for discounting local interests.[27] In short, the reactionary political mind-set of China's most conservative ruling groups threatens more than the Chinese people.[28] The chauvinistic discourse of such conservatives is ever more popular in China.

Because it is so vital to the peace and prosperity of all peoples in the Asia-Pacific region, including the American people, that action be taken to avoid war, to not allow a drift toward war, it is important to explore the explosive dynamics that, if not tamped down or out or turned in another direction could indeed lead to war. It is crucial now to rethink some assumptions about Chinese foreign policy so that war does not explode because of inattention.

China's nationalist mind-set focuses on Japan. The horrific NATO bombing of the Chinese embassy in Belgrade was instantly linked in China to Japan's bomb assassination of Zhang Zuolin in Manchuria, a prelude to Japanese invasion. In the minds of Chinese patriots, who assume that a great China should be predominant in Asia, being "beaten at the hands of such a small country as Japan" in war in 1894–95 in Korea was an insufferable humiliation. Still, as seen by post-Mao Chinese hardliners, the group around the Empress Dowager, at the turn into the twentieth century, that is, people similar to leaders of China at the turn into the twenty-first century, was correct to resist all-out reform. The still popular Kang Youwei and the 1898 constitutional reform movement are treated as unthinking disasters. China's destiny is served by unity, patience, and getting strong. The alternative, as with the loss of Taiwan, is disunity and dismemberment. China should not emulate Japan or the West, but hold to ancient verities, gain strength, and reassert itself.[29]

In conversations with members of China's ruling elites, I have been made aware of how much angry competition with Japan for hegemony in Asia infuses so much of what Beijing does. This is not always obvious from reading the censored Chinese press. Even Beijing's 1996 military adventures against Taipei should be understood in a significant part as emanating from the anti-Japan thrust of post-Mao foreign policymakers.[30]

This central fact of a felt Chinese need to keep Japan subordinated in Asia[31] is inconceivable to many. After all, Tokyo is Beijing's top source of bilateral development loans. Tokyo does not upset Beijing on human rights issues. Japan is a leading trade partner. Japanese investment in China has been rising quantitatively and qualitatively since 1992. The Japanese people have been, since the end of World War II, absolutely opposed to military adventures abroad. And, some add, Japan remains trapped both in war guilt toward China and in historic cultural subordination to the great achievements of Chinese civilization. For more than a quarter of a century, Japan has conceded to China on issue after issue to avoid confrontation. How then could China-Japan relations be fraught with explosive tensions, even perhaps a potential for war? Of course, no such potential dynamizes Japan. The question is China.

But surely a rational China needs peace. Interests of strong economic interdependence should make war impossible. Sadly, however appealing, this logic of "sweet commerce" promoting peace is belied by history, subverted by the strength of national chauvinism and the appeal of national glory. Statesmen just prior to World War I agreed that economic interdependence made an intra-European war impossible. They were wrong. There is no reason to believe that today's economic interdependence is more determinative.

Nationalistic mobilizations and security anxieties regularly turn mere economic self-interest into an experiential betrayal of patriotism. That is how it is increasingly imagined in the chauvinistic discourse in China. Beijing's nationalism makes Japan an enemy to be kept down in Asia for ever more people in China, including ruling groups. The threatening shape of this reimagined China-Japan relationship escapes the gaze of most analysts. Yet even people of Chinese descent living in America identify with the Chinese passion that China must keep Japan from hegemony in Asia. Wars between major powers such as China and Japan can and do originate in local issues which escalate and spread out of control, just as with World War I. A separate Taiwan, imagined in Beijing as part of a Japanese empire, is just such an issue.

Illusions obscure this dangerous possibility. These illusions include a myth that Beijing is not aggressive. Chinese nationalists even believe that China never has been expansionist. That is what school children in China are taught. Actually, all large nations are big precisely because they have been expansionist, whether it is the United States, Russia, China, Brazil, or any other. They all have conquered and killed. China's neighbors and minorities are painfully aware of a history, an auger, to which Chinese nationalists are blind. Even many Chinese democrats embrace this myth of a uniquely peace-loving Chinese defensiveness. They imagine China as a victim of invaders, never an invader.

In Chinese nationalism, Japan was invaded in the thirteenth century by Mongols, not by China's Yuan dynasty. Tibet, however, was at the same time incorporated by China's Yuan dynasty. That was not an immoral invasion by alien Mongols. The contradiction is invisible in China, but not in Japan.

In Chinese nationalist consciousness, Muslim rebels were merely put down by China's Qing dynasty. There were no incorporating massacres. The conquering Manchu Qing, by all accounts a very expansionist imperium, had to be overthrown by patriotic Chinese because Manchus supposedly were soft on imperialism. With Chinese patriots seeing China as a pure victim, they do not see that China has the frontier problems it has because of its insistence on holding on to all the imperialist conquests of the Manchus. China is an imperial successor state understood by many of its neighbors as resuming an imperial quest.

Patriots see none of this. They even tell each other that the only reason Deng Xiaoping ordered an invasion of Vietnam in 1979 was because American President Jimmy Carter made that invasion the price of recognition by the United States, of access to the American market, and of international financial institution money. Of course, this is untrue. Chinese cannot face up to central, nasty, ordinary truths about Beijing's foreign policy. Silence prevails on China's part in Kim Il-song's invasion of South Korea. China's all-out invasion of northern India in 1962, using the pretext of an actual Indian incursion at one border post as part of a feeble march north, is described in China as an all-out Indian invasion. There is no open democratic discussion to make Chinese conscious of how others see them.

Well-meaning Chinese cannot readily change course when they cannot even recognize where China has been and is heading. Taiwan President Lee Teng-hui is blamed for war dangers in the Taiwan Straits region; Philippines President Ramos is blamed for South China Sea confrontations with China; disarray in Washington, D.C. is blamed for the growth of anti-Americanism in China. Chinese believe America denied China the year 2000 Olympics, which went to Sydney, Australia, although no evidence supports such a conjecture. Australia seems to have bought its votes in the standard way. Is this nationalism of victimhood and vengeance worrisome?

To be sure, China's military might should not be exaggerated. But, ignoring the regional facts, places where China already is bullying neighbors is also a mistake. Illusions protect war-prone forces. Were China a democracy, there could be voices in a debate calling attention to millennia of Chinese wars of incorporation and expansion. A democratic debate in China might somewhat puncture virtually genetic notions of Japanese evil, Chinese purity, and an aggrieved China as the eternal victim. In a democracy, supporters of China-Japan reconciliation as more important than demands for endless Japanese apologies could ask, "Should Vietnam demand that China apologize and face history for the Ming [dynasty] invasion of Dai Viet in the fifteenth century, when Chinese commanders claimed 7 million killed and that the plains were turned red?" And should China apologize for any of the subsequent Chinese attacks on the Vietnamese state over the next four centuries. What should reparations be?[32] It might be possible in a Chinese democracy to get the viewpoints of China's anxious neighbors into China's policy debate. As in its 1999 view of war in Yugoslavia which brackets Kosovo victims of Serbian policy, Beijing sees no neighbors or minorities as victims of China.

China's expansionist chauvinism is not new.[33] Its invasion of Korea in 1950 was not a matter of simple defense; Mao very much wanted into that war.[34] Also, the Chinese side provoked the 1969 conflict with Soviet Russia. In addition, China invaded Vietnam in 1979 and then kept harassing Vietnam while putting out stories that Vietnam was provoking China with border incidents. Beijing was also the backer of the genocidal Pol Pot; Beijing was the major arms supplier of the murderous Khmer Rouge. It arms the murderous tyrants in Myanmar (Burma). It armed the perpetrators of genocide in Rwanda. Dictatorship precludes these huge facts from entering the political discourse in China.

It is therefore not true that the CCP rulership never has, and therefore never can, do anything offensive in Asia. China's neighbors are worried.[35] Singapore's elder statesman Lee Kuan Yew, at that September 1996 Twenty-First Century Forum in Beijing, reported that "Many medium and small countries in Asia . . . are uneasy that China may want to resume the imperial status it had in earlier centuries and have misgivings about being treated as vassal states having to send tribute to China as they used to in past centuries."

China long backed subversive forces throughout Southeast Asia. Of course, the PRC is not uniquely militaristic. The United States in the twentieth century intervened all over Central America and the Caribbean. Before 1898, however, when Britain ruled the seas, the United States was more cautious. It is not unusual for a major power to try to impose its will on smaller, weaker nations. But with China in the Asia Pacific, not all other nations are small and weak. Dangerously, in China, normal international relations dynamics combine with the superpatriotic path of relegitimation by frightened ruling groups without any legitimate dissenting voices in China pointing out that it is a quite secure, large, and powerful China that is seen as a bully, thereby making a rising and chauvinistic Beijing worrisome.

The logic of a security dilemma is already unleashed. China's neighbors talk to the United States and quietly prepare to fend off what frightens them. Singapore in 1998 invited the U.S. Navy in. Indonesia allied militarily with Australia. The Philippines, after asking the U.S. military to leave in 1991, invited it in 1999 to return.

Feeling innocent and purely defensive, rulers in Beijing see their neighbors' cautionary actions as threats to China and respond to defend China. A vicious cycle could grow out of control if each side sees itself as singularly responding defensively to provocations. Surely the American President did the right thing in 1998–99 in trying to reengage China in a more positive strategic direction. Forces opposed to peaceful partnership and conciliation, however, are strong in both Washington and Beijing.

Most of China's neighbors are already so anxious over Chinese expansionism and impending domination and so worried about further enraging Beijing that they will not even utter what they believe, for fear of provoking this China to strike out against neighbors sooner or harder. India was unique in *declaring* in 1999 that it feels threatened by China. Increasingly, in particular in Asian subregions, doubting the reliability or staying power of the American military in the Asia Pacific, seeing the weakness of Japan's political ability, Asian neighbors ruefully submit to China's words and policies.

Yet many American analysts treat Chinese words of pure defensiveness as gospel. It, however, was not Lee Teng-hui's alleged provocativeness, but changes in China, including a growing anti-Japanese nationalism that sparked Beijing's military action against Taiwan in Summer 1995 and 1996. Unless there are changes in Chinese politics, more military action should be expected from Beijing if Taiwan does not capitulate.[36] This threat to the peace is real and new.

There was no Chinese irredentism toward Taiwan from the Mao camp before the 1943 Cairo Conference, when Nationalist Party leader Chiang Kai-shek persuaded the Allies arrayed against Showa-era Japanese military expansionism to agree to give Taiwan to Chiang's Republic of China after imperial Japan's armies, which had first occupied Taiwan in the Meiji era, were defeated. It is not surprising that Taiwan had not been part of Mao's nationalism, since during the many millennia of Chinese history, Taiwan had never been a province of China until the expansionist imperialism of the Manchu Empire, and then, for just one decade. (Mongolia is unique in having regained its independence after the fall of Manchu imperialism in 1911.) When Chiang's forces fled from Mao's conquering army to safety on Taiwan in 1949, Mao treated Taiwan mainly as a home to a defeated civil war military force that wrongly sat in Beijing's rightful seat in international bodies. Mao saw no need for a war over Taiwan in his lifetime.

For the post-Mao generation out to build up China, Taiwan might be seen as a partner in a common project. After all, Taiwan is a major source of foreign exchange helping to speed China's economic growth, a partner in trade, a well-spring of foreign investment, a part of a huge tourist influx. There was no cross-straits civil war. Millions of people from the mainland of China and the island of Taiwan went back and forth peacefully. It is possible to imagine European Common Market–style mutual benefit. Indeed were China to democratize and federalize or confederate, it would swiftly become irresistibly attractive to Taiwanese. It is dictatorship in China which perpetuates war-prone division.

The benefits to Chinese unity of a federalist democratization are invisible in China because the people have accepted the Beijing propaganda that democratization in the Soviet Union caused political and economic disintegration. Actually, the Russian Communist Party still dominates the parliament entering the twenty-first century and is part of the problem. As for the economy, agriculture remains largely unreformed. In industry, Russia's particular situation forced Moscow to deal with the hemorrhaging of state-owned enterprises. Whereas in China, only 19 percent were on state payrolls, in Russia it was 91 percent. In short, the Beijing propaganda against democracy is not about Russian reality but about legitimating China's new authoritarianism.

The new authoritarian Chinese nationalism has a vengeful, militaristic edge. It fixates on despised signs of prior Chinese weakness, matters such as the linkage of Hong Kong to the British-initiated Opium War. At the return of Hong Kong in 1997, a moment when there was more per capita wealth in Hong Kong than in Britain, the British were vilified for having made Chinese poor and backward. Actually it was a multicentury decline of China, beginning in the Ming or Qing, depending on one's point of view, which left China so far behind in military technology that even puny, distant Britain could win the disgraceful Opium War.

In like manner, ignoring the fact that Chinese rulers had almost happily gotten rid of a Taiwan experienced as most alien, the Japanese and the treaty the Meiji rulers of Japan imposed in 1895 upon the Manchu imperium in China at Shimoneseki are blamed in post-Mao China for Taiwan's autonomy, taken as a continuing humiliation of a rising Chinese people. There is silence on Mao's decision to back the invasion of South Korea which actually led to American intervention in the Taiwan Straits region, changing the military balance. Until Mao made war in Korea his priority, nothing blocked his conquest of Taiwan.

Given Chinese nationalism's fixation on Japan, Chinese acts are ignored. Instead, visceral anti-Japaneseness incites outrage in Beijing toward Taiwan's 1990s President Lee, seen as pro-Japan. Lee Teng-hui is seen in China as a traitor to the Chinese people. That fact is painfully revealed to Chinese in President Lee's interview in Japanese to a Japanese reporter in which Lee expressed pride in his Japanese past and for which the Japanese reporter praised President Lee for being virtually an ideal Japanese. This Chinese outrage at Taiwanese treason is reignited regularly by pro-Japanese comments of countless Taiwanese citizens.

On the one hand, the Chinese passion against Taiwanese pride in its cultural inheritance from Japan is quite natural, similar to how a Jew or Pole might feel about someone proud of culture, life, and education acquired during the Nazi era. On the other hand, a nasty chauvinism is at work. A democratic South Korea, which suffered longer and far more from Japan's imperial militarism than did China, has reconciled with Japan and agreed to put the past behind it and build together for a better future. Despite all the continuing difficulties of Koreans, Seoul and Tokyo could still devise democratic ways of resolving issues in textbook disputes as authoritarian China cannot. Seoul and Tokyo can even cooperate to host the World Cup in Soccer. If China cannot reconcile with Japan as even South Korea, which suffered so much more from Japan, can do, then the reasons may well lie in China's nondemocratic system and its anti-Japanese ambitions in Asia. Once South Korea democratized, President Kim Dae Jung could find a formula for reconciliation and mutual benefit with Japan.

Were China a democracy, its anti-Japan passion might be cooled by the complexities of openness and transparency. Chinese specialists in Japanese history could add to the public debate large facts which Beijing's authoritarian censors suppress.[37] Japanese do not imagine themselves as eternal aggressors against China. Through much of Japanese history, as one Japanese analyst noted, "Japan tried to maintain diplomatic relations with China on an equal basis. China, however, never recognized Japan or any other nation under heaven as an equal, viewing the rest of the world as below itself."[38] That is, much of Japanese history is an attempt to end subordination to China. Chinese are not taught that China's neighbors have historic grievances toward an unwelcome Chinese hegemony.

The nineteenth century war between China and Japan was experienced by Chinese elites as an end to civilization and the Sinocentric tribute system, seen as encompassing civilization.[39] In Japan, instead, it was the culmination of a centuries-long struggle to win freedom from subjugation to Chinese dominion.[40] That war fought in Korea led to the Treaty of Shimonoseki. It was, as Tokyo saw it, a war played by the international rules of the time. In fact, Japan experienced itself then as a victim. "The Great Powers . . . betrayed [Japan] in the case of the Sino-Japanese War. After the signing of the Shimonoseki Peace Treaty, Germany, France, and Russia put on strong pressure forcing Japan to return the Shantung Peninsula which it had gained in the treaty." This exploded Japan's understanding "of international society . . . [as] the rule of the jungle and the equality of nations. The intervention . . . boosted the cynical view of 'might makes right' in international society which was 'dominated by the West.'"[41] Japanese experience themselves as the victim of Shimonoseki in a double sense, losing what they gained by treaty and energizing the revanchist forces that eventually defeated the constitutional process begun in the Meiji era, detouring instead on to the tragic and deadly path of militarism in Showa-era Japan. None of this can be discussed in a chauvinistic, dictatorial China. Anti-Japanese understandings fester.

The lack of democracy helps make Chinese blind to their own history, to the complex Japanese experience of China, and to the reality of an independent, democratic, and peaceful Japan. Instead, "Chinese analyses of Japanese foreign policy . . . assume an atavistic tendency in Japan to revert to militarism and expansionism."[42] The Beijing government has, as one Japanese commentator noted, made China's World War II anti-Japan war "into a symbol of the genesis of the modern Chinese people. In order to stir up nationalist feelings, Japan has been used as a scapegoat both by China's government and its [internal] opponents."[43] Indeed, Chinese nationalism is largely anti-Japanese.

In the 1996 *China Can Say No* books, Japan was treated far worse than America. As with America, Chinese are told to stop being so accommodating to Japan. But Japanese are portrayed as virtually genetically and unchangeably evil. "Japan is an immoral neighbor . . . immoral in the past, immoral in the present, immoral in politics, immoral in economics, etc." "Japanese lack Chinese generosity, kindheartedness, and modesty. Theirs is a different kind of blood . . . you can only be humane toward humans; toward beasts you can only be bestial."[44] Only a democratized China, made less nativistic by confronting its own repressed expansionist and inhuman activities and able to comprehend Japan as something other than inherently and cruelly militaristic, can realize the Tokyo-Beijing reconciliation required for prolonged peace and prosperity in the Pacific.

Japan is a demonical focus in Chinese nationalism also because it impedes Chinese predominance in Asia. Tokyo and Beijing competed to woo hard-hit Southeast Asian nations in the wake of the 1997 financial crisis. In the 1990s, China has chosen to highlight Chinese victims of Showa-era Japan's brutal invasion of China, from the extreme inhumanities of the Nanjing Massacre and monstrously inhuman medical experiments on prisoners, to the ubiquitous savageries of a colonial war. Chinese analysts iterate and reiterate that such a Japan as a leader in

Asia is absolutely unacceptable. Chinese will not accept that earlier militarily expansionist Japan is more dead in Japanese hearts than Manchu imperialist conquests are in Chinese hearts.

Even when Beijing insists its goal is to "forge [a] closer relationship" with Japan, it actually demands Japanese subordination. In the Chinese view, all problems in the relationship come from Tokyo which supposedly supports separatists in Taiwan, continues Cold War ties with America, and keeps alive glories of Japanese militarism instead of "working out a positive China policy" that recognizes "China's strategic position in the world."[45]

Without a democratized, self-critical China, Beijing misunderstands Tokyo. Japanese leaders naturally worry about Chinese military actions in Asia and about American military withdrawal from Asia. The Chinese are blind to Japanese anxieties. As one specialist put it, "The blind spot in the analysis is the inability to perceive that Japan's enhanced security measures could be stimulated by Chinese arms spending. The notion that Japan is the former rapacious predator of Nanjing precludes once and for all any possibility that China could conceivably threaten Japan. Thus . . . any increase of its [Japan's] responsibilities under the U.S.-Japan security treaty is perceived not as part of a dialectical process, but only as inborn revanchism,"[46] even though ASEAN, which also was a victim of World War II Japan, as one commentator noted, is also concerned with "the growth of Chinese power and how the countries of Southeast Asia can best cope with it."[47] Tokyo feels a "need to balance a re-emergent China . . . provide powerful incentives . . . forging stronger politico-strategic ties with Southeast Asia."[48] "Japan has begun to move away from sole reliance on the tools of interdependence toward 'hedging' strategies designed to offset China's growing power."[49]

Chinese leaders believe that the Japanese public's taboo against a normal foreign policy is very gradually disappearing. They conclude that China may have a short window of opportunity to take what supposedly is rightfully China's before Japanese militarism returns. This includes the South China Sea, Taiwan, and the Senkaku Islands. In the Beijing perspective, China is purely defensive, retaking what had always been Chinese, while Japan is inherently aggressive. Such attitudes and beliefs do not provide a solid foundation for reconciliation and preserving the peace.

Koichi Kato, then the secretary-general of Japan's Liberal Democratic Party, declared in Washington in July 1998 that China's goal was "to be equally strong as the U.S." He worried that China, to achieve its goal, would use force in the Asia Pacific, which would be alarming and unacceptable to Japan. Because of sea lane vulnerability, Japan has strengthened maritime security ties with the United States.[50] China's own analysis buttresses the case for Japanese concern.

Inside China, Beijing's Asian ambitions are proud boasts. A recent Chinese analysis, while suggesting "lying low" for a while "to break up the feeling within the Asia-Pacific region of the 'China threat,'" sees a world of national interest conflict, not mutually beneficial globalization ("empty talk") in which "in the twenty-first century, the fundamental conflict of interests between China and America will become more apparent." . . . "The rise of China will change the balance of power in the Asia Pacific. . . . Asia may well then become China's 'sphere of influence.'" Consequently, "the U.S. and Japan do not want China to gain in power."[51] China has been acting to gain that power. That is taken for granted in Beijing.

The present Beijing perspective, nonetheless, can find no Chinese actions that could have led strategic specialists in and out of government from America and Japan to conclude by January 1997 that "constructive engagement [with China] is no guarantee that China will not consider actions, including the use of military force, that are unacceptable to the United States or Japan. In these instances, the U.S.-Japan alliance also must be formidable enough to deter such actions, or, if deterrence fails to respond to them."[52] In July 1997, the Japanese Defense Agency, in its annual defense white paper expressed a need to respond to "Chinese actions" in the region. These Chinese actions included, the "modernization of nuclear forces, naval and air forces . . . activities in the high seas [i.e., South China Sea and East China Sea] and the Taiwan Strait."[53] Rulers in China treat such an approach to Taiwan and those maritime territories as Japanese aggression against sacred Chinese soil. That is a legitimate Chinese cause for war.

In imagining a return to past glories, Chinese patriots envision a Sinocentric Asia, one in which a less civilized Japan supposedly of course borrowed from the great civilization of China. Chinese still see Japanese, an analyst born in China found, as devoid of creative culture.[54] In a racist imagining of 5,000 years of greatness for a racially pure Chinese people, Japanese—as Koreans[55]—can even be imagined as Han by history, by culture, and by blood. Only a sinified Japan is a good Japan.

Japan's rise is portrayed as treason, abandoning Asia (China) for the alien and immoral West.

Japanese hear the Chinese discourse as a return to the Sinocentric tribute system, with Japan subservient to China, living in semi-enslavement, in fear of China. In China, voices of mutually beneficial interdependence[56] can be denounced as a return of Wang Jingwei, seen as the war era quisling who sold out to Japan. China-Japan reconciliation may therefore require sufficient democracy and openness in China such that Wang Jingwei might just seem very Chinese,[57] similar to earlier Chinese who accepted defeat by Mongols and Manchus, believing that ultimately China's great culture would conquer the conquerors, that such a peaceful change was better than shedding endless innocent Chinese blood in a losing cause. One does not have to agree with Wang. But it is vital for reconciliation that his choice, and the similar choice of many tens of millions of Chinese, be understandable, not just treasonable.

Such a change is not easy when the mythos legitimating the Chinese Communist dictatorship is that Communists earned the legitimate right to rule by fighting Japan, while lesser Chinese, let alone collaborators with Japan, were illegitimate. It would take a very different politics to be open to a discourse that could both declare that cooperation with Japan was not a crime, but even, at times, helpful to Chinese, as many in China's northeast actually feel, and that Japan also did most monstrous deeds worthy of the strongest condemnation. Reconciliation with Japan may first require reconciliation in China, almost inconceivable without democratization.

Only in a democratic atmosphere could Chinese contemplate that, say, what the Belgians did in the Congo was far worse than the truly barbarous savagery of Japan's Imperial Army in China, and yet reconciliation was possible.[58] This openness to reconciliation requires democracy, because only with democracy could Chinese confront the lies in their own textbooks, the stories they tell themselves to hide the history of inhumanity under communism. Also I look forward to one day seeing a Chinese textbook that accurately described America's role in defeating imperial Japan. China could use with some textbook revisions, too.[59]

As any student of American history should suspect, all governments have hands steeped in blood. Only with democracy can the Chinese learn that the extraordinarily inhuman practice of sexual slavery of Hirohito's Imperial Army, as with raping German Nazi officers, was not prosecuted in war crimes trials after World War II because, among other reasons, in

East Europe, as in China's northeast, there was a cover-up of the monstrous raping done by the advancing Russian Red Army.[60]

Communists did monstrous things, too; some would say equally monstrous; some would say worse. Reconciliation requires some understanding of one's own complicity in inhumanity for all peoples, Americans included. Democrats in power in Beijing might want to commemorate the victims of tyranny in China by Chinese, people murdered in land reform, the three and five anti's campaigns, the antirightist movement, the great leap, the four cleans, and the horrendous slaughtering movements, almost too numerous to count, during the Cultural Revolution. With consciousness of how many Chinese died unnecessarily under Mao, probably more than even under Japanese Imperial Army occupation, reconciliation would become far more possible. It is impossible as long as an authoritarian China seeks to focus singularly on the real cruelties of Hirohito's army to drum up a legitimating nationalism.

Obviously reconciliation will not be easy. Chinese patriots want to hear that they are victims and others are villains. Anything else, including this article, is all too readily experienced as confusing right and wrong, reversing truth and slander.

To get a feel for how dangerous these surging chauvinistic forces in China are, one need only talk with the most decent, caring, democratic, and human rights oriented Chinese living outside of China. Few can escape the pull of a Sinocentric nationalism legitimating the rise of an innocent and victimized China to a deserved and defensive greatness. Few Chinese would respond to the data and logic of this article with anything but denunciation. The popularity of China's patriotic passion makes politics very, very difficult for peace-prone ruling groups in China who prefer international reconciliation and cooperation to policies of chauvinism and belligerency. Military, hard-line, and conservative forces are enjoying seeing their discourse become hegemonic. In the 1980s they already defeated reformers Hu Yaobong and Zhao Ziyang. By the end of the 1990s they constrained Zhu Rongji and were criticizing the Deng Xiaoping reform line as soft on imperialism. Given the strength of these revanchist forces in China, the problem is how to avoid war.

That means how to advance genuine Tokyo-Beijing reconciliation. Chinese—even in Taiwan, even in America—can feel strongly that the Meiji-era rise of Japan was an abandoning by a hitherto Confucianized Japan of an ethically superior China-centered Asia for a rapacious West. Chinese patriots are blind and deaf to the actual comprehension of a historically hegemonic China as experienced by Japan and other Chinese neighbors. The emotion among patriotic Chinese is that Japan must end its treason and return to Asia, meaning a world centered in and led from Beijing.

So presuppositional is the logic of Chinese patriotism that its perverse consequences seem invisible or irrelevant. However, Chinese assertiveness is not winning friends. Japanese are "becoming fed up" with China's insistent demands for ever more aid and apologies.[61] Japanese public opinion has turned against China. Official visits to China by Japanese parliamentarians have plummeted. "The Sino-Japanese relationship has deteriorated since 1994 as both countries have resorted to semi and indirect military actions."[62] In 1995, Chinese insensitivities to Japanese feelings on Chinese nuclear testing led to a momentary freezing of some aid. Japanese see that it "is becoming chic in China to treat Japan as a weak, ineffectual power and to scoff at the passivity that results from the postwar [peace] constitution and from the public preference for pacifism."[63] The November 1998 visit to Japan by China's President Jiang was a public relations nightmare in Japan as he hectored the Japanese in the presence of a conciliatory emperor. And yet the popular Chinese response to President Jiang's Japan trip was that the Chinese side was absolutely insufficiently tough on Japan.[64] In like manner, by the way, the popular scuttlebutt in the provinces after the deadly NATO bombing of China's embassy in Belgrade, even after nationwide anti-American riots in China facilitated by the government in Beijing, was that President Jiang was too soft on the enemies of China.

Even democratically-minded Chinese nationalists do not readily comprehend Japan's security dilemma. They cannot hear the anxiety, as expressed by a Japanese Foreign Ministry official that "The Japanese used to view China as weak so Japan did not feel a threat from China, . . . the situation is 'different now.' "[65] To patriotic Chinese, it is almost inconceivable that anything Tokyo is doing could possibly be a defensive response to Chinese actions. Does anyone in Beijing argue that China was wrong in 1995 testing nuclear weapons or that China should pay heed to Japanese nuclear sensitivities? Does anyone among the CCP rulers call for an understanding of changing national identity in Taiwan? If not, then decision makers in Beijing cannot understand why a responsible international relations analyst in Europe could worry in 1997 that China may provoke war over Taiwan and that, therefore, Washington and Tokyo should act now to make that less likely. "A good case could be made that future Taiwan crises would be better served if the U.S. and other allies made clear that any [Chinese] threat or use of force would be met by overwhelming deterrence."[66] While I would not endorse such a provocative policy, the question remains, can China restrain itself if it pictures itself as pure innocence and unique victim? Such a passion will not be negated by economic success. Economic engagement alone will not win peace for Asia.

Beijing attempts to isolate Taiwan and bully Tokyo to accept China's view of justice in Asia. Chinese are continually reminded by rulers in Beijing of weakness as a spur to strength and assertion in the Asia Pacific. A rising power insisting on acting on emotions of righting historical wrongs does not bode well for future peace in the region. To be sure, China also acts on an economic calculus which includes an imperative for good relations with America, Japan, Taiwan, and Southeast Asia as part of a strategy to win the wealth needed to reform China, hold popular support, and raise the living standards of the people. The struggle in Chinese politics is real and deep. But a rise of hardliners or economic problems, or both, could facilitate total victory for expansionist chauvinists.

Post-Mao China embraces late nineteenth century social Darwinist nativistic values, absolute sovereignty, and racist understandings of a struggle of the fittest for survival.[67] All around the globe, politically threatened red political power has regularly tried to glom on to a brown nationalism in order to mobilize nativists in a power-entrenching and militaristic cause. Beijing's 1999 identification with Belgrade against Kosovo is, in part, a consequence of these Chinese political passions. This red-brown trend has been gaining force in China since the end of the 1970s when Vietnam was invaded and the return of Taiwan to the motherland was promoted to a top national priority.

Given great power dynamics in China, Bernstein and Munro suggest an explicit U.S.-Japan military alliance against China.[68] Christopher Layne suggests that "the United States should encourage . . . Japan . . . acquiring great power, including nuclear, military capabilities."[69] These, I find, are bad policies of desperation, guaranteed to make the already dangerous yet worse. They will entrench power in China for worst case forces which seek a militarized foreign policy.

Worst case forces, however, do not monopolize Chinese politics. There are plenty of Chinese, including powerful people among ruling groups, who accept a world of diffuse power among diverse nation-states, with

China one, albeit a great one, among many. There are even some Chinese who see anti-Japanese nationalism aimed at Chinese predominance in Asia as a distraction from the priority need for deals with neighbors to start exploiting the maritime resources of the South China Sea and energy resources elsewhere, to the mutual benefit of both China and its neighbors. In this perspective, the priority for the Chinese government is bettering the life of the Chinese people. There are also Chinese who have reimagined Sinocentrism so that it is less an ideological cover for the hierarchical subordination of others in Asia and more a legitimation for mutually enriching cultural and other exchanges, as in the era of exchange over the Silk Road and across the South China Sea. There thus is no reason for a policy of containment toward China when there still is the possibility of building peaceful, mutually beneficial relations. If engagement is in fact mutually beneficial, open interchange could win support from ever more Chinese, whatever today's balance of forces. Consequently, forces of political reform could yet win out. But they do not have it easy. Foreign governments interested in peace and prosperity should not make life harder for them.

Meanwhile China's anxious neighbors have to protect themselves. This gives rise to a vicious cycle that intensifies mistrust. Anxieties in Tokyo and Washington led to a strengthening of their alliance, which Chinese took as a threat to Chinese interests. Missile actions by Beijing and Pyongyang heighten interest around China in a theater missile defense, which China promises to overwhelm militarily. While democracy is not a panacea to such vicious cycles, dangerous Chinese tendencies could be eroded or even reversed by the transparency and trust and international cooperation and more critical self-understanding resulting from democratization.

Thus, if China wants peace and prosperity, it is in Beijing's interest to foster a more open political system. Yet China's rulers treat secrecy in virtually everything as a life-and-death issue. How then should China's peace-prone neighbors act to persuade Beijing to move in the direction of greater transparency; how to involve China in multilateral, confidence-building efforts? The alternative would be interactions that intensify mistrust and thereby strengthen the most vengeful forces in Beijing, unintentionally making war more likely.

The point surely is not that China is about to attack America. But lesser actions can go awry. The PRC has not done well in comprehending American foreign policy responses to Chinese ventures. In fact,

Beijing has a record of misunderstanding Washington and unintentionally provoking American military responses. Mao Zedong backed Kim Il-song's invasion of the Republic of Korea, never imagining Truman would respond with massive force. Mao was again shocked by Eisenhower's massive response in 1958 after Mao ignited a military crisis in the Taiwan Straits. Yet again, in 1996, when China bullied and harassed Taiwan with missile exercises just off Taiwan's two great ports, Beijing never expected Clinton's massive response. In short, Beijing has a record of not understanding how provocative, threatening, and dangerous its military initiatives appear to others in the region. Worse yet, the new nationalism in China and the almost natural arrogance that comes everywhere with economic success combine to increase the likelihood of more explosive misunderstandings.

Although tempered by the 1997 and later Asian economic crisis and the concomitant heightened importance of the American economy for continued Chinese growth, the combination of remnant Marxism-Leninism expecting America to suffer the final crisis of capitalist imperialism and a new chauvinism which absorbs the writings of American declinists and treats the United States as a paper tiger that flees at the loss of any American lives persuades many in Beijing that if China but stands up to America, it is America that will back down. In fact, the elite gossip in Beijing is that it was Washington that cringed in fear of China's military might in the 1996 Taiwan Straits crisis. America is portrayed as a pushover for patriotic Chinese willing to sacrifice to achieve nationalistic goals.

Beijing's historic underestimation of how threatening its armed actions appear in the Asia-Pacific region, and a wish to see America as weakening and becoming a pushover, can join with China's new nationalism to impel China in a more militaristic direction. After all, Chinese believe they are an inherently peaceful people merely trying to put an end to a long history of wrongs that victimized a previously weak China. Patriots in a stronger China have no right to rule, in this nationalistic perspective, unless they, at long last, stand up for China and use China's strength to right historic wrongs. Beijing, therefore, is again likely to be militarily active. Such action will force difficult choices on the governments of the Asia-Pacific region.

From the perspective of policy, it seems incontrovertible that Washington should be doing nothing to harm the better forces in China. It is not obvious that the worst case forces in China must win. Nonetheless, those forces are there. They are strong. They have persisted for many decades. And their anti-Japan logic almost seems hegemonic. What is most worrisome is the conventional wisdom which treats the powerful rise of a war-prone chauvinist discourse, a big change at the heart of Chinese politics, as a cause of but small problems and little tensions, things that are readily managed in the interests of peace and common prosperity with little effort by mere engagement.

A major change of inordinate import has occurred. Resurgent Chinese chauvinism is already weighty. It could win out totally if China's economy plummets. It could even have appeal in parts of Asia. In 1997–98 many Asians scapegoated America and the IMF (seen as American) as the cause of Asia's financial difficulties. It is possible to envision a victorious Chinese hegemony in Asia, just as Huntington suggests.[70] While it would be misleading in the extreme, a monstrous self-fulfilling prophecy, to treat this dangerous force as already victorious and exhausting all political possibilities emanating from China, it would also be a danger altogether to ignore it. This force could, starting with an incorporation of Taiwan, incite a rollback of democracy in Asia, an explosion of a horrible war in the Asia-Pacific region, and an intensification of cruel repression in China. Within Beijing's resurgent, popular anti-Japanese, Sinocentric nationalism, even some friends of political reform in China entering the twenty-first century can feel deep inside themselves that democracy is alien to Asia, an enemy of Asia, the camouflage of immoral Japan and traitorous Lee Teng-hui on Taiwan. Democracy seems a camouflage for alien hegemony. Although many Chinese seek democracy to cure the pervasive corruption and cronyism that allow so much of the Mao-era economy to remain unreformed so that ruling groups leech off the Chinese people, China's popular, antidemocratic nationalism may not swiftly abate. As in fascist ideology, liberal democracy is seen in China as a disease, a threatening plague to be wiped out so that our pure people can thrive.

Having absorbed Hong Kong, China, at the start of the twenty-first century, may confront the 22 million people in Taiwan's flourishing democracy, imagined as a traitor to the Han, a colony of Japan, with a timetable for reunification. President Jiang has promised to act on such a war-prone calculus. Beijing will also woo Taiwan's tycoons to betray Taiwan as Hong Kong's did. Beijing will intensify pressures to isolate Taiwan internationally. And it will use military force and economic destabilization to shake the support of the people of Taiwan from their government, all the time telling others in Asia that Taiwan is a unique issue with no larger significance. To prove this, Beijing temporarily may limit its South China Sea expansion and rely for the immediate future on huge oil deals with Kazakhstan and elsewhere.

The challenge for the nations of the Asia Pacific is how to keep China from imposing its military will in the region, without treating China as a hostile nation. That is, it is important to keep options open for the better forces in China to grab on to. In America, an irresponsible policy debate on China, which demonized China and was replete with racism against Americans of Chinese descent, made headway at the end of the 1990s. If such passions make the American policy choice containment versus isolation, that would make a responsible American policy discussion almost impossible. Worst case forces then could intensify the security dilemma. Engagement with quiet vigilance is called for.

Both Tokyo and Washington should be committed to full engagement with Beijing, to an equivalent of NATO member Germany's 1969 *Ostpolitik*. But that enlightened Germany policy that meant to enrich Germany's Communist neighbors and help them appreciate the virtues of peaceful cooperation (engagement) did not prevent the crushing of Solidarity in Poland in 1980 or block an intensification of a second Cold War in the 1970s caused by Brezhnev's militarism. It is worth recalling the tensions in Europe in the early 1980s as Pershing missiles were deployed to match Soviet Russia's SS-20 missiles. Engagement with vigilance has to be a long-term commitment despite nasty bumps along the way. Demagogues in Washington or Beijing could easily derail it. The road to peace and prosperity in the Asia-Pacific region will not be smooth. Growth will not by itself reverse the nasty chauvinistic dynamics pulsating in China. American policymakers, if they wish to preserve peace and prosperity, will have to face up to the real dangers that lie within resurgent Chinese anti-Japanese, Sinocentric chauvinism. Yet outsiders cannot change China. Only Chinese can do that. Only with a democratization of China by Chinese can Chinese develop the critical self-understanding that can facilitate a reimagining of Japan, thereby creating a peace-oriented foundation for genuine China-Japan reconciliation.

Notes

1. This article benefits from papers presented at a January 15–16, 1999 Harvard University conference on China-Japan-U.S. triangular relations.

2. Kent Calder, *Asia's Deadly Triangle*. London: Nicholas Brealey Publishing, 1997, pp. 137–138.

3. *Oppose the Revival of Japanese Militarism*. Peking: Foreign Languages Press, 1960, p. 1.

4. Ibid., p. 11.

5. Ibid., p. 48.

6. Ibid., pp. 115 and 117.

7. *Support the Just Struggle of the Japanese People Against the Japan-U.S. Treaty of Military Alliance*. Peking: Foreign Languages Press, 1960, p. 62.

8. Chae-Jin Lee, *China and Japan*. Stanford: Hoover Press, 1984, p. 7.

9. James Mann, *About Face*. New York: Knopf, 1999, p. 43.

10. Odd Arne Westad, Chen Jian, Stein Tonnesson, Nguyen Va Tung, and James G. Hershberg, *77 Conversations*. Washington, DC: Woodrow Wilson Center, Cold War International History Project, 1998, p. 145.

11. Quansheng Zhao, "China's Foreign Policy in the Post-Cold War Era," *World Affairs*, vol. 59, no.3, winter 1997, p. 117.

12. Westad, et al., *77 Conversations*, p. 179.

13. Greg Austin, *China's Ocean Frontiers*. St. Leonards, Australia: Allen & Unwin, 1998, ch. 6, "Japan's Superior Rights in the Senkaku Islands, pp. 162–176."

14. Quansheng Zhao, *Japanese Policymaking*. Oxford: Oxford University Press, 1993, p. 169.

15. Hidenori Ijiri, "Sino-Japanese Controversy Since the 1972 Diplomatic Normalization," in Christopher Howe, ed., *China and Japan*. Oxford: Clarendon Press, 1986, p. 70.

16. Allen Whiting, *China Eyes Japan*. Berkeley: University of California Press, 1985, p. 158.

17. Ibid., p. 183.

18. Edward Friedman, "Modernity's Bourgeoisie: Victim or Victimizer?" *China Information*, vol. 11, no.2–3, autumn/winter 1996, pp. 89–98.

19. Makoto Iokibe, "Japan's Democratic Experience," in Larry Diamond and Marc Plattner, eds., *Democracy in East Asia*. Baltimore: The John's Hopkins University Press, 1998, p. 85. In like manner, French President Mitterrand would not take responsibility for the crimes of the Vichy regime, treating it as "a parenthesis in the continuous history of the Republic" (W. James Booth, "Communities of Memory," *American Political Science Review*, vol. 93, no.2, June 1999, p. 250). Such views in democracies are popular and understandable, but, also, morally inadequate. In the political realm, a matter of lesser evils, when a tyranny is replaced by a democracy, it is ordinary practice for the imperatives of reconciliation to trump the demands of justice. In short, the Japanese immorality should be understood more as inherent in the tragic realm of politics and less as a Japanese peculiarity.

20. Martin Booth, "China's Oskar Schindler," *Far Eastern Economic Review*, April 1, 1999, p. 41.

21. One therefore could never infer from coverage in the Chinese media that Rabe's diary was a bestseller in Japan. Polls show most Japanese aware of and condemnatory of the horrible Japanese aggression against China.

22. The papers from that September 1996 Beijing conference were not published, to the best of my knowledge.

23. Charles W. Freeman, Jr., "Preventing War in the Taiwan Strait," *Foreign Affairs*, July-August 1998, p. 7.

24. The speech was downloaded from a web site.

25. Harvey Nelsen, *Power and Insecurity*. Boulder, CO: Lynne Rienner, 1989.

26. Yong Deng, "Chinese Relations with Japan," *Pacific Affairs*, fall 1997, pp. 373–391.

27. The reasons why federalism tends to be equated with weakness and disintegration are explored in Edward Friedman, "Does China Have the Cultural Preconditions for Democracy?" *Philosophy East and West*, vol. 49, no. 3, July 1999, pp. 352–353.

28. At an interview, carried on a web site, in Beijing following the May 1999 riots in China in response to the murderous NATO bombing of the Chinese embassy in Belgrade, Jia Qingguo, Beijing University international relations specialist, was asked "A journalist . . . told me that he is concerned that China will become like Japan before Pearl Harbor. How do you see this?"

29. Ma Yong, "Defeat in 1894 War and Radicalism and Predicament of Chinese Elite," *Strategy and Management*, no. 2, 1995, pp. 140–154.

30. Edward Friedman, "Chinese Nationalism, Taiwan Autonomy and the Prospects of a Larger War," *The Journal of Contemporary China*, no. 6, 1997, pp. 5–32.

31. Denny Roy, "Hegemon on the Horizon," *International Security*, vol. 19, no. 1, summer 1994, pp. 168–184.

32. Geoff Wade, "Facing History," *Far Eastern Economic Review*, December 24, 1998, p. 29.

33. See Alastair Johnston, *Cultural Realism*. Princeton: Princeton University Press, 1995.

34. Chen Jian, "Sino-American Relations Studies in China," in Warren Cohen, ed., *Pacific Passage*. New York: Columbia University Press, 1996, pp. 3–35; Shu Guang Zhang, *Mao's Military Romanticism*. Lawrence: University of Kansas Press, 1995.

35. Allen Whiting, "ASEAN Eyes China," *Asian Survey*, vol. 37, no. 4, April 1997, pp. 299–322.

36. On the rise of military hardliners, see Willy Lam, *The Era of Jiang Zemin*. New York: Prentice Hall, 1999.

37. See Xu Heming, *The Redefinition of the U.S.-Japan Security Alliance and Its Implications for China*. Washington, DC: Sigur Center for Asian Studies, 1981.

38. Onuma Yasuaki, "'Japanese International Law' in the Prewar Period," *The Japanese Annual of International Law*, no. 29, 1986, p. 24.

39. D. R. Howland, *Borders of Chinese Civilization*. Durham, NC: Duke University Press, 1996.

40. See the essay by Takeshi Hamashita in Peter Katzenstein and Takashi Shiraisha, eds., *Network Power: Japan and Asia*. Ithaca, NY: Cornell University Press, 1997.

41. Yasuaki, "'Japanese International Law' in the Prewar Period," p. 34.

42. Lowell Dittmer, "Unstable Outlooks," *Harvard Asia Pacific Review*, winter 1997–98, p. 16.

43. Hifumi Arai, "Angry at China? Slam Japan," *Far Eastern Economic Review*, October 3, 1996, p. 21.

44. Review essay by Peter Gries, *The China Journal*, January 1997, pp. 182, 183.

45. Cai Hong, "China, Japan Should Forge Close Relationship," *China Daily*, June 19, 1997, p. 4.

46. Dittmer, "Unstable Outlooks," p. 16.

47. Derek DaCuno, "Strategic Uncertainties," *Harvard Asia Pacific Review*, winter 1997–98, p. 19.

48. Andrew MacIntyre, "Can Japan Ever Take Leadership?" Japan Policy Research Institute, Working Paper No. 57, May 1999, p. 4.

49. Christopher Johnstone, "Japan's China Policy," *Asian Survey*, vol. 38, no.11, November 1998, p. 1080.

50. Koichi Kato, "View from the North Pacific," *Far Eastern Economic Review*, August 15, 1998, p. 28.

51. Liu Jinghua, "The Rise of China and the Choice of Strategy by the Year 2020–2030," *Strategy and Management,* no. 2, 1995, pp. 123–126.

52. Donald Zagoria, et al., *Revitalizing the U.S.-Japanese Alliance.* New York: The Ralph Bunche Institute of the United Nations, CUNY, Report of Workshop III, January 24–26, 1997, p. 10.

53. Cowen Robinson, "Call to Revise Japan's Pacifist Constitution," *Financial Times*, July 16, 1997.

54. Yong Deng, "Chinese Relations with Japan," p. 387.

55. On Chinese irredentism toward Korea, see "Open History, Open Nationalism," *Harvard Asia Pacific Review*, winter 1998–99, pp. 58–61.

56. Fang Zhaokui, an analyst at the Chinese Academy of Social Sciences' Institute for Japan Studies, averred at the September 1996 Beijing Forum on the Twenty-First Century, "the transferring of its [Japan's] traditional industries to other Asian countries has offered China a chance to speed up its industrialization. . . . Japanese direct investment in China has promoted China's export of industrial products to Japan. With income from exports to Japan, China has expanded its imports of capital goods from Japan, especially technical equipment. . . . In short, China and Japan [enjoy] a benign circle in which trade and direct investment promoted each other."

57. South Korea's military dictator, Park Chung Hee, is seen in China as a great mastermind of Korea's wonderful nationalistic economic rise toward independence of and competition with Japan, making invisible that Park, as Wang, served the imperial Japanese occupation forces. Even patriots could be collaborators, not an easy view to advance in China's anti-Japanese nationalism. But Burma's Aung San and India's Subhas Chandra Bose both allied with imperial Japan in the name of anti-imperialism, which complicates, but does not exculpate, Japanese militarism.

58. Adam Hochschild, *King Leopold's Ghost.* Boston: Houghton Mifflin, 1998.

59. See the special issue, "Textbook Nationalism, Citizenship, and War," *Bulletin of Concerned Asian Scholars,* vol. 30, no.2, April–June 1998.

60. Katherine H. S. Moon, *Sex Among Allies.* New York: Columbia University Press, 1997.

61. Osaki Yuji, "China and Japan in the Asia Pacific," in Kokubun Ryosei, *Challenges for China-Japan-U.S. Cooperation.* Tokyo: Japan Center for International Exchange, 1998, p. 106.

62. Ming Zhang and Ronald Montaperto, *A Triad of Another Kind.* New York: St. Martin's Press, 1999, p. 118.

63. Francis Godement, "Weighing up the Conflict Factor between China and Japan," *Asia Times*, June 10, 1997.

64. "Chinese Go Home" (in Chinese), *Shijie ribao* (weekend edition), December 20, 1998, pp. 16–17.

65. Banning Garrett and Bonnie Glaser, "Chinese Apprehensions About Revitalization of the U.S.-Japan Alliance," *Asian Survey*, vol. 37, no. 4, April 1997, p. 398.

66. Gerald Segal, "Japan's Have-it-Both-Ways Defense Policy Too Clever By Half," *Asia Times*, June 16, 1997.

67. Barry Sautman, *Relations in Blood: China's 'Racial' Nationalism*. Seattle: University of Washington Press, 2000.

68. Richard Bernstein and Ross Munro, *The Coming Conflict with China*. New York: Knopf, 1997.

69. Christopher Layne, "Less Is More," *The National Interest*, spring 1996, p. 73.

70. Samuel Huntington, *The Clash of Civilizations and the Remaking of World Order*. New York: Simon and Schuster, 1996, pp. 218–238, "Asia, China, and America."

Chapter 5

Human Rights
in China's International Relations

Samuel S. Kim

Taking Human Rights Seriously?

One of the most novel but generally overlooked aspects of China's post–
Cold War international relations is high-profile human rights diplomacy.
Beijing is no longer merely an object of other countries' human rights
diplomacy but is itself an active player in the domain of global human
rights politics.[1] That such diplomacy has come of age is shown in the
growing body of human rights literature including *Encyclopedia on
Human Rights in China*, the establishment of a human rights "nongovernmental" organization (NGO), the China Society for Human Rights
Studies), the publication of a series of white papers on human rights and
human rights–related subjects, the dispatch of governmental and NGO
human rights delegations to democracies, active participation in the UN-
anchored international human rights regime, and accession to seventeen
human rights conventions. In October 1997 and October 1998 Beijing
even signed—but has not yet ratified—two keystone human rights trea-

For helpful comments and suggestions on an earlier version, I thank Rosemary
Foot, Edward Friedman, Steve Levine, Barrett McCormick, Andrew Nathan, and
Peter Van Ness without of course holding any of them responsible for whatever
errors in fact or interpretation that may still persist.

ties: the International Covenant on Economic, Social and Cultural Rights (ICESCR) and the International Covenant on Civil and Political Rights (ICCPR).

What is the relationship between China's human rights diplomacy and democratization? What are their interactive effects? This chapter focuses on the changes and continuities in Beijing's human rights theory and practice as made manifest in the UN-anchored international human rights regime. In both transition and consolidation phases democratization is better seen as an outcome of strategic choices and interactions among political elites, institutions, societal forces at home, and the changing international environment. The question of Beijing's human rights theory and practice—whether the PRC will become more compliant with universal human rights norms—is crucial to any assessment of the future of Chinese democratization. It is also a question that is central to the debate over the shaping of a post–Cold War world order. In an era of globalization and the global transparency revolution, the international context matters more than ever.

Although human rights in both negative and positive terms are intrinsic to the democratization process, international pressures on China to democratize come indirectly via universal human rights principles and norms. For instance, the Universal Declaration of Human Rights (UDHR), while not using the word "democracy," nonetheless defines and asserts such democratic principles as "the right to take part in the government," "the right of equal access to public service," and the right to "universal and equal suffrage" via secret vote (Article 21) along with other enumerated rights as a "common standard of achievement for all peoples and nations."[2] In the ICCPR, such democratic principles are spelled out as a legal obligation (Article 25).[3]

In post–Cold War global politics, the United Nations shifted its primary attention toward a more synergistic concept of *human* security that focused on the performance of the state in the broadest sense. After having suffered from domestic and external legitimation blows—the Tiananmen tragedy and the collapse of communism at its Soviet epicenter—Beijing responded to foreign critics by trying to shore up its shaky legitimacy. The collapse of the Soviet Union, the third wave of global democratization (doubling the number of democracies from 44 to 107), and the rejuvenation of the United Nations normatively challenged the post-Tiananmen Chinese leadership. As Deng Xiaoping put it, "The human rights issue is the crux of the struggle between the world's two social systems. If we lose the battle on the human rights front, everything will be meaningless to us."[4] Human rights diplomacy was Beijing's response to "a smokeless World War III" allegedly waged against socialist China. Beijing's official position and strategy emerged in 1990–91,[5] culminating in its first-ever white paper on human rights issued by the Information Office of the State Council in October 1991.[6]

Getting Human Rights Theory Right?

Any human rights theory needs to address the *nature* of human rights (what they are), the *source* of human rights (where they come from), the *subjects* of human rights (to whom do they apply), the *scope* of human rights (whether they are universal or culturally relative), and the *prioritization* of human rights (which rights among different categories or generations of human rights enjoy preferred or priority status).[7] Although there is no such thing as an Asian theory of human rights just as there is no such thing as a Western theory of human rights, both theoretical debates and practical global human rights politics have revolved around (1) the theory of universality versus the theory of cultural or developmental relativism, (2) the right to intervene versus the principle of state sovereignty, and (3) the prioritization or the interdependence and indivisibility of different categories of human rights, especially the first generation of civil and political rights as against the second generation of economic, social, and cultural rights or the third generation of solidarity rights.[8]

Beijing's human rights theory is a strong version of cultural and developmental relativism.[9] Despite situation-specific modifications, Beijing's concept of the nature and source of human rights has remained largely unchanged. The claim of inalienable (natural) rights—human rights everyone has by virtue of being human—remains alien to PRC thinking. Two of the three major ends prominently stipulated in the preamble to the Charter of the United Nations deal with human rights—"to affirm faith in fundamental human rights" and "to promote social progress and better standards of life in larger freedom." The UDHR adopted and proclaimed by the General Assembly on December 10, 1948, the chief catalyst in the making of the International Bill of Rights between 1948 and 1976, states in Article 1, "All human beings are born free and equal in dignity and rights. They are endowed with reason and conscience and should act towards one another in a spirit of brotherhood."

Yet, in the PRC, the fundamental rights of "citizens"—not "individuals" or "humans"—specified in Articles 33–41 of the 1982 constitution—are compromised by the even more fundamental duties of citizens (Articles 51–54) such as not to "infringe upon the interests of the state," "to safeguard the unity of the country and the unity of all its nationalities," to "keep state secrets," and "to safeguard the security, honor, and interests of the motherland."[10] Article 36 stipulates that "the state protects normal religious activities" but "no one may make use of religion to engage in activities that disrupt public order, impair the health of citizens or interfere with the educational system of the state. Religious bodies and religious affairs are not subject to any foreign domination." There is no such thing as "natural human rights"—entitlements that inhere in persons—but only citizens' rights as defined and extended by the state. What the Chinese state gives, it can and often does take away in accordance with its definition of changing state interests. In short, human rights in China are whatever the state, or more accurately, groups with a monopoly of state power, say they are.

There is nothing distinctively Chinese about this approach. The PRC's human rights theory is derivative of Soviet theory. The emphasis on social/economic rights is the old position of socialist and many developing countries. What few public pronouncements on global human rights issues Maoist China made in the course of its UN participation in 1971–76 were largely confined to the claim that human rights abuses were an inevitable function of structural violence embedded in imperialism, colonialism, and hegemonism; human rights abuses were no more or less than violations of state rights.[11] This theme of collective human rights-cum-state rights—and the theory of cultural and developmental relativism—receded somewhat in the 1980s as Beijing began to participate in UN human rights politics, only to reemerge with greater vigor in post-Tiananmen foreign relations. The irony is that despite putatively universalist socialist values, Beijing posed itself as a self-styled champion of a cultural relativist approach in global human rights politics.

Cultural relativism rejects universalist claims asserting instead that human rights have always remained and will continue to remain *relative* to time, place, culture, social and economic condition, and so on. It contends (1) that human rights rules and norms vary from place to place; (2) that such diverse and varying human rights claims and rules can only be understood in terms of their cultural context; (3) that each culture is a self-contained entity which is itself the source of ultimate legitimacy; (4) that the principle of the universality of human rights is a disguised version of the moral imperialism of a particular culture; and

(5) that the UDHR is an exercise in futility between competing cultures in the United Nations. Thus, Chinese Communists presaged the Huntingtonian civilizational clash thesis.[12]

How does Beijing's human rights theory address the universalist versus cultural relativist debate? Just as Chinese citizens' rights are circumscribed by state-imposed duties in the PRC constitution, so too is rhetorical support of the UDHR qualified in the 1991 white paper:

> The Chinese government also has highly appraised the Universal Declaration of Human Rights, considering it the first international human rights document that has laid the foundation for the practice of human rights in the world arena. However, the evolution of the situation in regard to human rights is circumscribed by the historical, social, economic, and cultural conditions of various nations, and involves a process of historical development. Owing to tremendous differences in historical background, social system, cultural tradition, and economic development, countries differ in their understanding and practice of human rights. From their different situations, they have taken different attitudes toward the relevant UN conventions. Despite its international aspects, the issue of human rights falls by and large within the sovereignty of each country.[13]

In the prioritization of several competing categories of human rights, the second generation of social, economic, and cultural rights and the third generation of solidarity rights command preferred status. "The right to subsistence is the most important of all human rights, without which the other rights are out of the question. . . . Without national independence, there would be no guarantee for the people's lives."[14] It follows that international intervention is justified only in those cases "that endanger world peace and security, such as gross human rights violations caused by colonialism, racism, foreign aggression and occupation, as well as apartheid, racial discrimination, genocide, the slave trade and serious violations of human rights by international terrorist organizations."[15] The basic, recurring theme in PRC human rights thinking over the years is the primacy of state sovereignty—*no state sovereignty, no human rights.*

The proposition that individuals have finally become subjects of international law in the post-Holocaust and post-Nuremberg era is ruled out in Chinese international law literature and policy pronouncements. Such a view is considered theoretically untenable and practically infeasible, because it pits the principle of state sovereignty against the principle of human rights in mutually conflictive terms. The principle of state sovereignty is said to be always primary and superior to human rights, because only the former can guarantee the implementation of the latter.[16] Citing Hedley Bull's work with approval, a PRC writer argues that to take human rights as the basis of international relations is to reject the essence of the international order: "Although theories advocating the supremacy of human rights abound in the world, *modern* international law is *still* centered on national [state?] sovereignty and the nature of international relations *still* rests on the balance and coordination of interests between national states."[17]

The cultural and developmental relativist theory rests on the notion that communities come before individuals, duties and obligations before rights and privileges; hence, human rights inhere not so much in individuals as in collectivities. Even the much touted "right to development," one of the central themes in post-Mao China, inheres solely in the state, not in the individual. The gap between rhetoric and action— the double standard—is greater in this than any other domain of global politics. The cultural and developmental relativist thesis is not exclusively Chinese; the universalist theory is not exclusively Western.[18]

Still, Beijing's cultural and developmental relativist line—that human rights should be applied differently according to varying cultures and levels of development—is quite alluring for an authoritarian or repressive state.[19] But the theory is not without conceptual and logical problems. It proceeds from the dubious premise and mistaken logic that what is being practiced in various countries in varying cultural and developmental conditions should be accepted as international norms and standards. To accept varying human rights conditions and practices throughout the world as empirical reality (the "is") is one thing, but to accept multiple allegedly "culture-specific" (read: governmental) practices as normative reality (the "ought") is something else—namely, to have no international standards at all.

The cultural relativist theory assumes an incompatibility between civil and political rights and economic performance. In fact, a state does not have to reach an advanced stage of development to be able to grant its citizens civil and political rights as they are mostly negative "freedoms from" rather than positive "rights to." After all, a nation-state does not have to reach a certain stage to be able to leave its people alone or let them enjoy their rights as humans. This cost-effective logic—that civil and political rights are more readily accessible to both rich and poor countries—explains the universal appeal of civil liberties as embodied in almost every constitution of every country in the world today.

On the other hand, the right to subsistence or the right to development requires specific policies. The Chinese claim—no state sovereignty, no human rights, no guarantee for people's well-being—stands on shaky grounds. After all, it was not state sovereignty-cum-self-reliance that brought about post-Mao China's rapid economic growth. Maoist China's homicidal famine occurred during the heyday of self-reliance. If China's sovereignty-bound cultural and developmental relativist thesis were true, Hong Kong as a British colony (until mid-1997) and Taiwan as a sovereignty-lacking island would be languishing in civil, political, social, economic, and cultural misery waiting for sovereign China to lead them to the promised land of economic growth and plenty!

To be sure, post-Mao China has achieved remarkable economic growth, although at high equity and ecological costs. However, a recent World Bank study shows that some 257 million people or 22 percent of China's population still live in conditions of abject poverty—subsisting at the global poverty line of $1 a day, as against China's official figures of about 6 percent of the population (or some 70 million Chinese).[20] In addition, Beijing's cultural and developmental relativist line treats Tibetan Buddhism as a "foreign culture." According to the International Commission of Jurists based in Geneva and consisting of about forty lawyers, judges, and law professors, the rights of Tibetans, particularly Tibetan cultural rights, deteriorated sharply between 1994 and 1997. Since early 1996, repression escalated in Tibet, marked by an "intensive re-education drive in the monasteries at which monks were told that they would be required to sign loyalty pledges or face expulsion" and by a propaganda campaign to brand Buddhism as a "foreign culture."[21]

Beijing's cultural and developmental relativist line is alluring because it fills a vacuum left by a lack of international pressure on developing countries to make good on the right to subsistence and the right to development. The Chinese government has skillfully manipulated its status as a "poor global power," and a champion of the rights to subsistence and development in maximizing its special entitlements (the world's number one recipient of multilateral aid from the World Bank and the Asian Development Bank and number one recipient of Japan's bilateral aid) while minimizing its financial responsibilities as one of the Perm Five in the Security Council.[22] Beijing's real commitment to the right to subsistence and development is suggested by its reluctance to sign the

ICESCR until late 1997. Even after signing the covenant to coincide with President Jiang Zemin's trip to the United States, the Chinese government made it clear it will not implement the ICESCR (meaning there would be no immediate legalization of independent labor unions as required by the covenant) until it has been studied and ratified by its National People's Congress with all careful consideration and speed. Into 1999, the ICESCR remains yet to be ratified.

Despite privileging the right to subsistence and development over civil and political rights, Beijing's human rights literature contains little discussion of development-related environmental problems such as deforestation and acid rain. Nor was there any discussion of development-related issues like child labor or women's rights. The dark side of Beijing's claim of the right to subsistence was revealed by a detailed and searing report of Human Rights Watch/Asia in 1996, exposing a secret world of disease, starvation, and unnatural death—a world in which the victims are orphans and abandoned children in state welfare institutions run by the Ministry of Civil Affairs.[23]

In Beijing's post–Cold War perspective, Asia is now said to be the center of Chinese power and influence. China relies on Asia for its status and role as "a special power in the world." By conflating the cultural/developmental relativist line and the "Asian values" rhetoric, Beijing has posed as a champion of an Asian way in which civil and political rights are not as important as in "the West" and in which collectivism is more valued and essential.[24] Ironically, the Lee Kuan Yew-Mahathir-Li Peng line of espousing "Asian values"—which is being dubbed by some Southeast Asian neoconservative intellectuals as "situational uniqueness"—embraces the very Westcentrism that they criticize because their Manichaean assumptions are themselves the products of the Eurocentric spell of Orientalism—the Christian West versus Confucian Asia, the individualist West versus communitarian Asia, and so on.[25]

In fact, the defining feature of Asia is not singular Asian values but linguistic, cultural, and religious diversity. Such diversity is pronounced not only between Asian states but also within particular Asian states. The pre-1999 Asian Gang of Four in global human rights politics—China, Singapore, Malaysia, and Indonesia—whose governments had been most vocal in espousing the "Asian values" line are multicultural, multireligious, and even multinational. As Tokyo University Philosophy of Law Professor Tatsuo Inoue argues, the internal diversity "requires Asian countries to develop liberal democracy to accommodate the sharp conflicts and tensions it generates."[26] Contrary to Huntington's cultural clash thesis, in the post–Cold War world the chief divide is still within states, in authoritarian states in Southeast Asia, between the governments and their human rights nongovernmental organizations (NGOs).

The counterpoint to institutionalizing societal pluralism is Beijing's chaos (*luan*) complex, equating democratization with social and political instability. As Deng put it, "If we were to run elections among China's one billion people now, chaos . . . would certainly ensue. . . . Democracy is our goal, but the state must maintain stability."[27] Deng warned of serious (chaotic) domestic *and* international consequences if China were to adopt democracy and human rights. Democracy was described as a recipe for military factional fighting leading to a civil war that would bring about the world's biggest refugee exodus. If such domestic *and* international chaos is to be avoided, international relations must be conducted such that others refrain from interfering in China's internal affairs. To make sure that reform and openness lead to national strength and stability, human rights must take second place to sovereign rights.[28] In short, the legitimacy of the party-state dictatorship is the subordination of human rights to state sovereignty.

Closely connected to the problem of PRC chaos-causing theory is a means-ends dichotomy implied in the prioritization of human rights. Although the first and second generation rights are sometimes claimed to be indivisible and interdependent, PRC leaders justify their denial of civil and political freedoms in the name of long-term developmental imperatives. Yet, there is no empirical support for an incompatibility between the two types of human rights. The claim implied in the cultural and developmental relativism theory that dictatorial or authoritarian states are better at generating economic growth and well-being in poor countries and that, once these states have developed, their regimes will give way to democracy is false.[29] There is a well-established empirical evidence showing that democratic systems do far better than nondemocratic ones and even in democracies citizens of consistently democratic states were found to be 30 percent better off than those of inconsistently democratic states.[30] As Amartya Sen—the 1998 Nobel Prize Winner in Economics—has demonstrated, "no substantial famine has ever occurred in any independent and democratic country with a relatively free press. Whether we look at famines in Sudan, Ethiopia, Somalia, or other dictatorial regimes or in the Soviet Union in the 1930s or in China from 1958 to 1961(at the failure of the Great Leap Forward, when between 23 and 30 million people died) or currently in North Korea, we do not find exceptions to this rule."[31]

Beijing, however, still blames underdevelopment on the policies of rich countries. "If one really intends to promote and protect human rights . . . then the first thing . . . to do is to help remove obstacles to the development of developing countries, lessen their external debt burden, provide them with unconditional assistance."[32] While this proposition of unconditional aid may play like sweet music in poor nations, China has received the lion's share of bilateral and multilateral aid, with virtually no political strings attached.

The cultural relativist line is also culturally suspect. It proceeds from the primordialist notion that culture is preordained or immutable or a set of traits that people inherit passively from generation to generation. Yet, culture or cultural identity does not grow "naturally"; it has to be negotiated, transacted, and achieved. The seemingly unchanging Chinese culture is actually giving new meanings about being and becoming Chinese in a rapidly changing world.[33] Cultural determinism à la Huntington—that Confucian and Islamic civilizations or cultures pose insurmountable obstacles to democratization and that "clashes of civilizations are the greatest threat to world peace"[34]—stands on shaky historical grounds since many of the bloodiest wars have occurred within, not between, civilizations. In the postwar era, the remarkable democratic transformation of Japan's (and Germany's) hypernationalist and militarist social institutions and cultures is a powerful rebuttal of cultural determinism. This point also emerged from the rise and fall of the Chinese television documentary *He Shang* (River Elegy) in 1988–89, which generated a great stir of both horror and applause among Chinese at every level of society revealing thereby that there is no national consensus on the core symbols of Chinese national or cultural identity. In short, Chinese national identity can be reassessed, reappropriated, and reconstructed. If indeed culturally rooted democratic norms and beliefs were the necessary and sufficient conditions for the rise of democracy, then there would have been no such things as the first, second, and third waves of global democratization in numerous nations with largely authoritarian cultures (e.g., Japan, Taiwan, South Korea).

Huntington's clash of civilizations theory took the Chinese academic community by storm, reigniting the old debate about a Chinese essence needing protection. His theory generated more than forty commentaries and essays.[35] It exposed chauvinistic dangers embedded in the PRC's theory of cultural relativism. Huntington's clash thesis seemed to the Chinese commentators a variant of American exceptionalism, a version of cultural relativism. Most Chinese scholars rejected the clash thesis on empirical and policy grounds—that it turns a blind eye to multiplying economic ties and growing economic integration all over the globe and that, in an era of globalization, it is convergence, rather than clash, that looks increasingly more likely despite being circumscribed in the short term by cultural, political, and economic conflicts. Beijing's neoauthoritarian conservatives, however, welcomed Huntington's idea that democracy was incongruent with Chinese culture.

Beijing's cultural relativist line, as Huntington's clash of civilizations thesis, seems a rather poor fit for the increasingly universalizing discourse on human rights. It is difficult to regard post–Cold War global politics as emblematic of clashes of competing cultures or civilizations. At Vienna the United States for the first time expressed its willingness to move toward ratification of the ICESCR, even as South Korea—arguably the most Confucian place in the world—rejected Beijing's cultural relativism as an Asian perspective by embracing the universality of human rights. Even Beijing's invocation of cultural relativism in regional and global human rights politics is rendered dubious not only by its use of one set of "Western" ideas and principles (absolute state sovereignty) to counter another set of "Western" ideas and principles (human rights universalism) but also by the actual fault lines between authoritarian Asian states and their human rights NGOs as well as between and among those East Asian states in the supposedly Confucian civilizational zone—China, Singapore, Taiwan, Vietnam, North and South Korea, and Japan.

China's Human Rights Diplomacy

The pattern of the PRC's participatory behavior in the international human rights regime offers evidence of how Beijing's human rights theory has been affirmed, revised, or repudiated in practice. The international law of human rights, despite being hobbled by its implementation or monitoring problems, is a living political and juridical reality, "realist" protestations notwithstanding. Although rarely mentioned in PRC scholarly literature and policy pronouncements, there exists the International Bill of Rights consisting of the UDHR, the ICCPR, and the ICESCR. In addition, there are now in effect at least two dozen major human rights treaties on racial discrimination, rights of women, rights of the child, slavery, freedom of information, employment, marriage, genocide, torture, apartheid, nationality, statelessness, asylum and refugees, war crimes, and crimes against humanity.

A whole network of human rights treaties and institutional mechanisms and procedures has been developed to realize—however imperfectly—the charter mandate of protecting and promoting "fundamental human rights," giving rise to what is commonly referred to as the international human rights regime. The Commission on Human Rights, composed of fifty-three member states, is the main policymaking body dealing with human rights issues, but other organs such as the General Assembly, the Security Council, and an extensive network of subsidiary bodies (e.g., the Sub-Commission on Prevention of Discrimination and Protection of Minorities, the Commission on the Status of Women, the Commission on Crime Prevention and Criminal Justice) are also involved in the protection and promotion of human rights. The history of the International Bill of Rights suggests a common practice of the international human rights regime of establishing a broad conceptual and normative framework through a declaration, followed by normative specification and elaboration in the form of a multilateral convention. The so-called protection and promotion of human rights entail a multistage process involving norm creation, standard setting, treaty making, and implementation or monitoring. The two keystone human rights covenants—the ICCPR and the ICESCR—are legally binding human rights agreements. Both were adopted in 1966 and entered into force ten years later, making many of the principles of the UDHR legally binding.

Beijing had no part in the making of the International Bill of Rights and a host of other international human rights treaties because the PRC had been excluded from the United Nations. Since its entry in late 1971, Beijing was caught up *faute de mieux* in the global politics of human rights. From 1971 to 1979, Beijing refused to endorse a single multilateral human rights convention. What few public pronouncements on global human rights issues the Chinese government made were largely confined to the notion that human rights abuses were an inevitable function of structural violence embedded in imperialism, colonialism, and hegemonism.

A break came in 1979 when post-Mao China decided to participate in the Commission on Human Rights as an observer and in 1982 as a full member state. This second period, 1982–89, witnessed incremental shifts and modifications in PRC's human rights diplomacy. The government moved from outright denial to a more variegated and situation-specific response. Evidence of such tactical adaptation is seen in Beijing's slow, reluctant, and almost forced, modification and expansion of the concept of human rights; its greater participation in the activities of the international human rights regime; its increasing acceptance of certain select global human rights principles and norms (by signing and acceding to eight of the twenty-five major UN human rights treaties on women, racial discrimination, refugees, apartheid, genocide, and torture from 1980 to 1989); and its softer, albeit increasingly less effective, response to the growing human rights movements at home.

As late as 1979, the UDHR was dismissed as a means of safeguarding the bourgeois dictatorship of capitalist states and as a cover to legitimize ideological infiltration of socialist countries, China included.[36] By 1982 China seems to have accepted that human rights had become an integral part of world politics. Finding a new and dominant Third World majority in global normative politics, Beijing explained that the concept of human rights was being modified and expanded. The right to development was claimed to have emerged as a basic human right, thus creating a new facet to the old struggle against imperialism, colonialism, and hegemonism. While acknowledging that the first generation of civil and political rights played a fairly progressive role in world history, the second generation of economic, social, and cultural rights became the centerpiece of Chinese human rights pronouncements. Only socialism, Beijing claimed, not the capitalist system of exploitation of man by man, guaranteed the full implementation of collective people's rights.[37]

The years from mid-1986 to mid-1989 were the apogee of PRC human rights diplomacy. In 1986 for the first time a positive reference was made to the two keystone covenants in Foreign Minister Wu Xueqian's annual "state of the world" report before the UN General Assembly. Two years later, on the occasion of the fortieth anniversary of the UDHR in early December 1988, both Chinese delegates in the United Nations and Chinese scholars at home joined the global chorus of paeans with their own glowing commentaries on human rights.[38] The first and second generations of human rights—individual, civil, and political rights as well as collective economic, social, and cultural rights—were claimed to be interdependent and inseparable: "Giving equal attention and full respect to those two categories of rights," Chinese representative Dong Yuanhong declared at the forty-third session of the UN General Assembly in 1988, "constitutes an important condition of the comprehensive protection of human rights and fundamental freedoms."[39]

More tellingly, some PRC international relations scholars implicitly advanced the Wilsonian, not Leninist, Second Image explanation of war and peace—that democracy at home is the cause of international peace. Global activities to promote and protect human rights were now regarded as making major contributions to the cause of world peace.[40] As if to give some credence to this line of reasoning, the Chinese government took a first major step—indeed the most significant single step—in the protection of *individual* rights by signing in 1986 and ratifying in 1988 the Convention Against Torture and Other Cruel, Inhuman or Degrading Treatment or Punishment. Conceptually and legally, China thus crossed the Rubicon by ratifying this human rights convention requiring the signatory state to protect the human rights of individual citizens by taking "effective legislative, administrative, judicial or other measures to prevent acts of torture in any territory under its jurisdiction" (Article 2), as opposed to the social and economic rights of a group. As a matter of its international legal obligation, China could no longer seek the cover of domestic jurisdiction nor excuse itself by citing the structural violence of colonialism and imperialism or its own social, economic, and cultural constraints. Global thinking and local acting seem to have almost squared a circle in Beijing in May 1989 as the student-led democratization movement was nonviolently drawing upon new sources of knowledge and forming new linkages that few outside (and inside) observers would have thought possible only a few months previously. With the crushing of the movement in early June 1989, the government reverted to the 1979 position. In the world of international organizations, the Beijing Massacre made possible a human rights mission that had seemed impossible, condemning China, a permanent member of the Security Council, for human rights abuses at home.[41]

However, by 1991 Beijing shifted from defense to offense with the publication of a first-ever white paper on human rights on October 31, 1991. The implications of the white paper were that there is no longer any escape from human rights as a legitimate global issue and as a challenge to Chinese foreign policy. Sovereignty-bound pronouncements alone would no longer suffice. The 1990–91 Gulf crisis was a godsend for the PRC's human rights diplomacy. To secure a "voluntary" abstention in place of a possible Chinese veto, the Bush administration ignored the continuing repression in China and agreed to resume high-level diplomatic intercourse (by granting a long sought White House visit by

Foreign Minister Qian) and to lift the World Bank's sanctions by supporting its first "nonbasic human needs" loan ($114.3 million) since Tiananmen. President Bush also vigorously pushed for unconditional extension of the most-favored-nation (MFN) treatment of China to reciprocate for China's help in the Security Council in forging "the broad coalition that brought us victory in the Gulf."[42]

Beijing adopted a "divide and conquer" strategy in its human rights diplomacy. The strategy is to slice up the concept of universality little by little, region by region, to the point where there are few teeth left in the UN human rights monitoring and implementation mechanisms. The 1991 white paper "accepted" international human rights principles by redefining them in terms of state sovereignty and cultural, economic, and social relativism. However, in both absolute and relative terms China still remains far behind in terms of some of the rights claimed (e.g., China's global human development index and ranking dropped from 82nd place to 108th place in the first half of the 1990s).[43]

Beijing claimed in the white paper's final section that China had been active in the drafting of most human rights agreements of recent decades and had played a constructive role in promoting human rights for Palestinians, South Africans, and (less convincingly) in Cambodia. China actually led the way on behalf of some of the most oppressive Asian countries to keep the UN human rights regime small, fragmented (regionalized), ineffective, and downsized. The efforts to alter the structure and terms of reference of a World Conference on Human Rights held in Vienna in June 1993 to conform to China's minimalist view, however, received little support.[44] The Chinese delegation was also extremely active in the General Assembly's Third Committee and Fifth (Financial) Committee debates about financing the UN Human Rights Centre, attempting to alter UN plans and reduce the resources available, but again with little success. However, China pressed successfully for the General Assembly to include the relationship between development and human rights as one of the priority topics at the Vienna Conference as well as to hold regional preparatory conferences.[45]

As a result, Asia's first-ever regional human rights conference was held in Bangkok in late March 1993 and was attended by governmental delegates from forty-nine countries stretching from the Middle East to the South Pacific. That the chief delegates from China, Burma, and Iran made up the drafting committee of the Bangkok Conference—not to mention the fact that Asia still has no regional human rights regime—

strengthened a perception in the United States that this was a prelude to an Asia-led revolt against the universality of human rights principles.

The principal interstate division at Bangkok turned out to be between democratic Japan, Thailand, Nepal, South Korea, and the Philippines which assumed a more universalist interpretation of human rights, and authoritarian China, Indonesia, Iran, and Burma which took a more uncompromising cultural relativist stand. An even greater split, however, divided official state representatives and their NGOs, which outnumbered the governmental delegates by more than two to one. Contrary to Huntington's cultural clash argument that "the greatest resistance to Western democratization efforts" stemmed from Islam and Asia[46] and Beijing's cultural and developmental relativist line, as one human rights NGO observer at the Bangkok Conference put it, "there was no single 'Asian' position on anything, and that when it came to human rights, the most important distinctions [were] neither the East-West nor the North-South, but between the powerful and the powerless."[47]

The disagreement at Bangkok centered on the question of universality versus cultural and developmental relativism along with the indivisibility of human rights, aid conditionality (linkage), the role of NGOs, and the parameters of national self-determination. Beijing called on the Asian countries to demonstrate solidarity around two sets of priority rights: (1) collective Mao-era human rights notions of opposition to racism, colonialism, foreign aggression, and occupation, and (2) state sovereignty, defined as the basis for the realization of human rights and, as a corollary, precluding a people using self-determination to instigate or foment splits of a nation or state.[48] The final Bangkok Declaration was replete with contradictions and ambiguities. Japan voiced serious reservations, restating its stand that expressions of concern about human rights violations do not constitute interference in a state's internal affairs. Japan and Cyprus still registered serious reservations with some parts of the draft document but the draft Bangkok Declaration was allowed to be adopted by consensus due largely to the solidarity of governmental delegates from ASEAN, who played a critical bridging role between Japan, South Korea, Nepal, Thailand, and the Philippines and such hardline authoritarian states as China, Burma, and Iran.[49] Tokyo and Seoul found Beijing's articulation of its human rights stand as a common Asian view and Beijing's projection of an image that all Asian countries are united against "Western" hegemony on human rights an embarrassment, but did not feel able or willing to stand up to China for fear of damaging their bilateral commercial relations with the PRC.

Not surprisingly, the final Bangkok Declaration has engendered considerable criticism from democracies and Asian NGOs.[50] While paying lip service to the notion that human rights are universal, the declaration insisted "they must be considered in the context of a dynamic and evolving process of international norm-setting, bearing in mind the significance of national and regional particularities and various historical, cultural, and religious backgrounds." While paying lip service to all the major human rights treaties ratified by Asian governments, the declaration pulled out their teeth by stressing "the principles of respect for national sovereignty and territorial integrity as well as noninterference in the internal affairs of States, and the non-use of human rights as an instrument of political pressure." In addition, Beijing succeeded in having its position incorporated in the declaration expressing "opposition to racial discrimination, racism, colonialism, and foreign aggression as well as the right to development."[51] Although the conference politics revealed great differences between Beijing's hardline position and others in Asia, China, on paper (the final Bangkok Declaration), emerged as a winner.

Beijing pursued its "divide and conquer" strategy with greater vigor at Vienna than at Bangkok. The outer parameters of the Vienna Conference were defined by American exceptionalism and Chinese exemptionalism—the U.S. hortatory exaltation of the virtues of universal human rights principles colliding head-on with the formal hardline Chinese reaffirmation of the principles of sovereignty, self-determination of peoples from colonial domination, and noninterference in internal affairs.[52] China's official position at Vienna stressed core principles undergirding cultural and developmental relativism—namely, the priority of the rights to subsistence and development, the guarantee of each country's right "to formulate its own policies on human rights protection in the light of its own conditions," since "different historical stages had different human rights requirements," with international concern limited to gross, large-scale violations of human rights such as foreign aggression, colonialism, and apartheid.[53] The Vienna Conference also witnessed the debut of the China Society for Human Rights Studies, a first-ever human rights "nongovernmental organization" established by the Chinese government in 1993. At Vienna, the Chinese human rights NGO quickly acquired a new identity as a GANGO (Government Appointed NGO) or GONGO (Government Organized NGO). One of its delegates, Xu Yong, declared that "on the whole, China's human rights record is better than the United States." The chief divide at Vienna, as at Bangkok, was less between the states of the North and South and more between states, particularly those of the South, and their own human rights NGOs. Indeed, of all the regional NGO declarations preceding the Vienna Conference, the Bangkok NGO Declaration had been "the most unequivocal in its support for the universality and indivisibility of human rights."[54]

The Vienna Conference was reportedly saved from collapse only by the timely intervention of its secretary general and then director of the United Nations Human Rights Centre, Ibrahima Fall. Contrary to Huntington, China did not emerge as "the big winner" at Vienna.[55] From the perspective of democratic states and human rights NGOs, the achievements of the Vienna Declaration include:[56] (1) The recognition and reaffirmation of the core principle that "the universal nature of these rights and freedoms is beyond question" and that "it is the duty of states, regardless of their political, economic and cultural systems, to promote and protect all human rights and freedoms," something Beijing had worked vigorously against in the drafting process, something Beijing believes stands in the way of its cultural and developmental relativist line; (2) the recognition of the *human person* as the central subject of development since "all human rights derive from the dignity and worth inherent in the human person, and that the human person is the central subject of human rights and fundamental freedoms, and consequently should be the principal beneficiary and should participate actively in the realization of these rights and freedoms" and that "the promotion and protection of all human rights is a legitimate concern of the international community," all of which run counter to Beijing's primacy of state sovereignty line; (3) the interdependence and mutually reinforcing nature of democracy, development, and respect for human rights,[57] which collides head-on with China's insistence on the right to development as a priority right; (4) the recognition that the right to development or "the lack of development may not be invoked to justify the abridgement of internationally recognized human rights," which denies legitimacy to Deng's chaos theory; (5) the recognition of the role of NGOs in the international human rights regime, the supreme *bête noire* in Beijing's human rights diplomacy; and (6) the rights of minorities, something that is respected in China's rhetoric, if not in practice in Tibet, Xinjiang, and Inner Mongolia.

The weaknesses of the Vienna Declaration—the successes from Beijing's perspective—include: (1) The lack of any human rights linkage on aid conditionality—"the promotion and protection of human rights . . . should be universal and conducted without conditions attached"; (2) a serious dilution of language on the freedom of press; (3) the absence of a decision on the establishment of a post of UN High Commissioner for Human Rights (leaving this matter up to the General Assembly to consider); and (4) the failure to address the problem of enforcing human rights treaties, confining itself to the general statement that "every state should provide an effective framework of remedies to redress human rights grievances and violations." On the eve of the Vienna Conference, Beijing felt so threatened by a proposal of an international human rights regime strengthened by a High Commissioner for Human Rights that the *People's Daily* launched a preemptive attack: "All attempts to put in place a power or a supranational organization could compromise the foundation of modern international law and eventually lead to the disintegration of the international community."[58] And yet, Beijing's victory was Pyrrhic, as the General Assembly on December 20, 1993 adopted Resolution 48/141 without a vote (consensus) to create the post of the High Commissioner for Human Rights.[59]

Beijing's post-Vienna reactions were initially muted but became progressively strident. Two months after the Vienna Conference, Chinese representative Tian Jin, a leading Chinese human rights commentator, asserted at the United Nations Human Rights Sub-Commission that the final outcome of the conference—the Vienna Declaration and Programme of Action—satisfied no one (read: Beijing), meaning that China would continue to pursue its "divide and conquer" strategy as a self-styled champion of "Asian values." Another PRC analyst argued that "the real significance of Western states' emphasis on the universality of human rights is to use this universality as a means of applying pressure on states having different social systems to promote Western style democracy and freedom."[60] When Malaysian Prime Minister Mahathir called for reviewing and restructuring the UDHR in 1997, Chinese Premier Li Peng was the only voice saying this call reflected "vision and courage."

The PRC also put forward proposals for "reforming" the Human Rights Commission: (1) The commission needs a complete and thorough reform and "rationalization" (meaning further underresourcing of its already underresourced budget); (2) the commission has "an imbalanced seat distribution favoring certain regions over others" despite the fact that the fifty-three-member commission is as representative as any UN sub-sidiary organ can be, certainly far less unrepresentative than the UN Security Council which Beijing wants to keep exactly as it is; and (3) some "working groups or individuals of the commission have based their reports on biased views in disrespect of the specific legal system of a certain country" (China's cultural relativist line is not respected in the commission).[61] While Beijing is calling for "rationalization" (downsizing and underresourcing) of the Human Rights Commission, the overwhelming majority of the member states are "expressing concern that the underresourcing of the Centre for Human Rights of the Secretariat is one impediment to the human rights treaty bodies in their ability to carry out their mandates effectively."[62] The United Nations actually spends less than 2 percent of its budget on human rights activities not counting its expenditures for refugee humanitarian aid.

Beijing has also tried to slow down the establishment of an international criminal court in the General Assembly's Sixth Committee by advocating a "step-by-step evolutionary approach." Not surprisingly, at the United Nations Diplomatic Conference of Plenipotentiaries on the Establishment of the International Criminal Court (ICC), held in Rome from June 15 to July 17, 1998, Beijing expressed its strong opposition to the very idea of a permanent ICC based on the familiar self-serving sovereignty-bound arguments: (1) China could not accept the general compulsory jurisdiction of the ICC as the ICC Statute stipulates; (2) China harbored "great reservations regarding whether or not war crimes in armed domestic clashes should be included in the general jurisdiction of the Court"; (3) China held reservations concerning stipulations regarding the functions of the UN Security Council; (4) China harbored "serious reservations to ex officio power of prosecutors in investigations" on the crimes against humanity; and (5) China held reservations concerning the definition of crimes against humanity.[63] In the event, by a vote of 120 to 7, the UN Rome Conference agreed on a treaty setting up a permanent ICC with the United States left voting against it in the company of Iran, Libya, and China.

Although agreeing in principle that the international community could intervene in case of "large-scale human rights violations," in practice Beijing makes a first-order principle of *state* sovereignty. If a nation within a state demands interdependence or self-government, Beijing calls that a matter of state jurisdiction so that the principle of national self-determination is not applicable.[64] When faced in mid-1997 with Pol Pot possibly facing an international criminal trial for genocidal crimes during his forty-four-month reign of terror, a slaughter resulting in the death of perhaps two million Cambodians or a quarter of the country's population, Beijing insisted that the Pol Pot case was for Cambodians alone to manage, not an international human rights concern. In late 1998, Beijing likewise rejected with the same sovereignty-bound argument when the question of bringing the two defecting top Khmer Rouge leaders—Khieu Samphan and Nuon Chea—to an international criminal trial was raised. In mid-March 1999 Beijing cast a unit-veto blocking the creation of an international criminal tribunal for the trial of twenty or thirty surviving Khmer Rouge genocidal leaders.

The "divide and conquer" strategy was successful if measured by the failures of the Human Rights Commission even to consider a mild draft resolution on China. In the 1997 session, the vote on China's "no action motion" on a draft resolution alleging violations of human rights "in China by local, provincial and national authorities and severe restrictions on the rights of citizens to the freedoms of assembly, association, expression, and religion, as well as to due legal process and to a fair trial" was defeated 27–17–9—the widest margin of failure of the seven annual attempts to debate and eventually put a resolution on China to a vote. No other state under UN human rights scrutiny—including Cuba, Iran, Iraq, Russia, or the Sudan—ever advanced a "no action motion," preferring to debate draft resolutions on their merits. Despite repeated pronouncements about its willingness to engage in international dialogue on human rights issues, Beijing preempted the introduction of even a mild draft resolution, thus denying the raison d'être of the Human Rights Commission. Paradoxically, the key to the success of Beijing's "divide and conquer" strategy lies in linkage realpolitik, a politics that runs contrary to what Beijing has been saying publicly, especially to the United States; that is, that there should be *no* linkage between human rights and trade or aid. Beijing, in fact, has been practicing linkage-sanctions diplomacy against human rights action on China through promises of aid projects to developing countries and threats of withholding commercial contracts to industrialized countries. Beijing's battle cry to authoritarian Third World countries—"You could be next"—often finds receptive listeners and ready responses in the Human Rights Commission.[65]

In several respects the year 1998, the fiftieth anniversary of the UDHR, was perhaps the most momentous year as Beijing's human rights diplomacy experienced a series of unprecedented events. On February 23 the fifteen-member European Union (EU) foreign ministers decided not to introduce another draft resolution on China in the forthcoming annual session of the Human Rights Commission apparently based on growing realization that this has become an ineffective "rite of spring" in the international human rights regime. As a result, at the fifty-fourth annual session of the Human Rights Commission in Geneva in March-April, for the first time in eight years Beijing faced no challenge of any kind. As if to respond in kind, Beijing's "principled stand" shifted slightly toward the complementarity of the universality of human rights and cultural and developmental relativism. As far as the protection of human rights is concerned, according to the Chinese delegation, all the countries in the world now have at least four things in common: (1) all of them take human rights seriously, (2) they all accept the universality of human rights, (3) they all acknowledge that the human rights status in each country is in the process of continuous improvement and that no country has perfect human rights conditions, and (4) they all believe that human rights constitute an integral whole.[66] President Clinton's official state visit to China in June seemed made to order for highlighting a new air of tolerance and confidence among the Chinese leadership. The televised debate between Clinton and Jiang on human rights and democracy was warm enough to be dubbed a "Beijing spring."

In September UN High Commissioner for Human Rights Mary Robinson made a first-ever nine-day visit to China in the course of which an agreement on cooperation between her office and China was signed. The agreement offers China technical assistance, if requested, in resolving human rights issues and in developing plans to meet commitments under human rights conventions and the Vienna Declaration and Programme of Action. On October 5, the Chinese government through its UN ambassador in New York signed the ICCPR thus marking the end of a long journey from Maoist collective rights to the International Bill of Rights. After years of the divide-and-conquer strategy of rejecting that the world community had any right to interfere in domestic affairs, the Chinese government finally conceded the point, at least on paper, by signing onto the ICCPR. All the same, 1998 witnessed the publication of a series of human rights books including the *Encyclopedia on Human Rights in China*. At long last, we are told, more consensus has been reached on human rights in the international community and more progress of different degrees has been achieved by countries all over the world in the promotion and protection of human rights.[67]

By late December the "Beijing spring" suddenly turned into a harsher political climate—a "Beijing winter"—as the government launched a major but targeted crackdown. Jiang Zemin is reported to have told a December 23 party meeting in Beijing: "Any factor for instability, as soon as it raises its head, must be resolutely nipped in the bud."[68] Against this backdrop, in a rare show of unanimity, the U.S. Senate and House of Representatives voted 99:0 and 421:0 in February and March 1999 for a nonbinding resolution urging the Clinton administration to submit a censoring resolution at the annual meeting of the United Nations Commission on Human Rights scheduled to be held in Geneva, March 23 through April 30, 1999. What really started the firestorm of Congressional criticism was not just Beijing's human rights practices but a conflation of triple concerns about the accelerated deployment of ballistic missiles against Taiwan, a purported leap in the miniaturization of nuclear warheads with nuclear secrets allegedly stolen from a U.S. government laboratory, and another cycle of repression against democracy activists.

Once again a familiar annual rite of spring was performed in the UN human rights regime but with new twists. The Clinton administration was almost forced to bring China back on the agenda. This belated decision was at one and the same time approved and criticized by human rights NGOs as "too little, too late" since the decision was announced on March 26, 1999, a week after the annual meeting had already convened in Geneva. With the United States unable to get any country other than Poland to sign on as a cosponsor, China once again won enough support for a "no action motion" with a vote of 22 to 17, with 14 abstentions, quashing all debate on a U.S. draft resolution critical of Beijing's human rights practices.

Yet Beijing's tactical victory was a flash in the pan, compared to the epochal unveiling of a new doctrine—dubbed the Annan Doctrine—with profound implications for post-Kosovo international relations in the new millennium. The NATO airstrikes against Yugoslavia, UN Secretary-General Kofi Annan said at the century's last session of the UN Commission on Human Rights, showed that the world community would no longer permit any sovereign state intent on committing genocide to hide behind the UN Charter. The protection of human rights must "take precedence over concerns of state sovereignty." "As long as I am secretary-general," Annan asserted, the world organization "will always place human beings at the center of everything we do."[69]

NATO'S errant bombing of the Chinese embassy in Belgrade on May

7 was a tragic mistake, to be sure, but it helped Beijing in the short run on several fronts: to manipulate and redirect popular anger—the power of ugly nationalism—that would have surfaced at the tenth anniversary of the Tiananmen carnage on June 4 by depicting Western human rights concerns as a plot to spark internal chaos and/or a plot to stop China's march to superpowerdom; and, to forge a Beijing-Belgrade partnership of sorts in defense of state sovereignty including the right to commit ethnic cleansing bordering on quasigenocide; to leverage better terms and extract more concessions with the NATO countries on a host of China-specific issues in exchange for China's "cooperation" in the UN Security Council on the Kosovo peacekeeping formulas.

Whither China's Human Rights and Democratization?

Taken together, post-Mao Beijing's human rights diplomacy has mutated through several situation-specific stages. In the initial "continuity" period (1976–81), there was no change to speak of as Beijing stood firm on Maoist collective rights and nonparticipation in the international human rights regime. The second period (1982–88) witnessed China's participation in the international human rights regime, accession to eight of the twenty-five major UN human rights conventions, and a subtle but significant shift toward the interdependence and indivisibility of the first and second generations of human rights. The third post-Tiananmen period (June 1989 to the present) proved to be most confusing and turbulent.

A pessimistic conclusion is that despite the seemingly principled pronouncements in 1997–98 about the acceptance of the International Bill of Rights and the complementarity between the universality of human rights and cultural and developmental relativism, the gaps between promise and performance, between a rule-of-law facade and a repressive political reality, remain, ever widening and growing. All the situation-specific shifts and modifications in China's human rights diplomacy in the post-Mao era can be seen as tactical adjustments rather than any normative change. Beijing's participation in the international human rights regime for nearly two decades and accession to seventeen human rights treaties and signing of the two keystone covenants notwithstanding, there is no hard evidence yet of any fundamental learning or paradigmatic shift from the sovereignty-bound cultural and developmental relativism to the sovereignty-free universality of human rights. Indeed, China's divide and conquer strategy—and the pronounced tendency of using its international agreements as a bargaining ploy to be displayed or withdrawn at will rather than accepting and implementing them as a matter of legal obligations—seemed made to order for having human rights cake and eating it too by simultaneously rallying Third World support and appealing to the practitioners of geoeconomic and geopolitical realpolitik, especially in the United States. Given the unwillingness of the Chinese multinational state to allow its own citizens, especially those in Tibet and Xinjiang, a minimum of political freedoms, talking more and more about human rights achieves less and less.

An alternative and somewhat more optimistic evaluation from a longer-term historical perspective is that the absence of fundamental learning does not mean that China's sovereignty-bound views are immutably predetermined or that changes conducive to the enhancement of human rights and democratization cannot come about. While state sovereignty and cultural and developmental relativism have remained central in Chinese rhetoric, their unbridled premises have been chipped away in the first post-Tiananmen decade due to three types of changes, both intended and unintended consequences of China's growing enmeshment in the international system.

First, there is a sense in which the International Bill of Rights and the international human rights regime, for all their structural weaknesses and performance failures, have exerted a significant influence in the slow but steady modifications of China's theory and practice of human rights, thus improving long-term prospects of transition to democracy. Although the human rights clock was set back after the Beijing Massacre, China returned to global human rights politics with a proactive strategy, combining sovereignty-bound defense and resistance with selective situation-specific concessions. The seemingly slow process of domestic ratification notwithstanding, Beijing has taken the first critical step in signing the two keystone human rights covenants in 1997 and 1998. To a certain extent, Beijing's long march to the International Bill of Rights reflects a progressive erosion of state sovereignty in post–Cold War world politics, especially when it conflicts with human rights norms. In the 1990s universal human rights are becoming a major instrument for promoting collective security as made evident in the UN Security Council's actions in 1993 and 1994—the establishment of the International Criminal Tribunal for the Former Yugoslavia (ICTY) and the International Criminal Tribunal for Rwanda (ICTR). The indictment issued on May 27, 1999 by the ICTY charging President Slobodan Milosevic, the Serbian tyrant, and four other top Serbian leaders with crimes against humanity and the UN Security Council resolution of June 10, 1999 passed with a vote of 14:0:1 (China), which guarantees that the ICTY will have freedom of movement in Kosovo to carry out its mandate, reflect and effect the latest trend in world politics—no human rights, no state sovereignty!

The International Bill of Rights and the international human rights regime have engendered various "second-image reversed" consequences already made evident in the emergence of a human rights epistemic community, the publication of a flurry of white papers, the enactment of a series of criminal justice laws, and the incremental lessening of the scope of political repression. Participation in the human rights regime linked China's international legal behavior and its legislative politics at home. The National People's Congress in 1994–95 enacted a series of new criminal laws. As if to add more credibility to its acceptance of the Anti-Torture Convention, China's new criminal procedure law is now said to be drawing upon the rational portion of the Western criminal justice system to overcome the comparative disadvantage of China's original criminal procedure law, which has been criticized for its lack of probity in practice. As a fundamental principle, Article 12 in Part I of "General Provisions of the New Criminal Procedure Law" stipulates that "no one can be found guilty without a judgment rendered by the people's court according to law."[70] Thus, Beijing has taken a major step in the direction of accepting a "presumption of innocence" principle. The two keystone human rights treaties—the ICESCR and the ICCPR—that Beijing signed in 1997 and 1998 would surely provide a legitimating platform for China's emerging labor union and democratic movements for prodding their government to carry out its new legal obligations.[71]

Second, for all the habit-driven trumpery about socialism with Chinese characteristics, Beijing has become so dependent upon foreign trade, foreign direct investment, bilateral and multilateral aid, and technology transfers that there is no socialist exit from globalization that would not entail a major economic disaster. President Jiang Zemin in his political report to the Fifteenth Chinese Communist Party Congress on September 12, 1997 admitted just as much when he stated that there is no longer an escape from "the globalization (*quanqiuhua*) of economy, science, and technology" and that there is no choice but to reform, restructure, and open up state-owned enterprises to the "survival-of-the-fittest" competition. That Jiang's political report was issued two months after the eruption of the Asian financial crisis in Thailand and that the debate on or reference to the Asian values argument has disappeared from China's burgeoning globalization literature speak volumes about its poor "fit" for meeting China's globalization challenges. Indeed, the Asian financial crisis, the ascent of the anti-Asian values human rights champion Kim Dae Jung in South Korea, the demise of the Suharto dictatorship in Indonesia, and the collapse of a Sino-Malaysia "human rights" partnership in Yugoslavia where Mahathir sided with NATO, have all combined to discredit the Asian values argument. This is not to say that states are as constrained by globalization as many of the proponents of the hyperglobalization school would have us believe. Far from making states functionally obsolete or irrelevant, globalization has in effect redefined what it takes to be a competent and effective state in an increasingly interdependent and interactive world.

Third, a decade after the Tiananmen crackdown the greatest challenge to Communist rule comes from rising social discontent and protests from the peasants and workers, not from the high-profiled elite democracy activists. As post-Tiananmen China becomes increasingly less isolated and less regimented a society, as state control mechanisms continue to rusticate, as social, economic, and regional gaps widen , as unemployment, inequality, and economic insecurity deepen, as the two-thirds of Chinese living in rural areas continue to "experiment" with "village democracy," as more Chinese in urban areas are enjoying more social, economic, and academic freedom, social protests of all kinds, mostly from economic grievances, occur somewhere each day across the vast country. Chinese Justice Minister Gao Changli admitted as much when he said that in 1998 alone Chinese "mediators" stopped 36,000 armed fights amongst groups and helped to keep another 36,000 groups of complainants from taking to the streets.[72] As if all of this were insufficient to challenge Deng's chaos theory, some 10,000 members of a group known as Falun Gong made a surprise but silent sit-in demonstration outside Zhongnanhai (government headquarters) in central Beijing in April 1999, the largest demonstration in the capital since the prodemocracy movement of 1989. The many varieties of grassroots protests have evolved and mutated through cycles of repression and relaxation during the first post-Tiananmen decade further complicating the state's control of "human rights" movements broadly defined.

To borrow from the familiar Chinese refrain—"no state sovereignty, no human rights"—we can say, "no human rights, no or little chance of democratization." Viewing democratization as an ongoing and multistage process rather than a natural outcome of certain social, cultural, and economic preconditions, human rights can be defined as what David Held calls "empowering rights"[73] that are integral to strategic interactions among state, society, and international factors necessary to bring about a transition to democracy. Democracy in a minimalist procedural sense—universal and equal suffrage and free electoral competition—cannot come about without the citizens enjoying civil and political rights as guaranteed in the UDHR (Article 21) and the ICCPR (Article 25).

Human rights are empowering democratization in normative and substantive terms as well. There is no way or means of "seeking truth from facts" without an opposition. International legitimation no longer rests solely on the claims of state sovereignty by the powers that be. Increasingly, it rests on the condition of human rights, on how the government treats its own sovereign people.[74] Contrary to Deng's chaos theory, respect for human rights is not only a more reliable guide to a peaceful transition to democracy but also for domestic stability in the multinational Chinese state, especially for peaceful resolution of the simmering conflicts in Democratic Taiwan, Buddhist Tibet, and Muslim Xinjiang. There is also the normative/behavioral requirement of great power status: a great power abroad is and becomes what a great power does at home and abroad.[75] In short, a China that respects human rights would be a more democratic country, just as a more democratic China would become part of the world order solution in the Asia-Pacific region and beyond.

In substantive terms—enhancement of people's social and economic well-being—respecting civil and political rights could empower, not destabilize, the Chinese state in the provision of basic human needs. As shown earlier, democratic states perform far better than nondemocratic ones in this respect. In an era of globalization, the concept of a competent and effective state is increasingly seen as vital for development. Reflecting upon the benefits and the limitations of state action in the last fifty years, the World Bank embraced the notion that "the state is central to economic and social development, not as a direct provider of growth but as a partner, catalyst, and facilitator."[76] Most recently, the state capacity to absorb, generate, disseminate, and apply knowledge has come to be viewed as critical for economic and social well-being because everything one does in life depends on knowledge.[77] To enhance human rights is to enhance the state capacity to generate, disseminate, and apply knowledge in the service of social and economic growth and well-being. Herein lies the meaning of Sen's theory that no mass famine has ever occurred in any democratic country. Enhancing human rights could thus provide for a high degree of developmental creativity and productivity.

As matters now stand, democratization pressure is becoming more powerful than ever due to the synergistic effects of newly emerging forces. Domestically, power has been shifting from state to society. It is just a matter of time before demands for democratic political reforms begin to overwhelm the repressive power of the state. Internationally, with the collapse of rightist and leftist dictatorships from Southern Europe to Latin America to East Asia, the third wave of democratization has reached every region of the world accompanied by dramatic increases in normative, material, and strategic support for the causes of human rights and democratization.

What if China does not democratize? What if there is no linkage between human rights and democratization or between Chinese democracy and Chinese foreign policy? However valuable are peace and democracy, human rights are an intrinsic and inherent end goal. We should therefore become more concerned about and more actively engaged in the enhancement of the human rights of the Chinese people. Here the United States as the lone if perhaps fleeting superpower has an important role to play for the enhancement of human rights in China—not by asking China to follow what it says, nor what it actually does, nor by endlessly debating how to engage or contain China, but by cleaning up its own human rights act and by shifting its own post–Cold War foreign policy from a unilateral-cum-bilateral to a multilateral cooperative security approach—indeed, by acting like the responsible great power that it wants China to become.

Notes

1. Whatever reference to "China" is used throughout the chapter is merely for stylistic convenience. The chapter is about the PRC's theory and practice of human rights as made manifest in its international relations, not exactly about the "Chinese" human rights situation at home which, of course, is more diverse than unitary. For the place of human rights in post-Tiananmen foreign relations, see Ann Kent, *Between Freedom and Subsistence: China and Human Rights* (Hong Kong: Oxford University Press, 1993); idem, "China and the International Human Rights Regime: A Case Study of Multilateral Monitoring, 1989–1994," *Human Rights Quarterly* 17:1 (February 1995): 1–47; idem, *China, the United Nations, and Human Rights: The Limits of Compliance* (Philadelphia: University of Pennsylvania Press, 1999); Samuel S. Kim, "Thinking Globally in Post-Mao China," *Journal of Peace Research* 27:2 (May 1990): 191–209; Andrew Nathan, "Human Rights in Chinese Foreign Policy," *China Quarterly*, No. 139 (September 1994): 622–643; idem, "China: Get-

ting Human Rights Right," *Washington Quarterly* 20:2 (Spring 1997): 135–151; idem, "China and the International Human Rights Regime," in Elizabeth Economy and Michel Oksenberg, eds., *China Joins the World: Progress and Prospects* (New York: Council on Foreign Relations Press, 1999), pp. 136–160; James Seymour, "Human Rights in Chinese Foreign Relations," in Samuel S. Kim, ed., *China and the World: Chinese Foreign Relations in the Post-Cold War Era* (Boulder, CO: Westview Press, 1994), pp. 202–225; idem, "Human Rights in Chinese Foreign Relations," in Samuel S. Kim, ed., *China and the World: Chinese Foreign Policy Faces the New Millennium* (Boulder, CO: Westview Press, 1998), pp. 217–238; and Peter Van Ness, "Addressing the Human Rights Issue in Sino-American Relations," *Journal of International Affairs* 49:2 (Winter 1996): 309–331.

2. For the texts of the UDHR and other relevant human rights documents and treaties, see *The United Nations and Human Rights* (New York: United Nations, 1984); for the quote, p. 243.

3. Ibid., p. 254.

4. These remarks are attributed to Deng in Wang Renzhi, "CPC Takes Offense on HR Issue: CPC Central Committee Document," *Dangdai* (Hong Kong), July 15, 1992, pp. 39–41, in Foreign Broadcast Information Service, Daily Report [hereafter FBIS-CHI], July 22, 1992, p. 16.

5. For detailed discussion, see Samuel Kim, *China In and Out of the Changing World Order* (Princeton: Center of International Studies, Princeton University, 1991).

6. For the text of the white paper, see "Human Rights in China," *Beijing Review* (November 4–10, 1991): 8–45.

7. For discussion of the theoretical issues involved from various normative and methodological perspectives, see Jack Donnelly, *Universal Human Rights in Theory and Practice* (Ithaca, NY: Cornell University Press, 1989), chaps. 1–2, pp. 7–46; Richard Falk, *Human Rights and State Sovereignty* (New York: Holmes & Meier Publishers, 1981), chap. 3, pp. 33–62; David P. Forsythe, *The Internationalization of Human Rights* (Lexington, MA: Lexington Books, 1991), chaps. 1–2, pp. 1–54; Kent, *China, the United Nations, and Human Rights*, chap. 1; Samuel S. Kim, "Global Human Rights and World Order," in Richard A. Falk, Samuel S. Kim, and Saul H. Mendlovitz, eds., *The United Nations and a Just World Order* (Boulder, CO: Westview Press, 1991), pp. 356–376; and R. J. Vincent, *Human Rights and International Relations* (New York: Cambridge University Press, 1986), chaps. 1–3, pp. 4–60.

8. For further discussion on the three generations of human rights, see Kim, "Global Human Rights and World Order."

9. Jack Donnelly argues that the universalist versus cultural relativist distinction should be seen as a continuum rather than a dichotomy and that between the two ideal end-points—radical relativism and radical universalism—lies "strong cultural relativism and weak cultural relativism." See Donnelly, *Universal Human Rights in Theory and Practice*, pp. 109–110.

10. See "Constitution of the People's Republic of China, Adopted on December 4, 1982 by the Fifth National People's Congress of the People's Republic of China At Its Fifth Session," in *Renmin Ribao*, December 5, 1982, pp. 1, 4.

11. Samuel S. Kim, *China, the United Nations, and World Order* (Princeton: Princeton University Press, 1979), pp. 483–486.

12. Vincent, *Human Rights and International Relations*, pp. 37–57; Samuel P. Huntington, "The Clash of Civilizations," *Foreign Affairs* 72:3 (Summer 1993): 22–

49 and *The Clash of Civilizations and the Remaking of World Order* (New York: Simon & Schuster, 1996).

13. "Human Rights in China," pp. 8–9.

14. Ibid., p. 9.

15. Ibid., p. 45.

16. Wang Tieya, ed., *Guojifa* (International law) (Beijing: Falu chubanshe, 1981), pp. 267–268.

17. Yi Ding, "Upholding the Five Principles of Peaceful Coexistence," *Beijing Review* 33:9 (February 26–March 4, 1990): 13–16; quote at p. 16 with emphasis added. Bull was cited twice in the same article at p. 16. See also Hedley Bull, "The State's Positive Role in World Affairs," in Richard Falk, Samuel Kim, and Saul Mendlovitz, eds., *Toward a Just World Order, Studies on a Just World Order Series*, Vol. I (Boulder, CO: Westview Press, 1982), pp. 60–73.

18. For scholarly attempts to locate an area of common ground and to establish a core of "basic rights" which recognizes the priority claims of certain rights within the three generations of human rights rather than assigning preference to one set of rights, see Henry Shue, *Basic Rights, Subsistence, Affluence and US Foreign Policy* (Princeton: Princeton University Press, 1980), pp. 19–20, 23; Kent, *Between Freedom and Subsistence*, pp. 222–230; Donnelly, *Universal Human Rights in Theory and Practice*, pp. 28–46.

19. For a trenchant critique of the universality claims, see Xin Chunying, "Guoji renquan wenti redian shuping" (commentary on controversial aspects of human rights issues), *Zhongguo shehui kexue* (Chinese social science), No. 6 (November 1994): 132–141.

20. World Bank, *China 2020* (Washington, DC: The World Bank, 1997), p. 50.

21. Barbara Crossette, "Legal Experts' Group Says China Is Clamping Down on Tibetans," *New York Times*, December 27, 1997, p. A4.

22. For further analysis along this line, see Samuel S. Kim, "China and the United Nations," in Economy and Oksenberg, *China Joins the World*, pp. 42–89.

23. Human Rights Watch/Asia, *Death by Default: A Policy of Fatal Neglect in China's State Orphanages* (New York: Human Rights Watch/Asia, January 1996).

24. For critical appraisals of the Asian values argument in the setting of globalizing human rights and democratic discourse, see Edward Friedman, "What Globalizing Asia Will or Won't Stand For: Human Rights and Democracy," *Asian Thought and Society* 22:65 (May–August 1997): 200–229 and Joanne R. Bauer and Daniel A. Bell, eds., *The East Asian Challenge for Human Rights* (New York: Cambridge University Press, 1999).

25. See Tatsuo Inoue, "Liberal Democracy and 'Asian Values,'" in Bauer and Bell, *The East Asian Challenge for Human Rights*, pp. 27–59.

26. Ibid., p. 44.

27. Quoted in Andrew J. Nathan, "Is China Ready for Democracy?" in Larry Diamond and Marc F. Plattner, eds., *The Global Resurgence of Democracy* (Baltimore: The Johns Hopkins University Press, 1993), p. 281.

28. See *Deng Xiaoping wenxuan: di san juan* (Selected works of Deng Xiaoping, Vol. III) (Beijing: Renmin chubanshe, 1993), pp. 330–333, 344–346, 359–361.

29. Adam Przeworski, Michael Alavarez, Jose Antonio Cheibub, and Fernando Limongi, "What Makes Democracies Endure?" *Journal of Democracy* 7:1 (1996): 39–55.

30. Doh Chull Shin, "On the Third Wave of Democratization: A Synthesis and Evaluation of Recent Theory and Research," *World Politics* 47 (October 1994): 135–170, especially 156–157.

31. Amartya Sen, "Human Rights and Asian Values," *The New Republic* (July 14 and 21, 1997), p. 34. See also idem, *Resources, Values, and Development* (Cambridge: Harvard University Press, 1997).

32. "The Right to Development: An Inalienable Human Right," *Beijing Review* 35:51 (December 21–27, 1992): 13.

33. James Watson, "Rites or Beliefs? The Construction of a United Culture in Late Imperial China," in Lowell Dittmer and Samuel Kim, eds., *China's Quest for National Identity* (Ithaca, NY: Cornell University Press, 1993), pp. 80–103.

34. Huntington, *The Clash of Civilizations*, p. 321.

35. Huntington, "The Clash of Civilizations?" and *The Clash of Civilizations.* Twenty-seven of the forty commentaries and essays published as immediate reactions to Huntington's *Foreign Affairs* article were chosen and included in Wang Jisi, ed., *Wenming yu guoji zhengzhi—Zhongguo xuezhe ping Hengtingdun de wenming chongtu lun* (Civilization and international politics—Chinese scholars on Huntington's clash theory) (Shanghai: Shanghai renmin chubanshe, 1995). See also essays and comments by Wang Jisi, Wang Yizhou, Liu Jinghua, Jin Junhui, and Jin Canrong in *Shijie zhishi* (World knowledge) (May 1, 1995): 4–12 and Wang Jisi and Zou Sicheng, "Civilizations: Clash or Fusion?" and She Duanzhi, "East and West Mutually Complementary," *Beijing Review* (January 15–21, 1996): 8–13.

36. See Xiao Weiyun, Luo Haocai, and Wu Xieying, "Makesi zhuyi ren mayang kan 'renquan' wenti" (How Marxism views the question of 'human rights'), *Hongqi* (Red flag), No. 5 (1979): 43–48.

37. Shen Baoxing, Wang Chenguan, and Li Zerui, "Guanyu guoji lingyu de renquan wenti" (On the question of human rights in the international domain), *Hongqi*, No. 8 (1982): 44–48.

38. See *Renmin ribao*, December 3, 1988, p. 4; Tian Jin, "Guoji renquan huodong de fazhan he cunzai zhengyi de wenti" (The development of international human rights activities and some controversial issues), *Guoji wenti yanjiu* (International issues), No. 1 (January 1989): 4–7; UN Doc. A/43/PV.74 (23 December 1988), pp. 61–62.

39. UN Doc. A/43/PV.74 (23 December 1988): 61–62.

40. See Tian, "Guoji renquan huodong de fazhan he cunzai zhengyi de wenti."

41. In August 1989 the UN Sub-Commission on Prevention of Discrimination and Protection of Minorities, a subsidiary expert body of the Commission on Human Rights, passed by a secret vote of 15:9 the first-ever resolution in UN history censoring the PRC for human rights abuses at home. In February 1990, the International Labor Organization (ILO) added international delegitimation by endorsing the findings of an expert committee which were extremely critical of China's mistreatment of workers who had supported the prodemocracy movement.

42. For a detailed discussion about the behind-the-scenes horse trading in and out of the Security Council, see Kim, *China In and Out of the Changing World Order*, pp. 24–28.

43. See UNDP, *Human Development Report 1991* (New York: Oxford University Press, 1991), p. 120 and *Human Development Report 1996* (New York: Oxford University Press, 1996), p. 136.

44. This was the first global conference on human rights in twenty-five years. The General Assembly decided to convene such a conference pursuant to its Resolution 45/155 of December 18, 1990.

45. For the most comprehensive analysis of China's human rights diplomacy at Bangkok and Vienna, see Kent, *China, the United Nations, and Human Rights*, chaps. 6–7, pp. 146–193.

46. Huntington, *The Clash of Civilizations*, p.193.

47. Sidney Jones, "Culture Clash: Asian Activists Counter Their Governments," *China Rights Forum* (Summer 1993): 8–9, 22.

48. *Renmin ribao*, March 31, 1993, p. 6 and "Asia's Major Human Rights Concerns," *Beijing Review* 36:16 (April 19–25, 1993): 10–11.

49. Gordon Fairclough, "Standing Firm," *Far Eastern Economic Review* (April 15, 1993): 22.

50. For a cogent critique of the Bangkok Declaration, see Inoue, "Liberal Democracy and 'Asian Values.'"

51. For the text of the Bangkok Declaration, see Michael C. Davis, ed., *Human Rights and Chinese Values: Legal, Philosophical and Political Perspectives* (Hong Kong: Oxford University Press, 1995), pp. 205–209.

52. For a trenchant critique of U.S. human rights diplomacy as a contemporary variant of America's Manifest Destiny, see Hong Guoqi and Wang Xiaode, "Kelintun YaTai zhengce shoucuo de wenhua yinsu" (Clinton's Asia-Pacific policy thwarted by cultural factors), *Xiandai guoji guanxi* (Contemporary international relations), No. 5 (May 1995): 18–22.

53. For the text of Liu Huaqiu's speech, see "Proposals for Human Rights Protection and Promotion," *Beijing Review* 36:26 (June 28–July 4, 1993): 8–11.

54. Liu Baopu and Xiao Qiang, "The Poor Relations Push Their Way in at the Door: NGOs at the Vienna Human Rights Conference," *China Rights Forum* (Fall 1993): 17.

55. Huntington, *The Clash of Civilizations*, p. 197.

56. For the text of the Vienna Declaration and Programme of Action, see UN Doc. A/CONF.157/24 (Part I) at 20 (12 July 1993) (Internet version).

57. Revealingly, the most comprehensive UN report on this theme of democratization and human rights was produced by Secretary-General Boutros-Boutros Ghali just a few days before his forced retirement. See Boutros-Boutros Ghali, *An Agenda for Democratization* (New York: United Nations, 1996).

58. Liu Wenzong, "Lun zhuquan yu renquan" (On sovereignty and human rights), *Renmin ribao*, June 13, 1993, p. 5.

59. Resolution 48/141 of 20 December 1993, in *Resolutions and Decisions Adopted by the General Assembly During the First Part of Its Forty-Eighth Session, From 21 September to 23 December 1993* (New York: United Nations Press Release GA/8637, 20 January 1994), pp. 411–414.

60. Xin, "Guoji renquan wenti redian shuping," p. 133.

61. For excerpts from Tian's speech, see FBIS-CHI-95–040 (February 28, 1995) via WNC (Internet version).

62. General Assembly Resolution 51/87 (December 12, 1996). See also B. G. Ramcharan, "Reforming the United Nations to Secure Human Rights," in Saul H. Mendlovitz and Burns H. Weston, eds., *Preferred Futures for the United Nations* (Irvington-on-Hudson, NY: Transnational Publishers, 1995), pp. 193–219.

63. Xinhua, 28 July 1998 in FBIS-CHI-98–209 (July 28, 1998) via WNC (Internet version).

64. Wei Min *et al.*, eds., *Guojifa gailun* (Introduction to international law) (Beijing: Guangming ribao chubanshe, 1986), p. 247.

65. Barbara Crossette, "China Outflanks U.S. to Avoid Scrutiny of Its Human Rights," *New York Times*, April 24, 1996, p. A12.

66. *Renmin ribao*, April 27, 1998, p. 14 in FBIS-CHI-98–124 (May 4, 1998) (Internet version).

67. Wang Zaibang and Qiu Guirong, "21 shiji shijie renquan mianlin de tiaozhan—jinian 'shijie renquan xuanyan' 50 zhounian" (Challenges facing the universal human rights in the 21st century—in commemoration of the 50th anniversary of the 'universal declaration of human rights'), *Xiandai guoji guanxi* (Contemporary international relations), No. 11 (1998): 2–8.

68. "Beijing Chill," *Far Eastern Economic Review* (January 14, 1999): 12.

69. Cited in Judith Miller, "When Sovereignty Isn't Sacrosanct," *New York Times*, April 18, 1999.

70. Lu Zhongya, "New Criminal Procedure Law Adopts 'Presumption of Innocence' Principle in Conformity with National Conditions," *Faxue* (Jurisprudence) in FBIS-CHI-96–187 (June 10, 1996) (Internet version).

71. For instance, an incipient Czech human rights movement issued "Charter 77" in January 1977, drawing its legitimacy from the incorporation of the two human rights covenants into the domestic laws of Communist Czechoslovakia.

72. AFP on line, May 27, 1999.

73. David Held, *Democracy and the Global Order* (Stanford: Stanford University Press, 1995), p. 223.

74. W. Michael Reisman, "Sovereignty and Human Rights in Contemporary International Law," *American Journal of International Law* 84 (October 1990): 872.

75. Samuel S. Kim, "China as a Great Power," *Current History* 96:611 (September 1997): 246–251.

76. World Bank, *World Development Report 1997* (New York: Oxford University Press, 1997), pp. 1–15, quote on p. 1.

77. World Bank, *World Development Report 1998/99: Knowledge for Development* (New York: Oxford University Press, 1998).

Chapter 6

China and Its Neighbors

June Teufel Dreyer

The founding of the People's Republic of China (PRC) in 1949 was followed by a period of relative isolation. In the case of the United States, this was nearly total. Even relations with the Soviet Union, though cordial on the surface, were characterized by an underlying atmosphere of distrust. The PRC leadership was interested in spreading the communist revolution, recouping lost territories such as Tibet and Taiwan, and responding to perceived threats. It sent military forces into Korea in 1950 and into a border war with India in 1962. As evidenced by the country's seizure of the disputed Paracel (Xisha) Islands from South Vietnam in 1974, just before China's "fraternal ally" North Vietnam completed its conquest of South Vietnam, PRC leaders did not lack the ability to exploit international opportunity. Nonetheless, Beijing's orientation was basically inward. With a few exceptions such as Premier Zhou Enlai, even senior party and government leaders rarely traveled abroad. Relatively few foreigners visited the PRC, and those who were able to did so under carefully controlled conditions. As Mao Zedong explained, "we must first put our own house in order."[1]

This changed with Deng Xiaoping's accession to the position of paramount leader at the end of the 1970s. As part of sweeping economic reforms that repudiated communism in all but name, Deng opened China to foreign investment and encouraged large numbers of young Chinese to study abroad. Diplomatic relations improved not only with the capitalist states including Japan, but also with the Soviet Union and even, to some extent, with Vietnam.

By the late 1980s, however, the contradictions of Deng's reforms, including high inflation rates, pervasive corruption, and uneven distribution of prosperity, had led to simmering resentments and protests. After brutal suppression of the largest of these protests at Tiananmen Square in 1989, the legitimacy of the leadership was called into question. Its ideological claim to authority had been eroded by market reforms; the charismatic leadership of Mao was long gone; and old age was gradually claiming the remaining heroes of the revolution.

The leadership fell back on nationalism for support. When harnessed to the PRC's rapidly expanding importance in world trade, this caused concerns among China's neighbors about an emerging regional juggernaut. Napoleon's famous observation about China as a sleeping giant which, when wakened, would cause the world to tremble, was a *sotto voce* backdrop to sentiments publicly proclaimed by U.S. and Asian policy and opinion makers that a rising tide would lift all boats; that the twenty-first century would be the century of Asia; and that an economically prosperous China would lead to a stable, democratic China. The disposition of potentially troublesome territorial issues could hopefully be postponed until that utopian future arrived.

Actions

A series of developments that began in the 1990s called the optimistic outlook into question. These may be classified under three headings: military modernization, Chinese assertiveness in international issues worldwide, and a much stronger stance on regional territorial disputes.

1. *Military Modernization.* This term includes both higher defense budgets and purchases of advanced weaponry.
   - Military budgets rose steadily, quintupling from 20.37 billion yuan in 1987 to a budgeted 104.65 billion yuan (approximately U.S. $12.61 billion) in 1999. Actual military expenditures are estimated at three to five times this amount.[2]
   - Major weapons purchases were made, mostly from Russia. These included Su-27 and Su-30 fighter planes, Kilo-class diesel-electric submarines, and S-300 surface-to-air missiles. The PRC will eventually produce its own Su-27s under license from Russia,

and existing indigenously-produced Song class submarines will be retrofitted with the advanced sonar systems carried by the Kilos. The integration of these and other weapons acquired or indigenously developed will enhance the Chinese military's power projection capabilities and could allow the PRC to dominate the East China Sea, South China Sea, and Bay of Bengal.

• New weapons have been developed, including the several that American sources have charged were derived from secrets stolen from the U.S. These include a device used in missile-guidance systems, an artillery system that uses electrical energy and magnetism, satellite technology that can be used to launch multiple nuclear warheads, and the W-88 submarine-launched nuclear warhead.[3] The People's Liberation Army (PLA) also displayed interest in "acupuncture warfare," or techniques to destroy an enemy's command and control functions.[4]

2. *Assertiveness on International Issues.* China has strongly asserted its own interests on a variety of international issues, sometimes very much in opposition to a majority of other nations.

• The PRC became the leading supporter of Burma's State Law and Order Restoration Commission (SLORC), defending the SLORC's right to stay in power in preference to the democratically elected Aung San Suu Kyi. China sold more than a billion dollars of weapons to the SLORC and helped construct important infrastructure projects. These included the upgrade of several naval bases and installation of radars which will allow Chinese intelligence to monitor activities in the Indian Ocean area. The SLORC later renamed itself the State Peace and Development Council, though observers noticed no improvement in its attitudes toward democracy or human rights.

• In mid-1993, after preparing the Chinese population for a celebration when Beijing was chosen to host the Olympics in the year 2000, official media put forth bitter anti-imperialist invective and conspiracy theories when Sydney, Australia, was chosen instead.[5] These included strong racial overtones. For example, a Xinhua commentary blamed interference by Anglo-Saxon countries, and complained that the Olympics were a "white man's games." [6] This angry response conveniently ignored the fact that both Japan and South Korea had sponsored recent Olympic games.

- Despite continued protests by its neighbors and other states, the PRC continued to test nuclear weapons and, while participating in negotiations on the Nuclear Non-Proliferation Treaty, seemed deliberately obstructive. In April 1996, for example, the Chinese gave as reasons for continued testing both (a) the need to use nuclear detonations to dig underground irrigation canals in Xinjiang and Tibet[7] and (b) as a defense against giant asteroids on a collision course with earth.[8]
- In February 1996, the PRC strongly hinted that it would use its Security Council veto to prevent a six-month extension of the United Nations peacekeeping mission in Haiti, in retaliation against the Haitian government's invitation of China (ROC) to Taiwan's vice-president to attend the inauguration of President René Preval in Port-au-Prince earlier in the same month.[9]
- Vetoed a UN peacekeeping mission to Guatemala requested by that country's government to monitor a ceasefire to a civil war that had begun in the 1960s, since it had supported Taiwan's bid to enter the United Nations and invited an ROC representative to attend the ceasefire ceremony.[10]

3. *Territorial Disputes.* The majority of these disputes concern islands and the extent of territorial waters in the South and East China seas.
- In February 1992, China's National People's Congress (NPC) passed a law asserting China's ownership not only of the Paracel Islands, but the Spratly (Nansha) Islands, the Senkaku (Diaoyutai) group, and Taiwan. The same law claimed the right to "adopt all necessary measures to prevent and stop the harmful passage of vessels through its territorial waters," and for "PRC warships or military aircraft to expel the intruders."[11] Vietnam claims jurisdiction over the Paracels (Xisha) as well as China; claimants to the Spratlys include China, Taiwan, Vietnam, the Philippines, Malaysia, and Brunei. Ownership of the Senkakus is disputed by the PRC, the ROC, and Japan.
- In May 1992, China granted oil exploration rights in the Vanguard Bank disputed area of the Spratly Islands to a U.S.-based corporation, Crestone Energy.
- In early 1995, the government of the Philippines complained that China had built concrete structures, including radar installations, in the Mischief Reef area of the Spratlys claimed by

both the PRC and the Philippines. Boundary markers demarcating the PRC's territorial waters had been placed fifty miles from Palawan Island.[12]

- Shortly thereafter, the Indonesian government made public the existence of a Chinese map including the oil- and gas-rich Natuna Islands, which are formally administered by Indonesia, in the PRC's exclusive economic zone.[13]
- A series of war games, including live missile firings, in and around the Taiwan Strait area was held from July 1995 to March 1996 with the apparent aims of discouraging the efforts of the government of the ROC to enhance the country's international stature, and of disrupting the ROC's first direct presidential election.
- During the last several months of 1995, the PRC conducted oil exploration in the Diaoyutai/Senkaku Islands in what the Japanese media interpreted as a test of their country's resolve to defend its claims to that area.[14]
- In November 1995, a Chinese navy vessel was sent to pour more than a thousand tons of cement and stone onto a submerged reef in the Spratly area in order to bolster the PRC's claim to sovereignty thereto.[15]

While all of the above may be characterized as elements of a nationalistic agenda, it was the regional territorial disputes that caused the strongest reactions among the PRC's neighbors and the United States.

Reactions

Reactions ran the gamut from accommodationism to complaints to countermeasures. Those in the first category, the inevitabilists, tend to fall back on a false reading of history to justify inaction: China has "always" been the hegemon and by virtue of size and population is the "natural" dominant regional power.[16] In fact, however, the power of Chinese empires has waxed and waned over the course of millennia. Its leaders' goals were typically limited to the unification of *tian xia* (all under heaven), meaning the Chinese cultural area, and its defense against foreign invaders, who usually came on horseback from the north. Conquest of non-Chinese areas was not valued, and was largely confined to occasional control of the "Western Regions," that is, present-day Xinjiang. This was especially true under the Han and Tang. The broader empires of the Yuan and Qing might seem to contradict these generali-zations. Their respective rulers, however, were not Han Chinese but Mongols and Manchus who acted from distinctly non-Chinese values. Ming China's brief period of naval power in the early fifteenth century resulted from the ambitions of one emperor, who was opposed by his officials and reversed by his successor. Even then, the Ming voyages largely ignored Taiwan and the other islands whose status has recently become controversial.

China's regional influence in imperial times rested on its economy, which was usually the largest in the area. In the traditional tribute sys-tem, the Chinese empire usually paid more in gifts than it received in tribute. Non-Chinese put up with the humiliation of acknowledging the primacy of the Chinese ruler according to prescribed ritual since even the limited access this gave to the China trade was too valuable to be given up.

Also, to argue that China has always been the regional hegemon is to forget the dominant position held by Japan in the half century preceding World War II. To assume that size and population assure regional domi-nance ignores both the Japanese position in pre–World War II Asia and that of nineteenth century Great Britain, which was not only regional but global as well.

The second category, the complainers tend to concentrate their analy-ses on the injustices that have been perpetrated on them, usually adding that therefore some outside power, sometimes the United Nations, but more often the United States, has an obligation to help. How the former can do this, given the PRC's veto in the UN Security Council, is not addressed. Given the recent downsizing of the U.S. military and a gen-eral American reluctance to become involved in disputes where national interests are not clearly threatened, hopes for American intervention are perhaps overly optimistic as well.

While on a speaking tour of Southeast Asia in 1995, a professor at the United States Naval Academy was asked repeatedly why America did not bomb or shell the PRC's installations on Mischief Reef. Even those who did not call for armed aggression wondered why Washington did not tell Beijing that it would not tolerate the erection of such structures and demand their immediate removal.[17] Philippine diplomats have sev-eral times asked Washington to include the territories Manila contests jurisdiction over with Beijing within the scope of the U.S.-Philippines security agreement, thus far without success.

The third category, those who advocate countermeasures, has displayed great ingenuity, and acted both as individual states, bilaterally, and in multilateral fora. Countries often display elements of all three attitudes: publicly acknowledging the PRC's "natural" leadership while simultaneously expressing their resentment and fear of China privately, complaining to other countries and organizations that those countries and organizations should take action, and at the same time seeking to devise individual and collective coping strategies.[18]

To consider first actions by states acting individually, perhaps none of the PRC's moves concerned more countries than the NPC's 1992 unilateral declaration over a number of island chains and the waters surrounding them. Even those countries that did not contest sovereignty over any of the disputed islands were concerned with the right of free passage for their shipping. Discussions on the implications of the law were a standard feature in the media of many states, among which Japan was especially prominent.

Tokyo, which contests the ownership of the Senkaku/Diaoyutai Islands with China and has major shipping interests in the area, quietly made representations to Beijing. It had previously been understood that the two parties had agreed to postpone their differences over the islands and the rights of shipping in the waters surrounding them; joint exploitation of the resources thereof had been understood as a possible compromise. These unilateral actions by the NPC would, Japanese diplomats pointed out, inflame right-wing sentiments within their country and lend credence to the demands for remilitarization that right-wingers had been advocating for several decades. The new law could not only enhance the influence of such groups, but might also jeopardize a long-planned visit to China by the emperor and empress that had been scheduled for later in the year. Chinese leaders, since they were hoping to obtain an official high-level apology for Japanese aggression during World War II, strongly wished the visit to take place.

Within a month, the Chinese Foreign Ministry issued a "clarification" of the law, describing it as part of a normal domestic legislative process which did not represent a change in Chinese policy and would not affect the joint development of the islands in question with other parties involved in the dispute.[19] While at least publicly reassured, the imperial visit took place; the apology was somewhat less than the Chinese leadership had hoped for. The 1992 law remained in place and presumably in force, ready to be cited in any future dispute. And the nagging question remained of why, if the law did not represent a change in policy, it had been necessary to pass it in the first place. The issue of the significance of the law did, however, fade from the media.

The issue of sovereignty over the Senkaku/Diaoyutai Islands did not. Chinese concerns over the creeping remilitarization of Japan were reinforced in the fall of 1996 when Prime Minister Ryutaro Hashimoto announced his intention to visit the Yasukuni Shrine for the second time in less than three months. The shrine, which honors Japanese who died in all the country's wars, has nonetheless come to symbolize the country's aggression during World War II for many people, including pacifist elements within Japan. In July, Japanese right-wing groups erected a lighthouse on one of the disputed islands and placed memorials and flags on another.

The lighthouse, a temporary structure, was damaged during a typhoon, and in September, members of the right-wing Japan Youth Federation reappeared on the island, accompanied by Japanese news media, to repair it. Chinese sources, arguing that this event must have had official sponsorship if the media covered it, responded angrily. A vicious cycle of action and reaction seemed to be forming.

Popular indignation ran high enough in the PRC that the government feared that the dispute over the Senkaku/Diaoyu Islands might become the excuse for a new round of public mass demonstrations. It detained anti-Japanese activists, forbade protests outside the Japanese embassy, and increased security at universities considered likely sites for disruptions.[20]

Hong Kong and Taiwan activists could not, however, be similarly restrained. They determined to form a protest "armada" of small boats, which would land on the disputed islands and proclaim China's sovereignty over them. The boats set sail with great fanfare, but were turned back by the Japanese coast guard. A Hong Kong protester who jumped into the water to try to reach the island was drowned, thereby creating, in some minds at least, a martyr to the cause.[21] One Hong Kong magazine quoted the president of the Chinese Academy of Social Sciences' prediction that

> If the central authorities fail to handle the people's desires properly or fail to adopt a correct attitude toward the Japanese occupation of the Diaoyu Islands . . . , this could well lead to nationwide unrest against both a corrupt and incompetent government and the privileged stratum. This will cause serious consequences that are hard to imagine at this stage, and

may even bring about greater trouble than the political turbulence of 1989.[22]

While attempting to clamp down overt popular manifestations of anti-Japanese sentiment, the PRC left no doubt that it would not concede or compromise on the sovereignty issue. An unnamed senior military officer was said to have declared pointedly that the era of Li Hongzhang (the Qing dynasty official who signed the Treaty of Shimonoseki, ceding Taiwan and the Diaoyu Islands to Japan) had ended.[23] In mid-April 1997, the Japanese Foreign Ministry complained to Beijing that a Chinese marine survey ship had been operating near Miyako Island, Okinawa. Ministry sources noted that during the previous year there had been sixteen separate instances of PRC ships entering Japan's 200 nautical mile zone to conduct marine surveys.[24]

Another action taken by Japan alone was to suspend grants-in-aid to China until such time as the PRC agreed to stop nuclear testing.[25] The Tokyo government also decided to extend a major grant to Burma for infrastructure development. While ostensibly given as a reward for SLORC's having released democracy activist Aung San Suu Kyi from house arrest, government officials privately added that they hoped to be able to wean Burma away from its dependence on the PRC.[26]

The election of an outspoken right-wing independent candidate, Shintaro Ishihara, as governor of Tokyo in 1999, while certainly not planned by the Japanese government, was also indicative of rising anti-China sentiment. Ishihara not only used the derogatory term "Shina" to describe the People's Republic, but declared himself a supporter of Taiwan and a friend of Tibet's Dalai Lama. Prior to his election, Ishihara caused a minor diplomatic row when he disputed the Beijing government's account of the 1937 Rape of Nanjing.[27]

India raised defense budgets in response to a perceived threat from China; the 1998 budget represented a real increase of approximately 7 percent over 1997, with the navy's share up 22 percent as a reflection of concern with Chinese activities in the Indian Ocean.[28] Partly in reaction to the "China threat," a conservative Hindu group, the Bharatiya Janata Party (BJP), came to power. Its defense minister, George Fernandes, issued several provocative statements about China, including publicly proclaiming it India's "number one enemy,"[29] and of far greater concern than Pakistan—a country which has received significant military aid from the PRC. In May 1998, India detonated a series of nuclear tests, prompting Pakistan to do the same. Indian leaders argued that they felt compelled to test because the United States was so intent on pursuing constructive engagement with China that it simply disregarded India's fears.[30] A year later, India launched the Agni intermediate-range ballistic missile.[31] It is also developing a submarine-launched ballistic missile, the Sagarika, with Russian help.[32]

As for Vietnam, its ability to respond to the PRC's activities in the Vanguard region of the Spratlys was somewhat constrained because China had cleverly awarded exploration rights to an American-based corporation. Vietnam was at that point working toward formal diplomatic recognition with the United States, and seemed unlikely to complicate the process by taking military action against U.S. nationals. Vietnam did, however, counter by granting exploration rights in Blue Dragon, another part of the Spratlys with which it contests ownership with the PRC, to Mobil, another U.S.-based corporation. It also enlisted the services of a leading American law firm, Covington and Burling, to determine how the International Court of Justice might rule on the ownership of Vanguard and Blue Dragon.[33]

In March 1997, Hanoi protested the presence of a Chinese oil rig, Kantan-03, which was located 64 nautical miles off Vietnam's coast, but also 71 nautical miles from the coast of the PRC's Hainan province. Beijing promptly rejected the protest. Differences on the two countries' territorial sea baselines accounted for the dispute: the PRC had drawn its baseline from the Paracel Islands which it had seized from Vietnam two decades ago, but which Hanoi continues to claim.[34] In April, the rig was withdrawn and Vietnamese Vice-Foreign Minister Vu Khoan pronounced the Hanoi-Beijing relationship as "not so bad . . . moving ahead in different areas."[35] However, just a week after the two countries concluded an apparently cordial bilateral meeting in Hanoi, Vietnam complained that Chinese military planes were overflying the disputed area, apparently in coordination with fleets of communications ships. Tensions rose again.[36] A pattern had developed: the PRC pushed its claims to the brink of hostilities, then stepped back temporarily and pushed forward again, trying to turn its claims into *faits accomplis.*

Philippine reactions to the PRC's provocations showed a similarly inconclusive pattern. Remonstrations to Beijing regarding structures and radars on and near Mischief Reef produced the reply that they were for the use of fishermen and had no military significance. Then-president Fidel Ramos, a career military man and former chief of staff, rebutted this claim and set up a tour for the media so that they could see for themselves. He also ordered the boundary markers destroyed.

Beijing warned that, despite its principled stance, it would be unwise to assume that Chinese restraint would be of indefinite duration; any repetition of these actions, even another media tour, would invite retaliation. The Philippines must cease "bullying" China.[37] Meanwhile, Beijing suggested a fishing cooperation agreement to prevent the arrests of Chinese fishermen in what the Philippines regards as its territorial waters.[38] At the same time, Ramos submitted to his congress an ambitious and expensive military buildup plan designed to deter intrusion into the country's 200-mile exclusive economic zone. It was quickly approved by a legislature that had heretofore been reluctant to allocate funds for defense purposes.[39]

A period of relative calm ensued, punctuated by brief Filipino reports that Chinese naval ships had been sighted in the country's waters, followed by terse statements from Manila that, given imperfect weather conditions, it could not be sure that the ships actually belonged to the Chinese military. In November 1996, in what seemed a sign of improving relations, Chinese President Jiang Zemin paid a state visit to Manila. Agreements were reached to augment bilateral trade; the two countries agreed to set aside their conflicting territorial claims, and military attachés were exchanged.[40]

This impression was shattered a few weeks later when a group headed by Filipino military chief Arnulfo Acadera made a Christmas Day visit to the largest of the islands in the Kalaayan group claimed by the Philippines. Agence France Presse (AFP) reported that Arnulfo had announced plans to upgrade Kalaayan's airstrip and build a new garrison there as part of the country's military modernization plan.[41] Arnulfo subsequently said that the facilities were being upgraded simply to support scientific research— possibly the functional equivalent of the PRC's earlier-expressed concerns for the welfare of its fisherfolk on Mischief Reef—and that, as head of the Filipino military, he had a duty to visit military outposts.[42]

In February 1997, PRC Defense Minister Chi Haotian arrived in the Philippines for talks with his opposite number, Renato de Villa. The two agreed to resolve territorial disputes through dialogue and refrain from provocative acts in the Spratlys;[43] during the following month, Manila hosted a port visit by ships of the PLA navy.[44]

Comity was short-lived: in April, the Philippine navy forced three Chinese ships away from Scarborough Shoal. Filipino fishermen subsequently landed on the shoal, tore down Chinese markers, and hoisted the Philippine flag.[45] In May, Filipino fishermen claimed they had been fired on by Chinese naval vessels patrolling the Spratlys,[46] and three Filipino legislators made an inspection tour to one of the contested islands, vowing to help its defenders upgrade their arms.[47] In late June and early July, the Philippine navy discovered new Chinese boundary markers on Sabina Shoal, off Palawan Island, and destroyed them,[48] vowing that any future markers would be treated similarly.[49]

In 1999, the two countries were still arguing: Beijing strongly opposed a Philippine plan to bring the dispute to an international court, arguing that involving a third party would "complicate the problem."[50]

Indonesia, on discovering the Chinese map which included the Natuna Islands as part of China's exclusive economic zone, quickly dispatched its foreign minister, Ali Alatas, to Beijing. Alatas returned shortly, explaining that Chinese foreign minister Qian Qichen had told him that the PRC considers the Natunas to be under Indonesian jurisdiction, and has never claimed them.[51] Indonesian officials were well aware that this did not constitute a binding commitment. The Indonesian foreign ministry's chief maritime law expert subsequently made several frustrating trips to Beijing to try to clarify the issue. He later complained, "They tell us this is the national heritage of China. . . . They don't argue, they just go on talking about Chinese dynasties. . . . We have a great deal of difficulty analyzing what they're claiming."[52] As the minister was acutely aware, this was the language of expansionism.

Some months later, Beijing extended its maritime jurisdiction claim from 370,000 square kilometers off its main coastline to 3 million square kilometers, doing so only for the Paracels. Ali Alatas pointed out that this would be valid only if the PRC were an archipelagic state, which it is not. He added that he feared the PRC planned to follow up this claim of extended maritime jurisdiction with a similar claim with regard to the Spratlys.[53] A member of Jakarta's Center for Strategic and International Studies warned that China's actions were making it difficult for Indonesia, which is not a claimant to either the Paracels or Spratlys, to maintain its honest broker role with regard to the conflicting claims.[54]

Indonesian officials opined that the PRC was taking extreme positions in order to get more than it otherwise might be able to reasonably expect. In addition to the matter of baselines being calculated as if the PRC were an archipelagic state, they pointed out, China's claims with regard to the Paracels went beyond what was allowed under the Law of the Sea. Whereas it stipulates that the ratio of land to sea area within the baselines should not exceed one to nine, China's claim in the Paracels is one to twenty-six.[55]

In September 1996, Indonesia held its largest air, land, and sea military maneuvers in four years. The exercises were held in the Natunas. Foreign military attachés were invited; the PRC's did not attend. Indonesia also ordered F-16 fighter planes from the United States. A PRC spokesperson complained that Indonesia's attitude could "complicate" the situation in the South China Sea.[56]

Malaysia purchased MiG-29 fighter planes from Russia as well as American F/A-18 Hornets. It also constructed a new air force base.[57] Australia began Project Takari, a major fifteen-year upgrade of its armed forces that focused on introducing state-of-the-art equipment for information warfare.[58]

Bilateral efforts to deal with what the PRC's perceived aggressiveness included joint naval maneuvers between India and Indonesia, and between Malaysia and Indonesia.[59] In December 1995, Indonesia also concluded a defense treaty with Australia that sent a message to Beijing. An Indonesian newspaper noted with evident satisfaction that, whereas Australians had until recently thought of Indonesia as the chief threat to their security, they now believed that the country "serves as a defense front line for the land of the kangaroos."[60] A few months later, Australia concluded a defense agreement with the United States as well. It included upgrades to the satellite surveillance facility at Pine Gap and a ten-year extension of the American lease to it. A joint military exercise involving 17,000 U.S. and Australian personnel, the largest since 1976, was to be conducted in Queensland in 1997.[61] While no likely adversary was mentioned in the agreement, a respected Australian newspaper editorialized that ". . . the clear logic of maintaining U.S. power in the Asia-Pacific is that it balances the highly unpredictable power of China."[62]

In April 1996, Japan and the United States signed a "joint declaration on security alliance for the 21st century." While the only geographic area named in the crucial paragraph on regional tensions was the Korean peninsula, it was understood by all parties that concern with recent PRC démarches was a major factor in the rather bland language expressing concern with "unresolved territorial disputes, potential regional conflicts, and the proliferation of weapons of mass destruction and their means of delivery."[63] The commitments made therein were reiterated a year later when U.S. President Clinton met with Japanese Prime Minister Hashimoto, amid concerns from Beijing that Hashimoto had introduced "a dangerous note" by expanding the two countries' defense co-operation to include the Spratly Islands and Taiwan.[64] Chinese sources also complained that America's alliances with Japan and Australia were threats to peace in Asia aimed at encircling the PRC and motivated by a U.S. "hoping to see Asians bite Asians so it can hold its leading position in Asia-Pacific Affairs."[65]

At the end of May 1999, the Japanese government finalized guidelines for military cooperation with the United States, including aid in case of emergencies in areas surrounding Japan. Tokyo refused Beijing's demand to specifically exclude Taiwan from the scope of the guidelines. A Chinese foreign ministry spokesperson reacted sharply to Diet member Taku Yamazaki's statement that "if China liberates Taiwan by force, the move certainly will have an important impact on Japan's peace and security. For situations that have an important impact on Japan's peace and security, Japan will certainly support the United States."[66]

During the periods when the PRC was conducting missile tests and war games in and around the Taiwan Strait, the ROC government requested, and received, real-time information from U.S. satellites with regard to Chinese missile launches and troop movements; the U.S. also sent two carrier battle groups to the area. The Taipei government has also discussed participating in the Theater Missile Defense system being developed by the United States.

The Philippine Senate passed a military training agreement with the United States in late May 1999. While the pact had been under consideration for some time, passage occurred just at the time Beijing and Manila were engaged in an acrimonious dispute over a Philippine navy ship ramming and sinking a Chinese fishing boat near disputed Scarborough Shoal. Supporters of the agreement described it as Manila's "most potent weapon to deter Chinese aggression in the South China Sea."[67]

Multilateral efforts to cope with potential Chinese aggression included Vietnam's admission to membership in the Association of Southeast Asian Nations (ASEAN). Burma was also brought in, despite its leadership's poor record on human rights, with the aim of reducing Burma's international isolation and therefore excessive dependence on the PRC. Since several ASEAN states have been uncomfortable with a military role for the organization, the Asian Regional Forum (ARF) was created in 1994 to provide a mechanism for the discussion of security issues. China has become a dialogue partner of both ASEAN and ARF. Despite its initial adamance that it would discuss territorial issues only bilaterally, the PRC did agree that the Spratlys could be placed on the agenda for the next ASEAN meeting.[68] It is, of course, a long way between agreeing that an item can be placed on an agenda and the resolution of the problem.

In 1996, Japan took the initiative in creating an annual forum of top Asian defense officials to discuss outstanding security issues and regional confidence-building measures. While the PRC's representatives strongly defended their country's actions, they were also obliged to listen to other countries' sometimes blunt concerns about those actions. By 1998, representatives of twenty countries attended the forum.

The PRC's actions in the Security Council with regard to Haiti stirred a firestorm and created an unusual unanimity of opposition among Latin American and Caribbean states even including China's staunchest Latin ally, Cuba. PRC diplomats refused to comment on the coalition's statement that it was

> unacceptable that cold-war games should be played on this continent . . . this mandate must be renewed because it is what Haiti needs. Haiti has to be judged on its own merits and not because of a bilateral issue like its relations with Taiwan. It is for Haiti to decide in a sovereign fashion how to handle that.[69]

The message had been received. The PRC introduced a resolution calling for extending the UN peacekeeping force in Haiti for four more months with a maximum of 1,200 troops, as opposed to the original plan for six months and "about" 2,000 troops and police officers. The Chinese media subsequently described the agreement as indicative of the PRC's "adherence to principles and flexibility" that had been "hailed by the international community."[70] Whether this should be seen as a victory for Latin nations and an embarrassment for China, or as the PRC successfully sending a strong message to Haiti, whose peacekeeping mission it never actually intended to block, is unclear. The action did, however, create much commentary critical of China among nations that are typically not judgmental of its actions.

The same pattern appears with Guatemala. China agreed to lift its veto, but apparently only after Guatemala agreed to stop supporting the ROC's candidacy for membership in the United Nations. Since ROC diplomats have privately confided their conviction that UN membership is a lost cause which they must nonetheless pursue because it is extremely important to a highly vocal segment of public opinion in Taiwan, this is not in itself a great victory; the Guatemalan government remains close to Taipei.[71] But, as noted by a columnist for a Hong Kong magazine,

> China got what it wanted. But while its victory may taste sweet right now, there is a grave danger that in the long run China's move may turn out to be counterproductive. The rest of the world is unlikely to welcome the arrival of an emerging power that insists on getting its own way, even if it means browbeating smaller nations and weakening the UN itself.[72]

A parallel instance of the strategy of pushing an issue to the limits of tolerance and then withdrawing slightly in what the PRC claims is a compromise can be seen with regard to the PRC's conduct in nuclear nonproliferation negotiations. Stephen Ledogar, the American negotiator at the talks, termed the Chinese "quite outrageous" in purporting to present a flexible stand that was really hardline. He charged that China had made a concession to drop its insistence that peaceful nuclear explosions be permitted by the treaty with the aim of having other countries give ground on inspections. This would make it harder to verify possible Chinese violations of the treaty.[73] Ledogar imputed to China the same modus operandi that Indonesian diplomats had identified with regard to the PRC's baseline claims in the South China Sea.

A year later, in June 1997, in the face of severe international pressure, the PRC dropped its insistence on peaceful nuclear explosions, but rejected the provisions of the Comprehensive Test Ban Treaty (CTBT) for on-site inspections should suspected violations occur in signatory states. In August, Beijing and Washington reached an agreement wherein the PRC would first try to convince Pakistan to sign the treaty, and second help the U.S. to take the CTBT to the United Nations General Assembly if India also agreed to vote for it. The United States, in return, acquiesced to the PRC's demand to make it more difficult to initiate on-site inspections.[74]

As with China's willingness to have the matter of the Spratlys placed on ASEAN's agenda, it is not clear whether the PRC's participation will constitute a force for resolution of problems or provide it with a convenient forum for obstructing a solution. A leading analyst of Chinese foreign policy behavior feels that China's full compliance with the CTBT is dubious, and points out that, even if some way can be found to overcome India's unit veto, which is a prerequisite for the treaty to come into force, the PRC's participation in discussions is apt to cause as many problems as did its previous refusal to take part.[75]

Collective efforts to deal with perceived PRC expansionism were set back by the Asian currency crisis, which resulted in sharp cutbacks in defense budgets and, indirectly, caused tensions within alliance groupings. In Indonesia, violent demonstrations sparked by unemployment toppled the Suharto government and threatened to destabilize that of his successor. Beleaguered Malaysian prime minister Mahathir put deputy prime minister Anwar Ibrahim on trial for alleged crimes that included sodomy. Criticized by other members of ASEAN, he cancelled Malaysia's participation in the Five Power Defense Arrangement, essentially negating its usefulness. When Philippine president Estrada expressed sympathy for Anwar, Mahathir cancelled a defense consultation meeting that was to be held in Manila. Australia, responding to domestic criticism that its military exercises with Indonesian forces tacitly condoned human rights abuses by its members, announced that the exercises had been "deferred by mutual agreement."[76]

Doubtless encouraged by this disarray, Beijing resumed its probing. In fall 1998, the Philippines discovered that the Chinese navy was expanding the structures built on Mischief Reef in 1995, despite an earlier agreement between the two countries to take no further actions in the area. The Philippine defense minister protested a "creeping invasion," comparing the PRC's actions to a dog urinating on an area to mark its territory. President Estrada expressed his belief that Beijing had chosen this time to act so as to take advantage of his country's current weakness, saying that the matter would have to be settled through negotiations because the country could not afford to be confrontational.[77]

By mid-1999, with several countries seemingly on the way to recovery, Asian defense spending began to rise again.[78] For example, in April 1999 the Philippines reinstated the fifteen-year military modernization program it had suspended the year before due to complications attendant on the Asian currency crisis.[79]

China's Alliance System

While railing against attempts to encircle it, the PRC moved to solidify its ties with Russia, Burma, and Iran. After Russian President Boris Yeltsin's visit to Shanghai in April 1996, the two sides began speaking of their "strategic partnership," a posture reinforced by Jiang Zemin's trip to Moscow a year later. Border demarcations, troop reductions in border areas, and arms sales were agenda items, as was talk of a "long-term convergence of strategic aims."[80] The two sides share annoyance with the West, Russia because of the North Atlantic Treaty Organization (NATO)'s plans to expand eastward, and China due to pressures with regard to human rights and trade liberalization measures. The arms trade has been mutually beneficial as well; Russia and China also have a common interest in containing the Islamic fundamentalist influences that have contributed to instability in Central Asia.

Burma became an international pariah state in 1988 when the SLORC placed Aung Sang Suu Kyi under house arrest after she won the presidential election of that year; similar notoriety accrued to the PRC after its brutal suppression of unarmed civilian protesters the following year. In addition to the two governments' distaste for what they term Western notions of human rights, the relations between Beijing and Rangoon/Yangon have been reinforced by Chinese sales of military equipment to the Burmese junta and its development of roads and ports which could be commercially beneficial to both sides as well as to enhance the PRC's strategic reach. During the first half of 1997 alone, the two sides concluded military cooperation[81] and border management agreements,[82] and China contracted to construct a transport corridor linking Kunming, the capital of its Yunnan province, with Burma's capital Rangoon, leading on to the Indian Ocean.[83] China also agreed to build two sugar mills in Burma.[84] The sum total of these and similar actions upset prodemocracy forces in Burma, who saw them as strengthening the junta's position as well as facilitating a possible Chinese invasion of Burma. India, which had viewed the Indian Ocean as vital to its interests, was likewise perturbed.

China has also sold missiles to Iran, bought its oil, and participated in several infrastructure development projects including power generation reactors. In May 1997, Iranian president Hashemi Rafsanjani suggested to visiting Chinese Vice-Premier Li Lanqing that Russia, China, and Iran strengthen their mutual economic and political cooperation.[85]

Forces for Cooperation

While the above has concentrated on the sources of disagreement between China and its neighbors, there are also signs of cooperation. At the same time as the PRC and Vietnam were exchanging protest notes over the Spratlys, passenger service opened between Hanoi and Kunming;

freight service was reinstituted the preceding year after a seventeen-year hiatus.[86] Sino-Indonesian trade grew from 2.69 billion dollars in 1994 to 3.78 billion dollars in 1996; the two sides have been negotiating an agreement on avoiding double taxation.[87] Japan approved a $78 million soft loan for agricultural development in the PRC's Heilongjiang and Inner Mongolia areas.[88] Trade across the Taiwan Strait continued to expand, and an airline hijacker was repatriated. The two sides appeared to be cooperating in the search for suspects in the kidnap and murder of an ROC teenager.[89]

High level Sino-American military exchanges resumed, having been suspended since the Tiananmen incident of 1989. Although the Chinese side suspended them in June 1999 in retaliation for the U.S. bombing of the PRC embassy in Belgrade, it is believed that this represents a temporary situation.

Optimists hailed these signs of cooperation as indicative of a PRC which was evolving into a responsible international actor whose paramount need for a peaceful environment in which to pursue economic development would restrain it from military expansionism. Pessimists interpreted the same events as short-term expedients before the PRC's next phase of pressures against its neighbors. In either case, the driving force behind better relations appeared to be the desire for commercial and technological gain rather than a changed view of the international environment.

Intra-Alliance Tensions

None of the groupings—alliances may be too strong a term—discussed above is without its internal differences of opinion. Indonesian President Suharto, though worried about the PRC, cancelled his country's planned purchase of nine American-made F-16 fighter planes as well as its participation in U.S. military training programs in response to congressional criticism of his human rights policy.[90]

Moreover, though the Association of Southeast Asian Nations tries to speak with one voice internationally, the concerns of ASEAN members differ in many areas. Thailand, for example, is not a claimant to any part of the Spratly Islands. It is also mired in economic difficulties. When Bangkok asked China to purchase more of its goods, the PRC agreed to do so with the understanding that Thailand would help defend the PRC's interests internationally. In the words of Defense Minister Chi Haotian,

"China is hopeful that Thailand will help create understanding with neighboring countries."[91] The economic interests of ethnically-Chinese Thai citizens, such as those of the Charoen Phokphand conglomerate, in the PRC is another force pulling Thailand toward the PRC and away from ASEAN.[92]

There are also differences between the Philippines and Malaysia over how to deal with the Spratlys. In June 1999, Filipino defense secretary Domingo Siazon formally protested to Kuala Lumpur over Malaysia's construction on one shoal and occupation of two reefs in the disputed area.[93]

Nor is the Sino-Russian partnership without problems. Russians note that sparsely populated and mineral-rich areas of Siberia could be taken over by China's large and expanding population. This may appear unlikely to others—*The Economist* noted that sovereignty is leaking away from Moscow and accruing to Siberian local leaders rather than to Beijing[94]—but it is nonetheless believed, and is causing anxiety. Russian military leaders have also expressed concern about their country's weapons sales to the PRC, worrying that they may be arming people who may soon decide to attack them, complaining that civilian leaders are trading long-term security for short-term commercial benefits.[95]

On the Chinese side, Reuters reported friction among military leaders with the April 1997 communiqué signed between Jiang and Yeltsin. They complained that, while Jiang had supported Yeltsin's interest in opposing NATO expansion, the agreement did not advance the PRC's interests in any way; in order to boost his own standing within the Chinese leadership, he had allowed China to again become a card in the U.S.-Russian game.[96]

After a period of desuetude in 1998, Russo-China ties became closer due to a common interest in opposing U.S.-NATO behavior in Kosovo. The Chinese were concerned that the encroachment on a country's sovereignty in the name of human rights could be used as a precedent for international opposition to China with regard to assuming control of Taiwan or putting down separatist movements in Tibet and Xinjiang.

The developments described herein turn on realpolitik: they are driven by perceived national self-interest rather than ideology or shared cultural values. Huntington's clash of civilization does not apply, nor does his "west against the rest" hypothesis. Japan, a *sui generis* civilization in Huntington's categorization, cooperates with Confucian-civilization Taiwan and the Western-civilization United States against Confucian-civilization China. Buddhist-civilization Thailand cooperates with Confucian-civilization

China while carefully maintaining ties with Western-civilization America as well as Islamic-civilization Malaysia and Indonesia. Meanwhile, Confucian-civilization Vietnam has cultivated ties with Malaysia, Indonesia, and the United States to shore up its claims against fellow-Confucian civilization China.

The Future

China's recent international behavior has exhibited a fourfold pattern:

1. a strong, even extreme, assertion of China's position generally couched in the phrase "China's principled stance"
2. a willingness to make conciliatory gestures if resistance is encountered, but without conceding the substance of China's claims
3. attempts to keep other countries on the defensive through establishing structures and/or carrying out research and patrol activities in disputed areas; issuing threatening statements which are sometimes backed by military actions; threatening and sometimes using the PRC's veto power in the United Nations Security Council; and using access to the PRC's market as leverage to induce compliance with China's wishes
4. continued probing to test the limits of other nations' tolerance of its claims and behavior.

Behind this pattern is a nationalistic leadership manipulating a population to whom nationalism has strong appeal. This pattern is hardly unique to the PRC, though its diplomats have practiced it with considerable skill.

China's neighbors have responded with coping strategies. Indeed if the PRC has the goal of becoming an Asian or global hegemon, recent experience indicates that this will not come about quickly or easily. Nationalism is unlikely to diminish in the near term, and a democratic PRC may not differ greatly in its foreign policy behavior from that of the current authoritarian regime.

In fact, the advent of democracy, if it happens, may complicate the Chinese leadership's ability to control crises, as ingrained notions about the freedom to organize, to demonstrate, and to dictate policy choices to the government make it more difficult to squelch demands for policy choices vis-à-vis Japan that the leadership deems unwise: mobilized populations may demand that their government defend the nation's honor even when it may not be in the long-term interests of the nation to take the action the population demands. A legalized opposition party may seize on the leadership's perceived foreign policy weaknesses to goad it into a stronger stance or risk being turned out of power by the electorate.

The pressures faced by some of China's more democratic neighbors illustrate these potential difficulties. Nationalistic mobilized populations already exist among the PRC's fellow claimants for territory. In the Philippines, Fidel Ramos's predecessor, Corazon Aquino, regarded her country's claim to part of the Spratlys sufficiently unconvincing, and its military force sufficiently weak, that she considered abandoning the claim. Public opinion, doubtless stirred up by Aquino's political enemies, prevented her from doing it. More recently, the outcry in the Philippines following Singapore's execution of a Filipina maid convicted of strangling a fellow Filipina damaged relations between the two countries for a time; President Ramos was forced to recall his ambassador.

Other instances of mobilized populations complicating foreign policymaking in democratic states involve Japan and the ROC, respectively. In the former, Prime Minister Hashimoto was reportedly furious when, in May 1997, a group headed by an opposition party Diet member visited one of the disputed Diaoyu/Senkaku Islands and issued a provocative statement, but he could do nothing.[97] In the latter, during the "informal" Koo-Wang talks between the ROC and PRC held in Singapore in 1993, a group representing Taiwan's largest opposition party, worried that the majority party might make concessions unacceptable to them, staged a noisy demonstration outside the negotiation hall. Singaporean police removed them, but extensive media coverage made the point the demonstrators intended.

Populations mobilized by nationalism are likely to insist that disputes be resolved unequivocally in their country's favor. It is not easy for nationalists in the Philippines, Vietnam, or China to demand an international settlement in the Spratlys so that oil can flow for the benefit of all. It is also difficult to envision them demanding that their government compromise on the Diaoyu/Senkaku issue or on the matter of Taiwan's separate status to avoid bloodshed.

Though the PRC is not a democracy, already it has, partly through the efforts of its authoritarian leadership, an intensely patriotic group that is concerned that the government is not doing enough to advance China's rightful place in the world. The passionate rhetoric "China has stood up" that attended Hong Kong's reversion to the mainland, followed by unsubtle reminders to Taiwan that it is next on the list, may prove difficult to handle. The PRC leadership's decision to devote considerable attention to the commemoration of the sixtieth anniversary of the Marco Polo Bridge incident of July 7, 1937 that sparked the Sino-Japanese war, accompanied by media diatribes about the need for vigilance against revived Japanese arrogance and resurgent militance[98] may also prove unwise. So as well might the simultaneous opening of the Coastal Defense Museum, described as commemorating "the military exchanges between defending Chinese people and forces and Japanese, British, and French invading navies."[99]

Chinese leaders could easily have chosen to place major emphasis on the twenty-fifth anniversary of the normalization of Sino-Japanese relations and the benefits that a quarter-century of such relations have brought to both sides. The leadership presumably believed that the costs of not taking a strong stand in its negotiations with Japan would be greater than the dangers of reinforcing nationalistic sentiments within the Chinese population. While, in the short run, such moves may build support for the regime, they may constrain its freedom of choice, and that of any successor government, democratic or otherwise, in the future.

Party and government are in a difficult position in the PRC. The consequences of nearly two decades of economic reform strengthen the power of regions and provinces vis-à-vis the central government. Financially, for example, Beijing receives a much smaller percentage of tax revenues than before.[100] Guangdong has been able to evade government instructions on several occasions; Fujian was so resentful of the economic losses it suffered when it was the staging area for anti-Taiwan war games played in early 1996 that the central government agreed to reimburse the province's losses.[101] Rebellion and separatist sentiments in Xinjiang, Tibet, and Inner Mongolia have been increasing.[102]

Though nationalism is a useful adhesive to keep increasingly disparate provinces and regions loyal to the central leadership, it presents difficulties of its own. Empress Dowager Cixi's encouragement of extremist nationalist forces at the turn of the century led to the Boxer Rebellion and contributed to the fall of the Qing dynasty. Chiang Kai-shek's not paying enough attention to patriotic sentiment in the 1930s allowed the communist party to seize the high ground of opposition to Japan and contributed to the fall of Chiang's Kuomintang government. In fall 1996, the Shenzhen organizer of a signature campaign demanding Japan's withdrawal from the Diaoyu Islands could be ordered to call it off "to prevent an uncontrollable accident from happening because we don't have the ability to maintain order."[103] A similarly motivated movement in a democratic society might be much more difficult to control.

There is also the possibility that people able to demonstrate freely may have an agenda that is overtly patriotic but has other purposes as well, which the government may regard as more sinister. When prereversion Hong Kong protesters accused the Beijing government of being insufficiently patriotic because it did not push China's claims to the Diaoyu/Senkaku Islands assertively enough, PRC leaders suspected that they were using the anti-Japan issue as a weapon against the party in power—in this case the communist party. In Cultural Revolution terms, they were "waving the red flag in order to oppose the red flag," taking anti-Japanese actions that masked their real agenda of opposing the rule of the communist party.[104] At the same time that the party/government was instigating crowds to attack the U.S. embassy in Beijing in May 1999, in retaliation for the NATO bombing of its embassy in Belgrade, democracy activists were arrested to prevent their turning the anger of demonstrators to their own cause.[105]

How to use a mobilized population to advance its own interests in staying in power while not allowing that population to escape government control is already a problem. It is liable to become more so with greater democratization.[106] It has been tacitly assumed that a democratized China will be a force for peace and stability in the world. This is not necessarily the case.[107] A democratized China which is simultaneously a nationalistic China is apt to prove a contentious neighbor.

Notes

1. Quoted by Chen Jian. *China's Road to the Korean War: The Making of the Sino-American Confrontation*. New York: Columbia University Press, 1994, p. 10.

2. Calculated at 8.3 yuan to the U.S. dollar. Fiscal year 1999 figures in Pamela Pun, "Military Boost 'Surprisingly Low,'" *Hong Kong Standard*, March 6, 1999. Because the budgeted figure for FY 1998 was 90.99 million yuan, but 131.1 billion, was actually spent, the FY 1999 figure is apt to be higher than that budgeted. The 131.1 billion yuan figure was cited by Defense Minister Chi Haotian, quoted in "Mini-News" Column of *Cheng Ming* (Hong Kong), February 1, 1999, p. 21. For a summary of various attempts to estimate Chinese military expenditures, see June Teufel Dreyer, "State of the Field Report: Research on the Chinese Military," *AccessAsia Review*, vol.1, no. 1 (Summer 1997), pp. 5–29.

3. "How Much Does China Really Know?" *Straits Times*, May 22, 1999, via Internet.

4. Barbara Opall, "Beijing Pursues Acupuncture Warfare," *Defense News*, March 1, 1999, p. 4.

5. For example, primary school students in Beijing were told to go to bed early so that they could get up at midnight to watch the Olympic Committee's announcement from Monte Carlo, which was to be broadcast live by the central television station. A celebration party, including fireworks, had been arranged. After the announcement that Sydney had been chosen instead, the United States requested that the Chinese Foreign Ministry provide official protection for American installations in Beijing. See "Beijing Authorities Prepare for Olympic Vote," *Ming Pao* (Hong Kong), September 24, 1993, p. A/2 and "Citizens Gather After Vote," Kyodo (Tokyo), September 23, 1993, in United States National Technical Information Service, Foreign Broadcast Information Service: Volume I: China (hereafter, FBIS-CHI), September 24, 1993, pp. 1–2.

6. See, for example, Xinhua (New China News Agency; Beijing), September 25, 1993, in FBIS-CHI, September 28, 1993, pp. 6–7. Politburo member Li Tieying's official response to the International Olympic Committee was, however, polite and statesmanlike.

7. "Experts Propose Nuclear Blasts To Dig Underground Canal," Kyodo, April 20, 1996, in FBIS-CHI, April 22, 1996, p. 47.

8. Patrick Tyler, "Chinese Seek Atom Option to Fend off Asteroids," *New York Times*, April 27, 1996, p. 4.

9. Barbara Crossette, "Latin Nations at UN Insist China Change Stand on Haiti," *New York Times*, February 23, 1996, p. 5.

10. "Hopes for Lifting of Guatemala Veto," South China Morning Post (Hong Kong), January 20, 1997, via Internet; "China Undermines UN Council," *Far Eastern Economic Review,* February 6, 1997, p. 30.

11. The text of the law appears in Xinhua, February 25, 1992, in FBIS-CHI, February 28, 1992, pp. 2–3.

12. Nayan Chanda, Rigoberto Tiglao, and John McBeth, "Territorial Imperative," *Far Eastern Economic Review*, February 23, 1995, pp. 14–16.

13. John McBeth, "Oil-Rich Diet: Beijing Is Being Asked to Explain its Maritime Appetite," *Far Eastern Economic Review*, April 27, 1995.

14. Hiroyuki Sugiyama, "PRC Likely to Increase Activity in Japanese Waters," *Yomiuri Shimbun* (Tokyo), January 4, 1996, trans. in FBIS East Asia (hereafter, FBIS-EAS), January 23, 1996, pp. 7–8.

15. "Concrete Claims," *Far Eastern Economic Review* (Hong Kong), December 21, 1995, p. 14.

16. See, for example, the editorial on GMA-7 Radio-Television Arts Network (Quezon City), January 30, 1996, in FBIS-EAS, February 1, 1996, pp. 61–62. Other Filipino commentators welcomed the idea of a strong China, presuming that it would balance off U.S. dominance. See, for example, J.V. Cruz, "U.S., Taiwan Provoked the Current Crisis," *The Manila Chronicle*, March 12, 1996, p. 4, in FBIS-EAS, March 25, 1996, p. 63.

17. Stephen Wrage, "Mature Response to Chinese Moves Is Needed in Asia," *Asian Wall Street Journal Weekly*, May 8, 1995, p. 16.

18. As the reader will notice, the Philippines is an excellent example of this, with Malaysia a close second.

19. An English translation of the clarification appears in Ma Baolin, "Legislation Doesn't Mean Policy Change," *Beijing Review* (Beijing), March 30, 1992, pp. 10–11.

20. Matt Forney, Sebastian Moffett, and Gary Silverman, "Ghosts of the Past: China Tries to Keep a Lid on Diaoyu Protests," *Far Eastern Economic Review*, October 10, 1996.

21. See, for example, Bruce Gilley, Sebastian Moffett, Julian Baum, and Matt Forney, "Rocks of Contention," *Far Eastern Economic Review*, September 19, 1996, pp. 14–15; Commentator, "China Will Never Yield an Inch of Territory—Analyzing Diaoyu Islands Issue and Trends of Japanese Authorities," *Wen Wei Po* (Hong Kong), September 12, 1996, p. A2.

22. Lao Ping, "Notes From a Northern Journey: Army, Civilians Call Jiang Zemin into Account," *Cheng Ming* (Hong Kong), October 1, 1996, pp. 6–8 via Internet.

23. Staff reporter, "Attitude of Chinese Military: Not Yielding an Inch of Land," *Ming Pao* (Hong Kong), October 23, 1996, p. A6 via Internet.

24. Kyodo (Tokyo), April 18, 1997, via Internet.

25. Sugiyama, "PRC Likely to Increase Activity in Japanese Waters," pp. 7–8.

26. As well as, apparently, pre-empt South Korea from gaining a privileged place in Burma's economy. See "Tokyo Plans 4.8 Billion Yen in Loans to Burma," *Sankei Shimbun* (Tokyo), October 5, 1995, p. 1, trans. in FBIS-EAS, October 17, 1995, p. 15.

27. Agence France Presse (hereafter cited as AFP), Tokyo, "New Tokyo Governor Reinforces Animosity," *South China Morning Post*, April 15, 1999, via Internet.

28. Because the rupee was devalued, the dollar amount of the budget showed a slight decrease over 1997. See International Institute for Strategic Studies. *The Military Balance, 1998/99*. Oxford: Oxford University Press, 1998, p. 147.

29. See, for example, AFP dispatch (New Delhi), "Beijing No. 1 Threat, Says India Official," *South China Morning Post*, May 4, 1998, via Internet. Despite criticism from the opposition Congress Party, Fernandes repeated these comments on more than one occasion. At a public rally in Bombay in May 1998, he said he did not regret his previous statements, and added that China was a bigger threat to India than its traditional rival, Pakistan. Agencies, "Defence Minister Points Again to 'Biggest Threat,' " *Hong Kong Standard*, May 19, 1998, via Internet.

30. See, for example, Prem Shankar Jha, "India's Choice, and Pakistan's," *New York Times*, May 29, 1998, p. A19.

31. Ian Mackinnon, "Indian Test Fuels Arms Race," *South China Morning Post*, April 12, 1999, via Internet.

32. See *The Military Balance, 1998/99*, p. 146; Rahul Bedi, "India Denies Building Russian-Aided Missile," *South China Morning Post*, April 28, 1998, via Internet.

33. Barry Wain, "International Law Firm Hired by Hanoi Asserts Vietnam Is Entitled to Disputed Areas' Deposits," *Asian Wall Street Journal Weekly*, June 19, 1995, p. 5.

34. "Vietnam Protest at Oil Drilling Rejected," *South China Morning Post*, March 18, 1997, via Internet.

35. AFP (Huangshan, Anhui), April 17, 1997, via Internet.

36. Greg Torode, "Hanoi Anxious Over Build-Up in Spratlys," *South China Morning Post*, April 29, 1997, via Internet.

37. Merlinda Manolo, "PRC Warns, Offers Cooperation Pact in Spratlys," *Manila Standard*, June 23 1995, p. 4, in FBIS-EAS, June 27, 1995, pp. 59–60.

38. Merlinda Manolo, "Proposes Fishing Cooperation," *Manila Standard*, June 23, 1995, p. 4, in Ibid., p. 60.

39. Dario Agnote, "Reports on Planned Military Purchases, " Kyodo (Manila), August 13, 1995, in FBIS-EAS, August 14, 1995, pp. 79–80.

40. Associated Press (hereafter, AP) dispatch (Manila), "Exchange of Attachés Marks Thaw in Strained Relations," December 3, 1996, via Internet.

41. AFP (Manila), December 30, 1996, via Internet.

42. AP (Manila), December 31, 1996, via Internet.

43. AFP (Manila), February 18, 1997, via Internet.

44. AP (Manila), March 17, 1997, via Internet.

45. AFP (Manila), May 1, 1997, via Internet.

46. AFP (Manila), May 8, 1997, via Internet.

47. AFP (Thitu Island, Spratlys), May 10, 1997, via Internet.

48. AFP (Beijing), July 4, 1997, via Internet.

49. "Philippines Promises to Press on with Spratly Campaign," *Hong Kong Standard*, July 5, 1997, via Internet.

50. AFP, Manila, "Mainland Resents Portrayal as Threat," *South China Morning Post*, April 21, 1999, via Internet.

51. Antara (Jakarta), July 25, 1995, in FBIS-EAS, July 24, 1995, p. 75.

52. Ambassador Hashim Djalal, quoted in McBeth, "Oil-Rich Diet. . . ," p. 28.

53. "Questionable Claim," *Far Eastern Economic Review*, June 20, 1996, p. 12.

54. Rizal Sukma, "Indonesia Toughens China Stance," *Far Eastern Economic Review*, September 5, 1996, p. 28.

55. John McBeth, "Exercising Sovereignty: Indonesia Sends a Message from Natuna," *Far Eastern Economic Review*, September 19, 1996, p. 17.

56. Ibid.

57. "Completion of New Air Force Base Expected in December," *New Straits Times* (Kuala Lumpur), June 5, 1996, p. 9.

58. John Stackhouse, "Australia Learns Vital Lesson from Gulf War," *The Australian Financial Review* (Sydney), July 2, 1996, p. 49.

59. McBeth, "Exercising Sovereignty."

60. Ferdinandus R. Sius, "The Significance of the Republic of Indonesia-Australia Security Agreement," *Suara Perbaruan* (Jakarta), January 10, 1996, pp. 2–3, in FBIS-CHI, January 10, 1996, via Internet.

61. Craig Skehan, "Pine Gap Improvements, Exercises with U.S." *The Sydney Morning Herald*, July 27, 1996, in FBIS-EAS, July 29, 1996, pp. 105–106.

62. "Security Links with the U.S.," *The Australian Financial Review*, July 29, 1996, in FBIS-EAS, July 30, 1996, p. 99.

63. Text in Japanese, Ministry of Foreign Affairs web page, August 17, 1996.

64. Xinhua (Beijing), April 22, 1997, via Internet. The dispatch cited remarks Hashimoto allegedly made to a meeting of the political affairs investigation committee of the Japanese Liberal Democratic Party which had been quoted by a Japanese television report.

65. "U.S. Defence Alliances 'a Threat to Peace,'" *South China Morning Post*, May 27, 1997, quoting *China Daily* (Beijing), May 26, 1997, via Internet.

66. Xinhua (Beijing), English, June 25, 1999, via Internet.

67. See, for example, "Violence as U.S. Pact Wins Vote," *Hong Kong Standard*, May 25, 1999; "Estrada Dismisses Damages Demand," *South China Morning Post*, May 29, 1999, via Internet.

68. AFP (Huangshan), April 18, 1997, via Internet.

69. Crossette, "Latin Nations," p. 5.

70. "China's UN Vote on Haiti Shows 'Principles, Flexibility,'" Zhongguo xinwen she (Beijing), March 1, 1996, in FBIS-CHI, March 5, 1996, pp. 3–4.

71. Jason Blatt, "Taipei Wins Backing from Central American Allies," *South China Morning Post*, July 7, 1997, via Internet.

72. Frank Ching, "China Undermines UN Council," *Far Eastern Economic Review*, February 6, 1997, p. 30.

73. Stephen J. Ledogar, quoted in "U.S. Criticizes Beijing's Concession on Nuclear Testing as 'Outrageous,'" *Asian Wall Street Journal Weekly*, June 10, 1996, p. 20.

74. Samuel S. Kim, "China in the United Nations" in Elizabeth Economy and Michel Oksenberg, eds., *China Joins the World*. New York: Council on Foreign Affairs, 1999.

75. Ibid.

76. Reuters (Canberra), "Canberra Postpones Indonesian Military Exercises," *South China Morning Post*, October 27, 1998, via Internet.

77. AFP, "Manila Protests at Military Moves in Spratlys," *Hong Kong Standard*, November 6, 1998, via Internet; Reuters (Manila), "Navy Ordered to Seal off Spratlys," *Hong Kong Standard*, November 11, 1998, via Internet.

78. Reuters (Stockholm) "Asian Military Budgets Shoot Up as Global Average Falls in Real Terms," *South China Morning Post*, June 17, 1999, via Internet.

79. AP (Manila), "Military Assigned $1.2 Billion for Upgrade," *South China Morning Post*, April 14, 1999, via Internet.

80. "Arms Key Issue as Sino-Russian Embrace Tightens," *South China Morning Post*, April 26, 1997, via Internet; "Can a Bear Love a Dragon," *The Economist* (London), April 26, 1997, pp. 19–20, 22.

81. AFP (Hong Kong), January 23, 1997, via Internet.

82. Xinhua (Beijing), March 25, 1997, in FBIS-CHI, March 26, 1997, via Internet.

83. AFP (Hong Kong), May 6, 1997, via Internet.

84. Xinhua (Rangoon), June 24, 1997, in FBIS-CHI, June 25, 1997, via Internet.

85. AFP (Teheran), May 5, 1997, via Internet.

86. Reuters (Hanoi), April 19, 1997, via Internet.

87. Xinhua (Jakarta), July 8, 1997, via Internet.

88. Kyodo (Beijing), May 5, 1997, via Internet.

89. Central News Agency (Taipei), March 6, 1997, via Internet.

90. John McBeth, "No Meddling! Jakarta Sends Washington a Sharp Defence-Linked Message," *Far Eastern Economic Review*, June 19, 1997, pp. 16–17.

91. Quoted by Michael Vatkiotis in "Tributary Trade: Thailand's Chavalit Seals a Trade-Off with China," *Far Eastern Economic Review*, April 17, 1997, p. 19.

92. Ibid., p. 20.

93. Reuters (Manila), "Spratlys Danger Warning," *Hong Kong Standard*, June 25, 1999, via Internet.

94. "Can a Bear?," p. 21.

95. Ibid.; see also Sophie Quinn-Judge, "Common Cause: Russia and China Join Hands for Mutual Benefit," *Far Eastern Economic Review*, May 8, 1997, pp. 15–16.

96. Reuters (Beijing), May 20, 1997, via Internet.

97. Stella Lee, "Japanese Legislator's Diaoyu Landing Angers Hashimoto," *South China Morning Post*, May 6, 1997, via Internet.

98. Reuters (Beijing), July 7, 1997, via Internet.

99. Xinhua (Beijing), July 4, 1997, in FBIS-CHI, July 4, 1997, via Internet.

100. Tax income as a proportion of Gross Domestic Product (GDP) fell from 23.3 percent in 1985 to 10.3 percent in 1996. See Xu Yuegang and Xue Benbu, "Why Tax Receipts Have Declined as a Proportion of GDP," *Zhongguo Shiwu Bao*, (Beijing), April 10, 1997, in FBIS-CHI, June 26, 1997, via Internet. Despite strenuous central party/government attention to tax collection and stringent punishments meted out to those who failed to comply, central revenues barely reached 12 percent in 1997 and are apt to decline again in 1998. AFP (Shanghai), quoting Shanghai Securities News, "Poor Collection Frustrates Beijing," *South China Business Post*, November 19, 1998, via Internet.

101. Pamela Pun, "Fujian Receives Subsidies from PLA," *Hong Kong Standard*, April 11, 1996, p. 6, quoting Fujian governor Chen Mingyi. Chen refused to say how much compensation was involved.

102. See June Teufel Dreyer, "The Potential for Instability in Minority Regions," in David Shambaugh, ed., *Is China Unstable? Assessing the Factors*. Armonk, NY: M.E. Sharpe, 2000, pp.125–41

103. Staff reporters, "Beijing Said Ordering Cities to Curb Diaoyu Protests," *South China Morning Post*, October 18, 1996, via Internet.

104. Matt Forney, Sebastian Moffett, and Gary Silverman, "Ghosts of the Past: China Tries to Keep a Lid on Diaoyu Protests," *Far Eastern Economic Review*, October 10, 1996, p. 24.

105. Vivien Pik-kwan Chan, "Dissidents Fear Further Crackdown on Dissent," *South China Morning Post*, May 18, 1999.

106. President Lee Teng-hui of Taiwan argues that nationalism will hinder the mainland's democratization, since party and government use extreme nationalism to divert attention from solving the country's more pressing problems. Maubo Chang, "Nationalism Will Hinder Beijing's Democratization: ROC President," Central News Agency (Taipei), May 17, 1999, via Internet.

107. Subsequent to the production of the first draft of this chapter, an article by Fareed Zakaria described this kind of state as an "illiberal democracy." See Zakaria, "The Rise of Illiberal Democracy," *Foreign Affairs*, vol. 76, no. 6 (Fall 1997), pp. 22–43; the same point is made with regard to similar, well-established republics versus dissimilar less well-established republics by Spencer R. Weart. *Never at War: Why Democracies Will Not Fight One Another*. New Haven: Yale University Press, 1998. The classification of liberal versus illiberal and similar versus dissimilar republics, however, is likely to beg the question: belligerent states must be defined as illiberal, and republics that fight each other are dissimilar. These distinctions thus lose analytical usefulness. A cynic might be tempted to point out a subtext: since democracies and republics are inherently good and war is inherently bad, obviously no state that makes war can be a republic or a democracy. The major point, however, is that elections, freedoms of speech and press, and representative government do not immunize countries against dangerous jingoistic behavior.

PART II
A DEMOCRATIC PEACE?

Chapter 7

China's Democratization: What Difference Would It Make for U.S.-China Relations?

David Bachman

It is a widely shared belief, felt across the political spectrum, that "the single most important change, one that would, almost at a stroke, eliminate the sharpest areas of conflict between China and the United States, would be for China to follow the global trend toward democracy."[1] It is the central tenet of this chapter that this perception is wrong. Even if a democratic transition were to take place in the People's Republic of China (PRC), most areas of conflict in Sino-American relations would remain largely unaffected. Most important, at least for an intermediate period, the transition to democracy will not alleviate the danger of war. Areas of tensions, systematic misunderstandings, and differing national interests, purposes, and cultures will persist. Those who believe that democracy will substantially change the nature of U.S.-China relations conflate democracy as it is likely to be practiced in China (initially anyway)—a means of structuring and controlling political conflict—with the mythical attributes of American-style democracy or democracy as an ideal type.[2] Democracy is not likely suddenly to transform China's international interests, its economic system, Chinese nationalism, and some important domestic institutions. Indeed, the process of the demo-

cratic transition may make Chinese nationalism even more inflamma-
tory. The failure of a democratic China to conform to American expectations may in fact create a huge crisis in U.S.-China relations, as there
will no longer be any "excuse" for China not to so conform. (Similarly,
there will no longer be any excuse for American leaders not to accept
the complexity of the U.S.-China relationship.)

Obviously, China's transition to democracy is a hypothetical development, and while I share with the other authors in this volume the
belief that China can make a democratic transition, and the hope that it
will happen in the most expeditious and effective way, I am not centrally addressing current developments and forecasting them into the
future, in the ways, for example, Zhao, Pei, and Wang are. The nature of
China's potential democracy is not subject to empirical verification or
normal research methods. The same is true for the relationship between
a democratic China and the United States. What can be done is to discuss explicitly the current nature of U.S.-PRC relations and issues with
the PRC to which the United States takes exception. The sources and
reasons for these issues can then be examined. A thought exercise can
be undertaken to relate the current American critique of the PRC to the
types of changes that democracy might bring to China. Using logical
methods and comparative historical analogies, I can try to examine how
democracy might or might not affect U.S.-China ties.

Moreover, China's path to democracy can follow a number of possible roads. I shall examine five different, though not entirely mutually
exclusive, alternative paths to democracy which might have different
implications for U.S.-China relations. These paths are:

1. gradual reform and transition from below—the village democracy
   and rule of law path (similar to Pei's essay in this volume);
2. an overthrow of the regime by the people—"people power" as occurred in the Philippines and, to a somewhat lesser extent, South
   Korea;
3. gradual political reform from above led by the Chinese Communist Party (CCP);
4. a reforming coup instituting democracy; and
5. democracy as an outcome of an increasingly explicit federalist
   system.

Some forms of transition turn out to have more positive implications for U.S.-China relations than others, but none eliminate all areas of concern. The result of this analysis is an argument, particularly addressed to American political and opinion leaders, that the democratization of the PRC is not a panacea for all the problems in U.S.-China relations; for these same leaders to realize that there are courses of development for China other than democracy, and that these might be worse than the status quo; and finally that sobriety in examining U.S.-China relations is absolutely essential.

The American Critique of Contemporary China

The range of issues seen as problematic by at least some prominent Americans and a nontrivial portion of the public include the following general categories: human rights; trade and economic issues; Taiwan; the PRC's "rising power"; Beijing's "outlaw" international behavior; and "new world order" issues, especially China's environment and its effects on the global environment. The greatest or most important issue, as it is with all foreign policy, is the issue of war and peace. While others might typologize the issues somewhat differently, I believe the specific issues discussed below accurately reflect a consensus on what the issues are, no matter how they are delimited.

The following areas are contested, both within the United States and between the United States and the Chinese government. The accuracy or relative merits of different views is not important for the purposes of this essay. What is important is to record at least some of the American discourse on China, and from this critique of the PRC, imagine how a Chinese democratic transition might or might not affect behaviors in China and perhaps the discourse in the United States about China.

War and Peace

A central assumption at the heart of American foreign policy is that democracy breeds peace. It is in the U.S. national interest to promote democracy because this means the world will be more peaceful. This view is linked to Kant's ideas, and, in recent years, Michael Doyle has been its strongest promoter. (More on this below, and see the essays by Wang, Friedman, and McCormick in this volume.) In particular, the combination of the rising power syndrome with a vehemently antidemocratic regime is seen as a double threat to peace. Rising powers generate conflicts, if not wars; so too do nondemocratic regimes. Taken together, the PRC is variously portrayed as a rising Germany (either second or third reich), Japan between the wars, or a post–World War II Soviet Union.

There was, of course, no direct military conflict between the United States and the Soviet Union during the Cold War, so rising powers, even of a nondemocratic sort, do not inevitably engage in hegemonic war. But many fear (or in some cases, hope for) a new cold war with the PRC. Those fearful of the Cold War point to the costs and consequences it had on American society; those hoping for a new cold war see it as ineluctably leading to the collapse of communist power in China, and presume that democracy will replace communist power.

There are areas where U.S. and PRC national interests are in conflict, and where the range of conflict can expand as the United States might aid others who find themselves in conflict with the PRC. These areas are Taiwan, the South China Sea, and the Diaoyu/Senkaku Islands. In the latter two cases, the United States has vowed to defend the right of free passage through the South China seas, and it appears to have accepted as legitimate Japan's claims to the Senkaku. Korea is another possible area of conflict, as Beijing's defense treaty with the North still seems to be in force. PRC arms sales and proliferation of weapons of mass destruction are yet another area which might lead to a U.S.-PRC confrontation.

But these specific areas and issues are merely the surface manifestation of the deeper issue of the PRC's growing power: can Beijing be accommodated into the existing international system, or will China's rise bring about a hegemonic war (see the Kim and Nelsen chapters for further examination of this issue)? Obviously, there might be other answers to this question—a changed international system that the PRC accepts peacefully for example—but scenarios about war between the PRC and the United States are receiving mass readings, as seen in Bernstein and Munro and in Huntington.[3]

Human Rights

American (and Western and other) criticisms of the Chinese government's violation of human rights are extensive, and there is a consensus view in both official and nongovernmental sources.[4] The points of criticism include: denial of basic political, social, legal, and cultural rights—lack of religious freedom, lack of freedom of speech and press, lack of due process, discrimination against women, minorities, and the disabled;

use of torture and cruel and inhumane means of punishment; lack of freedom of assembly; controls on personal mobility; imposition of the "one child" policy and the effects of its implementation; suppression and forced assimilation of non-Han Chinese cultures, especially in Tibet, Xinjiang, and Inner Mongolia; denial of workers' rights; fear that the PRC will take away the rights of the people of Hong Kong, and so on. The violations are systemic, extensive, and in the view of the Department of State, the PRC was more successful at suppressing dissent recently than at any time since 1989, if not 1976.

Trade and Economic Issues

If anything, the list of U.S. complaints about PRC trade and economic practices is even longer than the kinds of human rights abuses in China, though length reveals little. Again, the U.S. government provides a useful summary statement of many of the issues at hand.[5] Complaints about the PRC's trade and economic system include the following:

- a huge PRC trade surplus;
- protected domestic markets and regulated foreign trade;
- lack of "national treatment" for foreign enterprises;
- lack of protection of intellectual property rights;
- diversion of imported technology to proscribed uses;
- industrial espionage;
- unreasonable demands for technology transfer;
- violation of textile quotas;
- lack of transparency in the trade regime;
- industrial policies that discriminate against foreigners;
- unreasonable standards for testing and certifying products;
- export subsidies;
- a not totally convertible currency;
- corruption affecting business operations;
- lack of developed property and labor markets for joint ventures; and
- the lack of the rule of law for handling trade and investment disputes.

Many of the complaints about Beijing's trading practices can be challenged, but there are also real grounds for concern. Many Americans are dissatisfied with aspects of the China market, but despite the perceived short-term orientation of American business, many U.S. firms are committed to the China market for the long haul. Yet, the basic fact of the trade deficit with the PRC, its growth, the projection that it will soon surpass Japan's to make it the largest surplus trader with the United States, with the PRC in contrast to Japan, not a democracy, not an ally, and not completely capitalist, means that the trade surplus is becoming politically very hard to accept.

Taiwan

There is somewhat more ambiguity about the Taiwan issue than either human rights or trade in the American political spectrum. It has been policy since the Nixon administration to see some validity to Beijing's claims to Taiwan, and to see no need to recognize the independence of Taiwan. On the other hand, the U.S. government is opposed to the use of force to resolve PRC-Republic of China on Taiwan (ROC) issues, and under U.S. law, the United States has serious commitments to provide Taiwan with defensive weapons and to view threats to Taiwan's security as grave threats to peace and stability in Asia.

In general, nonexecutive branch opinion is more positive about Taiwan, and is prepared to go further. Former House Speaker Newt Gingrich gave an all but unconditional statement of America's commitment to come to Taiwan's defense should it be attacked by the PRC when he visited the island in March 1997. For many, Taiwan's transition from a hard authoritarian state to a democracy with vibrant public debates and protests in a Chinese cultural context makes Taiwan a symbol of the types of changes that are to be hoped for and promoted in China. At the very least then, Taiwan is a card or tool to be used to reform a nondemocratic China, and as such, needs to be protected. Others, accepting Wilsonian ideals about self-determination, are willing to consider Taiwan's independence and perhaps recognition.

There is a fundamental clash of values and interests on Taiwan questions. The PRC believes that Taiwan is an integral part of China and that principle is nonnegotiable. A growing segment on Taiwan does not accept the legal and the ethnic dimensions of the PRC's claims. Given ties and commitments to both sides, the United States is stuck in the middle, admiring Taiwan's achievements (and U.S.-Taiwan economic interactions, where U.S. exports to Taiwan are at least 150 percent of U.S. exports to the PRC), but accepting of Beijing's importance, though hoping that the PRC will look more and more like Taiwan over time.

The PRC's Rising Power

Throughout the past twenty or so years, China's economy has been the world's fastest growing. (Rapid growth of the Chinese economy is a much longer term phenomenon than a simple Mao China/Post- Mao China dichotomy.[6]) This has led to projections of the PRC as the world's largest economy at some date in the relatively near future. While some have seen this growth as a tremendously positive development,[7] others see the PRC's growth as particularly threatening, especially if a rising China is not or will not commit to upholding democratic values and international norms (see Kim's and McCormick's chapters and Friedman's on Sino-Japanese tensions).[8] Scholars of international relations note that there is often extensive international conflict when a rising power, perhaps desirous of becoming a hegemonic power, runs up against the existing hegemonic and status quo power.

For whatever reason, there is considerable concern within the United States about many elements of Beijing's rapid economic advance. The PRC's official military budget has grown at double-digit rates since 1989. The Chinese government continues to use force or threats of the use of force as part of its foreign policy. The PRC is modernizing its military doctrine and purchasing advanced military equipment to increase its ability to project power. Beijing's claim to territory—whether Taiwan or the South China Sea—brings it into conflict with other states, and threatens or at least calls into question the freedom of the seas to Japan and other places deemed vital to U.S. national interests. The PRC is trying to procure technology by whatever means to enhance its capacities. The PRC's neighbors have in the past feared that their overseas Chinese populations may not be entirely loyal to their place of residence, and fear the large influx of Chinese traders and others who cross their borders for various reasons.

That the PRC's capabilities will increase as it grows is hardly surprising. Given China's huge population, it is also not surprising that in aggregate terms, China ranks very high on many gross economic dimensions. In many ways, the PRC's rising power is an inevitable result of economic growth. What is under dispute and what is seen as frightening are the ends to which this rising power might be put, and what the PRC's "real" intentions are for the present and the future. Pessimists, realists, "orientalists," racists, and others all see the potential for the bad or the worst—the need for a new cold war to contain or rollback Beijing's rise, or a hegemonic war.

Outlaw International Behavior

The PRC is accused of acting in ways that are seen as harmful to U.S. international interests, particularly by maintaining reasonably close relations with states considered by the United States to be "outlaw" regimes. The accusations include the sale of ballistic missiles to hostile regimes (and violation of the Missile Technology Control Regime), proliferation of weapons of mass destruction, illegal interference in American politics through campaign contributions, buying weapons that destabilize the Asian and Middle East power balance, and selling weapons that destabilize regions or strengthen regimes seen by the United States as hostile. Indeed, in 1997, the CIA called the PRC probably the world's largest supplier of technology related to weapons of mass destruction.[9] In addition, accusations that Beijing or its intermediaries may have provided campaign contributions to the Democratic Party and President Clinton in 1996 are also seen as a different kind of outlaw behavior.

New World Order Issues

International transformation and the ending of the Cold War, coupled with reform in China and economic dynamism, have led to increasing discussions involving the PRC and emerging issues associated with a "new world order." Whether in terms of environmental issues, broader global common questions, flows of illegal drugs, activities of international criminal organizations, illegal flows of migrants, and so on, the PRC is seen as an increasingly important actor, victim, accomplice, or source of problems. Without Beijing's cooperation, these issues cannot be satisfactorily addressed. In some cases, PRC cooperation has been forthcoming, if less than totally effective (illegal emigration). In other cases, Beijing acknowledges the problem, but its response is unsatisfactory (and acknowledged as such domestically)—in regard to environmental issues. In this last example, given China's size, growth, reliance on coal as the major source of energy, and so forth, the PRC may soon be the world's largest source of greenhouse and ozone-depleting gases, making any serious attempt to deal with global warming and other atmospheric issues dependent on Beijing's cooperation. The PRC will adopt pollution control policies and measures (especially if their implementation is subsidized by outsiders, but it will not fundamentally alter its pattern of growth for the sake of the international environment or its own environment).

The United States has complaints with all other countries, and some of the categories of issues mentioned above appear in American complaints about many other states. They reflect some of the to-oing and fro-ing of diplomacy and American ideals, values, and ideology about the way the world should work. But while many areas of dispute are manageable, it is also true that probably no other country has all these problems as severely as does the PRC (at least in American eyes), and given China's population and growth, no other country's behavior can be construed to be as potentially hostile and aggressive as the PRC's.

Democracy and U.S. Complaints

How and why would democracy affect these issues? Part of the answer would depend on how Chinese democracy is imagined. I would anticipate that a Chinese democracy would confront the following basic issues and have the following characteristics: (1) it would have a fundamental problem with its authority and especially with its power; (2) it would be nationalistic; (3) it would be committed to rapid economic development; (4) there would be a proliferation of political parties, and political parties would be factionally based; (5) the bureaucracy would remain largely unaffected by a democratic transition; and (6) social control and order would decline.[10]

While an actual transition would have additional specific dimensions, let me first justify these points and think through what they might mean for U.S.-China relations.

The new regime would have a problem with authority and especially with power. It is conceivable to imagine a broadly popular moderate democratic regime coming into being through a grand state-societal compact, and thus it might have great authority. But it is far from clear that this authority will automatically translate into effective government capacity and the requisite state power. My conclusion here grows out of the current weakness of the existing regime, its lack of revenue, and a natural testing of the limits of power of the new regime by powerful interests, groups, regions, and individuals which/who have emerged during the years of reform. Will the successor to the People's Liberation Army (PLA) respond to the command of potential noncommunist civilian leaders? Will Guangdong be more responsive to a new democratic regime? Will the banking system or taxation system actually become autonomous? Many other questions of a similar nature might be asked. My answer is that the creating of government capacity for the new regime will be a long-term process, and certainly not one that is unilinear. Moreover, actual democratic politics may further weaken the power of the state. Work in progress by Tun-jen Cheng, Yun-han Chu, and others suggest that the new democracies in Taiwan and South Korea pursued expansionary fiscal policies without raising taxes.[11] Jack Snyder argues that nationalism can become more virulent and aggressive during the process of democratization, as less than fully free and comprehensive marketplaces for ideas have emerged in places like Germany before and after World War I.[12] The issue of state enterprise reform will bedevil a Chinese democracy, even if it is able to carry out a "big bang" transition for the remaining nonmarketized elements of China's economy.

The central weakness of a Chinese democratic regime is likely to be the issue of the rule of law. It is assumed by many in the United States and elsewhere that either the rule of law can be rather easily constructed in China, or that a democratic regime can bring about the rule of law rapidly.[13] Such a view is naïve. The institutionalization of the rule of law requires many things: a complete set of laws; trained legal personnel capable of interpreting the laws correctly and carrying out their duties according to law; institutions that carry out the will of courts; and most important it requires broad societal and elite acceptance of the primacy of law over other sources of the regulation of human behavior. As Pei's essay points out, there has been significant progress in some of these areas over the last several years. But I am particularly skeptical about progress in the last area—social acceptance of the primacy of law—even though many Chinese recognize its importance. To paraphrase Durkheim about the "noncontractural basis of contracts,"[14] the nonlegal bases for the rule of law have to be created within Chinese society. In short, attitudes and values about the primacy and legitimacy of universal legal principles will have to be embedded within popular consciousness, for there is no true rule of law when external enforcement of the law is the principal aspect of law. The transition from patrimonial sources of authority to rational legal forms is a profound social and cultural change that will take time and effort, and the prospects for success are less than certain.[15] Nowhere has that transition been instantaneous. Until there is the rule of law in China, the Chinese government's ability to comply with World Trade Organization (WTO) requirements, to give one example, is problematic. Without the rule of law in China, there is no rational-legal authority, suggesting a weak democratic regime.

China will remain nationalistic under democratic rule. Partly this is because the rise of nationalism has been one of the great historical trends in modern Chinese history, and there is no compelling reason why this should stop. Chinese ideas about the historical boundaries of "China" are reasonably fixed. Politically it would be extremely difficult for leaders to make territorial deals that sacrifice areas widely conceived of as belonging to "China," such as Taiwan and Tibet, and it is easy to imagine that the "nationalist card" would be used against them, as Zhao suggests it already is in his essay. Democratic rule (as authoritarian rule) can be and often is very demagogic about nationalist issues. Given the crisis of values in today's Chinese society undergoing rapid change (which an actually existing Chinese democracy is probably incapable of addressing), nationalism and perhaps xenophobia are convenient substitutes. Assuming also that the transition to democracy does not tear what was the PLA apart, it will remain a very powerful actor in Chinese politics, and a champion of Chinese nationalism.

This is not to say that there is one "Chinese nationalism." The contents of Chinese nationalism have been deeply contested over the past hundred or so years, and given the diminishing threat to China's security over the past fifteen years, the intensity of the competition to try to define Chinese nationalism has increased. A democratic China with a dominant nationalist ideology is not necessarily a belligerent or aggressive China. But I find it unlikely that any kind of democratic Chinese nationalist regime could easily continence an independent Tibet or Taiwan, or easily give up claims to the Diaoyu Islands.[16]

A Chinese democracy would be as committed to rapid economic growth as is the current regime. Economic growth usually contributes to government revenues, provides benefits that can be distributed for political support, and furthers the nationalist agenda. It can provide the foundation for performance-based legitimacy. Declining economic growth will lead to political difficulties for incumbents, and to broader problems of consolidation.

Given the lack of a widely known potential opposition leader to the heads of the CCP, division within opposition movements both in China and abroad, and other cleavages, it is unlikely that a democratic China will have only two or three major parties. Obviously, the voting system will have some effect on the formation of parties and the nature of the party system, as will the way the legislature would be constituted. But politics in China, in Taiwan and Hong Kong, and among Chinese émigrés abroad suggest that personalistic parties or faction-based parties are the most likely result of democratization in China, at least in the short run. Indeed, it is the "sheet of loose sand" view of Chinese political life, which Sun Yat-sen railed against in the early part of the twentieth century that has caused Lee Kuan Yew and his colleagues in Singapore to prevent real democratization there.

One may take exception to the ways factional models of the CCP have been codified; no one would deny that clientalistic ties and personality have shaped important aspects of intra-CCP politics in Mao and Deng's time. As the power of the top leader diminishes by political generation, so too does the top leader's ability to control or curtail clientalism and factionalism.

On Taiwan, for comparison, there has not been a huge proliferation of parties per se (though there have indeed been splits), but party discipline is weak in all parties in the legislature. Personal rivalries and factions have dominated intra-KMT politics, and the DPP's weak showing in the 1996 presidential election was partly attributed to splits in that party as well. In Hong Kong, the advent of regionwide elections led to a proliferation of political groupings and parties, and even the most popular parties have very small numbers of party members. It is important to note that the key issues in Taiwan and Hong Kong politics are more sharply drawn and fewer than there are likely to be in a postcommunist China. The postcommunist states of Europe have also seen at least an initial burst in party formation, though there has been some consolidation and merging of parties over subsequent national elections. Finally, the inability of Chinese émigrés to form an effective united front in their opposition activities in the United States and Europe is a warning of what might happen on a much broader scale in a democratic China. If a highly educated group of refugees with many common views on Chinese politics cannot work in a relatively unified way, what happens when politics becomes open and issues less sharp?[17]

The bureaucracy would be unaffected in important ways. The most basic reason is that there is not a large pool of people with the requisite skills and learning available to replace large portions of the existing bureaucratic apparatus. It may be that a large portion of the existing apparatus would not be needed in a democratic China. On the other hand, the growth of the market in China has stimulated the growth of the size of the cadre corps.[18]

Again, the record elsewhere in East Asia is instructive. Throughout East Asia, whether Japan, South Korea, Taiwan, or Hong Kong, strong relatively or highly autonomous bureaucratic administrations have shaped and guided state affairs despite the activities of their respective legislatures. Certainly China's current bureaucracy is nowhere nearly as qualified as the civil service in Japan, etc. Nonetheless, given the likely proliferation of political parties and factions and China's size, it is hard to imagine the legislature providing much careful oversight of administrative affairs in a democratic China.

Of particular salience is the judiciary and public security forces. As is well known, the number of lawyers and trained jurists in China is very small, and the qualifications for becoming a lawyer are rather perfunctory (a college graduate can become a lawyer after an intensive summer training program). Who can replace the existing legal personnel, many of whom are deeply linked to the CCP (all judges are nomenklatura appointees)? The public security agencies may be sufficiently powerful to negotiate an amnesty and a very limited change of personnel, as in Russia where successors to the KGB remain close to the center of power, with minimal personnel turnover. Moreover, it is not clear that the types of people who would want to replace the existing police forces would necessarily be any better in terms of defending and protecting rights. (Similarly, which college-educated youth would want to become officials of whatever task or rank in rural areas?)

Over time, these constraints would lessen. The workings of a free press would help expose the worst abuses and encourage greater democratization of the state apparatus of a democratizing China. Education would supply a growing cohort of educated people to staff the bureaucracy with people not closely tied to the CCP regime. Many local notables may desire to supplant CCP leaders in the rural areas. Moreover, many CCP cadres in the local state corporatist mode may be quite happy to stay in power, with the support of their communities. But will such people have the power and ability to bring about national integration in new ways? If they are able to do so, I believe it will again be a long-term process, not easily achieved.

Finally, social control and order would decline. This has been the record everywhere in postcommunist regimes, and there is no reason why China would be any different. Indeed, the decline of social order is a fact of life in China today, and a source of no little dissatisfaction with the regime. Given the uncertainty about power and authority which the new regime would face, it is hard to argue that it could deal better with social order than did the CCP. It might be suggested that during the Beijing Spring of 1989, social order actually improved in Beijing, and therefore, democracy writ large would bring about a reduction of social problems. I believe that the Beijing Spring was exceptional in terms of social order because it was exceptional politically. An ongoing democratic regime would not draw the focus and commitment that were characteristic of Beijing in 1989.

If these assumptions about the nature of a democratic China are correct, what implications do they have for U.S.-China relations in the event of such a transition? How would a democratic China deal with U.S. complaints and fears about war and peace, human rights, international trade issues, Taiwan, China's rising power, outlaw international behavior, and new world order issues?

The growing conventional wisdom is that democracies do not go to war against each other, or in more extreme form, democracies do not initiate wars. However, these views have recently been challenged by Edward Mansfield and Jack Snyder.[19] As they note, "virtually every great power has gone on the warpath during the initial phase of its entry into the era of mass politics." The propensity of democratizing regimes to be involved in war is the highest in their statistical analyses, and the effects of democratization on war last at least ten years after the onset of the transition to democracy. In short, one fundamental conclusion to draw from this research is that China's transition to democracy will not guarantee the democratic peace. Thus, in contrast with Friedman's essay in this section, I am skeptical that the benefits of the democratic peace will accrue to the world in the short run, if and when China makes a transition to democracy.

This is not to say that democratization or democracy itself causes war. Rather an incompletely consolidated democracy faces challenges from within from antidemocratic (former) elites and often from external sources which may be hostile to a democratic transition. War results because, in many cases, domestic and external sources of power are unreconciled to democracy, and domestic opponents of democratization use the structural opportunities of democratic processes to pursue antidemocratic ends. However, external challengers to democratization may no longer be as important as they once were, when democratic governments were a minority of all states. With a majority of all states now democratizing if not fully democratic, and with the exception of the PRC, no great power is nondemocratic, it is unclear what external source could or would oppose democratization in China.

What this means for a democratizing China is unclear. Once China's democracy is consolidated, arguments about the democratic peace should apply to China. But when new democratic regimes become consolidated is not easy to determine until well after the fact. But until consolidation has taken place, Mansfield and Snyder warn, there is good reason to believe that any democratizing great power will have a greater war prone-ness than other types of regimes. In short, the mere coming into exist-ence of a China with a democratic constitution and nascent democratic institutions does not insure the democratic peace.

It is likely that democracy will improve China's human rights record, but less so than many might believe. Certainly there would be less arbi-trary persecution, and, by definition, most basic political rights would exist in law (whether they would be protected is another question). The one-child family policy and formal restrictions on migration would likely end, but the latter might be seen as contributing to a further deteriora-tion of social order and the demand for "something to be done." But, as suggested above, the rule of law is far from guaranteed. Would the idea of the presumption of innocence take hold? Would the deterioration of social order lead to crackdowns on crime? Would courts protect the rights of the accused? Would court judgments be executed by other agencies?

It is also unlikely that a democratic China would fundamentally change its view of Tibet, Xinjiang, Inner Mongolia, and probably Taiwan as integral elements of China. A democratic China may treat these areas somewhat better and there might actually be some real autonomy in these areas. It is conceivable that a democratic Chinese government might accept a federalist confederation, but one that acknowledges in some vague way sovereignty by the Chinese regime, presumably based in Beijing. But a democratic China would still be a majority Han Chinese state, and Han chauvinism as well as nationalism would suggest that there would be little sympathy for Tibetan or any other form of identity and independence from China.

On balance, there would be significant improvement in the human rights of the Chinese people under democratic rule, but the improve-ment would not be total. Human rights activists would still have grounds for complaint. Cultural attitudes—of male chauvinism, of Han chauvin-ism, of denigration of the handicapped, of presumption of guilt of those arrested, among others—are likely to persist. Democracy provides the potential to address these issues through open politics, but many of these prejudices are held by a large majority, and it is not clear that an attack on them would be a successful strategy in the political marketplace. A strong judicial system might be able to protect rights, but a strong court system is more common in the United States and Europe than it is in Asia, and only the United States has the kind of judicial review that is so forthright in checking abuses of power by electoral majorities or strong democratic leaders.

Whether trade and other economic issues would be more easily solved between a democratic China and the United States than is currently the case depends on whether a democratic China tries to bring about a rapid complete transition to capitalism. One thing is sure, China's trade surplus will remain large. Given the large absolute size of the disparity ($52 billion of Chinese exports to the United States versus $12 billion of American exports to China in 1996, and growing larger in 1997, 1998, and 1999) and realistic expectations about the growth of trade on both sides, it is unlikely that the deficit would decline dramatically. Moreover, China's low labor cost comparative advantage is not going to go away anytime soon, while it is not clear that per capita income in China will grow rapidly enough to greatly increase the demand for American products.

It is not clear that on other trade issues a democratic China would be more forthcoming than the current regime. There are political reasons to believe that postcommunist China will protect its domestic markets and industries. As long as nationalism and a sense of destiny persist, the government will protect high technology defense-related industries. Indeed, its effective protection of these sectors may grow. A new regime may be even less able to enforce textile quotas (which are due to be phased out under the WTO by the end of 2004 anyway) or intellectual property rights. Could a new Chinese regime actually enforce "national treatment" for foreign companies?

The PRC and a postcommunist China will differ in important ways from the developmental states of East Asia. But it is not unlikely that a democratic China will resist market opening pressures from the United States, as have Japan, Taiwan, and South Korea, and the results of the Asian financial crisis are likely to reinforce caution on the part of the current and probably future Chinese regimes about reliance and vulnerability to international capital markets. This is not to say that issues cannot be resolved over time, in an ad hoc way, but the pattern of confrontation, threats of 301 actions, and other patterns of U.S.-China interactions on trade issues are likely to persist across a regime change. Even a Chinese entry into the WTO that seems to concede to almost all important U.S. demands will not be implemented smoothly, if only because of problems with the lack of rule of law.

If China does undertake a "big bang" to complete its economic transition, then that China would have many fewer trade disputes with the United States. That does not mean that the United States would be all that well positioned to take advantage of the China market, given limited funding for exports and doubts about the continued existence of the Export-Import Bank, and so on. But a big bang that allowed China to join the WTO is probably suicidal for a Chinese democracy, as most domestic heavy industry and state-owned enterprises would be all but wiped out and tens of millions would lose their jobs.[20]

It is likely that a democratic China would offer Taiwan better and more credible terms on reunification. But a democratic China would find it hard to accept Taiwan independence (how it would make its views on independence credible would be a major problem for the new regime). Bernstein and Munro (and many others) assume that Taiwan would go along with reunification with a democratic China.[21] This may be wishful thinking. My sense is that Taiwanese identity is now so strongly established on the island that there is almost no conceivable arrangement that would win majority approval from the people of Taiwan on reunification with China. But a Taiwan reluctant to negotiate with a democratic China may risk losing U.S. support, leaving Taiwan isolated.

Thus projecting how the Taiwan issue would play out were China to democratize is difficult, and could go in several directions, including armed conflict. It would be a mistake to assume that democracy for China will ensure peaceful reunification. But it would also be a mistake to assume that there would not be peaceful reunification.

It is not clear that Chinese democracy would end concerns about the rise of China. The optimists would point to the Kantian view, as discussed in this volume by Friedman and McCormick.[22] It is clear that there is no reason to believe that China's democratization will stop the rise of Chinese power. (The wag's view that the 102 countries that have MacDonald's franchises have never gone to war with each other may suggest that the causal mechanism in the Doyle view may need some further specification.) China, (with Russia) bordering on more states than any other, will continue to modernize its military. It will seek to increase its technological capabilities, whether it is democratic or authoritarian. It will see itself having a special place in the world and especially in Asia that may fundamentally conflict with the United States's image of its role in Asia. It is unlikely that a China of any political stripe will be fully committed to open international institutions that reached their apogee at Bretton Woods and with the UN Charter (see Kim's and Dreyer's chapters).

An often unstated element of concern about China's rise is apparently racism. This may take other names: Huntington's "civilizations"; those who deliberately magnify a "China threat" such as California Congressman Dana Rohrabacher, Senator Jesse Helms, the Cox Commission; or a view in the corridors of power in Washington, D.C. that sees very few Asian-Americans in said corridors—"Yale, male, and pale"— that carries over into the world outside the United States.[23]

If the projections are borne out, China will be one of the two great powers at some point in the twenty-first century, and many predict China will be the greatest of the powers in the not-too-distant future. In the twenty-first century, military power may well be bipolar, and arguably the say of nonwhite males in setting the terms for world order will be greater than at any point since the heyday of the Mongols. Asians— nonwhites—coming to a leading position in the international system is deeply troubling to many (whites), who in true orientalist fashion project their hopes and fears onto China's rise in ways that have been much less common with the rise of other powers, especially those ruled by whites. Thus it seems to me that the statements of Lee Kuan Yew or Mahathir Mohamad, or of those who argue that Japan or China can say no, draw particular opprobrium in the Western media. While indeed a number of the things the people mentioned above said seem silly, wrong, and yes, racist (as indeed they are in some cases) to many Americans, the point that they are reacting against a world order that they find uncomfortable and overbearing, at least in part because they and their countrymen played no role in its creation, is usually missed.

The rise of a PRC that can appear to thumb its nose at U.S. sanctions, that appears to make U.S. companies make concessions to beat out international competitors, that will not apologize for its actions on June 4, 1989, and that continues to grow strong, all are deeply troubling to many. This is seen in popular literature and movies, where the PRC and its agents, or in some cases, China, are the villains. It is a short step, glossed over in many contemporary movies, to go from castigating and attacking the PRC to coloring the Chinese with the same brush. Truly the rise of China is seen as posing the threat of an alien order (which is one of the reasons the United States and Britain found the Hong Kong transition so hard to accept).

A transition to democracy may not have a decisive effect on outlaw international behavior by China. A great deal of the way this issue is handled would depend on the practical politics associated with such a transition. The major issues that would need to be clarified include the role, power, and autonomy of the successor to the PLA; the political power of the military industrial complex; and the economic policies and economic strength of the new regime. If the PLA and the military industrial complex remain relatively strong politically, and the economic health of China declines, then continued transfers of technologies associated with weapons of mass destruction will continue. If the PLA breaks up after or during a transition, if the reform of state-owned enterprises continues and gradually accelerates, and if the economy remains buoyant, then prospects for decreasing such sales and transfers increase. My view is that the PLA will likely remain a powerful interest in Chinese society after the transition; that any Chinese government would have an interest in seeing to the modernization of and profitability of the military industrial complex; and that the economy would have to be very robust indeed, if the regime was prepared to forgo foreign sales of any sort, particularly to states that share some strategic interests with China or that can supply China's growing petroleum needs.

Finally, it is not clear that a democratic China would be all that willing to do more than the current regime on new world order issues. A democratic China might do more to fight pollution, but in terms of domestic Chinese politics, water pollution problems may be a more likely target for government action in the short run than air pollution would be. Of course air pollution in all its ramifications is a more "common" issue than is water pollution. A democratic China would share with the United States a desire to attack the international drug trade, but it is unclear that a democratic China would be any more effective at it than either the current Chinese regime or the American democratic regime. To the extent that a democratic transition further weakens government capacity and social order in China, illegal emigration, drug smuggling, and other issues related to transborder flows through China might all worsen.

Thus, in general terms, the United States would see a democratic China performing better in some areas than is the case now, but the improvements would not be uniform across all issues. In a number of cases, there might not be any changes at all or actual deterioration; perhaps most ominously, the statistical chances for armed conflict might increase, though few Americans are likely to accept this. In other cases, the results might be highly contingent on how the actual transition takes place. But it is clear that the PRC's transition to democracy is not a panacea for all the issues in the Sino-American relationship. But might the type of transition make a difference?

Types of Transitions and Sino-American Relations

We imagine five different paths to a Chinese democracy. There might be a gradual transition from below, relying on the spread of local institutions of democracy, use of the legal system, and so on as one type.[24] Another transition from below would be more in keeping with a repeat of either Tiananmen 1976 or Tiananmen 1989. A mass protest might lead to either a popular takeover of the government or the regime's collapse. Three scenarios might be imagined for transition from above: gradual state-led transition by a reforming leadership; a coup that replaces ineffective and/or conservative leaders with a new leadership that promotes rapid democratization, or democratization as the outcome of an increasingly regularized federalist economic system. Obviously, some of these scenarios might work in conjunction. It is also conceivable that a mass uprising from below could follow after a period of gradual reform from above. Nonetheless, I will treat each as an ideal type and see what the characteristics of each type of transition might be and what implications it might have for Sino-American relations. It remains important to remember that this does not exhaust the types of ways that China might become democratic (though the most likely to me) and that democracy is not an inevitable outcome for regime change at least in the short and medium term.

Gradual Transition from Below

This type of transition would, like the others, have both advantages and disadvantages to the stability of democracy in China, but on the whole, a gradual transition of whatever sort is preferable to abrupt transitions. (See also Minxin Pei's contribution to this volume.) The gradual extension of local elections would help to inculcate participatory norms and at least partially transform political culture.[25] It would provide time for more Chinese to obtain legal and other educational credentials necessary to make a democracy practicable. But it would probably not allow for the national aggregation of interests and nationwide parties until the very last stages of the transition. This makes coherent electoral politics less likely; it implies that the constitutional construction of post-communist China would reinforce the province as the basis of cleavages, and a gradual transition of this sort might reinforce localism. The PLA would probably survive as a relatively unified institution and constrain the actions of the civilian leadership, who would have little contact with the PLA leadership until the civilians were close to coming to power. One can easily imagine a Chinese democracy of this sort looking quite a bit like Thailand, with numerous political parties, a key role for the military in politics, and shifting, unstable coalitions.

Rapid Takeover from Below, or Tiananmen III

Here, the PLA would either be fractionated by the protests or it would join with the people. Without at least the tacit support of the military, the people would be unable to topple the CCP. The real issues here are who would lead China and how could authority be recreated if the party fell abruptly. It is possible that the mass movement would find a champion within the party who would become the leader of the fledgling Chinese democracy—a Chinese Yeltsin perhaps (though the Yeltsin years are not all that positive an example). Afterall, in 1976, had the protestors prevailed, Deng Xiaoping would likely have come to power, and Zhao Ziyang would likely have come to power in 1989. It is impossible to predict who would be the leader(s) of the popular movement that would overthrow the regime. Given the precedents of 1976 and 1989, whoever the protestors were who brought down the regime, they would not be well known, they would be young, their leaders would be well educated, and the protestors would have a primarily urban constituency. Unless one strong leader emerged from the movement that overthrew the party, China likely would face several years of intense political infighting as effective institutions and leaders tried to prove themselves in the course of elections and actual democratic politics. Even a former party leader coming to the fore would likely be a transitional figure, as he would find it hard to ride the tides of political change. No current CCP leaders combine relative youth with palpable democratic credentials to be anything but a transitional figure in a rapid mass takeover of the political system.

Gradual Reform from Above

Some prominent observers see gradual reform emerging from above. Younger, better educated, more sophisticated leaders are inclined to open the political system, and are reasonably confident about their holding on to power with competitive elections.[26] The return of Hong Kong to Chinese sovereignty may set precedents relevant for Guangdong, Shanghai, and elsewhere in China that may encourage gradual reform.

Gradual reform from above would be a difficult political process to manage. It invites opposition from anti-economic reform conservatives within the regime and more democratically or radically inclined members of society. But should it work, it has many advantages. It provides for general stability. It does not create a further erosion of authority, and may contribute to some limited expansion of authority for the regime. But it also means that most leaders will be members of the CCP; the leadership of the PLA is likely to be unchanged, as would the other agents of coercion. It is not fully clear how the rule of law would emerge in such a transition. The bureaucracy would be largely unchanged and the party's commitment to democracy would always be subject to question until it was voted out of office. How a national opposition and political parties would form, what access to the media they would have, and other critical issues are all unclear. The relevant historical case here is Taiwan, but without the issue of independence to define parties, coherence for an opposition is even less possible in China than it is in Taiwan, and thus gives the CCP great institutional advantages in the short run.

Radical Reform from Above

In this scenario, some party leaders, whether civilian or military, come to power and rapidly push a transformation of the Chinese political system with early national elections and direct election of China's leadership. Unless there was consensus within the CCP on this policy, this form of transition is probably the most destabilizing transition China could make. Some members of the CCP would undoubtedly resist the potential loss of their power. How would the reforming leadership bring about compliance with its edicts? Again, how could effective political parties arise to contest national elections? Would the commitment of radical reformers to democracy be perceived as credible? Is such a reform likely to lead to a replay of Yuan Shikai and the subsequent period of national disintegration? The Meiji restoration is the best case historical model here, with Portugal after 1974 perhaps a more typical example.

Fiscal Federalism Leading to Political Federalism

Arguably, this is a variation on the theme of gradual reform from above, but this scenario need not have a long-term time frame. It has been argued that China is already characterized by fiscal federalism, though this has not been codified constitutionally or even in many regulations and statutes.[27] It is not all that farfetched an idea that out of a more or less well understood agreement about central and provincial responsibilities toward the economy, a more explicit political pact might emerge that specifies central and provincial political responsibilities. Such an arrangement would bear a distinct resemblance to the Magna Carta that was the beginning of a democratic evolution in the West, an evolution that many see as the best or the only true path toward democracy. It would mark an institutional division of labor and presumably a check and balance system that might make China a political system with multiple centers of legitimate political power.

While sharing many of the advantages of the gradual reform from above scenario, this scenario has some distinct problems attached to it. First, the result of a federalist China, at least in the immediate term, is not necessarily a democracy. It would mark an important milestone of Chinese constitutional development that can contribute to democratization, but it is not yet equivalent to democracy. Second, given the relative strength of the provinces vis-à-vis the center, Chinese federalism might resemble the United States under the Articles of Confederation (or one country, 31 or 32 systems) rather than the United States under the Constitution of 1787. Even in federalist systems with the rule of law, there is constant jockeying for power between the center and the constituent units. Without a strong commitment to a shared understanding of and commitment to make federalism work, federalism will lead to political crises, not to a smooth system of rule. There are good reasons to believe that the center's fiscal strength is insufficient for the provision of key public goods, and key national constituencies like the military and the military industrial complex will demand more spending, almost all of which will come from the center. In short, Chinese federalism is likely to be unstable.

How are these various types of transition likely to influence U.S.-China ties? Each of the types of transitions would involve different kinds of tradeoffs. U.S. commentators and much of the public might not see a transition as genuine until the CCP is out of power, and pushed out of power rapidly. Would Americans accept a national election in China won by the CCP as really reflecting Chinese popular opinion? Yet, a rapid transition is much more potentially destabilizing than a gradual transition. Many more areas of authority come under attack, and who exercises authority and by what means are much more problematic than when the transition is more gradual. A rapid transition, whether from above or below, would have a positive effect on the human rights issue, at least at the rhetorical level. But it would remain unclear whether rights would be protected, or whether there would be any actual change in behavior. To the extent that extensive disorder ensues from a rapid transition, then arguably, human rights in China would deteriorate.

Through a rapid transition, the Taiwan issue would not lose its rhetorical salience, but with great questions about China's constitutional development left to be decided, China might not be in much of a position to do anything, at least until democracy was institutionalized. Or, if there was a superficial calm to the transition, democratic rulers in China, as a stratagem to mobilize nationalist support that would appeal to many elites, old and new, might pressure Taiwan for rapid talks and progress on reunification. On trade issues, it is hard to see a rapid transition having much immediate positive effect. With authority uncertain, actors in China might see how much they can get away with. This may mean more U.S. imports, but it also may mean even more exports, more corruption, and so on.

On the rise of China and outlaw international behavior, if the PLA were fractured in the transition, this might lessen some of the international behaviors the United States finds objectionable, and delay the modernization of the PLA's successor. On the other hand, with unclear political authority, bureaucracies and enterprises may continue to see how far they can go, and the export market, even for items related to weapons of mass destruction, as in democratizing Russia, might be attractive if there is substantial uncertainty in China. If the PLA was a participant in a rapid transition, its modernization and the rise of China's military strength would continue largely unaffected.

On new world order issues, it is not clear a new regime would be in any position to do much about them for a considerable length of time.

Certainly, it is not likely to be any better at these issues than is the current regime.

A transition that leaves a largely unified PLA is one that, almost by definition, is more threatening than one where the PLA splits under the pressure of the transition. The division of the PLA creates its own threats to peace and stability—more in China than anywhere else—but with potentially great spillover effects. As noted above, almost all transitions will see the use of nationalist rhetoric and attempts made by many to use the nationalist card. Any transition will bring about a hyper-politicization of China, one that even a well-meaning foreign country can blunder into, and then find it hard to extricate itself.

While much work has been done in recent years on the relationship between democratization and war, and undoubtedly more will be done in the future, to the best of my knowledge no studies evaluate the effects of different types of transitions on war proneness. Thus, unfortunately, there is no comparative study that sheds any light on whether one particular kind of transition in China would be better for international stability than others (or that one type of transition would be more dangerous than other kinds).

However, as noted, it is not clear that a gradual transition with the CCP still an important political actor in Chinese politics would be accepted as genuine in the United States. This would be particularly true if the PLA emerged essentially unchanged and an amnesty was granted to those who abused human rights in the past (which has been the pattern in most, but not all, transitions to democracy). Nonetheless, a gradual transition is likely to contribute to greater government capability than would a rapid transition. Yet, with federalism and a gradual transition from above, there would be fewer changes of purpose for the regime, meaning that, with the exception of human rights, there might not be any improvement in the issues that concern the United States. The implications of gradual transition from below are harder to predict, but it is difficult to see how, other than in the area of human rights, things will change all that much.

Conclusion: Implications for the United States

While a Chinese transition to democracy would not fundamentally remove all of the issues on the agenda of Sino-American relations, and conceivably not resolve any of them, a transition would do several things for the United States. First, it would expand the variety of policy tools available for influencing Chinese behavior. Second, it would make it easier for the United States to build a consensus on China policy. Finally, it would make it easier for everyone to think about China and China policy in fresh ways.

Were China to become democratic, it would expand U.S. policy tools. China would be admitted to the successor to the G-7 and the Summit of the Eight. China would become eligible for certain types of U.S. aid (should the United States have aid to provide). Some of the residual sanctions on China might be lifted. The United States would find it easier to consult with China realistically about international developments and to consider international institutions and arrangements that fully incorporate China. Whether this greatly expands U.S. influence on China is another matter, but at least the United States would have positive means to employ to reward China, as opposed to the current situation where threats seem to be the only tool of influence anyone thinks of.

Again, were China to become a democracy, there would be much self-congratulation and triumphalism in the United States. History may be over after all. It would be much easier for Americans to come together on China policy. China's democratization would seem to mark the culmination of one of the longest and most deeply held American concerns about the world, the realization of the changing of China, more or less in our image. To be sure, organized labor, Tibetan activists, and others would still be wary or critical of a democratic China, but at least in the short run, there would be a willing suspension of criticism of a China under democratic rule that would resemble the general lack of sharply drawn criticism about developments in the former Soviet Union. Chechnya did not reverse United States engagement with Russia.

But such a positive view of China would not last, because ultimately, China would not live up to American ideals (ideals Americans often do not live up to). Again there could be another cycle of attraction and then repulsion in American attitudes toward China. China's transition to democracy simply will not immediately afect many of the issues where the United States has criticisms of China, and it may be that democratization will never influence these areas of concern. (A similar process of disillusionment is likely to take place on the other side of the Pacific.) This is both an opportunity and a challenge for people on both sides. They must be prepared for eventual disillusionment on the parts of their populace toward the other nation-state. They must know that real problems always exist among states, businesses, and peoples. Problems of varying degrees of severity are natural in international interactions, and amity and total agreement are the real rarities. Farsighted leaders on both sides need to consider this, and make such international facts of life known and accepted by their citizens. This will not be easy for leaders on both sides, who, coming to power in large and powerful countries with strong images of their nations' specialness, will be more absorbed by domestic affairs than international developments. China's democratization would allow both the United States and China to develop fresh approaches toward the other. It is up to our leaders to do so in positive ways.

Notes

1. Richard Bernstein and Ross H. Munro, *The Coming Conflict with China* (New York: Knopf, 1997), p. 204. In this essay, I try to keep distinctions among China, the People's Republic of China, and the Chinese fairly clear. China refers to the geographic and historical entity about the same size as the United States on the eastern coast of the Eurasian land mass. The People's Republic of China (PRC) is the name of the current state in China's historical and geographic space, and will be used either as the formal name of the current Chinese nation-state, or to refer to the particular regime governing the country currently. (I will use Beijing as a synonym for the PRC, referring in most cases to the regime and its leadership.) The Chinese generally refer to the people living in China.

2. That China will conform to some model of what foreigners want for it has been a recurring theme, and has produced several important cautionary tales. See Jonathan Spence, *To Change China* (New York: Penguin, 1984); Harold R. Isaacs, *Scratches on Our Minds* (also published under the title, *Images of Asia*) (New York: Harper Torchbooks, 1972); and Richard Madsen, *China and the American Dream* (Berkeley: University of California Press, 1995). Needless to say, China has yet to fulfill such hopes, and by its resistance has been deemed to be an enemy.

3. Samuel P. Huntington, *The Clash of Civilizations and the Remaking of World Order* (New York: Simon and Schuster, 1996). The "logic" of Huntington's argument is war with the Chinese (and the other members of "Sinic" civilization), but his discussion focuses on war with the PRC. See pp. 313–316.

4. For the official view, see the U.S. Department of State, *Human Rights Report 97: China,* available on the excellent USIA Hong Kong website, www.usconsulate.org.hk/uscn/#hr. Annual reports from human rights organizations, such as Amnesty International and Human Rights Watch/Asia, among many others, are all in general agreement on the nature of human rights violations in China.

5. The Office of the U.S. Trade Representative publishes an annual National Trade Estimate for all countries. For the China report, see: "Text: National Trade Estimate Report for China," available at the following internet address: www.usconsulate.org.hk/uscn/trade&investment.

6. See Thomas Rawski, *Economic Growth in Prewar China* (Berkeley: University of California Press, 1989) and Barry Naughton, *Growing Out of the Plan* (Cambridge: Cambridge University Press, 1995), especially pp. 26–74.

7. William H. Overholt, *The Rise of China* (New York: Norton, 1993).

8. There are many writings that could be cited here, but Samuel P. Huntington, *The Clash of Civilizations,* is one of the most influential. See also Bernstein and Munro, *The Coming Conflict with China.*

9. *New York Times*, July 2, 1997, A4 (national edition).

10. This assessment is influenced by Andrew Nathan's projection of a Chinese democracy in his *China's Crisis* (New York: Columbia University Press, 1990), pp. 208–211.

11. Based on personal communication in Taipei in early May 1997.

12. Jack Snyder and Karen Ballentine, "Nationalism and the Marketplace of Ideas," *International Security* 21, no. 2 (Fall 1996).

13. For example, Greg Mastel, "Beijing at Bay," *Foreign Policy*, no. 104 (Fall 1996): 27–34; and Thomas L. Friedman, "China, Part III," *New York Times*, March 10, 1997, A-15. The subtitle of Friedman's column is "The rule of law must be established in China before any march toward democratic capitalism can begin."

14. Emile Durkheim, translated by George Simpson, *The Division of Labor in Society* (New York: The Free Press, 1964), esp. pp. 381–388.

15. On this point, see Barrett L. McCormick, *Political Reform in Post-Mao China* (Berkeley: University of California Press, 1990), esp. chapter 2.

16. On some of the dimensions, types, and issues related to Chinese nationalism, see Edward Friedman, *National Identity and Democratic Prospects in Socialist China* (Armonk: M.E. Sharpe, 1995) and Jonathan Unger, ed., *Chinese Nationalism* (Armonk: M.E Sharpe, 1996).

17. Ed Friedman points out to me that factionalized émigré communities are characteristic of all such communities. His point is well taken, but the fact of the ubiquitousness of émigré factionalism does not mean that upon a return to China, the Chinese émigré community will be able to act together in a Chinese democracy.

18. On the growth of local bureaucracy during the reform period, see Dali L. Yang, *Calamity and Reform in China* (Stanford: Stanford University Press, 1996), chapter 7.

19. Mansfield and Snyder, "Democratization and the Danger of War," *International Security* 20, no. 1 (Summer 1995): 5–38. The quotation later in the paragraph is found on p. 6.

20. Nicholas R. Lardy, "The Role of Foreign Investment and Trade in China's Economic Transformation," *China Quarterly*, no. 144 (December 1995): 1065–1082. See p. 1077.

21. Bernstein and Munro, *The Coming Conflict with China*, p. 205.

22. Doyle's most recent statement on his views are found in Michael W. Doyle, *Ways of War and Peace* (New York: Norton, 1997), chapter 8.

23. Huntington, *The Clash of Civilizations*; Congressman Rohrabacher played up the fear that the leasing of the closed Long Beach Naval Base to COSCO (China Ocean Shipping Company) was a PRC bridgehead in the United States and that China could learn valuable secrets from the former base [as if the Navy leaves secrets lying around when it closes bases]. Similar types of remarks about the Panama Canal, and elsewhere, have been made by retired military personnel. Senator Helms's views are widely known. On "Yale, male, and pale," see Tyler Marshall, "Asian

Americans Scarce in U.S. Corridors of Power," *Los Angeles Times*, October 21, 1997 (Internet edition). Some of the discourse of the congressmen and senators involved in the campaign funding investigations reveals some overt and more disguised racism.

24. The works of Minxin Pei and Kevin O'Brien are particularly instructive here.

25. See Edward Friedman's important arguments on this point in his essays in his edited volume, *The Politics of Democratization* (Boulder, CO: Westview Press, 1994), pp. 1–15, 19–57, and 249–258.

26. For example, Andrew J. Nathan, "China's Path from Communism," *Journal of Democracy* 4, no. 2 (April 1993): 30–42.

27. Gabriella Montinola, Yingyi Qian, and Barry R. Weingast, "Federalism: Chinese Style," *World Politics* 48, no.1 (October 1995): 50–81.

Chapter 8

Immanuel Kant's Relevance to an Enduring Asia-Pacific Peace

Edward Friedman

To explore what happens if the party dictatorship of the People's Republic of China (PRC) does not democratize, three questions will be asked. First, is the Kantian hypothesis, usually summarized as, "democracies don't fight each other," in fact true? That is, will successful resistance to democratization by ruling groups in Beijing greatly increase the likelihood of war in the Asia-Pacific region?

Since 1996, in future-oriented works on a PRC rulership that treats the United States as its primary enemy, analysts imagine China igniting a war over Taiwan[1] or over Chinese territorial claims to the South China Sea.[2] Would a democratic China be significantly less war prone?

Samuel Huntington previously embraced the idea that democracies do not fight each other.[3] Yet in *The Clash of Civilizations*, he contradictorily predicted that a democratic China would actually be more war prone than a despotic China, an assertion also made by a number of authors in this book. Since both claims about China and democracy cannot simultaneously be true, it seems worth returning to Kant's original argument to see what is at issue.

Democratization was initially imagined by Huntington as largely coterminous with the spread of Protestant cultures.[4] For him, Catholicism has recently been infused with Protestantism and this new Christianity has facilitated democratization in Taiwan and South Korea. Huntington's viewpoint is detested throughout Asia, in India and Japan, as well as in Taiwan and Korea. Local citizens take pride in their own rich cultures which they find replete with democratic possibilities.[5] Consequently, Huntington's Eurocentric analysis of Kant's hypothesis, conventionally taken to mean that "democracies don't fight each other," is of little import to peoples in Asia. It is therefore worth going back to Immanuel Kant himself to grasp the logic behind the famous conjecture that democracies don't fight each other.

Second, with rulers in Beijing describing the promotion of human rights and democracy in Asia as a nefarious American campaign to weaken and contain China, has Beijing become the leader of an authoritarian grouping of nations whose purpose is to push America, democracy, and human rights out of Asia? Since the Bangkok conference on human rights in 1993, discussed by Samuel Kim in this book, Beijing has sought allies in places such as Singapore, Malaysia, and Indonesia to join in denouncing the notion of universalistically applicable human rights as cultural imperialism. Beijing has insisted that, given China's level of development and cultural peculiarities, China has an admirable record on human rights because it feeds and houses its people, a claim mocked by democratically oriented Chinese as treating humans as if they were zoo animals. The empty Beijing boast also ignores the famines fostered by China's Leninist political system, the most deadly famines in human history.

Any nation that seeks to probe China's actual human rights performance risks being treated, since 1993, as an enemy by the government of the PRC. Although American presidents seldom work vigorously for human rights in China, the United States is Beijing's enemy number one, understood to be trying to bring about a peaceful evolution of China to democracy, as Beijing explains it, to spread chaos, keep China weak, and make China dependent on America. Popular Chinese turn-of-the-millennium chauvinism, discussed in this book by Suisheng Zhao, makes this antidemocratic litany appealing. Antidemocrats have been reimagined as pragmatic patriots.

In May 1997 when Denmark moved to cite China before a UN body as a massive violator of the human rights of the Chinese people, Beijing canceled a Danish trade mission, costing Denmark hundreds of millions of dollars in contracts. France, which took the lead in breaking with European Union unanimity on human rights was rewarded by China with billions of dollars in contracts. Beijing has used similar carrot and stick tactics with Europe's Airbus and America's Boeing. Democrats in Asia worry that big businesses will succumb and pressure their governments to toe China's antidemocratic line to the detriment of the cause of democracy in Asia. Many fear this is already happening.

Because China has been the most rapidly growing and largest emerging market since 1978, its economic clout has led democratic trading nations in Europe to back off from human rights activism. But is China also succeeding beyond its borders in Asia in rolling back human rights and democracy? Samuel Kim's chapter shows it is. This may touch vital American interests.

After all, the spread of fascism in Europe in the early part of the twentieth century eventually dragged the United States in to a world war. It would be irresponsible not to inquire whether China's work to roll back human rights activism in Asia (e.g., Myanmar) could also eventually drag America into a major conflict. The American economy entering the twenty-first century is far more enmeshed with Asia than the American economy of the 1920s was with Europe. The democratic world's ability to grapple with its social problems depends on continuing growth, which, in no small part, is linked to a friendly and prospering Asia-Pacific region.

China has growing influence in Asia. Already, Beijing has used its power to sustain dictatorship or block human rights efforts in North Korea, Myanmar, and Cambodia. It has bailed out a friendly Bangkok. While China is far from matching America militarily in an all-out confrontation, that will almost never prove decisive in a particular Asian conflict. China has been using its power to impose its territorial claims and to promote antidemocratic and anti-American purposes. In sum, China's opposition to democracy makes war more likely.

Third, and finally, what if there is nothing to the idea that economic engagement engenders interests (a middle class, mobility, civil society, private property) that will eventually force a breakthrough toward political democratization? Democratization is a political matter of grasping infrequent opportunities.[6] Quite often these breakthrough opportunities, as in Latin America and Leninist command economies, have resulted from economic decline. Some analysts, looking at places like Singapore and Saudi Arabia, even find that wealth expansion makes political oppression easier, since there are fewer dissatisfied people to oppose the despotism. The harsh truth is that China's economic boom has not advanced the cause of democracy. Democracy advocates have been arrested, jailed, and terrorized. China combines economic openness with political repression. When President Jiang Zemin proclaims that he will continue the legacy of Deng Xiaoping, he means precisely this.

Actually, economic growth neither causes nor precludes democratization. Politics is decisive because democracy is a mode of organizing governance. The political arena is a largely autonomous one. Hence, to argue for engagement, because it supposedly furthers democratization, is to tout a fraud. That rationale is increasingly seen as a fraud which leads some pundits to conclude, erroneously, that engagement is a failure and that containment is the only alternative.

Despite engagement, repression in China intensified after late 1997, producing a backlash in America against engagement because the policy had been sold based on impossible promises of democratic political evolution. Still, engagement can advance the cause of reducing the likelihood of war, even if China does not democratize in any foreseeable future.

Democracies Don't Fight Each Other

Immanuel Kant never actually claimed that democracies do not fight each other. Much recent social science literature on that proposition[7] misses the heart of the philosopher's 1795 argument,[8] which is as much about political will and economic interest as it is about political system. Democracies do go to war, even with each other. This was as true for ancient Athens[9] as it is for modern India, the world's most populous democracy, whose foreign adventures are overlooked in the conventional literature. Democratic India has been militarily engaged with both Sri Lanka and Pakistan, even when they were democracies. Is the notion that democracies don't fight each other based on indefensible counting rules? Should one count the War of 1812 as a war between democracies? What about earlier Dutch/English wars? How should one categorize American attempts to overthrow democracies in Guatemala in 1954, Chile in 1973, and Nicaragua starting in 1979?

Why not see these instances as decisive in disproving the claim that democracies don't fight each other, since most wars are fought between neighbors, and there have been few democracies throughout most of history sharing land boundaries for long periods of time? Typically democracies are isolated in a region, India in South Asia, Israel in West Asia, Botswana in southern Africa and Costa Rica in Central America.

The large number of democracies that are islands in both the South Pacific and the Caribbean obviously do not have land borders with neighbors. Therefore the correlations of democratic polity with less war may be circular or not significant.

Surely there is little reason to doubt international relations notions about the priority of vital national interests. In the Cold War era in which Washington saw friends and allies of Moscow as America's enemies, Washington could side with authoritarian Pakistan against democratic India and with authoritarian forces opposed to Moscow-related democratic adversaries, however tenuously linked, anywhere in the world, not only Guatemala, Chile, and Nicaragua. In sum, an absolute claim that democracies do not fight each other is unpersuasive.

Yet all studies show that wars between democracies and even wars of democracies against nondemocracies are much less likely, except where, as with the war of monarchical Europe against the French Revolution, the antidemocratic side in a fledgling democracy reaches out to foreign friends to intervene militarily against the new and fragile democracy.[10] That is, it is antidemocratic politics which deserves the onus.

Yet the post–World War II experience of the European Union puts before us most seriously the hypothesis that democracies do not fight each other. As with the Iroquois League, which kept the peace among nations for centuries,[11] the Kantian peace followed prolonged pains of war. The peace was a commitment to change, to learn, to do better, the consequence of many generations of painful lessons about war. The confederation of enduring peace was consciously worked at and institutionalized, especially among the Iroquois, in historical commemorations that kept alive in contemporary memory the cruel lessons about the horrors that were the alternative to peace.

The strategic American Cold War foreign policy toward a democratic India, Guatemala, Chile, and Nicaragua was very different. It was an experience with distant others, a realm of ordinary realpolitik. It was not transformed by prolonged epochs of massive, mutual killing between Americans and Russians. Therefore, a history of peacemaking involving warring neighbors may have little relevance for China except in dealing with Japan. As I argued in the chapter in this book on "Preventing War Between China and Japan," a democratic China engaged with a democratic Japan could build understandings to buttress a structure of peace premised on a shared desire to avoid a repetition of past horrors and ancient humiliations.

But what is a neighboring nation-state? Entering the twenty-first century, our planet is shrinking because of communications and transportation revolutions. Steam transport and telegraph shrank the planet in the nineteenth century, facilitating world wars in the twentieth. China may be much nearer now to America than Managua, Nicaragua, was to Washington, D.C. before the building of planet-shrinking 747s, huge container ships, and instantaneous electronic communications. Given this new reality, can the prior experience of war between Washington and Beijing in Korea, the frequent nearness of war in the Taiwan Straits and in formerly French Indochina serve as learning experiences to move ruling groups to cooperative efforts to prevent war? While one might hope so, the suffering imposed on and by Americans and Chinese seems insufficient, given what dense, slow learners are mere human beings. An architecture of peace therefore needs to be built by careful and prolonged craftsmanship.

Light is thrown on a link between peace and political system in Kant's extraordinary essay on "Eternal Peace" (note 8). Kant's work is indeed a classic. He wrote from a strong realpolitik perspective, accepting as true that states glory in their wars, that they seek "continued increase of power by any and every means" (p. 431), and that the security dilemma is indeed dangerous. That is, even where volunteer armies are meant merely to protect "their fatherland against attacks from without" (p. 432), their mere existence cannot help but be "looked upon by other states as a threat of war" (p. 433). This is part of the Japan-China vicious cycle of mutual suspicion.

In addition, a state that suddenly had far more money at its disposal constituted "a dangerous money power" (p. 433) because the rulers of such a state could feel an infinite enhancement of already existing inclinations to war. Contrary to the overly optimistic notion that growth leads to democracy, which in turn facilitates peace, Kant found that growth could actually make war more likely. Kant's hypothesis suggests, however, that if a state loses tax power and experiences a deep budget crisis, that is, experiences a money crisis, as some analysts already find true of China, then that state will be less prone to war. If China is a state with a budgetary crisis, then, given the high cost of contemporary war, Beijing may be less prone to engage in war than prophets of gloom and doom suggest. But the forces at work have nothing to do with some imagined virtuous cycle where all good things come automatically from economic growth.

From a Kantian perspective, if Beijing, on the other hand, experiences its huge foreign exchange reserves, the world's second largest holdings by 1999, as evidence of an almost infinite ability to finance wars, that enhances the likelihood that rulers in Beijing might initiate war. Kant's realpolitik conclusion is that war "constantly threatens" (p. 436) in an international world where there is no secure appeal to law and punishment. Consequently, "peace must be founded" (p. 436). Peace is not an automatic consequence of anything, not growth, not democracy.

Kant at first blush seems to argue that a founding of peace was possible only in law abiding, constitutional, representative republics. Despots could readily persuade themselves that the costs of war, both blood and treasure, could be imposed on others in their realm and that ruling groups, a private, small body that monopolized power, could escape the pain of war. Hence dictatorships were more prone to war than democracies. Kant's general hypothesis is supported by all statistical studies.

Nonetheless, being democratic in no way guarantees peace. Intentional political action is required. A constitutional republic has to found peace. It can do this only by treaty, by forming a union in a federalistic direction. That is Kant's specific hypothesis. Most analyses err in not distinguishing Kant's general hypothesis from the specific hypothesis.

Clearly the European Union fits Kant's specific hypothesis. But how about the Association of Southeast Asian Nations (ASEAN)? Is it a Kantian "union of nations which maintains itself, prevents wars, and steadily expands" (p. 445)? That indeed seems to be the case. Peace was, in fact, meant to be the purpose of ASEAN. Consequently, ASEAN and the ASEAN Regional Forum (ARF) process may hold a promise of peace in the Asia-Pacific region which the mere existence of democracy in, say, Japan or India does not, that is, assuming there is something to Kant's specific hypothesis which focuses on formal relations between governments and not on the automatic impact of a particular kind of polity, as does the general hypothesis. Arguing that "democracies don't fight" confuses the two hypotheses. If there is significant truth in Kant's specific hypothesis, then it may be far more important than many American analysts recognize for Washington to lend its full support to the ASEAN/ARF process. The same could hold true for Asian Pacific Economic Cooperation, APEC, or for an Asian human rights regime. While not all engagement promotes peace, membership in certain multilateral bodies might provide mutual benefit and deter war.

To be sure, China can refuse to join such a union. It can reject binding multilateralism. It can insist on preconditions on the South China Sea, Taiwan region, and East China Sea that make a peace-prone confederation including China impossible. China has indeed been wary of the peace process, preferring the realpolitik logic of power aggrandizement, insisting on bilateralism where Chinese might well force decisions. China is already very engaged globally, but seldom in multilateral ways that further a structure of peace. Kant's perspective clarifies why Beijing's actions appear worrisome to smaller neighbors.

Kant's point on what is today called democracy was merely that the "gradual" expansion of a peace-oriented union is made far more likely by "a republican form of government." He believed that a law-abiding polity could more readily put its faith in "a law of nations" (p. 444). Dictatorial China prefers bilateral power politics. Hence the question of a constitutional republic is central for Kant to the founding of peace. Where does that leave ASEAN or the ARF, since those multilateral fora are not constituted singularly by democracies? Was Kant's specific hypothesis too restrictive?

Perhaps it is the contemporary notion of democracy that is too restrictive.[12] Kant is a subtle thinker. He notes that "A state may be governed as a republic even while it possesses despotic power to rule" (p. 460). That is, rulers may act on their self-interest in a peacefully confederated pact even before realizing full constitutional legality at home. Kant even approved delay in a democratic transition if that transition threatens too much chaos at home.

For Kant, lawfulness matters, while China is a "lawless state," as Kant understood the term. In China entering the twenty-first century, police and judiciary and legislature seem less weighty, while violence spreads. But there is broad repugnance in China toward this lawlessness and a passionate, popular desire, one shared by many among ruling groups, to enhance the rule of law. How much progress in that direction is needed before the Kantian peace process can include China? That a despotic government can join in founding peace, something Kant insists upon, does not, however, mean that dictatorship is better for a peace process than is republicanism.

Kant ruled out of bounds the argument that Beijing urges upon the Chinese people, the claim that disorder in Russia proves democracy itself inherently is bad. Kant found that politicians "do not deserve to be listened to" who give "examples of badly organized constitutions . . . to prove their contention" that the constitutional republic was bad (p. 467). Such foolishness is like arguing that because the Communist Pol Pot or the Emperor Hirohito was a patriot, all patriotism is murderous.

Kant was suspicious about claims that the good evolved automatically. He would laugh at the claim that capitalism builds peace. He did not find that the expansion of commerce brought peace. Instead, the pursuit of wealth carried with it greed, theft, and conquest. Typical was the West Indies where "the sugar islands . . . are the seat of the most cruel and systematic slavery" (p. 447). In themselves, neither democracy nor the market brought peace, which was something that states had to work at to obtain.

Peace is human artifice (p. 448). "War . . . [is] grafted upon human nature" (p. 451). But if mutually beneficial economic interchange persists, if ever larger numbers of people in states see their selfish interests met in peaceful exchange, then, over time, selfishness can begin to serve the interests of peace. This is the core of the notion that engagement can eventually facilitate peace.

But the process takes time and it is not clear how much time the chauvinist passions that inform Chinese ruling groups leave. Besides, engagement does not automatically strengthen an experience of mutual benefit. This centrality of "mutual self-interest" in Kant's theory suggests the importance to the Kantian peace of Beijing-Washington economic negotiations succeeding—and being seen as succeeding—to the benefit of both. If, however, the Chinese government propagandizes so that the Chinese people see, as Beijing nativists insist, that economic interchange is spreading AIDS and juvenile delinquency, and subverting the family, while exploiting vulnerable young Chinese women, and if Americans experience their economic dealings with China as a one-sided theft of the American patrimony by a cheating and exploitative Chinese state, as supposedly proved by China's trade surplus or China's export of prison labor goods to America, then trade engagement will not seem mutually beneficial, will not seem in the popular interest, will not serve the cause of peace. Economic mutuality is something that the two governments must work at, too. In short, chauvinists who treat a potential partner as an enemy, who work continually to persuade people that the other is evil incarnate, deserve the onus for blocking the peace-prone forces shrewdly analyzed by Kant.

But, and this was Kant's basic point, and it is the essence of the ASEAN achievement, if one sees how much the nation will suffer from the high cost of war-prone forces, if one sees the potential gain of mutually beneficial peaceful exchange,[13] then there should be plenty of practical statesmen to act selfishly on the side of peace. In Kant's perspective, it is inevitable that there will be powerful Chinese who will, in the self-interest of their nation, opt for the constitutional republic and mutually beneficial economic exchange, while avoiding the monstrous costs of war. Thus, Kantian engagement offers an ideal that is also true realpolitik.

There are, however, strong antipeace forces at work in China. Kant's analysis suggests that a rising Asia, which rulers in Beijing imagine as a Chinese-led twenty-first century, will seek power over peace, because "a continent if it feels superior to another one . . . will not leave unutilized the opportunity of increasing its power . . . by dominating the other" (p. 459). It is misleading to gainsay the war-prone forces within Chinese nationalism, as do a couple of articles in this book.

Much of East and Southeast Asia does not imagine itself or its region as centered on China, as do chauvinists in Beijing. Much of prospering Asia imagines itself as part of an ocean-bound region, the Asia-Pacific, not locked on a continental land mass which lacks a capacity to generate great commercial wealth across an ocean which unites through trade, tourism, and exchanges, both cultural and scientific. This is a world of open, cross-border relations.

Identity is crucial. It helps shape the national policy project. Beijing's ruling groups who make sovereignty an absolute, who imagine borders as Great Walls, are not promoting the kind of engagement that would further a structure of peace. Prudential self-interest in China, however, can, over time, promote the cause of peace if Chinese understand themselves in an open, peace-prone way.

But Beijing's nativistic conservatives reject that peace-prone understanding and promote a racist notion of Chineseness, 5,000 years of continuous blood purity. That identity, that project does not serve the interest of a Kantian peace. The issue of war and peace rests heavily on who and what rules in China. Peace is linked less to whether China today is democratic and more to whether Chinese rulers believe China capable of a republican peace project. The one unacceptable action of a despotism for Kant is "pretending that human nature is not capable of the Good" (p. 461). The most dangerous ploy is the claim of authoritarians that their culture and people are inherently incapable of a transition to a democratic republic. That was the tragic understanding of the Showa-era emperor of Japan who launched his imperial army against the Chinese people.

Kant has taken us into serious issues of international relations, taken us far from the ignorant sound bites where "capitalism causes democracy" and "democracy causes peace." There are, therefore, good reasons for returning to the enduring wisdom of the classics and not being overwhelmed by simplifying and distorting popularizers.

Kant concluded his essay with a call for "courage" by statesmen in regard to the need to face up to the imperative of "publicity" (p. 468). Kant's worry was that without a constitutional republic, a lack of transparency could legitimate worst-case readings of the intentions of neighbors, a tendency that could lead on to preemptive strikes and war. His essay on "Eternal Peace" reads as a contemporary commentary on the dangers inherent in Beijing-Tokyo relations. In a relationship pervaded by secrecy and suspicion, a great growth in strength of the neighbor will produce a policy imperative of acting to prevent the rising neighbor from doing the evil of which it is increasingly capable and presumed willing.

This is in fact how Beijing rulers often discuss Japan. The Chinese dictators regularly claim to know, as shown in the chapter in this book, "Preventing War Between China and Japan," that Japan's rulers seek a return to hegemony in Asia. China's dictators analyze Japanese intentions as if the long term is not on China's side, as if it is only a matter of time before Japan acts on its hidden, expansionist objectives.

Why won't China's rulers take the popular attitudes of the Japanese people who are overwhelmingly against getting involved in war, who show few willing to fight even if Japan were invaded, as proof that it is extremely unlikely that Tokyo will act in a war-prone way? A vicious cycle in Chinese politics makes such a reading of Japanese policy very difficult. Popular nationalism blames the rulers in Beijing for being soft on Japan. Anxious rulers respond by being tough on Japan. Even in Hong Kong, people try to establish their patriotic Chinese credentials by militant opposition to Japanese foreign policy. The same holds for some few on Taiwan. There is a deep feeling among Chinese that Japan caused a holocaust in China in which at least 11 million Chinese died and that Japan is ruled by holocaust deniers.[14] Young men in China are filled with proud anger that resurgent Chinese strength guarantees that such horrors will never again be allowed to be inflicted on Chinese by Japanese. They rage against Japan, much as young Israelis might rage against Germany if Germany were seen as a rising, holocaust denying nation and Israel were a neighbor, the size and weight of a rising China. In short, the nationalist forces at work in China are not unusual. But they add up to a battle cry, never again to us!

In addition, although the Japanese citizenry has been persuaded by the open political debate that Showa-era Japanese militarists did indeed cruelly invade and barbarously occupy China,[15] nonetheless, in China it seems that mistrust is caused by Japan's refusal to face the truth. This is not a basis for mutual trust.

To be sure, Japan too deserves blame. Foreign policy is not made in Japan in a robust, open debate. Instead, small elites in the ruling parties, in the bureaucracies, and among nongovernmental analysts meet and talk and decide in secret. Worse yet, the structure of the ruling conservative parties in Japan often gives large clout to ultraright, superpatriotic, militaristic factions. The truth therefore is that Japan, which rightly calls for more transparency in China, could also do with far more of the courage and honesty that Kant finds is the basis of an international relations that makes possible the building of an enduring foundation for peace. Kant's point is that a linkage must develop such that palpably obvious lawful processes at home tie up with the foundations of mutual interest and trust abroad. Instead, mistrust is intensifying. China-Japan relations are not dynamized by peace-prone forces.

The fly in the ointment of China-Japan relations buzzes most nastily in Beijing. Given their institutionalized paranoid secrecy that can make even a street map or phone book in China a classified document, Beijing acts in ways which compel foreign neighbors to imagine that whatever Beijing publicly says, the hidden truth just might lie in worst case possibilities. Even as Presidents Yeltsin and Jiang toasted strategic partnership, Russian analysts could not help but be anxious about "China's geopolitical pressure on the Russian Far East."[16] In like manner, the majority leader of the Philippines Senate found that China's "political and military posturing in the South China Sea does not encourage confidence among its neighbors. As China assumes sovereignty over Hong Kong and makes no apologies for the way it has used 'missile diplomacy' to send messages to Taiwan, it would take a highly specialized and dedicated effort to raise that level of confidence."[17]

China's political machinations make neighbors feel it is necessary to give credence to leaks which aver that Beijing's goal is regional hegemony, that its public statements are meant to get neighbors to lower their guard, that military hardliners are gaining in strength,[18] that Beijing intends to talk to distract while arming and acting to impose its will in the many regions of territorial disputes with neighbors. These neighbors, and rulers in China, aware that the American military has been ousted from Thailand, that antibase sentiment is strong in Okinawa, and that the U.S. Congress is cutting back on overseas missions, worry that it may be dangerous to rely on an America that may not be reliable for the long haul. Increasingly China has the capacity to impose its will on its neighbors while America seems an unreliable deterrent, no matter how strong may be the total weaponry of the American military.

Peace, however, is not merely a matter of military balance. One should stress Kant's concern, the need of states to found a basis for peace. First and foremost, that founding requires Beijing to act toward Japan as a potential partner in Asian-Pacific prosperity. It does not. The challenge, which indeed Kant noted, requires courageous statesmen in Beijing, ending a politics premised on revving up passions of revenge against Japan. Despite China's just historical grievances, the onus is on Beijing to advance a multilateral peace-prone process aimed at establishing transparency and building trust.

Kant saw the propensity of all states to legitimize self-interest, greatness, and aggrandizement. This includes democratic states. Democracy alone is not determinative. Kant's specific hypothesis leads elsewhere. What is required to make the Asia-Pacific region an area of peace is that all ruling groups, including those in a secretive, superpatriotic, and rising China, desire to build a structure of peace and take the risks and steps, as ASEAN has, as ARF does, as APEC tries, to build mutually interested relations of trust, transparency, and mutual benefit. That is the Kantian prescription, one easiest, he found, for constitutional republics, but one open, he concluded, to all states willing to work for an enduring peace. Kant's analysis is a reminder of how dangerous it is when nations do not actively strive to build a peace.

China Rolls Back Democracy

While rulers in Beijing claim that they oppose interference in sovereign affairs, they have nonetheless created the impression that their goal is to intervene all over the region and roll back the forces of human rights and democracy in Asia. Deng Xiaoping crushed China's democracy movement in 1989. In 1993, Beijing joined with others in Asia to oppose human rights efforts at the international human rights conferences in Bangkok and Vienna. Beijing is the major military prop of the military tyranny in Yangon. It supports the Stalinist regime in North Korea. It disbanded the democratically elected Hong Kong legislature in 1997. Beijing looks upon democracy in Taiwan as a splittest treason to be reversed. Beijing keeps propagating the Leninist-Stalinist line about political democracy merely being bourgeois dictatorship and China's one party dictatorship being the truest democracy. Official PRC statements describe human rights and democracy as a foreign plot to subvert China's successful economic policies, with success supposedly resting on authoritarian rule. The goal of this nefarious foreign plot, the Chinese people are told, is to reduce China to the chaos, civil war, and economic misery said to characterize post-Leninist Russia. In word and deed, theory and behavior, the Beijing government has been working to roll back democracy and human rights.

A leading European human rights activist concluded in 1997:

> Every year, for the last six years, the European Union has sponsored a motion to censor China at the annual UN Human Rights Commission. This year, France and Germany backed off and China was let off the hook. "Conditionality" and "linkage" have lost all credibility as economic ties and strategic importance are cited as reasons for noninterference and only poor states, with few rich pickings or international friends, are censured and subjected to economic pressure.[19]

Beijing boasts that it has done well in deflecting and defeating human rights activism. Communist Party rulers intend to increase pressure to turn Taiwan into another Hong Kong, an event which some foreign realpolitik strategists readily persuade themselves is a unique policy for a piece of Chinese territory, with no larger regional consequences. Democratic internationalists, in contrast, tend to hear the claim about Taiwan as part of China as similar to what was once said about the German Sudetenland.[20] Beijing's worrying military and political actions serve the interests of the least democratic and most chauvinistic forces in Tokyo. A very vicious, antidemocratic spiral might be sparked; indeed, it could already be underway. It could help reverse initial democratic breakthroughs all around Asia, from Indonesia, Thailand, and Cambodia to Korea and Mongolia. China is, after all, a great and rising power. Its regional influence is ever greater. Beijing is using that influence to roll back democracy. What a nation of 1.3 billion with the weight of China, projected by the World Bank as the world's largest economy by 2040 or so, does is of global moment. Beijing's policies of global opposition to democracy and human rights should be treated with the respect they merit. China is already a major power whose influence is shaping the Asia-Pacific future.

Yet, the most populous democracy in the world, India, has done little to challenge China's antidemocratic program. While New Delhi openly describes China as a threat, this threat is usually understood in India in narrow realpolitik terms. India imagines itself as uniquely democratic, surrounded almost preternaturally by nondemocracies. While India's society is rich with nongovernmental organizations that are very active on domestic Indian human rights problems, India's anti-imperialist nationalism combines with large problems at home, including most centrally Pakistani aid to Kashmiris, to make India almost an absolutist on noninterference in the affairs of other once-colonized nations. To protect itself from scrutiny, India will not vote to look into human rights abuses in China. India is not an international human rights leader.

Indians imagine democratic Japan as a world away and democratic Americans as a sometimes ally of India's adversary (and China's friend) Pakistan. Consequently, Indian analysts expected the United States to accede to China's 1996 intimidation of Taiwan because, in India, the United States, supposedly following a policy of merely positive engagement with Beijing, was seen as a tool of Chinese interests, doing nothing to block China's help to Pakistan's nuclear program, picking instead on India, and voting in the World Bank to have China replace India as the number one recipient of soft loan money. America was not seen in India as sharing India's principled approach to world affairs premised on anti-imperialist developmentalism, but as on the side of the property rights of individuals which harmed third world development.

If America and India are to reach out to each other, Americans too would have to change, abandoning the culturally chauvinist position advanced by Huntington that democracy has to do with individualistic Protestant consciences and instead realize how much of human rights from the outset (e.g., ending slavery, ending religious persecution) was a matter of group rights. While New Delhi was happily surprised when the United States sent its navy to the Taiwan region in 1996 in response to Beijing's military actions, America could do more to put itself in tune with a responsible third world approach to human rights. To help woo India out of international human rights passivity, Americans would have to reconsider the American focus on human rights as mainly about individual political rights. That is, American participation in building a human rights regime for Asia as part of a structure of peace may require some fundamental cultural reinterpretation in the United States, freeing Americans from myths about their own political development.[21]

As with India, there likewise is little human rights activism emanating from Tokyo, and not only because the anti-Japanese politics of Beijing discourages Tokyo by denouncing Tokyo as the home of unrepentant war criminals, Asia's biggest nonremorseful violator of Asian human rights. Far more important are the actual domestic political forces of Japan where conservatives, in contrast to in Germany, did not experience the Cold War as a struggle between freedom and tyranny.[22] In Europe, an Iron Curtain was experienced as separating a democratic Europe from a Europe suffering the pains of despotic oppression. Not so in Cold War Asia. To conservatives in Tokyo, the Cold War pitted communists against anticommunists, capitalists against socialists. Into 1960 the Japanese left had to struggle against an anticommunist Kishi who just might reverse democratization. There could be no socialist Willy Brandt in Japan to win power and open up to communist neighbors. The anticommunists in Asia, democratic Japan's Cold War partners, included unpalatable military tyrannies all around Asia, from Pakistan and Indonesia to Taiwan and South Korea, which were not friends of democracy. In contrast to Europe, the Cold War in Asia was not a struggle for and against political freedom. The wars fought by Americans on the side of authoritarians in Korea and Vietnam against communist governments intensified the feeling of many Japanese rightists that they had been on the side of justice in their earlier war in Asia against so-called communists and that it was America that had erred in the Pacific War part of World War II in supposedly siding with the communist forces instead of with Tokyo. During the Vietnam War, America was seen by many conservatives in Japan as getting its just deserts for having reached out in World War II to Mao's forces in China and Ho's in Vietnam.

Since socialist forces in Japan long held to odd notions, such as North Korea as a good, socialist, anti-imperialist nation and South Korea as a suffering, exploited imperialist puppet of America, the left in Japan never was a viable alternative internationally on the side of democracy and human rights, even as its weight against militarism helped institutionalize constitutional democracy in Japan. Consequently, there has been no great Asian human rights thrust in the dynamics of Japanese politics since both right and left in Japan included major forces which identified with gross violators of human rights, the former with the Park dictatorship in Seoul, the latter with the far more brutal Kim dictatorship in Pyongyang, the left with those who insisted that anti-imperialism was the real basis of human liberation.

The failure of Asia's two great democracies, India and Japan, to act on behalf of human rights in Asia has given Taiwan's prodemocratic activities an unusual weight in Asia. It is Taiwan that took the lead in responding to the claims of some ruling groups which insisted that Asian values were incompatible with democracy. Beijing's efforts to isolate Taiwan from its Asian neighbors is an attempt to silence the most eloquent voice in Asia on behalf of the view that Asian cultures in their robust humanisms are rich with the seeds of democratization.[23] Consequently, a rollback of democracy in Taiwan by Beijing can have a major impact on the democratic forces in Asia, lending credence to the notion that there is no alternative to surrender to the authoritarians in Beijing, enormously strengthening the antidemocratic weight of Beijing.

And yet, while the discourse of hardliners, conservatives, and nativists is hegemonic in China, the authoritarians in Beijing have not yet won totally. While the future is unknowable and politics is unpredictable, it is so easy to imagine shifts in the democratic direction within Asia that that possibility should be seen as worthy of support. With the Cold War over and Mongolia, South Korea, Taiwan, and the Philippines democratized, it is easier for human rights forces in Japan to build on a long history of human rights concerns going back to the Meiji and Showa eras. In India, with the reform opening to the world economy since 1991, foreign investment increasingly seems a positive good and not evil imperialism. That change could facilitate openness and Indian human rights international activism. In fact, everything could change in the direction of democracy in Asia if India and Pakistan reconciled, if a moderate progressive party grew in Japan, and if Indonesia institutionalized its political breakthrough to democracy. Merely a successful transition in Indonesia could encourage the already strong democratic forces of Singapore and Malaysia to fulfill the democratic project of those nations. ASEAN then could turn into an alliance of democracies. Its Kantian peace character would be greatly strengthened. The reaching out of both Japan and India to ASEAN and ARF easily could then make Asia a leader in global human rights efforts and peace promotion.[24] Misconstruing Asia as a region supposedly defined by antidemocratic civilizations is both dangerously wrong and not in the vital interests of peace, democracy, and the United States. More important, a more democratic

Asia, precisely as Kant's specific hypothesis suggests, would be one where ASEAN would be the center of a project of peace and prosperity that would further humane prospects in Asia and everywhere.

It is self-defeating to assume that China is eternally a tyranny bent on aggression. Such presuppositions should be understood as a threat to better possibilities. Such a perspective, embedded in much of the work of Huntington, expresses a position which since the 1960s has lost faith in the West's own democratic citizenry.[25] Such conservatives in the 1960s claimed first that democracy had gone too far and should be limited in the United States, Japan, and Europe. They then, still in the late 1960s, insisted that Asia was rising because it was disciplined (Confucian) and the West was declining because it had allowed freedom to go too far. These conservative Americans invented the concept of Asian authoritarianism. Their future projections have invariably been wrong. In 1981 Huntington found, as always, that a too democratic America suffered from disharmony, whereas an unreformed Leninist "Soviet Union, China, and Japan have a substantial degree of consensus or ho-mogeneity . . . the stress . . . is on the pervasiveness of inequality, the 'sanctity of authority,' the subordination of the individual to the state. . . . [T]he prevailing political values and social norms reinforce the authority of central political institutions . . . and enhance their ability to compete."[26]

Huntington has almost invariably proved an apologist for authoritar-ian virtues. For his type of conservative, democracy was a deservedly endangered species. The 1980s focus on a somehow dangerously com-petitive Soviet Union is a reminder that this kind of conservative fear of the weakness of democracy is more ideology than fact.

These conservatives claimed through the 1970s and 1980s that de-tente and Ostpolitik in East Europe aiming at political liberalization were losing policies because, Huntington wrote in 1984 and repeated a year later, there simply would be no further democratization in the world; there especially could never be a democratization of totalitarian com-munist states. In the 1990s American cultural conservatives saw China in the same distorted way. Surely the record of those who have made dire predictions about the lack of a staying and growing power in de-mocracy suggests that it is not a good idea to base policy on their jer-emiads about democracy's alleged unattractiveness or about cultures supposedly deeply antithetical to democratic possibilities.

Somehow, miraculously, in 1991, Huntington discovered that while he had been writing about the decline and demise of democracy, actually a great wave of wondrous democratization had been washing all over the planet earth since 1974. How had he been blind to it? Still he noted, as always, that democracy had major cultural limits and strong preconditions. Consequently democracy could not reach Asia where civilizations such as Confucianism were inherently antidemocratic. Huntington, as other Eurocentrists, never took seriously the central fact that throughout the second half of the twentieth century the most populous democracy in the world and the third most populous were both in Asia.

In the 1950s Huntington announced that Japanese democracy could not hold because, he could tell, as a student of political culture, that Japan was a deeply militaristic civilization infused by Bushido and the Samurai warrior culture. For Huntington, since culture persists, so would Bushido militarism. He bet on no change "in essentials from that which prevailed [in Japan] prior to 1945."[27] For twenty-five years or more, Huntington has also been predicting an end to Indian democracy since that supposedly Western political form was said to be alien to Indian culture. Huntington apparently was deaf to the voices of Indian democrats who contrasted their glorious and historically tolerant culture with the intolerant sixteenth-century Europeans that India encountered in the age of the inquisition, religious wars, and witch burnings. It is important for the forces of democracy elsewhere at last to heed the discourse on human rights in Asia and cooperate with those forces. It is an Asian human rights regime of Asian democracies, especially if Indonesia joins, that would be the strongest force capable of preventing a rolling back of democracy and human rights in Asia.

This does not mean trying to recapitulate the great human rights achievements of the late 1970s and early 1980s. That global movement reflected a unique confluence of forces—a joining of Muslim and African states against an Israel that would not recognize the PLO and against an apartheid South Africa; a belief of anti-imperialist governments that the United States, complicit with right-wing military tyrannies in Latin America, would suffer from a human rights campaign; and burgeoning internal movements in the United States premised on civil rights activism to end racial and gender discriminations. That confluence of issues and forces is gone. Attempts to continue that human rights movement in an era ravaged by communalist strife threatening genocide has drawn international human rights groups into maelstroms and quicksand whose politics often swallow up and drown good intentions before good results are possible.

A human rights effort to be effective will have to be reborn. It is therefore worth listening to Asian human rights concerns. What are the issues? Do they require taking group rights more seriously? Religious freedom? Migrant labor? Sexual slavery? Child labor? Cultural survival? Listening does not mean forgetting the abiding value of political freedoms. But instead of nagging Asians from the Capitol Building in Washington, D.C., American legislators should seek to cooperate with parliamentarians from democratic Asia on a shared interest on which Asians can and should take the lead. Americans should be willing to learn and to change. Americans are wrong when they imagine democracy as the fruit of a culture of individualism. After all, freedom requires discipline and sacrifice and "has nothing to do with selfishness." "The idea that the people should govern themselves is hardly an individualistic or selfish one. It supposes that a political community must act as a kind of partnership in which each citizen accepts some responsibility for collective decisions . . . which means . . . that none can be denied a voice in collective deliberation."[28] It is a logic of inclusiveness. It is a political logic that can include China.

Can China Democratize?

The goal of American diplomacy and of Asian human rights efforts should not be to pressure China into democratizing. To be sure, in Asia and all over the planet, it is worth building a human rights consensus on matters such as religious freedom and on behalf of particular victims of arbitrary state power. But if China is to democratize, that transition will have to be the result of change brought by the great Chinese people themselves. Democracy is a political possibility open to all humans who wish to escape the pains of authoritarianism. If peoples as benighted and authoritarian as those of Europe—the people who gave the world the genocidal Hitler, the mass murderer Stalin, and the inquisitorial torturer Torquemada—could democratize, then there does not seem much reason why the great humanitarian civilizations of Asia should not do at least as well. Only an ignorant, arrogant Eurocentric chauvinist could think otherwise.

Yet naysayers argue that democracy is "contrary to the Chinese political culture."[29] That would mean that the people enjoying democracy in Chinese Taiwan, in Confucian South Korea, and in Japan are decultured. The antidemocratic claim misunderstands culture, presumes

244 • WHAT IF CHINA DOESN'T DEMOCRATIZE?

an ethnocentric notion of democracy, and essentializes Chinese society. A culture is a repertoire of possibilities, from the almost angelic to the completely demonic. The same culture contains antitheses. Confucianism contains some elements conducive to democracy and some not.[30] In some situations you draw on "look before you leap." In other situations, wisdom is "he who hesitates is lost." In choosing one, the other is momentarily blocked out. You forget it exists and persists. Cultural preoccupations are momentarily, but only momentarily, blinding. Sometimes, one opines, "absence makes the heart grow fonder." Yet other times, wisdom is "out of sight, out of mind." Thus, a culture is always far more than fixated on a moment. The same Dutch Reformed Church can nourish great republican liberty in Holland and apartheid oppression in South Africa. Cultures are not this or that. They are this and that. Some Christian churches in the nineteenth century found that God blessed slavery, while others found God demanding the abolition of slavery.

Likewise, it is an ethnocentric error to imagine democracy in terms of individualistic Protestant consciences and forget that democracy prospered in Athens centuries before Christ. Democracy is but a political mechanism by which citizens select governors in an experientially fair way that allows officials to be held publicly accountable. In China, as everywhere, including even Europe, germs of such institutional possibilities have appeared over the millennia. The evidence for this pan-human possibility has been educed so many times such as to put the factual claim about cultures lacking democratic potential to rest as a deadly error worth burying once and for all times. How strange it is that cultural conservatives who rightly inveigh against the type of multi-culturalism which is romanticizing the non-European and separationist, who insist on commonality, at the same time romanticize a West that is separate and special and not part of a common humanity. Conservatives of the Huntington type are guilty of the sin they preach against. They wrongly argue that Chinese and American political cultures are, in fact, antithetical, a contrast of "discipline instead of freedom . . . tradition instead of innovation."[31]

Claims about how culture blocks democracy (various naysayers offer their own idiosyncratic list of antidemocratic peculiarities) are baseless. Such claims are rhetoric meant to fixate on one momentary aspect of a diverse, contested, and changing reality, while ignoring the rest. Actually, in the late Qing era, when Chinese first contemplated building a constitutional republic, rather than being blocked by being too disci-

plined (like democratic Germany?), they envied democracies in Europe
for their democratic discipline and hoped that democracy, by forcing
Chinese to stop being narrowly selfish, would channel energies into
building a national platform to unite groups and to put before voters the
discipline of democratic party building, agenda setting, and campaign-
ing for seats all over the country in order to help end a disintegrating
China's indiscipline and fractiousness, an extreme anarchy in which
China seemed no more than a sheet of loose sand.[32] Democratic Europe
was discipline. Authoritarian China was freedom. If one understands
the breath of cultural possibility, it will not seem odd that opposites
reside in cultures.

Likewise, in contrast to the notion that Chinese are inherently incapable of democracy because they are bound by tradition, actually, far
from being incapable of innovation, when European sailors first reached
the shores of China in the sixteenth century, Chinese had innovated more
major technological advances than the whole rest of the world combined.[33] Chinese have not forgotten that reality. That technological
achievement is a living part of the culture.

Political culture is not a fixed and inhuman essence. That was the
self-serving error of genocidal Europeans treating the indigenous peoples
of the Americas as savages and cannibals. It is also the way powerholders
in Beijing discuss Tibetan culture. In fact, the rapid removal of Leninist
obstacles to democratization in China finally persuaded Huntington to
back off his long-articulated position that Confucianism blocks democratization in China.[34] It really is absurd to think that the rich and ancient
culture of a glorious civilization such as China could be alien to or threatened by some particular form of governance. It is like thinking that Japanese or Indians stop being Japanese or Indian because of a democratic
form of polity. I will confess to not fully comprehending how intelli-
gent, informed, and cosmopolitan people can imagine a magnificent civilization as inherently and permanently antidemocratic.

This does not mean that democratization is easy. It is especially difficult to democratize a nation dominated by large rural estates—debt pe-
onage latifundia, slave plantations, or socialist collectives—which bind
most of the people to dependency to an arbitrary and unaccountable
master.[35] But decollectivization in post-Mao China has provided sufficient mobility and independence for rural households that they now know
that democracy is preferable to dependency. They have been economically freed so as to be mobilizable against authoritarians. To claim that

villagers are too conservatively tradition-bound to participate actively in elections is to deny what by the late 1990s was a weighty fact to the contrary in village China.

In addition, Leninism, as other overcentralized and impoverishing tyrannies, is almost impossible to democratize when status, wealth, and power are all narrowly concentrated in the hands of narrow elites. Such rulers have too much to lose to negotiate a peaceful opening toward democracy. If they lose power, they lose everything.

But the economic rise of China has created large pockets of wealth and prestige all over the country. The heirs of the despots, the princelings, have learned that they can do well outside the orbit of a centralized dictatorship. Hence, losing political power through gradual democratization can come to seem an acceptable risk. The princelings have closely followed how well ex-Communists have done in democratic elections in East Europe.

This Chinese democratic potential is less obvious in America than it should be because of the rise of forces which have lent a patina of credence and respectability to the kinds of appeals against democracy made since the 1960s by conservatives who fear democracy, that make it seem that democracy is not good for a people. Pessimistic about democracy, they worry that America is but "a dysfunctional patchwork of self-double communities," such that "the crash of American civilization" is predictable. Chinese authoritarians love to read and cite such jeremiads about how "democracy will fade away" and "western civilization itself is bound to collapse."[36] This lack of faith in democracy in existing democracies should be worrisome to democrats, far more so than ignorant claims that demean the great culture of China. This lack of faith in democracy infects American analysts of China too. It is almost the conventional wisdom to understand China's great 1989 democracy movement in derogatory terms. The movement is described as an emotional outburst caused by the death of Hu Yaobang, thereby ignoring all the thinking, writing, and analyzing that went on in salons, the *World Economic Herald*, and numerous think tanks. The democracy movements' leadership is dismissed by the naysayers for acting in a nondemocratic way, as if political parties or lobbying groups have to be democratic in a democracy. That new requirement for a democratic reality would empty the world of all its democracies.

Furthermore, the Chinese democracy movement is derided by these pessimists for having made lesser demands than a full democracy, for not having understood democracy, and for not having been willing to compromise with ruling groups, thereby supposedly causing the June 4, 1989 massacre. It is disheartening to have to point out the absurdity of these condescending charges that diminish the contribution of heroic pioneers of democracy.

In the 1989 movement, courageous democrats risked careers and lives. It is indeed true that their demands were quite minimalist. That, however, is the norm with fledgling democracies. The United States, after all, did not begin by abolishing slavery, the most undemocratic institution imaginable. But, since China's democracy movement was, in fact, minimalist, clearly the finger of blame for no graceful compromise should be pointed at China's paramount leader who refused to conciliate the Chinese people. It is the regime that would not compromise and instead ordered a massacre to teach a lesson. It was the dictatorship that blocked democratization. As for the notion that Chinese somehow are unfit for democracy because democracy activists did not understand democratic theory, in fact, by that criteria no democracy qualifies. Democracy is a set of political institutions, not a high grade on an exam on constitutionalism.

In teaching a course on democratization, I have learned that students believe that democracy is a matter of majority rule, although, in fact, no major matter of national governance in the United States of America is decided by a simple majority. Not one. Murky thinking is so pervasive about and in democracies that even the most sophisticated analysts will believe simultaneously that democracy is about elections and that the West has been democratic since ancient Athens, not noticing that Athens chose none of its leaders by popular election. As numerous scholars have documented, going back to the late Qing, Chinese, comparatively speaking, have been unusually well informed about constitutional democracy. What blocks democracy in China is not a lack of knowledge. It is worth remembering the level of democratic knowledge in actually existing democracies. In the United States, people asked to sign the Bill of Rights regularly brush it away as an alien document.

China's democracy movement was not a sudden irruption caused by the death of Hu Yaobang. The documentation of how much the democracy movement's leadership and/or more senior advisers in China had thought hard about democratization is actually voluminous. Consequently, two serious questions follow from examining the dismissive tirades against China's democratic heroes and martyrs: why are such views so popular, and will antidemocratic forces outside of China hinder the constructing of democracy in China?

None of us can foretell the future. My hunch is that antidemocratic views are popular outside of China because the late 1970s through early 1990s era when human rights and democracy seemed a hegemonic ideology, a future project that seemed unstoppable, in fact, was a unique era that has passed. Conservative realpolitik and the economy are once again center stage. That consensus, however, will not block the forces of democratization in China. Democratic breakthroughs invariably emerge to the surprise of the realists. Democracy in China will be decided by outraged people in China. The intensifying repression in China in the late 1990s, a harsh reality ignored by simple-minded rationales for engagement with China that expect economic growth automatically to transmogrify into political democracy, a harsh reality detailed in numerous human rights reports and explained by Su Shaozhi and Michael Sullivan in this volume, would not seem to be a cause for optimism about Chinese democratization in any short or medium run. And yet the impact of that inhumanity against Muslims or Buddhists will have an impact on China's neighbors. This alienation was already clear following Beijing's late 1990s military activities in the South China Sea and the Taiwan region. Watching wary neighbors quietly act to block worst case Chinese possibilities can lead Chinese rulers to prefer cooperation over confrontation. In short, there are reasons for long-term optimism, however dangerous the short-term dynamics. Chinese are not trapped in a one-dimensional culture. Therefore, there are major reasons that neighbors should not act to harm the prospects of forces in China that would be conciliatory both at home and abroad.

Only a Pollyanna, however, would not notice that there also are powerful racist, expansionist, and repressive forces of great influence among Chinese ruling groups. These forces could yet win and incite war in the region while acting cruelly within China.

But that development is far from inevitable. Since it is true that China, just as Kant described, can benefit from participation in the multilateral institutions of the region which aim to perpetuate peace and prosperity for the Asia-Pacific, the wise policy is to welcome a rule-abiding China within the cooperative efforts of those multilateral bodies. That approach requires no special China policy. Any policy aimed especially at China will be experienced by rulers in Beijing as anti-China. That includes engagement, which is described by sensitive Chinese patriotic authoritarians as having as its goal the subversion of the respect-worthy government that is bringing wealth, power, and pride to the Chinese people.

It will not produce a good outcome in China for others to have to choose between a policy of containing China or engaging China. The containment policy follows from believing, as argued in an April 1996 debate in *Foreign Affairs* by Ross Munro and Richard Bernstein, that China's quest for "dominance in East Asia" in league with "states, many of which have [antidemocratic] goals and philosophies inimical to the United States" requires an American response in cooperation with Japan to Chinese "aggressive behavior" in order "to prevent China's . . . regional hegemony." The perspective of Robert Ross, who would accommodate China, finds, in contrast to containment theorists, that China's "preeminence" in both northeast and southeast Asia is a given, such that others must "compromise . . . over the future of Taiwan" and accommodate China's military ties with Pakistan. To accommodationists, this China is "too weak to challenge" vital American interests which are mainly (merely?) in the maritime parts of the Asia-Pacific.

The latter description of a "weak" and "constructive" China is actually not so different from the containment theorists' view of a disruptive and expansive China. To the accommodationists, America should conciliate and engage a China which supposedly prefers to focus on economic growth, treating aggression such as a 1995 Chinese invasion of maritime Philippines territory as an "anomaly." Neither analysis pays sufficient attention to Kantian insights about peace as self-interest. These remind us that China's expansive acts of supposed security win both military-oriented defensive responses and the building of multilateral structures of peace from China's neighbors that can lead Chinese rulers to choose to build in mutual benefit with neighbors on the latter initiatives, even, indeed, especially Japan, and to do so via the multilateral structure of peace and prosperity that ASEAN has pioneered. Thus, while containment theorists are right that there are war-prone forces in China, they are still wrong to depict these as representing China's one and only possible political path. The United States should not act to turn pessimism into a self-fulfilling prophecy.

Narrow chauvinist groups in China are challenged by others, powerful people who do not wish to risk action that would undermine China's extraordinarily successful effort to keep rising economically and swiftly to become the largest economy in the world. Which group will win will be decided essentially by Chinese in China. The policy imperative for

China's neighbors in the Asia-Pacific region should be not to act to strengthen inadvertently the side of nativism and expansionism in China. The main goal should be not to worsen the problem for Chinese committed to improving the lives of the people and to working in peaceful cooperation with neighbors of China.

Other actors in Asia, including ruling groups on Taiwan and in Japan, find that a policy meant to contain a Chinese threat would be taken within Chinese politics as proof that China's expansive nativists are correct in treating America et al. as opposed to the rise of China. America then would be found culpable in Asia for causing a reactive Chinese threat. America thereby would alienate Asia. Containment is bad policy advice. It will make an iffy situation far shakier.

Yet strategists of accommodation through mindless engagement are too sanguine. They mischaracterize the view of China held by other Asian ruling groups, wrongly contending that China's neighbors are content to accommodate a Chinese hegemony in northeast and southeast Asia. Actually, these proud and patriotic nations do not welcome a world in which they are alone and vulnerable to China's whims.[37] Ruling groups in the regions of Asia seek a quiet, reassuring American presence, not merely to balance China or to preclude having to jump to the will of rulers in Beijing, but also to buy time for the forces of economic mutual benefit and peaceful openness, explored in Kant's specific hypothesis, to win the Chinese people to cooperative policy options of joining multilateral structures of peace in the region.

American policy should be aimed at making that happier outcome more likely. More policy attention should be given to Asia-Pacific Economic Cooperation. There already are major Chinese forces working in that healthier direction, although they are slighted by containment theorists who see Chinese culture as inherently nativistic and hegemonic. In fact, dynamic Asian-Pacific forces hold the promise that in Asia, as in Europe and North America, nations will do best when open interaction provides political transparency, a diminution of military tensions, and economic mutual benefit. American policy should be Kantian so that Chinese ruling groups, as the other nations of the region, see the superiority of an open and cooperative world order rather than one based on strategic secrecy or on revenge against neighbors treated mainly as adversaries. The key issue is China-Japan relations. The policy question is how to work for a long-run dispersal of, and end to, nasty China-Japan tensions and to promote a world of mutual benefit.

At a February 20, 1997 New York City commemoration of the twenty-fifth anniversary of the Shanghai Communiqué, the Ambassador from the PRC informed the American participants that "What we are concerned about is if the bilateral military arrangement between Japan and the United States is directed against China."[38] It, however, will not be easy to reverse the workings of the security dilemma which is leading each side to treat the actions of the other as threatening. It is, nonetheless, crucially important to dynamize peace-prone forces. Therefore, America's policy priority in APEC or the World Trade Organization, as elsewhere, should be building a world in which all can benefit from peaceful, open economic cooperation. Is it inconceivable that a cooperative arrangement of all parties claiming the maritime resources of the East China Sea and the South China Sea, as well as nonuse of force anywhere in the West Pacific, including the Taiwan region, could facilitate a redeployment of U.S. marines out of Okinawa? Surely diplomats on all sides should be able to craft policies through which all sides win.

To be sure, Chinese actions in an era of heightened and expansive nationalism could prove disastrous for peace and prosperity in the region. However, a policy of containment of China would be seen in the region as provocative. It would make the dangerous yet more volatile and explosive. Policy must not be mesmerized singularly by the military and the strategic or by the serious negatives in Beijing-Washington relations. More stress is needed on Kantian policies of economic benefit, of building pacts of peace, and on the detoxification of Japan-China relations so that the happier reality based on a conscious building of multilateral institutions of cooperation can bring future blessings to all the peoples of the Asia-Pacific region.

Sadly, on this key matter of not seeing Japan as a continuing and growing menace, it is not obvious that democratization in China would immediately change much. Political reformers deeply experience Japan as cruel, wily, and out to control Asia. Victim consciousness in China is strong. However misleading, the ploy of elites of blaming Chinese weakness and backwardness on the nineteenth century western narcotraffickers who imposed a war on China for the right to prevent Chinese from making opium imports illegal, and of blaming Japan for humiliating the Chinese at Shimonoseki and continuing to do so in supposedly making Taiwan part of a Japanese neocolonialist empire, those portrayals play to popular preconceptions and ignitable passions. Chinese nationalism is dangerous and popular.

There is little consciousness in China of China having ever been an arrogant center imposing a humiliating subservience on neighbors for centuries. Chinese do not discuss how Japan's rise, starting in the sixteenth century, was popular in Japan because it freed Japanese of humiliation by Chinese. There seems nothing problematic to most politically conscious Chinese in the sixteenth century policy of sending troops into Korea to defeat Japan, with vassal Korea thought of as a subordinate part of the Han. In short, it is not obvious that democratization would immediately bring to power in China people who might put a high priority on China-Japan reconciliation, although that is the prerequisite of an enduring Asian-Pacific peace. Chinese elites do not readily see that other peoples in Asia, who long suffered the humiliations of the hierarchical Sinocentric international system, might even welcome Japan as a balance against renewed Chinese hegemonic might.

Consequently, as Kant suggests, one might as well begin this effort of building a multilateral union of peace-prone states with an authoritarian China, hoping that the fruits of that policy enhance the likelihood of changed attitudes and policies, of Japan-China reconciliation, taken as a long-term imperative of peace whoever or whatever rules in Beijing. Democratization could speed that project, but it would be a project that would take time. The issue of preventing a war that would implode Asian-Pacific peace and prosperity should, whatever the difficulties, and precisely because of the difficulties, be a highest priority, whether or not China democratizes.

Hence, America, and China's nearer neighbors, should merely act as Kant long ago prescribed. That is, they should comport themselves in ways that are universalizable because actually they are in the mutual interest of all the parties involved. This means understanding that trade-oriented nations which can accept abiding by international norms can help construct these plus/plus unities even before governments have become constitutional republics. Kant's hope was that over time, through gradual evolution, without violent disruption and civil chaos, which were extreme evils to be avoided, this process could fulfill the logic of its premises. War is so devastating and peaceful prosperity is so attractive that for Kant more than two centuries ago, as for the nations of the Asia-Pacific today, governments should promote policies which not only can make war less likely but which also are conducive to transitions within nations that make massive, cruel repression less likely. These policies offer a safer direction for the ship of state, alternatives for charting a course seeking a peaceful and prosperous Asia-Pacific region in the near future, even if China does not democratize.

Notes

1. Richard Bernstein and Ross Munro, *The Coming Conflict with China*. New York: Knopf, 1997.
2. Samuel Huntington, *The Clash of Civilizations and the Remaking of World Order*. New York: Simon and Schuster, 1996.
3. Samuel Huntington, *The Third Wave*. Norman: University of Oklahoma Press, 1991.
4. In contrast, Daniel Chirot in a study of *Modern Tyrannies* (Princeton: Princeton University Press, 1994) notes that "Monotheism seems to be congenial to the exercise of ideological tyranny" (p. 17) and that "Marxist prophecy strongly resembles Christian teleology" (p. 57).
5. The articles in Larry Diamond and Mark Plattner, eds., *Democracy in East Asia* (Baltimore: The Johns Hopkins University Press, 1999) make no mention of Christianity or Western culture as sources of Asian democratization. The article on Korea actually finds Western culture an obstacle to democratization. See Edward Friedman, "Asia as a Fount of Democratic Universalism," in Peter Van Ness, ed., *Debating Human Rights* (New York: Routledge, 1998), pp. 56–79. See also, Wm. Theodore de Bary and Tu Weiming, eds., *Confucianism and Human Rights* (New York: Columbia University Press, 1997) and David Kelly and Anthony Reid, eds., *Asian Freedoms* (New York: Cambridge University Press, 1998).
6. Edward Friedman, *The Politics of Democratization*. Boulder, CO: Westview, 1994.
7. William Dixon, "Democracy and the Peaceful Settlement of International Conflict," *American Political Science Review*, 88, March 1994, pp. 14–32; Kurt Gaubatz, "Democratic States and Commitment in International Relations," *International Organization*, 50 (1), Winter 1996, pp. 109–139; Joanne Gowa, "Democratic States and International Disputes," *International Organization,* 49 (3), Summer 1995, pp. 511–522; William Thompson, "Democracy and Peace," *International Organization,* 50 (1), Winter 1996, pp. 141–174; Spencer Weart, *Never at War*. New Haven, CT: Yale University Press, 1998; Stephen Walt, "Never Say Never," *Foreign Affairs*, 78 (1), pp. 146–150; R. J. Rummel versus Ted Galen Carpenter, "Democracy and War," *The Independent Review*, 3 (1), Summer 1998, pp. 103–110; Miriam Fendius Elman, ed., *Paths to Peace*. Cambridge, MA: MIT Press, 1997.
8. "Eternal Peace" in Immanuel Kant, *The Philosophy of Immanuel Kant*. New York: Modern Library, 1949, pp. 430–476.
9. Bruce Russett, *Grasping the Democratic Peace*. Princeton: Princeton University Press, 1993, pp. 54–59.
10. Edward Mansfield and Jack Snyder, "Democratization and War," *Foreign Affairs*, May/June 1995, pp. 79–97.
11. Neta Crawford, "A Security Regime among Democracies; Cooperation among Iroquois Nations," *International Organization*, 48 (3), Summer 1994, pp. 345–385.
12. Cf. Friedman in Van Ness, "Asia as a Fount of Democratic Universalism."
13. China's historic greatness is built on exchange (see Andre Gunder Frank,

ReORIENT. Berkeley: University of California Press, 1998), but most Chinese have been taught to believe the opposite, that commerce threatened a culture that was inherently superior.

14. The number of Chinese killed by Japanese invaders has risen from 11 million, a popular number at the end of the war, to 40 million, a popular number entering the twenty-first century. It is imperative for Chinese patriots to find that more Chinese were slaughtered in Japan's Nanjing Massacre in 1937–38 than Japanese died in America's atomic bombing of Hiroshima and Nagasaki.

15. This Japanese reality of a democratic country, one apparent in opinion polling, is hidden from Chinese because Beijing's propaganda focuses on the apologetics of Japanese textbooks put out by forces beholden to ultraconservatives in the Ministry of Education. Again, democracy, which could allow an unfettered flow of information, could strengthen the forces of peace.

16. A. Voskressenski, "The Perceptions of China by Russia's Foreign Policy Elite," *Issues and Studies*, 33 (3), March 1997, p. 8.

17. F. Tatad, "Philippine Security Based on U.S. Presence," *Asia Times*, June 6, 1997, p. 7.

18. Willy Wo-lap Lam, *The Era of Jiang Zemin*. New York: Prentice Hall, 1999.

19. Caroline Moorhead, "All rights Reserved," *Index on Censorship*, 26 (3), May/June 1997, p. 204.

20. This is in no way even to hint at the absurd idea that Beijing in the post-Mao era faintly resembles domestic Germany in the post-Weimar era. Mass murder was the result of Mao-era policies which post-Mao reform ended.

21. See Joanne Bauer and Daniel Bell, eds., *The East Asian Challenge for Human Rights*. New York: Cambridge University Press, 1999.

22. John Dower, *Embracing Defeat* (New York: The New Press, 1999) argues that it was the American occupation's decision to use Emperor Hirohito, surely a war criminal, as a symbol of democratization that peculiarly confused the issue of war guilt in Japan.

23. He Baogang, *The Democratization of China*. London: Routledge, 1996.

24. Edward Friedman, "What Asia Will or Will Not Stand For: Globalizing Democracy and Human Rights," *Asian Thought and Society*, 22, May–August 1997, pp. 200–229.

25. Ian Buruma, "God Bless America," *Index on Censorship*, 26 (3), May/June 1997, p. 158.

26. Samuel Huntington, *American Politics: The Promise of Disharmony*. Cambridge: Belknap Press, 1981, p. 239.

27. Samuel Huntington, *The Soldier and the State*. Cambridge: Belknap Press, 1957, p. 139.

28. Ronald Dworkin, "Forked Tongues, Faked Doctrines," *Index on Censorship*, 26 (3), May/June 1997, pp. 151, 150.

29. Bernstein and Munro, *The Coming Conflict with China*, p. 15. Compare Andrew Nathan, *China's Transition*. New York: Columbia University Press, 1998.

30. He, *The Democratization of China*, pp. 160–163.

31. Bernstein and Munro, *The Coming Conflict with China*, p. 36.

32. Edward Friedman, *Backward Toward Revolution*. Berkeley: University of California Press, 1974.

33. Frank, *ReORIENT*.

34. Huntington, *The Clash of Civilizations*, p. 238.

35. Barrington Moore, Jr., *Socialist Origins of Dictatorship and Democracy*. Boston: Beacon Press, 1966.

36. Jacques Attali, "The Crash of Western Civilization," *Foreign Policy*, Summer 1997, p. 61.

37. Allen Whiting, "ASEAN Eyes China," *Asian Survey*, 37 (4), April 1997, pp. 299–322.

38. "Looking Back to the Future of U.S.-China Relations," *Notes from the National Committee*, 26 (1), Spring 1997, p. 17.

PART III
CONCLUDING OVERVIEWS

Chapter 9
Caution: Rough Road Ahead

Harvey Nelsen

Introduction: Will China Democratize, and If So, When?

Democracy has been sweeping the globe in a series of waves beginning in the late 1970s and intensifying since the end of the Cold War. Rich countries, poor countries, formerly communist countries, and former dictatorships have adopted democratic forms. Their historical backgrounds and cultural legacies do not seem to matter. The People's Republic of China (PRC) has not entirely escaped the influence of these democratic waves. But which democratizing influences are most relevant to the PRC?[1]

For years the conventional wisdom in America held that Confucian ideology and democracy were antithetical. Confucianism carries with it a respect for hierarchy, authority, and consensus. The rooting of democracy in postwar Japan opened the first crack in that argument. The more recent democratization of South Korea and Taiwan totally destroyed that belief.[2]

To the extent that wealth is a prerequisite for democracy, the PRC should soon qualify. Over one million families in the wealthy province of Guangdong earn over 100,000RMB per year. (That figure is equivalent to only $12,000, but it represents purchasing power far greater than that amount.) In cities throughout China, earnings exceeding 1,000RMB are reported by 76 percent of households.[3] But if a relatively equitable distribution of wealth is seen as easing the way for democracy, then China is going the wrong way. Inequities are growing between regions and between the newly rich and the newly poor.[4] The latter are often people who have lost jobs in the fading state-owned industries.

If grass roots democratic practices are the preconditions to the institution of a national democratic government, then China is on its way. Village elections have become commonplace and should soon be conducted throughout China or at least in the Han-populated regions. The Communist Party leadership realized democratic governance at the village level saved money, and avoided the problems inherent in direct rule. In 1998, Beijing proposed expanding elections to the township level. However, local self-governance for minorities such as the Tibetans and Moslem Uighurs will remain problematic for a regime worried about separatist tendencies.

The National People's Congress currently plays a role unimaginable twenty years ago. Rather than serving as a rubber stamp to decisions made in the Communist Party Politburo, the Congress debates policies and expresses displeasure by voting against the appointment of unpopular government officials. The Congress also accepts cases brought by citizens against governmental misrule. An "administrative litigation law" went into effect in 1990. Citizens can sue government offices for abuse of powers. The law is most often invoked against arbitrary police actions and the settlement claims are frequently in favor of the plaintiffs.[5]

One school of thought correlates democracy with the growth of a middle class and the emergence of a "civil society." The latter stems from the growth of nongovernmental organizations, and thus takes longer to emerge after an era of repression which systematically eliminated nongovernmental economic and social organizations. Civil society is growing in conjunction with the growth of the market economy. Not only are business associations growing in numbers, so too are social groups such a sports clubs, professional associations, foundations, and federations. But the Ministry of Civil Affairs keeps track of such groups and requires their registration with the state. The organizations have virtually no lobbying power in terms of influencing governmental policies. Central to the role of civil society organizations in creating democracy are features such as autonomy, spontaneity, voluntariness, and self-regulation. These are all deficient in contemporary China.[6] (For a more optimistic view of prospects for civil society in China, see Minxin Pei's chapter elsewhere in this volume.)

Another theory supporting the eventual democratization of China is known as "neo-liberal institutionalism." Based on the rising importance of international trade and global communications, this theory postulates that national governments are becoming less able to control their own destinies.[7] Over 25 percent of China's gross national product is now derived from international trade, so the approach would seem applicable to the PRC. But the neo-liberal institutionalist theory does not predict how soon democratization will follow internationalization of the economy.

In 1998, the *Journal of Democracy* published a symposium on the future of democracy in China. Ten well-known China scholars were asked to address a number of questions which can be summarized as (1) will the CCP still be in charge of the PRC ten years from now? (2) what are the prospects for democratization? and (3) what is the likelihood of chaos and possible territorial disintegration of the state?[8] There was significant agreement among the contributors. All but one believed that the PRC would still be intact in ten years and most believed that some form of CCP would still be in charge.[9]

The symposium generally agreed on the eventual democratization of the PRC, but no one could predict how long the process might take. The authors seemed to predicate the eventual attainment of democracy on neo-liberal institutionalism. (These arguments include the rise of a "civil society," the growth of the middle class, high levels of education, and the homogenizing effects of international capitalism.)

In his concluding article, Andrew Nathan, whose preface graces this volume, reviewed the analyses of his colleagues. He found that the contributors were unable to discover actors in the Chinese political-economic system who both represent democratic values and have real power to accomplish their goals.[10] Neo-liberal institutionalism looks to the rise of a bourgeoisie as an important factor in eroding authoritarianism. But the Chinese bourgeoisie is neither autonomous nor anti-state. The emerging Chinese middle class is not apt to challenge the state since it takes the form of a bureaucratic-business elite network.[11] Wealth is generated through special prerogatives, quasi-monopolies, and in general, the use of political power to achieve economic benefits. Politicians from the local level to the nation's capital work hand-in-glove, (and hand-in-pocket), with entrepreneurs. They have a symbiotic relationship.

Factors Impeding the Development of Democracy in China

I am in agreement with the contributors to the *Journal of Democracy* symposium. Regime change in the PRC does not seem imminent. Communist authoritarianism will characterize national and provincial politics in the PRC for years to come. A number of factors contribute to this end:

(1) The fear of anarchy has deep historical roots. China's long history has seen many periods of economic and political collapse. Even anticommunist supporters of the 1989 student democracy movement feared a loss of order. In fact, the students called for a cleaner, more responsible government rather than an immediate transition to a pluralist political system.[12] There was no institutional answer to the question, "If not the communists, then what?"

(2) Rapid economic growth dates from the early 1980s. Deng Xiaoping concluded that to save party rule, capitalism had to be adopted. His policies worked. De-collectivizing agriculture, opening the door to foreign investment, and allowing the growth of an urban private sector combined to produce rapid economic development. Chinese citizens like the consumerist results. Might pluralism slow the gravy train?

(3) Nationalism in China has waxed while communism—as an ideology—has waned. As a mobilizing ideology, communism has been dead in China since 1989, if not earlier. Nonetheless, the communist leadership soldiers on. It promises to develop prosperity. Equally important, it promises a "myth" of redemption from national humiliation. (The word myth is used in the sense of a powerful underlying belief conditioning the thinking of a society like the myth of American individualism.) As Edward Friedman put it: "It is as if American politics were still premised on passions of revenge for the humiliations of the Alamo, the Lusitania, Pearl Harbor and the helicopter evacuation of the U.S. embassy in Saigon."[13] Beijing promises to restore China to its rightful place in Asia and the international order. It has made a great deal of progress toward that goal especially since the death of Mao. Taiwan remains the major unfulfilled objective. This nationalistic rallying cry unites Chinese behind the current government (see the chapter by Suisheng Zhao). To the extent that the United States hinders China's mythic restoration to greatness, Washington will serve as a useful whipping post for Chinese nationalism. The spring of 1999 saw a case in point: the massive anti-U.S. demonstrations in reaction to the accidental bombing of the PRC embassy in Belgrade.

(4) While wealth accumulates, institutional development lags. Regional disparities partly explain this gap. The urban areas of coastal China and the adjacent rural areas are prosperous. Poverty remains strong

in interior provinces whose residents obtain remittances from migrant labor to the rich cities and a gradual "trickle in" economic process.[14] The government of the PRC is still state-centric and actively discourages the creation of interest groups. Thus, as noted above, civil society remains stunted. The press must be cautious when undertaking investigative journalism. Meanwhile, the rule of law makes progress in the PRC, but at a slow pace.

(5) Dissent and dissenters face severe treatment in the PRC. No Chinese Sakharovs remain free in China. Although this dike against democratic development receives the lion's share of attention in the U.S. media and government, it is a dike made of clay. Suppression collapses quickly. Whether in East Germany under Honecker or South Korea under the military juntas, once conditions favored the development of democratization, authoritarian controls quickly collapsed. That so many dissidents reside in jail or in exile reflects the vulnerability of the Beijing leadership rather than the strength of its tyranny.

(6) PRC corruption is among the world's worst. This provides perverse incentives to maintain the current system. The pathological mix of Stalinist politics and market economics offers marvelous opportunities for power holders to enrich themselves. The People's Liberation Army (PLA, encompassing all the armed forces), the Chinese Communist Party (CCP), and the governmental apparatus all conspire to protect their share of the corruption pie. In the summer of 1998, President Jiang Zemin announced a major effort to reduce corruption in the PLA. Over the years, the armed forces had become involved in tens of thousands of businesses ranging from arms manufacturing to houses of prostitution. It has also been involved in smuggling operations and the pirating of intellectual and artistic properties. Some of the most successful CD manufacturers operated their pirate plants in areas protected by the PLA. In addition to corrupting the personnel, especially the officers, such activities detracted from military readiness and training.

As of the summer of 1999, President Jiang's orders have largely been implemented. But many of the firms previously run by the military have been taken over by government offices so there is no guarantee of decreasing corruption or increased efficiency. In the absence of a rule of law and a free press, corruption will continue to fester in spite of repeated national campaigns to eliminate it. As the problem continues over time, the resultant popular disgust and weakening of governing institutions will probably hasten the democratization of the PRC. Hence it is a double-edged sword, supporting communism in the short term while undermining it in the long run.

So when will China become democratic? It will probably be a process, not an event, so it is unlikely that there will be a distinct date like the tearing down of the Berlin Wall. But the process will make only slow progress under the current generation of political leadership. There is no guarantee that pluralism will follow hard on the heels of Jiang Zemin and Zhu Rongji. The democratization which begins to emerge will likely look like that of Singapore. One party will remain dominant, but other parties will be allowed to compete in the political process, albeit under handicaps. The democratization process may well be from the bottom up, so the national government may be the last holdout of authoritarian, single-party rule.

We will probably have to deal with a corrupt, authoritarian, increasingly powerful, and slowly democratizing China for at least the next decade. What does this mean for the Chinese, their neighbors including Hong Kong and Taiwan, and for the United States?

China's Mid-Range Future: Politics and Nationalism

China will be authoritarian, not totalitarian.[15] Beijing has let much slip away from government and party control in the post-Mao era. The growth of a market economy, massive foreign investment, the birth of thousands of privately financed newspapers and magazines, and the overseas education of hundreds of thousands of students combine to prevent any possibility of the government controlling the lives of its citizenry as in the Mao era. These developments belie the assertion that the PRC will become a fascist state.[16] Yet when Beijing targets individuals or small groups, it can and does crush their ability to be heard or even to remain free.

Secondly, the centrifugal forces in China will not cause the country to break apart in the foreseeable future. The factors degrading national unity include: (1) serious gaps between wealthy coastal provinces and their poor cousins in the interior. Deepening economic ties bind regions of China with neighboring countries. (2) The national government receives a decreasing share of the gross domestic product, and lacks ideological legitimacy. (3) Social tensions are growing in Chinese society as the market economy creates winners and losers not simply among rich and poor provinces, but also within the wealthy provinces. (4) Ethnically based separatism, primarily in Tibet and Xinjiang autonomous regions, poses a challenge to Beijing's authority. Terrorist incidents based on Islamic separatism have broken out sporadically in the 1990s.

These forces are more than counterbalanced by the centripetal factors. Most important is the myth of national humiliation. Aspirations for regaining national pride would be stymied if China were to break up. Nationalism serves as a powerful bond. An ethnic Han nationalism is a bedrock upon which the more fragile state nationalism is built. This nationalism will prevent secessionist movements from developing except in the minority regions. Secondly, political power is still centralized in Beijing, especially through the power of appointment. Thirdly, a break-up into regions would not sustain economic prosperity; it would destroy it. The Chinese economy is too regionally interdependent to allow even the richest provinces to prosper on their own. Fourthly, the military serves as a powerful final bastion to prevent political dissolution. Finally, China is not the former Soviet Union. It has a common written language and thus a common culture even though there are mutually unintelligible dialects and languages spoken in China. Domestic difficulties, some of which will be violent, will preoccupy the PRC in the future, but they will not destroy the nation-state.

The long-term future of Tibet and Xinjiang remains to be seen. Who in the 1970s would have dared to predict that the Baltic States would be independent from Moscow's control in the 1990s? Ethnic nationalism is an incredibly durable force whose roots deepen during periods of suppression. Chinese imperial control of Tibet and Xinjiang guarantees the survival and the increasingly anti-Han nature of nationalism in those regions.

If the PRC remains united and authoritarian, how will it operate? Kenneth Lieberthal provides a valuable tool in his concept of "fragmented authoritarianism."[17] China has the world's largest bureaucracy. Both vertical and horizontal ties form complex matrix systems. An office chief will usually have several people in authority over him, party and government, regional and national. Depending on the issue at hand, one of these bosses will have more authority and relevance than others. This fragmented authority makes it relatively easy in China for the bureaucracy to frustrate the will of political leaders. As effective governments go, the PRC ranks among the worst.

Accurate information is a problem. The leadership has every reason not to trust its own official statistics. Beijing only recently learned that it had 20 to 25 percent more land under cultivation than was being reported and taxed. This information came from the United States which produces spectrographic satellite images of crops to evaluate the size of coming harvests. In 1997, Beijing began a new agricultural census. If it had continued to rely on its own internal bureaucratic reporting, how long would it have taken to discover this ancient tax dodge? Bureaucrats are aided by the cult of secrecy which restricts free access to information. If information is not directly related to one's responsibilities, then access may be denied. The "need to know" causes problems even in relatively open systems such as the United States. In China, secrecy enables bureaucrats to hide information easily, and to use limited access to information as a tool of power. The system also results in corruption and petty dictatorial behavior as bureaucrats find opportunities to enrich themselves and abuse the powers of their office while easily covering up such malfeasance.

The system is state-centric. In Lieberthal's words: "Neither in theory nor in practice is individual advocacy or interest group activity regarded as legitimate. . . . Only the leaders have the right to determine what is in the 'real' interests of the peasants and of other groups and to create appropriate official organs and assign appropriate tasks to them." [18] The confusion of lines of authority and responsibility also results in decision-avoidance behavior. Problems get shoved up the chain of command, overloading the system at the top and glutenizing the political process. Decisions reached at lower levels require consensus. Extensive consultations and bargains among bureaucrats reinforce the lack of responsive government in China.

Economics constitute an important exception to the centralization of decision making. For these matters, the provincial level has become a key decision maker. Deng began economic decentralization as a means of stimulating growth and allowing local leaders to take advantage of unique conditions and assets. But decentralization snowballed, resulting in reduced economic controls from Beijing and more power for the provinces than at any time since the communists assumed national power.

In the past, state controls over ordinary citizens relied heavily on the work unit and the residence permits. The work unit provided housing at little cost and offered job security, but the worker was not free to quit and change jobs. The residence permit controlled population distribution and prevented millions of peasants from moving into Chinese cities. Both of those control measures have lost much of their effectiveness with the rise of a labor market and the mobility of the current Chinese work force. Well over 100 million migrant workers live in Chinese cities today, virtually all of whom have come from the countryside and/or from poor provinces.

What is the operational outcome of these forces and factors? The Chinese will be preoccupied with economic development. Urban job creation has been a major focus in the 1990s and that will diminish only slightly over the next decade. Housing will be of increasing concern as privatization proceeds apace, and low-cost subsidized housing gradually becomes as hard to find as a rent-controlled apartment in Manhattan. Cleaning up a disastrously polluted environment may be the biggest single-budget item in China's future and it will be a necessity for public health. The central government will also be preoccupied with fiscal difficulties. Its problem is the decreasing share of the GNP flowing into tax coffers controlled by Beijing. Structural reforms are underway, including a new national value-added tax, and the cash-flow to Beijing did improve in 1999. Keeping a tight control on the money supply to prevent the return of runaway inflation will require relatively high interest rates and some austerity measures.

The rule of law will make progress in China, but the most rapid advances will be in the civil, commercial, and business sectors. (See Minxin Pei's chapter for advances made to date.) Those sectors will receive legal protections to insure the continued development of the market economy and magnetism for foreign investments.

Improvement in the human rights situation may well be a slow process. The "democracy movement" of spring 1989 will probably be positively re-evaluated, but no one can predict how long this might take. Beijing's 1997–98 signature on two United Nations international covenants looks potentially promising. It first signed the Covenant on Economic, Social and Cultural Rights and later signed the Covenant on Civil and Political Rights. These have yet to be ratified by the National People's Congress so they still have no legal force in the PRC. Even if ratified, enforcement is yet another question. However, the signatures seem to be a step in the right direction. (See Samuel Kim's chapter for a detailed discussion of China's human rights from an international perspective.)

The PRC will increase its military muscle over the next two decades. As a result of its export-oriented economic policy and favorable trade balance, the PRC has a large reserve of hard currency. The 1998 figure was about $125 billion. If the current account balance remains favorable, China can buy a great deal of modern military equipment in the coming years. Russia has been and will continue to be the primary supplier. A continuing annual growth rate at around 7 percent will enable China to double its military budget in ten years without robbing Peter to pay Paul. Modernization is badly needed. While new aircraft have been acquired, the bulk of the PLA air force looks like a flying antiques show, and the navy is not much better. Modernization includes force projection capabilities. The PRC will eventually be able to threaten its Asian neighbors with air and naval forces, but it will not be able to dominate the East Asian region.

The centrality of Chinese nationalism will guarantee that Beijing will develop a credible military force, including an advanced nuclear arsenal. Democratization or the lack thereof will probably have little relevance to the military budget. Of course, experience has proven that powerful military forces led by democratic governments are less dangerous than those of authoritarian regimes.

China's Neighbors: Hong Kong and Taiwan

The lynchpin for Beijing's relationship with "greater China" and, to a lesser extent, the rest of the world will be Hong Kong. If the "one country, two systems" program works and Hong Kong continues to prosper, the prospects for a Taiwan settlement will improve. If Hong Kong falls under the pall of repression and corruption, and capital flight takes place, then the Beijing government will have shot itself in the foot. Foreign investment would diminish sharply as a result of Hong Kong capital flight. Hong Kong has been the source of most foreign investment in the PRC. A loss of confidence in Hong Kong would drive most capital overseas. Some portion of Hong Kong's wealth would, however, end up in the PRC. The amount would depend upon Shanghai's ability to supplant Hong Kong as a major Asian financial and trade center.

The gloom and doom scenarios for Hong Kong seem unlikely. The "special administrative region" as it is now called faces numerous problems most of which are related to the general Asian financial crisis but none of these appear life threatening. The biggest concern is the probable growth of corruption. Hong Kong under British rule was hardly a paragon in this regard, but the playing field for the business community was pretty even. Now it seems that companies with mainland political connections are apt to find the field tilted in their favor. Over a period of time, this could diminish the dynamism and adaptability of the economy.

If things go badly in Hong Kong, the chances for a peaceful resolution of the Taiwan problem will be much reduced. Neither the Nationalist authorities—the Kuomintang (KMT)—nor the opposition Democratic Progressive Party (DPP) have any confidence in Beijing's "one country, two systems" formulation for Hong Kong's future. The DPP continues to oppose any eventual reunification with the PRC. However, in 1999, it adopted a platform opposing a declaration of independence for the island. Both the DPP and KMT in effect support a continuation of the status quo. That is the *de facto* political separation from the mainland. But in February 2000, the PRC made a dramatic and unilateral announcement. If Taiwan failed to pursue reunification talks with the mainland, that would be sufficient reason for China to use military force.

The policy of the United States, Taiwan, Japan, and virtually all other actors involved with the PRC has been to defer the Taiwan issue. The hope has been that fundamental political reforms in China would make reunification less odious to the Taiwanese. Now the PRC has declared an end to that approach. When the new urgency for reunification is combined with Chinese military modernization, it poses the frightening prospect of a war in the Taiwan Straits. This could easily involve the United States, given the generalized commitments of the Taiwan Relations Act. It is not a defense treaty, and there are no defined "triggers" which would automatically commit U.S. forces to the defense of Taiwan. American support for Taiwan seemed to fade in the summer of 1999 after President Lee Teng-hui announced his "two state" conditions for negotiations with the mainland. His demand for future talks required that Beijing deal with Taiwan as a negotiating equal rather than as a political entity inferior to the PRC. He did not declare Taiwan to be an independent nation, but the Chinese language was ambiguous. The term in Chinese for "state" is *guojia*. The same Chinese term is used for "nation." So Lee's position seeemed perilously close to "independence" which the United States had consistently renounced since the time of the 1972 Nixon visit to Beijing. The PRC has repeatedly warned that a Taiwanese declaration of independence would justify the use of military force.

President Lee's statement probably contributed to Beijing's new hard line. The clock is ticking. Taiwan's democracy is less than ten years old, but it has strengthened the Taiwanese sense of their own self-identity. Moreover, authoritarian political figures can no longer make deals with the mainland over the heads of the citizens. The virulent anticommunism on the island makes it suicidal for any Taipei government to get too close to Beijing. It would seem that the passage of time does not favor Beijing.

In the interim, an arms race has begun. Beijing's military modernization has been proceeding at a moderate pace. But the new weapons systems include ships, submarines, and aircraft which enhance the ability of the mainland to project military power against Taiwan. So far, the PRC has made little effort to build a major sea-lift capacity which would be needed for an invasion of the island. But the thinking may be that an air and naval blockade would be sufficient to bring down the government on Taiwan. The U.S. response has been to approve additional arms sales to Taiwan. Currently Taiwan looks like an iceberg in the path of the Titanic of Sino-American relations.

The ultimate irony of the Taiwan problem is democracy itself. If the PRC were to become a democratic nation, Taiwan would be far more interested in confederating with it. However, the Beijing leadership is not about to commit political suicide in order to accomplish national reunification. (How many of the surviving members of Gorbachev's Politburo hold responsible political positions today?) Yet democratization in Taiwan also poses a problem. If a reformed Mr. Beijing, respectful of the rule of law, freedom of the press, and pluralistic political processes, offered marriage to the lovely Miss Taipei, how long would she want to wait before setting the date? Would Taiwan turn coy? What would it take to generate the necessary level of trust to tie the knot? It takes two parties to make a marriage, and one party will be in no hurry. Realistically, the best outcome for the Taiwan issue was to postpone it. But in light of Beijing's February 2000 pronouncement, that course of action seems increasingly problematic.

China's Neighbors: Southeast Asia

The most important entity for China in this region is the Association of Southeast Asian Nations (ASEAN). This organization recently consists of Burma (or Myanmar as the current military junta calls it), Laos, Thailand, Malaysia, Singapore, Indonesia, Brunei, Vietnam, Cambodia, and the Philippines. ASEAN has made little progress over the last few decades in integrating the economies of its members. It has been more successful at building tariff and non-tariff barriers to imports from abroad while fighting to protect its export markets. A few years ago the organization added a political dimension to its economic role. It established the ASEAN Regional Forum (ARF) to discuss political and security concerns affecting the area. Participation in the ARF is not restricted to members of ASEAN. China initially declined to participate, but after it became clear that ARF discussions and potential decisions would impact on China's interests, it joined the group.

China's interests in Southeast Asia are predominantly economic. Overseas Chinese communities in ASEAN nations contribute an important portion of the foreign investments flowing into the PRC. Imports and exports to and from the region amount to approximately $15 billion. The most important source of conflict between China and the ASEAN members are overlapping territorial claims in the Spratly and Paracel Islands. These complex claims would be trivial but for food, oil and natural gas potential. Multiple sovereign claims twist the problem into a Gordian knot. The best hope is to defer the issue of sovereignty while seeking joint economic exploitation of the seabed resources. Such agreements will be very difficult to construct, but Beijing has at least said it would work toward that end.

Commentators have often noted that Asia lacks an organization such as NATO which helps insure stability in Europe. But ASEAN plays an important role in that regard. Since economic relations are so central to Beijing's concerns in the region, Beijing is unlikely to act like a neighborhood bully (but see the chapter by June Dreyer for a less sanguine view). The worst case scenario for the PRC would be joint ASEAN policies sanctioning Beijing for its behavior in the region. That would require highly provocative actions on the part of China; but the threat of collective economic sanctions still serves as a restraint against rash action.

Again the degree of democracy in the PRC has little relevance to the issue. Resource diplomacy and territorial claims could hardly be renounced by a democratically elected government in Beijing—not if it wanted to stay in office.

China and Japan

The future of Sino-Japanese relations may prove as troubled in the future as it has been in the last few decades. Objectively, the two nations should be "as close as lips and teeth" (as the Chinese saying goes). They are natural trading partners. Japan provides high value-added goods, China provides raw materials and labor-intensive products. Japan provides investment and technology transfer, China provides a large market with an immense growth potential. Japan provides foreign aid in part to protect its own environment from acid rain.

The problems stem from conflicting political cultures. China sees itself a morally superior but victimized nation. The myth of national humiliation is especially powerful in Sino-Japanese relations. In Chinese eyes, Japan owes debts which it has not begun to repay. These derive from the 1931–1945 occupation and war and from Japan's failure to fully confess its historical sins. The PRC seeks more than a confession of guilt. Japan must pledge itself to sin no more and must continue to so pledge and apologize over and over again. Japan's U.S.-imposed constitutional ban on war as a diplomatic tool is seen as an insufficient barrier to a militarily resurgent Japan. China suspects the worst when Washington and Tokyo alter their defense alliance to make Japan's role more pro-active as they did in 1996–97.

Japanese vary in their responses to Chinese paranoia and hostility. However, more and more feel that Tokyo has gone as far as it should in kowtowing to China.[19] The Japanese emperor visited China in 1992 and apologized for World War II. Many Japanese feel that China raises one issue after another, and that there is just no way to satisfy the moralists on the mainland. The issue of the "comfort women," (women forced into prostitution for the benefit of Japanese occupation forces during World War II), was just the latest in a long series of such Chinese demands for continuing Japanese contrition.

The difficulty of overcoming these historical and cultural conflicts was clearly demonstrated in President Jiang Zemin's visit to Japan in November 1998. While the Chinese leader availed himself of every opportunity to call for Japanese penitence for past wrongs, his message found an unresponsive audience.

A territorial dispute over the Senkaku (in Japanese) or Diaoyu Islands further complicates bilateral relations. These uninhabited rocks encompass known undersea oil reserves, though the size of the deposit is believed to be rather modest. There is no possibility of resolving the conflicting sovereign claims, and unlike the Spratly Islands, very little possibility for joint exploitation of the resources. Taiwan compounds the problem with its own claims to the Diaoyu Islands. It is easier for Beijing to share the seabed spoils with other nation-states than it is to share "its" resources with what Beijing considers a "renegade province."

Beijing seemed willing to let sleeping dogs lie regarding the islands. Unfortunately, right-wing Japanese activists stirred up trouble in 1996 by building a lighthouse on one of the larger rocks. This led to a great deal of heat, but not much light. Some of the heat came from Hong Kong. Citizens groups organized on the issue and a delegation traveled to Beijing to lobby the PRC in favor of a tough stance against Japan. This was the first case of spontaneous Chinese nationalism in Hong Kong which pressured Beijing to take action. It was noteworthy that Beijing did not attempt to inflame the Senkaku/Diaoyu issue. Anti-Japanese student demonstrations were kept in check and Sino-Japanese relations continued apace.

The ultimate dividing line between the two nations relates to power. The Chinese fear a revival of Japanese militarism more than any other real or potential threat. Most Chinese will accept the fact that the Japanese political environment has been remarkably pacifist since the end of World War II. But at the same time, the Japanese have only grudgingly expressed contrition and seem to lack guilt for their actions in World War II. Thus there is a visceral fear that aggressiveness may be revived at some time in the future. Would a democratic China be more comfortable with Japanese power and its growing sense of nationalism? (See Edward Friedman's chapters for a positive answer to that question.)

The United States and China: The American Perspective

The biggest problem for the United States if China does not democratize is not with the PRC. Americans put China into the special category of nations whose affairs are important to our self-image as the protagonist of democratization and human rights in the world.[20] Two other countries which share this misfortune are Cuba and Israel. Americans cannot distance themselves from the affairs of these countries without degrading their own international moral leadership as they perceive it. Bernstein and Munro premise their argument in *The Coming Conflict with China* on the rise of a neo-fascist government bent on establishing Chinese hegemony in Asia. This leads inevitably to clashes of national interest with the United States.[21] The authors could just as well have based their argument upon the nature of the U.S. polity and its paternalistic attitudes toward the Chinese.

Political demagogues target China as an emotional and easy way to prey on American sentiments. Bill Clinton accused President Bush of "coddling dictators in Beijing." In 1997, House Minority Leader Dick Gephardt took demagogy to new levels. He described the PRC as "totalitarian" and called for trade sanctions against Beijing similar to those undertaken against the USSR following the invasion of Afghanistan. "Only corrupt bureaucrats and brutal generals profit from trade with the United States."[22] The ballooning trade deficit is taking away American jobs, said Gephardt, ignoring the low unemployment rates in the United States and ignoring the labor-intensive nature of most Chinese exports. Are American workers standing in line waiting for jobs in garment sweatshops at below minimum wages?

A new crisis emerged in May 1999 with the release of the Cox Report —a congressional investigation into Chinese nuclear espionage in the United States. The findings were shocking in terms of how effective the intelligence collection effort was, and how long it had been going on (for about twenty years). Many in Congress were outraged at this Chinese breach of trust. Others more sensibly called for improved counter-intelligence efforts at U.S. nuclear labs. As the world's most advanced nation in terms of both strategic and conventional weaponry, the United States should expect to be the target of scores of foreign intelligence services. If the chief of Chinese intelligence did not put top priority on penetrating U.S. secrets, he should have been fired.

This has led to a growing distrust of China in Washington. The stolen nuclear secrets scandal was just the last in a series of events. These include arms proliferation (especially nuclear technology to Pakistan), illegal campaign contributions in the 1996 elections (both congressional and presidential), missile tests in Taiwanese waters in 1996, and the 1999 Chinese veto in the UN for continued peacekeeping forces in Macedonia. The latter came at a critical moment, just prior to the influx of Kosovar refugees and seriously complicated handling the flood of humanity. Last but not least was the February 2000 announcement that Taiwan could not indefinitely delay reunification talks without facing military reprisals.

The current levels of hostility and distrust toward China have forced the Clinton administration to retrench its China policy. In the presidential politics year of 2000, candidate Al Gore is less than enthusiastic in support of Beijing's entry into the World Trade Organization (WTO). Congress is divided on the permanent implementation "normal trade relations" legislation—formerly known as "most favored nation." This began as an annual exercise and legal requirement at the height of the Cold War when all communist nations faced various levels of trade restrictions with the United States. WTO trade relations among all members are supposed to be "normal." If the Congress insists on keeping the annual review of economic relations with Beijing, retaliation can be expected. Thus the main objective of the WTO—freer and more open trade—would be negated in Sino-American relations. Other member nations would then have a major advantage over the United States in terms of penetrating Chinese markets.

The White House no longer talks about China in terms of a "strategic partnership." Even the more neutral term "comprehensive engagement" has temporarily disappeared from the U.S. political lexicon. But relations are not damaged beyond repair. The regularly scheduled summit meetings will continue and Chinese cooperation will be needed on a host of future international issues. Also, no responsible politician in the United States wants to see China in an economic crisis nor does he/she want to see a new Cold War with the PRC.

How would a democratized China change its current negative image in the United States? First, and most importantly, Americans would no longer carry the image of the PRC government as "the butchers of Beijing." But it is unlikely that such a China would cease its drive for military modernization and the use of espionage for that purpose. Foreign arms sales would also continue since this is a significant contribution to China's overall favorable trade balance. Of course, as the world's largest arms merchant, it is hypocritical for the United States to point fingers at China. As noted in a previous section, Chinese democratization would probably reduce the tension over Taiwan, but patience would still be required of all the actors involved.

China and the United States: Beijing's Perspective

America views China with distrust. China views America as malevolent. The post–Cold War environment left the United States as the only superpower and American hegemony threatens Chinese interests. These include security, economic development, political stability, and Chinese national pride. The top threat from the security dimension is Washington's plans to develop a missile defense force for the continental United States and a theater missile defense force for deployment abroad. Discussions are currently underway to deploy a theater missile defense in Taiwan, even though the antiballistic missile technology is still only in the research and development phase. Those missile defense systems would weaken China's nuclear deterrent. The United States could attack China with impunity knowing that the PRC could not retaliate with missiles. This is one reason explaining China's nuclear espionage. Beijing wants to update its warhead designs. The ultimate aim may be a "multiple independently targeted re-entry vehicle" (MIRV) warhead which can penetrate all current missile defense technologies.

On the economic front, the United States put one road block after another in the path of China's efforts to enter the WTO and its predecessor, the General Agreement on Trade and Tariffs (GATT). When Premier Zhu Rongji visited Washington in 1999, he offered major concessions in return for American support. Not only was he turned down, the highly concessional terms he offered were made public. This embarrassed the Premier and seemed like a calculated American affront to Chinese pride. In late 1999, the breakthrough was finally achieved in WTO negotiations and both sides agreed to terms by which the PRC could join the club. But as noted above, congressional politics and a presidential election year in the United States may result in Beijing being snubbed again.

Beijing's great success in developing a market economy and decentralizing authority away from the national government has—in some ways—worsened relations with the United States. Beijing has lost control over activities at local levels. Intellectual properties, piracy, false labels of origin on textile manufactures, drug smuggling, and illegal immigration operations are flourishing. High levels of corruption in the PRC mean that such illegal operations often are protected by local officials. As with Washington D.C.'s efforts to end drug trafficking in the United States, the Beijing government can do little about these developments, even though it often makes good faith efforts. If Beijing could control such activities, would it stand idly by as the crime rate goes up in the PRC year after year and drug addiction spreads among its youth?

In terms of political malevolence, Beijing believes that the United States pushes human rights issues in China in order to weaken the government and bring on the collapse of Chinese socialism. Religious freedom provides a good example of the differing perspectives between the two nations. In July 1997, the State Department released a report on repression faced by Christianity around the world. A good deal of the report dealt with China. The main thrust of the complaints did not deal with actual suppression or persecution. It dealt with *regulation*. The PRC requires that churches be registered with the state. There are at least fourteen million practicing Christians in China, ten million Protestant and four million Catholics, who worship in over 12,000 churches.[23] So the registration requirement is not a ruse for refusing to allow churches to operate. Rather the requirement stems from a government fear that foreign evangelism might serve to undermine loyalty at home. Chinese churches, regardless of what religion is involved, are required to be "patriotic" churches. This is seen by the State Department as an intolerable persecution of Christianity.[24]

The religious issue is problematic in the Sino-American relationship because of the differing historical legacy with Christianity. The PRC sees Christianity as an appendage to imperialism. As early as 1742, a papal bull prohibited Chinese Catholics from participating in various Confucian rites.[25] Cultural imperialism is bad enough, but Pope John Paul II is famous for his role in assisting Solidarity to overthrow the communist leadership of Poland. Little wonder that the CCP leadership is reluctant to allow Chinese Catholics to be led by the Vatican. In the nineteenth century, protected by the military power of foreign nations, Catholic and Protestant missionaries raged throughout China. They undermined the legitimacy of the Manchu dynasty in a number of ways.[26] Still worse, a bizarre version of Christianity served as the religious ideology in a massive peasant uprising and civil war which killed tens of millions of people in the 1850–65 period. Inchoate mass hatred of foreign intervention and Christianity led to the Boxer Uprising of 1900 which saw many Chinese Christians murdered. Exclusive, evangelical religions whose deities are transcendent rather than immanent are dangerously divisive. The two major religions which fit that profile are Christianity and Islam. The religious war history of both compares very unfavorably to the traditions of religious tolerance expressed in Daoism, Buddhism, and Confucianism.

Meanwhile, Americans emphasize the good works done by Christian missions, ranging from humanitarian assistance to economic modernization. Since the ultimate ambition of the missionary movement is the saving of souls, it is hard for some Christian Americans to resist targeting an officially atheistic nation of nearly 1.3 billion people. These widely divergent perceptions of Christianity and of missions will continue to trouble Sino-American relations.

Chinese persecution of the Buddhist sect, Falun Gong, in 1999 also troubled Sino-American relations. The issue has parallels to the contemporary treatment of Christians in the PRC. The new sect was approved, and there was no major problem until 1988. At that time, the founder had a falling out with the national religious association which supervised the disparate elements of Buddhism. It is not clear whether Falun Gong pulled out from state sponsorship, or if they were ejected. But in either case, the religion had lost its credentials in the eyes of the state. In 1999, a mass demonstration of the Falun Gong faithful in Tiananmen Square caught the authorities off guard. From that point on, the government declared war against the sect. It had not only abandoned regulatory authority, it had the temerity to protest its treatment in a public demonstration, and in Tiananmen Square to boot! Beijing is intent on destroying the Falun Gong organization. It will not succeed, but it will take additional heat for human rights abuses. In this instance the case against the PRC is stronger than the protests regarding their treatment of Christianity.

Chinese national pride has been repeatedly wounded by the United States in recent years. The biggest wound is undoubtedly the continued military support for Taiwan. But more symbolically painful was inviting Taiwanese President Lee Teng-hui to Cornell University to give an alumni reunion address in 1995. That highly politicized trip seemed to set Washington toward a "two China" policy course, and infuriated the Beijing leadership. Other real and perceived slights include China's failed bid for the 2000 Olympic games, and the treatment and judging of Chinese athletes at the 1996 Atlanta Olympic games. In 1995, President Clinton refused to accord President Jiang Zemin a state visit to Washington. These accumulated grievances, all of which reinforce the myth of Chinese humiliation, came to a boiling point with the U.S. bombing of the Chinese embassy in Belgrade in May 1999. The popular outrage, albeit supported by the Beijing regime, was widespread. An anti-American demonstration even occurred in Taiwan.

In summary, China sees the United States as dangerous and Chinese concessions to American power never seem to be adequate. American hegemony is becoming the latest form of international imperialism. It tramples on the sovereignty of others as seen in the Kosovo intervention. It demands that the rest of the world adhere to its standards. The guiding principle for Beijing's foreign policy over the last several years has been "multipolarity." All reasonable measures should be undertaken to undercut American global hegemony.

Conclusion

Democracy has limited relevance to the policy issues which threaten to sour China's relations with foreign nations. As Harry Harding put it:

"Democratization, especially in immature countries, can permit expression of nationalism that authoritarian regimes once suppressed, and such activity may not lead to peaceful foreign policies."[27] Elections in the component states of the former Yugoslavia brought to power radical antidemocratic nationalists whose dedication to peace is dubious at best.

The big issue which democracy might help resolve would be Taiwan. It might clear the path for reunification or confederation, but the process would still probably be protracted. The threats to Hong Kong derive more from corruption than from loss of civil liberties which the citizens of Hong Kong never had until the 1990s. Ethnic nationalism, resource diplomacy, and corrupt economic practices would not disappear as a result of democratization. Nor would democracy convince Beijing to loosen its controls over Tibet and Xinjiang where the largest scale human rights violations have occurred. The regions are considered strategic to the long-term defense of Han China, and their natural resources have only recently begun to be seriously explored.

Samuel Huntington's *Clash of Civilizations* quotes approvingly from Michael Dibdin's novel, *Dead Lagoon*: "There can be no true friends without true enemies. Unless we hate what we are not, we cannot love what we are."[28] This is a moot statement; but for the sake of argument, assume that it is true. Democratization or the lack thereof in the PRC will have little impact on such "us-them" divisions between China and foreign countries and cultures. A democratized China would still look very different from the political cultures of the United States and Japan. Political demagogues would still roil the waters between themselves and the United States. PRC policies which trouble others would remain largely unchanged. The liberalization of China to date has generated almost as many problems as it has resolved. In general, a democratized government in Beijing would still find American power to be an obstacle to the pursuit of its national interests.

The editors of this volume, Barrett McCormick and Edward Friedman, make a clear distinction between popular nationalism in China and nationalism as an instrument of control and manipulation as used by the regime. This is important, but it is not clear that the one form of nationalism is benign and the other aggressive. McCormick, in the conclusion to this volume, correctly emphasizes that Han nationalism is ethnic. The other type is "civic nationalism" which requires a democratic government, rule of law, and a wide array of nongovernmental institutions. This form of nationalism is not in China's foreseeable future. The "myth of national humiliation" is used by Beijing to orchestrate its "official" nationalism, and it seems to play well with the mass audience. Both official and ethnic nationalism combine together to perpetuate Han control over minority regions—especially Tibet and Xinjiang. They also combine in support of reunification with Taiwan.

Bernstein and Munro conclude their *The Coming Conflict with China* by arguing that the United States should support the re-creation of Japanese armed forces as a balance to growing Chinese military power. That course of action, more than any other, would guarantee the realization of their book title. It would inflame Han nationalism and greatly strengthen the appeal of "official" nationalism. A strong Japanese military might force Beijing and Moscow to form a new alliance with one another. South Korea might abandon its alliance with the United States in favor of one with China. The United States and its Japanese partner would face widespread Asian opposition.

However, China must carefully avoid creating a self-fulfilling prophecy. Japan has thus far not sought force projection capabilities. But if Chinese military modernization combined with political hostility against Japan, then Beijing's nightmare of a remilitarized Japan could be quickly realized. Moreover, if China were seen as the cause of Japan's re-arming, the PRC would find few if any allies in Asia.

But these sorts of "if-then" security scenarios read like fairy tales in the face of reality. Economics drives international relations in the post–Cold War era. A recent highly revealing book was written by a former member of Beijing's Ministry of Foreign Affairs. Lu Ning repeatedly makes the point in *The Dynamics of Chinese Foreign Policy Making* that economic considerations are foremost in the minds of policy makers.[29] Beijing's eagerness to finesse the Diaoyu Islands crisis with Japan is a recent example showing the priority of maintaining good economic relations with its major partners.

The PRC will continue to enrich itself through international trade and investments. For that to happen, it must have political stability at home and regional stability in Asia. One squall on this otherwise smooth sea concerns arms sales. The PLA keeps much of the profits from overseas deals. Chinese missiles tempt foreign buyers who are unable to buy such equipment from the advanced industrial democracies. Beijing agreed some years after its inception to abide by the terms of the "missile technology control regime" but the government has not kept that pledge. The future will probably see additional violations hopefully less serious than in the recent past.

China's rise will be troubled by Taiwan, by a corrupt and often inept government, by continued human rights violations, by expanded arms sales, and by territorial disputes. But so long as its rise continues, the myth of national humiliation will be assuaged. Because the myth includes wealth as well as power, China will make every effort to pursue its present course of economic development. Belligerency will not serve that purpose. Economic development implies increased interdependence with the United States and other democratic nations. This developing interdependence provides the most important note of concluding optimism. The anti-China histrionics in Washington and the anti-U.S. histrionics in Beijing are very shrill in the year 2000, as this written. But the economic interests of both nations will work toward cooperation rather than confrontation. Neither a clash of civilizations nor a coming conflict with China looms on the horizon, unless mutual fears lead to a self-fulfilling prophecy.

Notes

1. In unusual cases, democracy may be a sudden development (see David Bachman's chapter). An institutional evolution is much more common, and that is the democratizing model assumed in this chapter.

2. Hu Shaohua, "Confucianism and Western Democracy." *Journal of Contemporary China*, vol. 6, no. 15, July 1997, pp. 362–63.

3. "China's Urban Families Enjoy Swift Rise in Annual Income." *China News Digest* (Internet: www.cnd.org), June 13, 1997.

4. "Poverty Spreads and Deepens in China's Cities." *New York Times*, October 4, 1998, p. A3.

5. "A Day in Court and Justice, Sometimes, for the Chinese." *New York Times*, April 27, 1998, p. A1.

6. Jude Howell, "An Unholy Trinity? Civil Society, Economic Liberalization and Democratization in post-Mao China." *Government and Opposition*, vol. 33, no. 9, Winter 1998, p. 65.

7. Suisheng Zhao, *Power Competition in East Asia.* New York: St. Martin's Press, 1997, p. 60.

8. "Will China Democratize?" *Journal of Democracy*, January 1998, pp. 1–64. The scholars who contributed their views were Robert Scalapino, Zbigniew Brzezinski, Suisheng Zhao, Juntao Wang, Andrew Nathan, Yizi Chen, Harry Harding, Arthur Waldron, Thomas Metzger, and Michel Oksenberg.

9. Yizi Chen was the exception. He believes that contradictions inherent within "market-Leninism" will cause national economic collapse prior to the ten-year time horizon stipulated in the symposium.

10. Andrew Nathan, "Even Our Caution Must Be Hedged." *Journal of Democracy*, January 1968, p. 64.

11. Ibid. p. 61.

12. The student demands to the government, which they were never able to officially deliver, were (1) the "re-evaluation" of the fired communist reform leader Hu Yaobang, who had just died; (2) to get rid of the oppressive "spiritual pollution" campaign intended to protect Chinese against "decadent" foreign influences; (3) to report incomes of leaders' children; (4) to cease press censorship and allow private newspapers; (5) to abolish the ten rules forbidding demonstrations in Beijing; (6) to provide more government money for education and improve the living standards of intellectuals; (7) to report the true nature of the "Democratic Patriotic Movement" as the students called themselves. This last point called upon the government to remove the "anarchical" description which the *People's Daily* had attached to the students in an April 26 editorial.

13. Edward Friedman, "Chinese Nationalism, Taiwan Autonomy and the Prospects of a Larger War." *Journal of Contemporary China*, vol. 6, no. 14, March 1997, p. 15.

14. Remittances from temporary workers in boom towns now constitute about one-fifth of the rural income for some of the poorest interior provinces. *The Economist*, vol 340, no. 7973, July 6, 1996, p. 33.

15. Authoritarianism is used here in the sense of Max Weber's "legal-rational authority," (as opposed to traditional authority), and bureaucratic authority but without the centrality of the rule of law. It is the latter which has given rise to democratic forms of authority. Andrew Heywood, *Political Ideas and Concepts.* New York: St. Martin's Press, 1994, pp. 91–92.

16. Fascist in the sense of dehumanizing and demonizing the "other." The other can be one or more religious, racial, or ethnic groups, or foreign nations. This maximization of us/them divisions justifies power transfer to central authority, results in chauvinism, and ultimately leads to wars and massive violations of fundamental human rights.

17. Kenneth Lieberthal, *Governing China: From Revolution Through Reform.* New York: W.W. Norton, 1995, p. 169.

18. Ibid. p. 181.

19. Sibata Tetsuji, "Japan's New Nationalism." *Asiaweek*, May 21, 1997, p. 74.

20. Richard Madsen, *China and the American Dream: A Moral Inquiry.* Berkeley: University of California Press, 1995.

21. Richard Bernstein and Ross Munro, *The Coming Conflict with China.* New York: A.A. Knopf, 1997.

22 "Dick Gephardt's China Ploy." *The Economist*, vol. 343, no. 8019, May 31, 1997, pp. 26–27.

23. Brian Palmer, "Caesar vs. Christ in China." *U.S. News and World Report*, Aug. 4, 1997, p. 41.

24. "United States Assails China Over Suppression of Religious Life." *New York Times*, July 22, 1997, p. A1.

25. Charles Horner, "China's Christian History." *First Things*, August–September 1997, p. 42.

26. Paul Cohen, "Christian Missions and Their Impact to 1900," in John K. Fairbank (ed.), *The Cambridge History of China,* vol. 10. New York: Cambridge University Press, 1978, pp. 543–90.

27. Harry Harding, "Breaking the Impasse Over Human Rights," in Ezra Vogel (ed.), *Living With China: U.S.-China Relations in the Twenty-First Century.* New York: Norton, 1997, p. 176.

28. Samuel Huntington, *The Clash of Civilizations and the Remaking of World Order.* New York: Simon and Schuster, 1996, p. 20.

29. Lu Ning, *The Dynamics of Chinese Foreign Policy Making.* Boulder: Westview Press, 1997.

Chapter 10

Aggressive Engagement, Not Containment: Political Repression's Role in Sino-American Relations

Su Shaozhi and Michael J. Sullivan

Sino-American relations have been in flux since the brutal suppression of the 1989 democracy movement and the 1991 demise of the Soviet Union. Gone is the anti-Soviet security consensus that cemented U.S.-China relations since the 1970s. The relationship is now more characterized by potentially destabilizing conflicts over security (e.g., missile sales to the Middle East and Taiwan), economics (e.g., World Trade Organization [WTO] membership and intellectual property rights), and human rights (e.g., most favored nation status and the UN Human Rights Commission). The 1996 confrontation in the Taiwan Straits and the 1999 accidental bombing of the Chinese embassy in Yugoslavia threatened to throw the relationship backward toward the antagonistic 1950s and 1960s. Subsequent efforts to tone down tensions, such as the 1997–98 exchange of presidents, stabilized and restored bilateral cooperation.

International relations specialists perceive this volatile relationship to reflect a natural confrontation between a reigning superpower and a rising power.[1] Profound economic growth over the past decade has bolstered China's resolve to challenge the United States and to implement strategies to enhance its regional military and economic power. We argue that Sino-American relations, however, are largely determined by domestic political factors within each country.[2] Anti-China groups in the United States and anti-U.S. groups in China are pitted against accommodationist groups, such as American senior military and business leaders and Chinese promarket reformers, seeking bilateral cooperation. After twenty years of reform, Chinese domestic and foreign policies are still heavily influenced by Leninist-authoritarian political structures as well as by the Jiang regime's continuation of the Dengist reform formula of "economic development with political repression." This entrenched set leads us to be cautious about the impact of Jiang Zemin's new course for economic reform and for limited political and legal reform following the Fifteenth Party Congress.

A focus on the impact of authoritarianism on Chinese foreign policy has direct implications for U.S.-China policy. Policy analysts disagree over whether engagement or confrontation would best allow each country to realize its national security objectives.[3] A crucial dynamic usually omitted from these policy debates concerns the repressive and authoritarian nature of the Jiang Zemin regime and how it influences Chinese foreign policies. During the 1996 Taiwan crisis, the Chinese leadership from Li Peng to Qiao Shi unanimously adopted a hardline nationalist military strategy to thwart a supposed move toward Taiwanese independence. Jiang Zemin's own switch from promoting dialogue on reunification with ruling groups on Taiwan to supporting aggressive military actions demonstrates the constraining impact of authoritarian politics and of the Jiang regime's use of nationalist propaganda. The hardline foreign policy toward Taiwan, as well as toward other countries and international organizations, corresponded with increased authoritarianism in the mid-1990s. While partly reflecting the succession struggle to Deng Xiaoping, the intensification of political repression reflects a concerted effort to maintain political stability while continuing Dengist economic reforms and enhancing the political security of top ruling groups. Top ruling groups lack the legitimacy of democracy and equate their own political survival with the national security of the PRC.

Nonetheless, in considering the domestic and foreign policy ramifications of Chinese authoritarianism, we conclude that the United States should adopt an aggressive engagement policy. This policy would cultivate areas of mutual concern (especially Asian regional trade and security concerns) while standing firm in areas of disagreement (e.g., WTO, environmental protection, and human rights). To advance the causes of

international peace and domestic political liberalization, the United States
and China both need to bury Cold War legacies.

A New Cold War?

An aggressive engagement policy encourages a "win-win" situation for
the United States and China. In the past several years, policy discourses
have been dominated by "win-lose" debates over the "China threat" and
the need to "contain China."[4] Containment proponents argue that authoritarian China's assertive nationalism and desire for regional and world
superpower status threaten America's long-term national security interests in Asia. Engagement proponents seek to integrate China into the
world order and, thus, into a cooperative bilateral relationship. The
Clinton administration's formal adoption of the engagement strategy
has helped to stabilize the relationship for major U.S. business interests.
But, this engagement policy is piecemeal and reactive. It fails to aggressively promote U.S. interests and the interest of liberal reform during
bilateral crises.

In China, groups disagree over foreign policy toward the United
States.[5] A cooperative group seeks common ground while standing steadfast against perceived "hegemonist" behavior by the United States. The
oppositionist group, relying on hardline Leninist ideology, favors a tough
stance on human rights, trade, and security since it perceives the United
States as a direct threat to Chinese Communist Party (CCP) domestic
rule. Elite and popular nationalist responses to the Taiwan situation allowed the oppositionist group to solidify an anti-U.S. policy up to the
Fifteenth Party Congress. The continual rise of anti-U.S. nationalism, as
exemplified in the May 1999 attacks on the U.S. embassy, continues to
shape Chinese policy debates toward the United States.

The American arguments for containment illustrate how neglecting
domestic political forces can distort understandings of China's foreign
policy behavior. China's assertive foreign policy and the PLA's intensified modernization efforts provide some evidence to legitimate a policy
of containment of China. However, many experts on Chinese security
have demonstrated that logistical and technical obstacles limit the PLA's
ability to achieve naval, air, and land superiority in East Asia.[6] This
means that China cannot be a serious threat for several decades. A theoretical basis for the containment school emanates from cultural arguments as in Samuel Huntington's "Clash of Civilizations" theory. In his

1993 *Foreign Affairs* article "The Clash of Civilizations?" and his 1996 book *The Clash of Civilizations and the Remaking of World Order*,[7] Huntington argued that China is destined to seek regional hegemony while continuing rapid economic growth. He believes deep-seated Confucianist forces will obstruct democratization and give rise to an autocratic China that might become a threat to the Asian balance of power.

Huntington's theory is premised on three main points about the linkage between China's domestic politics and foreign policy behavior. First, he argues that global conflicts between civilizations, which are supposedly supplanting ideological and other forms of conflict, will be more frequent, more sustained, and more violent. These violent conflicts between different civilizations are "the most likely and most dangerous sources of escalation that would lead to global wars."[8] The potential long-term conflict between Confucianist Asia and the Christian West would most likely emerge in a conflict between the People's Republic of China (PRC) and the United States. Second, Huntington posits that China's stupendous growth and Greater China's pervasive economic networks will, despite Japan's current economic weight, propel the PRC to emerge as a new regional and global industrial, commercial, and financial epicenter.[9] He predicted in 1996 that the handover of Hong Kong and Macao to China and the future reunification with Taiwan would lead to China's hegemonic rise in Asia. Third, China's Confucian cultural tradition of hierarchy, authority, community, and loyalty, Huntington argues, is inimical to political democracy.[10] Autocratic China would stir up nationalist and patriotic sentiments to mobilize popular support and to modernize its military forces. Huntington concludes that a "central focus of conflict for the immediate future will be between the West and several Islamic-Confucian states."[11]

Based on these new global trends, Huntington argues that the West must adopt two broad strategies. It needs to keep its own house in order and to expand its alliances with similar cultures. Huntington specifically emphasizes the need for America to cement cooperation and unity within its own civilization, to draw Eastern European and Latin American countries into the Western civilization camp, and to maintain cooperative relations with Russia and Japan. The second strategy involves implementing strategies to thwart threats to the West by hostile Islamic and Confucian countries. Huntington advocates balancing the military strength of Confucian and Islamic states, maintaining military superiority in East and Southeast Asia, taking advantage of differences among

Confucian and Islamic states, supporting groups sympathetic to Western values and interests, and strengthening international institutions that reflect Western interests and values. In the long term, the West will need to implement strategies to enhance its military and economic power because the rise of non-Western civilizations will bring parity with Western powers by civilizations that promote different values from the West.[12] Huntington's arguments and proposals embody cultural arguments made by procontainment groups. If the Clinton administration and the Jiang Zemin government had not taken major steps to arrest deteriorating bilateral relations, these containment arguments might have legitimated groups seeking a new Cold War.

Huntington's theory is based on a misunderstanding of the interaction among cultures and on a misinterpretation of the relationship between Chinese culture and political democracy. While world history is full of differences among civilizations, wars between nations are not inevitable. Exchange often is mutually enriching. As Arnold J. Toynbee demonstrated in his famous work *A Study of History*, the introduction of Islam into the Iberian peninsula allowed Muslim scholars to contribute unintentionally to the philosophical development of medieval European Christians by introducing the works of the Hellenic philosopher Aristotle.[13] The interaction of ideas and models continues to occur due to the high level of cultural exchanges and the technological advances in communication. No culture or civilization should be perceived to be anything but a melting pot.

The interaction between China and the world is multifaceted.[14] Early Chinese inventions, such as gunpowder and printing, were introduced into Europe by Muslim and European travelers. In the sixteenth century, Jesuit missionaries Matteo Ricci and Johann Adam Schell introduced European advances in the natural sciences and the calendar system to China. Perceiving a philosophical commonality in humanity, Matteo Ricci even suggested a combination of Confucianism with Roman Catholicism. German philosopher Gottfried Wilhelm Leibniz's interest in the binary arithmetic developed by the *Yi Jing* and French philosopher Voltaire's interest in Confucianism were integrated into their respective political philosophies.[15] Exchange went in both directions. Western political thought and experiences, such as Marxism, political liberalism, and anarchism, heavily influenced twentieth-century Chinese political leaders and activists. Dr. Sun Yat-sen's *Three Principles of the People* was deeply influenced by democratic thought. Even autocrat Mao

Zedong, in his early years, identified his theory of New Democracy not only with Dr. Sun Yat-sen's *Three Principles*, but also with Abraham Lincoln's idea "Of the people, by the people, and for the people" and President Franklin Roosevelt's "Four Freedoms." This interaction between China and the West continues today. Post-Mao intellectuals from liberal democrats to neoconservatives find inspiration in foreign writings and models in developing China's political, economic, cultural, philosophical, literary, and artistic realms.[16]

Huntington's "Clash of Civilizations" theory promotes a one-sided and deterministic argument on Confucianism's negative impact on democratic struggles in China. This argument reflects, in part, the lingering affects of Occidentalism. Some scholars have used Max Weber's *The Protestant Ethic and the Spirit of Capitalism* to argue that non–Northern European Protestant countries, such as Roman Catholic Latin America and Confucian China, lacked the preconditions for capitalism and political liberalism. Such Occidental thinking leads to an erroneous belief that political democracy cannot succeed in countries with Confucianist and Islamic cultures. As Edward Friedman has argued, perceiving political democracy as a quintessentialist Western project obscures the domestic forces leading the democratic projects in countries influenced by Confucianism (Japan, Taiwan, and South Korea) as well as other Asian countries (India, Thailand, and the Philippines).[17] More people in Asia than Europe enjoy the blessings of democracy. The democratization process in Asia clearly demonstrates that Confucianism and democracy are not inherently conflictual.

The relationship between culture and democracy is multifaceted and complex. Even Huntington admits in *The Third Wave*,

> Great historic cultural traditions, such as Islam and Confucianism, are highly complex bodies of ideas, beliefs, doctrines, assumptions, writings and behavior patterns. Any major culture, including even Confucianism, has some elements that are compatible with democracy. . . . The question is: What elements in Islam and Confucianism are favorable to democracy, and how and under what circumstances, can these supersede the undemocratic elements in those cultural traditions?[18]

Some of the philosophical concepts that were useful as a theoretical basis for political democracy, like the sovereignty of the people, did not carry much weight in Chinese imperial politics. Even so, alternate concepts that could provide a theory of democracy (e.g., "Minbenzhuyi" were in common usage. In contrast to Plato or Hobbes, Mencius believed that "the people are more important than the ruler" and that "the people are the foundation of the state." Admitting a premise of human equality, Mencius advocated the right of the people to revolt against a state that denies basic human principles. His emphasis on the people as the basis of the state can be interpreted as the promotion of humanitarian governance, which can be read large on behalf of the democratic principle that treats people as the subjective force and masters of the state. Confucius similarly promoted humanism and humanitarian government as reflected in his statement "Don't do to others what you don't want to be done unto you" and "to feel responsible for the hungry and the drowning of the people." These ancient and universal ideas are compatible with the spirit of tolerance and respect for personal freedoms. As Lin Yu-sheng has shown, inherited concepts of the primacy of the people and humanism can be creatively transformed and re-created to support projects for political democracy and liberty.[19] The theory of a "Clash of Civilizations" and other approaches insisting on insurmountable cultural impediments to democracy obscure the main factor hindering democracy in China–the political system of post-1949 China.

The Obstacles to the Transition to Democracy in China

The lack of democracy in post-1949 China directly results from the "partyocracy" (party/state) system, which the Chinese Communist Party (CCP) adopted from the Soviet Union. In this system, the state swallows society and the party dominates the state. Power is concentrated in the party, which is legitimated as a vanguard dictatorship. Within the party, powers are fused at the center, which is itself dominated by a supreme dictator. Dissent is forbidden and suppressed. Sprouts of democracy (e.g., the Hundred Flowers Movement and the 1976 Tiananmen protests) are smashed. During the Cultural Revolution, Mao Zedong's unfettered power resulted in a dangerous personality cult. The terror and inhumanity of the Cultural Revolution led many to see how the absence of democracy causes tremendous economic and political suffering. Some scholars rightly trace these tragedies to the CCP's tyranny prior to the capture of state power in 1949.[20]

Deng Xiaoping's ascent in the late 1970s brought hope of a broad revival of humanism. The pillars of Deng's reform and openness policy were broadly outlined as the economic transformation of a command economy into a market economy and the political realization of democracy and legality. The four objectives of political reform were (1) to separate the party and the state, (2) to transfer power to the local level, (3) to simplify the administration structure, and (4) to improve government efficiency. Deng and his political allies believed limited political reforms would bolster societal stability and the CCP's own political rule. Dengist reforms turned out to bring economic development without democratic political reform.

Deng Xiaoping's refusal to abolish the "partyocracy" has had a profound negative impact on political reform. Beginning in 1979, Deng hesitated and reversed course on his previous call to implement meaningful political reform.[21] Despite hopeful signs in 1986 and 1988, Deng and top party elites feared that substantial political reforms would seriously undermine the CCP's power and upset societal stability.

Even so, the China of the 1980s was substantially different from the Mao era. Two new phenomena have had a fundamental impact on the struggle for democracy. First, beginning in the rural areas and the coastal regions, economic reform freed many localities and enterprises from the state's heavy-handedness and its irrational policies. A certain degree of autonomous power was created as a market economy began to develop. Second, the rigid ideological control associated with the Maoist era became increasingly flexible. The 1979 Democracy Wall Movement and the 1983 Human Alienation debate, while failing initially, succeeded later in opening up political discourses on political system reform, Chinese culture, liberal democracy, Confucianism, and authoritarianism.

These cracks in the partyocracy are openings out of totalitarianism. Some analysts optimistically conclude that these developments signify substantial progress toward the gradual establishment of political democracy. The continuation of Dengist market-oriented economic development, they argue, will eventually create the socioeconomic requisites for political democracy.[22] Political democratization throughout the world demonstrates that sustained economic growth without democracy's accountability of elites and the protection of individual liberties will end badly.

The openness of political discussions in the late 1980s and the 1989 democracy movement did provide a glimmer of hope for successful democratization. If Deng and top party elites had chosen to implement meaningful political reforms, China might have gradually achieved top-down democratization. But Deng Xiaoping slammed shut the door he himself had partially opened. After the 1989 Beijing massacre, Deng and his chosen successor Jiang Zemin led other top party leaders to table all proposals aimed at systematically reforming the partyocracy system. The 1989 democracy movement reconfirmed to party elites that policy measures should be employed to protect and to stabilize the CCP's rule.[23]

Two Trends in the Jiang Zemin Regime[24]

Elite resistance to democracy does not guarantee that future democratization efforts will fail. The deaths of paramount leader Deng Xiaoping and his fellow "old guard" revolutionaries provide China with several possibilities for further political change. The Jiang Zemin regime does have an opportunity to open up the political system to democracy by allowing the systematic implementation of political reforms. This path would allow for greater equity and political freedoms through the establishment of uncorrupt and accountable political procedures, effective legal institutions, and independent government agencies to regulate China's domestic economy.

Another possibility would continue basic Dengist economic reforms while recentralizing party-state power and mobilizing support through appeals to wealth and nationalism.[25] Rather than striving to establish more humane politics, this path would strengthen authoritarian politics, the party's own stability and repressive security apparatuses. Within a year after Deng's death, Jiang Zemin outwardly bolstered his reign with Hong Kong's return to China and a 1997–98 exchange of visits with the president of the United States. In domestic politics, Jiang has continued the basic strategies of the Dengist era of sustained economic reform, limited political reform, and targeted political repression. Political democracy is still perceived as disruptive to party rule and societal stability.

After his promotion to party general secretary by Deng Xiaoping after the Beijing massacre, Jiang Zemin has toed the Deng position of "economic development with political repression." The Fourteenth Party Congress, however, demarcated a change for the Jiang Zemin regime. Step by step the Jiang regime has slid onto the track of intensifying focused political repression and of recentralizing party and state controls. Jiang Zemin should be understood, though, as relying on "neoconservative" strategies rather than on the hardline policies once associated with Maoist hardliners Deng Liqun and Wang Zhen. Neoconservatism seeks to rely on political authoritarianism to guarantee social stability and to implement controlled economic reforms. In this regard, Jiang and the party leadership have reemphasized the political and ideological systems of democratic centralism. This strategy rejects Deng's early appeal to localize power and, in effect, signals movement back toward the partyocracy system and toward repressive and erratic authoritarian rule. Jiang Zemin solidified his "core" status when the sixth plenary session of the Fourteenth Party Congress declared the successful transfer of power from the "Second Leading Group" (with Deng as the core) to the "Third Leading Group" (with Jiang as the core). The partyocracy system of autocratic dictatorship dating back to the Mao Zedong era continues unabated.

President Jiang and Premier Zhu Rongji's proposals to reform state-owned enterprises (SOE) indicate a commitment to Dengist reform strategies. Like rural reform in the late 1970s and urban reform in the 1980s, the Fifteenth Party Congress signaled further initiatives to reform SOEs. The South Korean experience provides the Jiang regime with an economic model. Internationally competitive SOEs will be supported by the state. Other state workers will be laid off. Unrest will be suppressed by China's security apparatuses, especially by the People's Armed Police. The then-still undemocratic South Korean government's ability, prior to 1987, to achieve high economic growth rates despite worker unrest has been closely analyzed by policy advisers in the Jiang regime. They have relied on the predemocratic-era South Korean model in proposing the establishment of state conglomerates in key industries. While ideologically significant, these proposed reforms remain within the rubric of the Dengist reform logic of political order and substantial economic reform that solidified after Deng's 1992 southern tour and at the Fourteenth Party Congress. There is no guarantee that SOE reforms will herald democratic political change.

Political repression constitutes a distinguishing trait of the Jiang Zemin regime, which has quite limited tolerance for political dissent. As a former head of the Shanghai party's propaganda department noted in spring 1997,

> Now, the control of ideology by the leading group has reached the standard of the Cultural Revolution. The relationship between the party and intellectuals is as bad as in the Cultural Revolution.[26]

Human rights organizations have documented the intensification of political repression under the Jiang regime.[27] Political dissidents have been unlawfully detained, sentenced, and harassed by security organizations. In 1993–94, more than 200 dissidents were arrested, which was the highest number since the nationwide 1989–90 antidemocratic crackdown.[28] While the exile of high-profile human rights leaders, such as Wang Dan and Wei Jingsheng, is a reminder of China's dismal human rights situation, the intensification of political repression hurts lesser known proponents of democracy, religious practitioners, protesting workers, resisting peasants, devout Muslims, and peaceful Tibetans.[29] The severity of political repression reflects the CCP's effort to protect its rule in order to maintain social stability.

Village elections, albeit welcome, should be seen less as a consequence of a democratization process and more as a calculated effort by the CCP to arrest rural unrest. Labor unrest due to layoffs, police brutality, and corruption resulted in an estimated 10,000 public labor disputes in 1993 and 12,000 labor protests in 1995.[30] A "strike hard" (*yan da*) campaign to crack down on criminal activities resulted in an estimated 6,100 death sentences and 4,367 confirmed executions in 1996.[31] The draconian tools of the partyocracy systems are still relied upon to deal with the problems emanating from China's social and economic transformations.

The techniques of repression have become more sophisticated under the Jiang Zemin regime. False and frivolous charges are used to arrest and convict political activists.[32] Common charges include sex offenses, traffic violations, embezzlement, tax evasion, and hooliganism. Dai Xuezhong, a member of the Shanghai-based Chinese Human Rights Association, was detained in May 1994 for his human rights activities. He received a three-year jail term in December 1994 supposedly for evading taxes. Beijing dissident Zhou Guoqiang was sentenced to three years of "reeducation through labor" (RTL) on the charge of disrupting public order. He printed T-shirts with labor rights slogans. Criminal charges are employed to discredit dissidents while hiding the actual number of China's political prisoners. Other repressive tactics used include bribery, threats, demolition of unregistered property, frivolous fines, and arbitrary detention and interrogations. The regime tars political opponents as ordinary criminals, a tactic that wins popular support.

The PRC officially denies that it has any political prisoners. It claims that all prisoners in China have violated criminal laws. One high-level official admitted in May 1997, however, that China had 2,026 counter-revolutionary criminals. The new criminal law implemented in March 1997 replaced "counterrevolutionary" with provisions on "treasonous acts designed to threaten national security." This new criminal law was used in the sentencing of political dissidents. While representing progress in legal reform,[33] the new criminal law did not eliminate the use of "reeducation through labor" as a repression tactic. RTL permits detention and sentencing without trial. It is still used by the CCP to silence and sentence dissidents to terms of one to three years in labor camps. As several establishment Chinese human rights scholars openly admitted, PRC laws aimed at increasing the legal protections for certain rights will remain ineffective until enforcement procedures are legitimately implemented.[34] The intensification of repression illustrates how the Jiang Zemin regime continues to rely on repression to maintain political and social stability.

Top party leaders disagree over a return to old totalitarian politics. When Deng Xiaoping was alive, party factions and the citizenry, especially intellectuals, were afraid "to kill the rat for fear of damaging the vase in which it is hiding." Very few were bold enough to take a clearcut stand, let alone express opposition. Deng's death broke the silence of political factions. Thus, Jiang has faced pressure from different groups, forcing him to reconsider his political tactics and policies. Hardliners led by Deng Liqun attempted to roll back reforms. Immediately after Deng Xiaoping's death, this group attacked reforms as exhibiting the tendency of "bourgeois liberalization,"[35] hoping to pull Jiang steadily into the antireform camp and to undermine the theory and practice of Deng Xiaoping's reform and openness. Jiang resisted these efforts because he uses Deng Xiaoping's theory of building socialism with Chinese characteristics as a protective umbrella. Jiang privately refuted Deng Liqun's position. But, unlike Deng Xiaoping's attack on hardliners in 1992, Jiang has never openly refuted Deng Liqun's position. Although Jiang opts to follow the autocratic traditions established by Mao and Deng, he lacks the power to impose his stamp on elite politics.

Reformers also have not remained silent under the Jiang regime. Intellectuals began breaking theoretical restrictions after Deng's death. They called for the implementation of political reform to protect and promote economic reform and openness. These intellectuals might unite with liberal reformers in the party to pressure Jiang to accept more political reform. Jiang has suggested several times a need for limited political reform. It was reported that a research project on "mild authoritarianism" approved by Jiang himself had been completed prior to the Fifteenth Party Congress. This neoconservative project would maintain party rule while allowing the controlled implementation of economic reforms. Political reforms are designed to depoliticize the economic reform process, to enhance the state's economic regulatory functions, and to promote the party's legitimacy and rule. Reforms introduced at the 1998 National People's Congress (NPC) include major cutbacks in the state bureaucracy and measures to salvage endangered state banks. Accompanying Premier Zhu Rongji's political rise and the Asian financial crisis, these reforms constitute an effort to reduce harmful state interference in the market and to prevent the financial collapse of China's banking system. These reforms do address outstanding problems confronting China's economic performance. But they do not address the democratic reform of the partyocracy. Jiang remains committed to the continuation of the Dengist project of "economic growth with political repression."

Some limited political reforms are being implemented. The 1997 criminal law would replace totalitarian methods with procedures designed to institutionalize centralized authority and power. Politically, Jiang's policies attempt to balance elite political conflicts in order to strengthen his own authority, to manifest a certain degree of tolerance, and to promote stability and unity. The limited political reforms adopted by the Jiang regime cannot be equated with political democratization. They mainly continue the Dengist reform agenda, adding small steps toward political liberalization.

Despite steadfast resistance to democracy by top party elites, three societal dynamics could facilitate future democratization. First, China's reform experience generally reconfirms the free-market principle that "open markets equal open societies." Twenty years of a market economy have allowed for the creation of relatively autonomous socioeconomic groups. Once there is a democratic opening, these groups could form into political interest groups. As has been the case in other parts of the world, these interest groups would be a major force in the realization and protection of political participation, political pluralism, multiparty elections, and political democracy. Second, the abolition of the commune system and the implementation of rural village elections provide a rural basis for future democratization. While the CCP intends these elections to maintain rural stability, these elections have raised peasants' understanding of political participation and electoral procedures. This constitutes a learning process, which is potentially an important step in a democratization project. If the CCP ever lost control of these elections, popular elections could spread to county, provincial, and national levels.

Third, increasing numbers of intellectuals, policy advisers, and even high CCP officials want existing constitutional provisions implemented. The constitution states that "All power of the People's Republic of China belongs to the people. . . . The National People's Congress is the highest organ of state," and "People should enjoy freedom of speech, press, religion, assembly, and association." The constitutional legitimacy for democracy in China exists on paper. These rights and freedoms, however, directly conflict with the actual political logic associated with the partyocracy. Struggles to promote the enforcement of the constitution can be part of other efforts to limit the CCP's arbitrary, personalized power and to monitor the government.

Chinese society is ever more ripe for democracy. If, however, one relies on an intangible socioeconomic evolution for the maturation of democratizing factors, the achievement of democracy may take an eternity. The Jiang regime resists efforts to democratize key structures of the partyocracy system. The combination of ripe democratic conditions with repressive totalitarian techniques and authoritarian tendencies produces a China caught in an early moment of a transition away from totalitarianism. A democratic breakthrough would require that Jiang not treat the stability of the partyocracy as a fundamental priority; but he does. The smooth transition after Deng Xiaoping's death prevented destabilizing power struggles. Despite standing firm through Deng's death, the turnover of Hong Kong and Macao, and the Fifteenth Party Congress, the Jiang regime still faces potentially destabilizing problems, such as the loyalty of the military, an insolvent financial system, bankrupt state enterprises, a population explosion, an increase of unemployment, and the polarization between the rich and poor. The Chinese government sees every problem as a potential crisis that could threaten widespread turmoil. Given that perspective, Jiang is not about to shift from repression to democracy.

Authoritarian China's Domestic and Foreign Policies

What direction will China's foreign policy take under the current authoritarian system? At the fifth plenary session of the Fourteenth Party Congress in September 1995, Jiang stated that "Development is the firm principle. . . . Reform is the strong motive force of economic and social development, . . . [and] stability is the prerequisite of development and reform. . . . Development and reform must have a stable political and social environment.[36]

Jiang's regime prioritizes stability. This neoconservative agenda's primary objective is to enhance economic growth, to defend central authority, and to consolidate the Jiang regime's power. This logic will not accept the fact that political and social stabilization has proven to be best achieved by political reform aimed at the development of democracy and by enticing groups to participate politically to commonly address and overcome pressing problems. Jiang and top party leaders simply fear political democracy.

Since the Fourteenth Party Congress, four broad measures have been adopted by the Jiang regime that have direct repercussions for Sino-American relations. First, Jiang seeks to enforce the control of politics and ideology, especially the repression of dissent, and to limit political participation. These measures continue to harm the human rights of people in China and often lead to conflict with international standards of democracy and human rights. The Jiang regime has aggressively attacked efforts by the United States, the European Union, and international human rights nongovernmental organizations (NGOs) to improve China's human rights. Although successfully rebuffing such international efforts, continuing political repression in China will further invigorate groups in the United States opposed to repression in China. Gross human rights violations directly conflict with American political values.

Second, to counter short-term and long-term foreign policy challenges, the Jiang regime adheres to an "active defense strategy." This strategy includes the build-up of China's national defenses, importing high-tech weaponry, and developing a more technologically advanced and indigenous military-industrial complex. In order to obtain the hard currency to support militarization, the People's Liberation Army has exported weapons of mass destruction to powder-keg countries, like Pakistan, Iran, and Iraq. These actions conflict with the U.S. commitment to support international efforts to restrict the proliferation of advanced weapons, especially nuclear technology.

Third, the Jiang Zemin regime strives to promote sustained economic growth to raise the living standard of the people and to increase the wealth and power of the state. Wealth and consumerism are intended to mobilize popular support and deflect popular discontent. To achieve these goals, the regime depends on direct foreign investment, foreign loans, and the import of advanced technology and equipment. China's reliance on its export economy has resulted in trade tensions with the United States. The United States's insistence that China's entry into the WTO depends on the opening of China's domestic economy will be a major continuing source of tension.

Fourth, Jiang's regime stirs up patriotism, including blaming American interference in China's domestic affairs, in order to legitimate Jiang's rule and policies. This regime is not inherently ultranationalistic. It has tempered criticisms of the United States and suppressed anti-Japanese nationalism when desiring to improve relations with the United States or Japan. Yet, it uses anti-U.S. nationalism, as in the 1999 attacks on the U.S. embassy, to shore up popular support and to thwart reactionary right-wing attacks on economic reform. Jiang and other top party leaders openly praised the protestors as patriots. Similarly, the top leadership adopted policies, such as limiting protests that passed by the U.S. embassy, to channel the protests and to protect their own power status.

As with domestic policies, Jiang has adopted foreign policies to further bolster economic growth, to prevent political disintegration, and to protect CCP rule, thus preserving authoritarianism. The Jiang regime seeks to promote China's national security interests, which ruling-power groups define as including the security of the CCP as well as the defense of the PRC's borders. Diplomacy is contradictory in that it is both aggressive and cooperative. In reality, this diplomacy consistently "bullies the weak and fears the strong."

China has had difficulties directly confronting U.S. actions against China's human rights abuses. But, when Denmark stood tough against China's human rights policies, the Jiang regime imposed economic and diplomatic sanctions on the Danes. Similar actions did not occur when the United States continued to criticize China's human rights violations. Likewise, the Jiang regime has muted criticisms toward Japan even when right-wing Japanese occupied contested East China Sea islands, the Diaoyutai. Generally speaking, this regime seeks to maintain regional peace to achieve its policy goals. Since April 1996, China and Russia have entered a strategic cooperative companion relationship facing the twenty-first century. China desires to use the "Russian card" to counter the United States. China and Russia's opposition to the use of American military forces to compel Iraq to comply with UN regulations on weapon inspections exemplifies this new tie. Even so, this relationship has limitations. Russia does not desire to directly challenge the United States since it relies on good relations with the United States to assist domestic reforms. China has benefited from cheap, high-tech Russian weaponry, which cannot be bought elsewhere. This does not constitute a direct threat to the United States since the weaponry is backward compared to America's. Even so, this weaponry has been and can be used to intimidate Taiwan and Southeast Asian countries, which illustrates the aggressive, bullying part of Jiang's diplomacy.

Sino-Japan relations are complicated. For the past several years, this relationship has been "warm in the economic field and cold in the political field." Reform of the Chinese economy depends on support from Japanese financial sectors and the Japanese government's aid programs. China has used Japan's desire to invest in China to counter U.S. efforts to improve the Chinese human rights situation. Japan was the first G-7 country to bolt from the international economic sanctions imposed on China following the 1989 Beijing massacre. Still, the continuing impact of Japanese brutality in China during World War II hinders closer bilateral relations. While unable to say no to Japanese economic assistance, the Jiang regime remains suspicious of Japanese diplomatic and military developments, such as the recently enhanced U.S-Japanese security agreement. Actions by Japan can easily arouse strong public indignation in China. Here too, despite China's desire for peace and cooperation, conflict with American interests is quite possible.

Conclusion: Implications for U.S. Policy Toward China

NATO's accidental bombing of the Chinese embassy in Yugoslavia appears to have undone Jiang's and Clinton's previous efforts to reverse the intensification of conflict between the United States and the PRC. One victim of this destabilizing relationship has been the delinking of human rights and democracy from U.S.-China policy. U.S. policy makers have generally come to "accept the fact that political reform and human rights in China remain essentially Chinese matters and do not necessarily produce a peaceful Chinese foreign policy."[37] Increased political repression and assertive foreign policies discredit the hypothesis that the futures of Chinese domestic and foreign policy are primarily influenced by how the United States and others deal with China. Beijing's behavior will be mainly determined by the degree and the manner to which China's own political and economic systems are reformed or not reformed.

Uncertainties in China cannot be squared with projections in which China is said to resemble Bismarckian Germany before World War I or Nazi Germany in the 1930s. One scholar argues, "The rapid rise of Chinese economic power and military power together promise to disrupt the Asian balance of trade and the Asian balance of power, just as Germany's rise disrupted the European balance after 1866."[38] But the ability of China's backward economy to catch up with the advanced countries will depend on the economic and political reforms to undo the irrational partyocracy system. Such reforms are not yet in the cards.

References by containment theorists linking present-day China with an aggressive Nazi Germany threatening all of Europe deny many of the conclusions reached in this chapter. China lacks the industrial base that gave rise to an aggressive Germany. China continues to confront obstacles to its economic growth, such as its huge population and its low gross national product (GNP) per capita. China generally seeks a peaceful international environment to facilitate domestic economic growth. In contrast, Nazi Germany linked economic growth to military aggression. Again, unlike Germany, China's reliance on foreign suppliers such as Russia for advanced weaponry does not pose a direct military threat to the United States or even perhaps to the other countries near China. Beijing lacks the naval and air support for conquering the South China Sea. To be sure, Chinese military build-ups deserve constant vigilance, but, unlike Germany prior to World War II, China at the turn into the twenty-first century dwells in a very different international context. Rulers in Beijing will have great difficulty resisting the global trends of democracy, cooperation, and economic development.

Policies based on an equation of China and prewar Germany do not bode well for U.S.-China relations. If the United States were to adopt containment policies, there would be a massive popular reaction within Chinese politics. Containment policies would provide party hardliners and ultranationalists an opportunity to propagate extreme nationalism and to undermine basic Dengist economic reforms. PLA factions would use such a U.S. position as an excuse to further expand military expenditures. Such developments would threaten the Asian balance of power. Containment policies toward China would thus harm China's fragile democratic movement and expose liberal intellectuals. Surely, it is in the interest of the United States and China to prevent success for hardline positions that would injure the relationship between China and America.

The United States should instead aggressively engage China on matters of security, economic trade, and human rights and democracy. The United States should craft policies most likely to promote a "win-win" outcome for the United States and for Chinese reformers, liberals, and dissidents. Criticisms of China's domestic political situation should not be muted. Nor should criticisms provoke reactions that would fuel anti-U.S. sentiments and policies in China. Despite the press given in China to anti-American sentiments in recent years, Chinese groups exist that welcome U.S. criticisms of China's domestic political and economic conditions. U.S. policy should not fall prey to Huntington's inability to distinguish between the regime line of the moment and the underlying dynamic that gives hope to so many Chinese people. Struggles for democracy should be supported by programs aimed at the development of a market economy, the progress of direct elections at the local level, the development of business law, and the legal enforcement of the constitution.

The United States must concretely affirm mutual interests while aggressively confronting issues that run counter to U.S. national interests. An engagement policy without bite only satisfies the moment while allowing future destabilizing conflicts to foster unabated. If this aggressive engagement policy is complemented by good relations between China and the United States, mutually beneficial interests can overcome tensions in the relationship.

Notes

1. See David Shambaugh, "The United States and China: Cooperation or Confrontation?," *Current History* 96 (611), September 1997, pp. 241–245; Paul H.B. Godwin, "Uncertainty, Insecurity, and China's Military Power," *Current History* 96 (611), September 1997, pp. 252–257; and Wang Jianwei, "Coping with China as a Rising Power," in *Weaving the Net: Conditional Engagement with China*, ed. James Shinn (New York: Council on Foreign Relations, 1996), pp. 133–174.

2. See John Kurt Jacobsen, "Are All Politics Domestic? Perspectives on the Integration of Comparative Politics and International Relations Theories," *Comparative Politics* 29 (1), October 1996, pp. 93–115; and Peter Van Ness, "The Impasse in U.S. Policy Toward China," *The China Journal* 38 (July 1997), pp. 139–150.

3. See Andrew Nathan and Robert Ross, *The Great Wall and the Empty Fortress: China's Search for Security*. New York: W.W. Norton & Company, 1997; Richard Bernstein and Ross H. Munro, *The Coming Conflict with China*. New York: Alfred A. Knopf, 1997; David Shambaugh, "The United States and China: A New Cold War?" *Current History* 94 (593), September 1995, pp. 241–247; and Shinn, ed., *Weaving the Net: Conditional Engagement with China*.

4. See Richard Bernstein and Ross H. Munro, "China I: The Coming Conflict with America," *Foreign Affairs* 76 (2), March/April 1997, pp. 18–32; Robert S. Ross, "China II: Beijing as a Conservative Power," *Foreign Affairs* 76 (2), March/April 1997, pp. 33–44; Shambaugh, "The United States and China: Cooperation or Confrontation?"; and Avery Goldstein, "Great Expectations: Interpreting China's Arrival," *International Security* 22 (3), Winter 1997/1998, pp. 33–73.

5. Shambaugh, "The United States and China: A New Cold War?"

6. See Samuel S. Kim, "China as a Great Power," *Current History* 96 (611), September 1997, pp. 246–251; and Godwin, "Uncertainty, Insecurity, and China's Military Power," pp. 252–257.

7. Samuel P. Huntington, "The Clash of Civilizations?," *Foreign Affairs* 72 (3), Summer 1993; and Samuel P. Huntington, *The Clash of Civilizations and the Remaking of World Order*. New York: Simon and Schuster, 1996.

8. Huntington, "The Clash of Civilizations?," p. 48.

9. Ibid., p. 28.

10. Samuel P. Huntington, *The Third Wave*. Norman: University of Oklahoma Press, 1991, p. 71.

11. Huntington, "The Clash of Civilizations?," p. 48.

12. See Huntington, "The Clash of Civilizations?"; and Huntington, *The Clash of Civilizations and the Remaking of World Order*.

13. Arnold J. Toynbee, *A Study of History*. London: Oxford University Press, 1961.

14. See John King Fairbank, *China: A New History*. Cambridge, MA: Belknap Press of Harvard University Press, 1992; and Benjamin I. Schwartz, *The World of Thought in Ancient China*. Cambridge, MA: Belknap Press of Harvard University Press, 1985.

15. See Gottfried Wilhelm Leibniz, *Writings on China*. Chicago: Open Court, 1994, pp. 8–9.

16. For the impact of Western political thought, see Michael J. Sullivan, "The Impact of Western Political Thought on Chinese Political Discourse on Transitions from Leninism," *World Affairs* 157 (2), Fall 1994, pp. 79–94.

17. Edward Friedman, *The Politics of Democratization*. Boulder, CO: Westview Press, 1994.

18. Huntington, *The Clash of Civilizations and the Remaking of World Order*, p. 310.

19. Yu-sheng Lin, *The Crisis of Chinese Consciousness*. Madison: University of Wisconsin Press, 1979.

20. See David E. Apter and Tony Saich, *Revolutionary Discourse in Mao's Republic*. Cambridge, MA: Harvard University Press, 1994.

21. See Su Shaozhi, "A Decade of Crises at the Institute of Marxist-Leninist-Mao Zedong Thought," *China Quarterly* 134 (June 1993), pp. 335–351.

22. See Yasheng Huang, "Why China Will Not Collapse," *Foreign Policy* 99 (Summer 1995), pp. 54–68; and Jianwei Wang, "Coping with China as a Rising Power."

23. For a similar analysis, see Merle Goldman, "Is Democracy Possible?" *Current History* 94 (593), September 1995, pp. 259–263.

24. This section draws heavily from Su Shaozhi, "Xiangjiquan zhengzhi huigui de dao lu" (The return to totalitarian politics), *Xin Bao*, December 5, 1996; and Su Shaozhi, "Zhonggong shiwuda pouxi" (An analysis of the Fifteenth Party Congress of the Chinese Communist Party), *Zheng Ming*, October 1997, pp. 19–27.

25. For analyses on the rise of neoconservatism, see Sullivan, "Impact of Western Political Thought"; Joseph Fewsmith, "Neoconservatism and the End of the Dengist Era," *Asian Survey* 35 (7), 1995, pp. 635–651; and Feng Chen, "Order and Stability in Social Transition: Neoconservative Thought in Post-1989 China," *China Quarterly* 151 (September 1997), pp. 593–612.

26. Quoted in *Ming Bao*, May 1997.

27. See *China Rights Forum News Update*, Winter 1997; *Amnesty International Country Report, 1997*. London: Amnesty International, 1997; and *China Country Report on Human Rights Practices for 1997*. Washington, DC: U.S. Department of State, January 30, 1998.

28. John F. Cooper and Ta-ling Lee, *Coping With a Bad Global Image: Human Rights in the People's Republic of China, 1993–1994*. New York: University Press of America, 1997, p. 43.

29. See *China: State Control of Religion*. New York: Human Rights Watch, 1997; Cao Changching and James D. Seymour, "Tibet Through Chinese Eyes: Dissidents Speak Out," *Chinese Studies in History* 30 (3), Spring 1997; and Lin Lin, "How Does the People's Regime Face the People," *China Focus* 5 (3), March 1, 1997.

30. Jennifer Holdaway, "China's Dissenters: What's Happened Since Tiananmen?" *Dissent* 44 (Winter 1997), pp. 17–21.

31. "China Death Penalty Breaks New Records," Amnesty International News Release, August 26, 1997.

32. See Michael J. Sullivan, "Development and Political Repression: China's Human Rights Policy Since 1989," *Bulletin of Concerned Asian Scholars* 27 (4), October–December 1995, pp. 24–25; and *China: Use of Criminal Charges Against Political Dissidents*. New York: Human Rights in China, 1994.

33. See Minxin Pei, "Is China Democratizing?" *Foreign Affairs* 77 (1), January/February 1998, pp. 68–82.

34. See Errol P. Mendes and Anne-Marie Traeholt, *Human Rights: Chinese & Canadian Perspectives*. Ottawa: The Human Rights Research & Education Centre, 1997.

35. *World News*, New York, May 5, 1997.

36. Jiang Zemin, "Correctly Handle Some Important Contradictions of Socialist Construction," *Document of the 5th Plenary Session of the 14th Central Committee of the CCP*. Beijing: People's Publishing House, 1996, pp. 10–11.

37. Fei-ling Wang, "To Incorporate China: A New Policy for a New Era," *The Washington Quarterly* 21 (1), Winter 1998, pp. 67–81.

38. Quoted in Edward Friedman, "How to Avoid War with China? Containment, Appeasement, or Engagement," paper presented at the conference "What if China Does Not Democratize," Marquette University, July 1997.

Chapter 11

U.S.-PRC Relations and the "Democratic Peace"

Barrett L. McCormick

Democratization in China would lead to better relations between the United States and China. This is because the present atmosphere of mutual suspicion and hostility between China and the United States is more the result of perceptions and institutions than unchanging culture or immutable national interests. Far from being inevitably driven to conflict by culture or realpolitik, China and the United States could derive mutual benefit from economic and cultural exchanges and cooperate to achieve common diplomatic goals. As the democratic peace argument suggests, democracy offers the best hope of ameliorating institutional conflicts and negotiating mutual understanding between the United States and China. As Bruce Russett and others have argued, democracy fosters a climate of negotiation and compromise. An open public debate offers the best chance of introducing new information and changing perceptions.

In addition, democracy is especially important in the emerging international system. The present world economy rewards open borders and the free flow of information. Multinational corporations and international institutions value rule of law and transparency. Secrecy, corruption, and arbitrary rule engender suspicion. Governments like China's government that define security primarily in terms of building a strong state and enforcing a Westphalian standard of sovereignty will not only be at odds with the emerging international system, but will be weaker and less secure for their trouble.

Democracy, however, is not a "magic bullet." Even the quickest consideration of American politics and American foreign policy offers overwhelming evidence that democracies can harbor chauvinists and pursue narrow national interests. These reflect human failings that cannot easily be eliminated from any society, whether democratic or not. Democracy would not instantly eliminate Chinese nationalism or anti-American attitudes. Some of the disagreements between the United States and China are based in the distinctions between rich and poor, between being a pillar of the existing international system and a rising power, the continuing relevance of different cultures and histories, and geopolitical considerations. But in both China and America, democracy offers a better chance of overcoming these problems than dictatorship.

Conflicts are no less "real" for being rooted in institutions and perceptions, as the democratic peace argument suggests they often are, than for being rooted in culture or realpolitik. Wars can result from domestic politics gone awry as well as from international politics gone awry. When nationalist grandstanding in either country evokes a similar response from the other, relations deteriorate and repeated rounds of the same could even lead to a war that is not in the "real" interests of either country.

But conflict between China and the United States is not yet inevitable. The existing Chinese leadership has made some bad decisions, but has also made some good decisions and has the potential to make more good decisions. Washington is similarly divided. In the meantime, Americans cannot make the United States secure or democratize China by demonizing Chinese leaders. To the contrary, only Chinese can build democracy in China and demonizing China will most likely prove a self-fulfilling prophecy. In the meantime, Americans need to be aware of potential threats, but these are as much of a reason to promote the best possible relationship as to adopt a hostile tone.

The Democratic Peace

A number of scholars including Michael Doyle, Bruce Russett, and John M.Owen have amassed persuasive evidence that democracies seldom go to war with each other.[1] Bruce Russett and his collaborators, for example, have established an empirical foundation for this claim that stretches from ancient times to the present.[2] Russett defines "war" as a conflict between internationally recognized sovereign states that produces more than a thousand battle deaths and "democracy" as a political system in which a substantial fraction of the citizens are enfranchised, governments are brought to power in contested elections, and the executive is either popularly elected or responsible to a popularly elected legislature.[3] Using this definition, Russett finds a few ambiguous cases, but nonetheless concludes that there have been no wars between democracies since 1815.

Various related reasons have been advanced to explain this finding. Some argue that citizens in democracies tend to identify with each other. Owen argues that the key is the perception of shared liberal values.[4] Russett argues that democracy teaches habits of negotiation and compromise. There are important similarities between the democratic peace argument and Hannah Arendt's discussion of violence and democracy.[5] Arendt argues that democracy provides a means of establishing legitimate authority, while violence is inimical to both democracy and legitimate authority.[6] Samuel Huntington made a similar point in *Political Order in Changing Societies* when he argued that political violence is indicative of weak political institutions.[7] As Edward Friedman argues in this volume, Kant's seminal argument was that democracies would be inclined to extend this preference for institutions over violence into international affairs.[8]

Mansfield and Snyder criticize democratic peace theory in a manner that has important implications for China.[9] They accept the claim that democracies seldom go to war with each other, but find that democratizing regimes (which according to their definition includes regimes moving from autocracy to a mixed form of government) are more likely to be involved in wars than regimes whose form of government is stable.[10] Even so, they agree that the solution to this problem is more democracy, not less.

This finding points to the important and ambiguous relationship between nationalism and democracy. On one hand, nationalism is an integral and necessary part of democracy. Unless citizens believe they belong to an important and valuable community, and unless they are committed to the welfare of that community, democracy is not possible. Yet very similar sentiments can result in violent and destructive chauvinism that not only threatens neighbors but that can also be turned against democracy itself. The passions that led the American revolutionaries toward Canada or the French revolutionaries to war with their neighbors were part and parcel of the passions that led to declarations of liberty and equality.

As regards China, this confluence is a source of both hope and concern. The same sense of concern for the welfare of China that blinds too many Chinese patriots to the ways in which China threatens its neighbors can also motivate a search for political reform within China. On the other hand, a democratic China will certainly include a potential for chauvinist foreign policies. To cite a pressing example, while many have noted the apparent contrast between the democracy demonstrations of 1989 and the anti-American demonstrations of 1999, both can find precedents in the May Fourth movement which was both nationalistic and democratic.

While the democratic peace argument should only be said to hold out a little hope, it is relatively optimistic when compared to cultural determinism and realpolitik, the perspectives considered below. Cultural determinism posits that there are no universal truths and that different cultures are essentially irreconcilable. In this perspective, democracy is not a means to reconcile different points of view, but a product of some cultures that is not suitable for other cultures. Cultural determinism thus counsels us to prepare for a future of enduring conflict with little or no prospect for mutual understanding. Realpolitik views international relations as an amoral quest for national interests, and posits that strife and anarchy are normal. Particularly if China is understood to be a rising power in a world presently dominated by the United States, realpolitik similarly suggests that conflict between the United States and China will be difficult to avoid. Is conflict as inevitable as these perspectives would suggest?

Realpolitik

Since the collapse of the Soviet Union, the United States and China have struggled to define common interests. Nixon and Mao found a common interest in resisting an apparently increasingly powerful Soviet Union. But now the U.S.-China security relationship is troubled. Both sides do have a common interest in peace in East Asia but are divided by a series of anxieties. From Beijing's perspective, the United States's 100,000 troops in East Asia, the U.S.-Japan security relationship, American commitments to Taiwan, and U.S. support for interventions such as in Kosovo are all worrisome. From Washington's perspective, Beijing's territorial claims to Taiwan, the Senkaku/Diaoyu Islands, and the Spratly Islands, increasing military expenditures, the lack of transparency regarding military affairs, and sales of sensitive arms and technology to sensitive countries all similarly raise security concerns.

China's phenomenal economic growth provides a credible alternative to security cooperation. Large American corporations with a stake in the China market have been the leading supporters of reconciliation and patience,[11] winning notable victories such as persuading President Clinton to abandon his campaign promises and remove the linkage between most favored nation status and human rights. Moreover, American investment in China and trade between China and the United States are not just exploitation or exporting jobs, but truly do help to bring prosperity to both sides.

The post–Cold War U.S.-China economic relationship is more intimate and complex than their former security relationship. As will be discussed at greater length, China's authoritarian leaders have committed themselves to a Westphalian standard of sovereignty. Sovereignty and security are more compatible than sovereignty and economics. Sovereignty, claims such as China's claims to Taiwan, can raise difficult security issues, but traditional security politics is primarily about guaranteeing sovereignty. However, economic exchange tends to undermine sovereignty, particularly in the increasingly integrated contemporary international economy. China's leaders are not alone in having to struggle to cope with eroding state sovereignty, but the considerable importance of sovereignty to their post-totalitarian institutions makes this issue all the more delicate in China.

American concerns about China do impinge on a wide range of issues that strict Westphalian logic would relegate to domestic politics. In terms of economics, opening markets to international trade would most likely further weaken some already insecure state-owned enterprises. Enforcing intellectual property rights entails adjusting relationships between the center and the provinces. Establishing impartial and transparent procedures for adjudicating economic disputes could have enormous implications for the entire political system. Human rights, including the treatment accorded to dissidents, the status of religious groups, the rights of labor organizations, the integrity of judicial processes, and not least the status of minorities such as Tibetans most certainly involve domestic politics and institutions. Even some issues that are seemingly international involve delicate domestic politics. For example, U.S. concerns about missile and weapons exports impact firms with close ties to the Chinese military. If Beijing were to accede to American demands for greater transparency regarding the PLA's funding and operations, it would set a precedent that could have huge implications for the rest of Chinese politics.

Given the range of international issues that run against the government's domestic interests, it is not surprising that Chinese leaders have ambiguous attitudes toward the international system. Many in Beijing believe that the international system is anti-China. After the 1989 demonstrations, the Chinese government made a determined effort to blame the "disturbance" on the interference of Western governments, and broadcast a steady stream of warnings regarding an alleged "peaceful evolution" plot whose goals were to overthrow Chinese socialism and block the rise of China. These claims appealed to the long history of Chinese xenophobia, including Mao's radical anti-imperialism. Though they were moderated during Jiang Zemin's visit to the United States in 1997 and Clinton's visit to China in 1998, these warnings have remained a constant theme in the Chinese media. Most Chinese are now familiar with a long litany of anti-American complaints ranging from sabotaging Beijing's attempts to host the 2000 Olympics to the allegedly poor treatment of the Chinese women's soccer team in the 1999 World Cup.

Beijing has been skeptical of Washington's efforts to promote international intervention in various world conflicts, seeing intervention as unwarranted interference in another country's domestic affairs and Washington as a self-appointed global policeman. Because of the clear violation of Yugoslavia's sovereignty, Beijing voiced determined opposition to the intervention in Kosovo. Official papers even doctored photographs to make Clinton look like Hitler.[12] Against this backdrop, the bombing of China's Belgrade embassy confirmed widely held fears.

Kosovo is only one of many areas where Beijing has been skeptical of what Washington likes to call "the international community." While many in Washington perceive regulating the world arms trade as fundamental to world peace, Beijing argues that American attempts to regulate the international arms trade are tailored to protect American interests, and above all, to maintain the U.S. arms industry's dominant position in the world arms trade. While from Washington's perspective China's lukewarm response to international efforts to curtail nuclear testing is worrisome, Beijing sees itself as a weak power that still has far fewer nuclear weapons than Washington. While many in Washington believe that admitting China to the World Trade Organization (WTO) without securing increased access to Chinese markets would compromise fundamental principles, Beijing officially claims that Washington is unfairly demanding that Beijing meet standards properly reserved for developed economies.

Beijing is particularly sensitive to Washington's international security arrangements. While Washington's internationalists see troops in East Asia as part of a multilateral network that maintains peace and stability,[13] Beijing now expresses fears that Washington will use these forces to pursue a policy of "containment."[14] Where Beijing once viewed the U.S. presence in Asia as a means of preventing the rebirth of Japanese militarism, Beijing now sees the strengthening of U.S.-Japanese security ties as promoting Japanese militarism.

It is critically important not to overestimate Beijing's opposition to the existing international system. International trade and investment has had a critical role in China's rapid economic growth which is in turn critical for maintaining the existing government. China has also become the world's leading recipient of inexpensive loans from international financial institutions. Prior to the war in Yugoslavia, it was the Chinese Prime Minister, Zhu Rongji, who brought concessions to Washington in an attempt to move the WTO negotiations forward only to be rebuffed by Clinton. Even in as sensitive a matter as human rights, while the Chinese government has rejected criticisms from the United States and others, it has not rejected the principle of universal human rights, but has instead issued white papers offering its own interpretation of how such rights should be defined, and has recently signed two UN covenants on human rights. Jiang Zemin has gone to great lengths to present himself to the Chinese people as an internationally esteemed leader. Nor is China a serious military threat to the United States. The U.S. military retains hundreds of times more nuclear missiles than the PLA, and despite alarmist reports in the American media, the Chinese army remains poorly equipped and has at best limited capacity to project power beyond China's borders.

Some Americans are tempted to overlook this ambiguity and construe China as an inevitable or even immediate threat to American security. Bernstein and Munro's book, *The Coming Conflict with China*, for example, finds that "China is an unsatisfied and ambitious power whose goal is to dominate Asia" and portrays China as "a rogue nation, unbound by the usual rules of diplomatic moderation, unbound even by its own stated commitments."[15]

More restrained academic commentators have portrayed China as a rising power and drawn analogies to Germany and Japan before World War II. In the terms of this argument—drawn from widespread international relations theory—the question is whether the existing international regime can adapt to accommodate the ambitions of a rising power that makes new demands. From this perspective, the United States is saddled with the task of "weaving the net" to incorporate China within the existing world system.[16] Such commentaries generally agree that the United States embodies norms that the Chinese government does not yet respect and, further, that the United States government has a major interest in guaranteeing these norms.

The Chinese government has expressed outrage over arguments that see China as a threat. The Xinhua News Agency, for example, labeled Bernstein and Munro's book racist, slanderous, and ill-informed.[17] The Beijing government argues that in all its history China has never been an aggressive power, and that since the Opium War, it has been a victim of imperialism. The theory that China—which the Chinese government argues remains poor and weak—is now becoming a threat is said to be a remnant of Cold War thinking whose cynical purpose is to prevent China's return to dignity and prosperity. One official commentary claims that the purposes of the "China Threat" argument are to seek public support for increased spending on arms, to prepare the public for high military budgets, and sow discord between China and other Asian countries. It concludes: "As long as the Communist Party refuses to give up its leadership, Western countries will not lower their guard against China"[18]

Both Beijing's and Washington's perspectives agree with important aspects of the theory of the hegemon struggling to deal with a rising power. The current Chinese government's ambiguous attitude about the existing international order and about the United States's role in maintaining that order has some foundation. Fears that Washington will use its power to further narrow interests without serious regard for China's interests must be taken seriously. On the other hand, Washington's ambiguous attitudes toward China also have a foundation. The Chinese government's emphasis on national sovereignty is profoundly contrary to the contemporary international economy and has enormous implications for the protection of human rights. Beijing's various territorial claims could well lead to broader conflicts. The withdrawal of American forces from East Asia would undoubtedly provoke tremendous uncertainty and quite possibly lead to insecurity.

In sum, the U.S.-PRC relationship has a potential for serious conflict. There are important groups in both capitals that are prone to demonize the other. These "demonizations" have enough of a foundation that either could come to dominate their country's domestic political scene. The Kosovo crisis cannot be understood as an isolated incident. In the next few years, Washington and Beijing will undoubtedly face disputes that will create opportunities for hardliners in both capitals. Both countries' domestic politics offer at least short-term rewards for leaders who will take a tough line. There is a real danger that the United States and the People's Republic of China (PRC) could develop increasingly hostile relations.

Cultural Determinism

In recent years Samuel Huntington has been a leading proponent of cultural determinist theories of international relations. Huntington foresees a future of irreconcilable conflict among the world's great civilizations.[19] While Huntington would probably agree that democracies seldom go to war with each other, he would attribute this to the democratic countries' ostensible common European heritage rather than the impact of democracy per se. Thus, in Huntington's perspective, the "democratic peace" could be subsumed within his claim that the world's most important conflicts are between civilizations, not within civilizations.

Huntington argues that democracy is not a universal value, but is instead a product of a European tradition that other civilizations do not share. From this perspective, attempting to foster a democratic peace would be both futile and unethical. It would be futile because non-European civilizations lack the cultural traditions required by democracy and are likely to prove indifferent or hostile to democratization. It would be unethical because when Western countries attempt to foster democracy in non-Western countries, they are imposing their values on others. He thus views attempts by the United States to foster democracy abroad as a form of nationalism that is both naïve and arrogant. He writes:

> Western concepts differ fundamentally from those prevalent in other civilizations. Western ideas of individualism, liberalism, constitutionalism, human rights, equality, liberty, the rule of law, democracy, free markets, the separation of church and state, often have little resonance in Islamic, Confucian, Japanese, Hindu, Buddhist or Orthodox cultures. Western ef-

forts to propagate such ideas produce instead a reaction against "human rights imperialism" and a reaffirmation of indigenous values. . . .[20]

Huntington's perspective has much in common with the official position of the Chinese government. The Chinese Communist Party (CCP) retains enough Marxism-Leninism to make a purely cultural perspective embarrassing. Culture, however, does retain a role in that the Chinese leaders publicly assert that definitions of terms like "democracy" and "human rights" are culturally specific. This not only refers to national traditions, but, in terms that introduce a note of political realism, also includes each country's "national situation."

No country, China's leaders say, has the right to impose their culture's definitions of democracy or human rights on another country which is in a different situation or which has a different culture. In the official Chinese perspective, the foreigners who call for democracy and human rights in China are directly descended from those who waged the Opium War. Official statements frequently accuse international human rights advocates of willfully distorting facts in order to slander China. The United States government in particular is singled out as hypocritically condemning others despite its own notoriously bad human rights record.[21] Foreign governments that raise human rights concerns are accused of trying to undermine the sovereignty of the Chinese state, impede China's economic development, and block China's return to its rightful status as a great power. A sympathetic Hong Kong source stated: "Human rights is nothing more than a big stick to use to impose pressure and sanctions on others, a pretext for the interference in other countries' internal affairs, and a tool for their political plots."[22]

China's national situation—according to China's leaders—is that China remains poor and is in urgent need of further development. The CCP argues that, in this situation, the primary individual right is the right of subsistence. The CCP claims that this right can only be realized through economic development, which in turn makes "the right of development" a similarly fundamental right. The CCP then argues that individual civil and political rights are both alien to Chinese culture and an impediment to development.[23] Thus, official CCP claims that their government is a world leader in human rights are based on evidence of rising standards of living.[24]

Chinese leaders argue that only a powerful state can protect the Chinese people from predatory foreign powers, guarantee China's development, and thus secure the fundamental rights of the Chinese people. This follows from their belief that the international system is dangerous and hostile. They then argue that democratic institutions such as a multiparty system, a popularly elected executive, or even what they would call Western-style freedom of speech are deceits designed to undermine the ability of the Chinese state to protect the Chinese people. Thus contrary to the democratic peace argument, the Chinese government holds that strong authoritarian states, not democracies, maintain peace.

Huntington and the CCP have different purposes but arrive at similar conclusions. Huntington presents his thesis as a somber warning about how to get along in difficult times. His *Clash of Civilizations* ends with a scenario in which the West loses a world war. Foreseeing a future dominated by irreconcilable conflict between cultures, he argues that the West should strengthen and purify itself, thus essentially reaching realist conclusions. The Chinese leadership, on the other hand, conflates maintaining its authoritarian grip on Chinese society with protecting the rights of the Chinese people from an ostensibly predatory world. This conjunction serves to construe those who question authoritarian political institutions as traitors and enemies to the whole Chinese people.

Both Huntington's and the Chinese government's criticisms of the "democratic peace" argument raise critical questions. While their differences are important, both agree that the attempt to promote democracy abroad will not be successful and will lead to conflict rather than peace. Are they right?

Is Democracy Possible in China?

Overwhelming evidence shows that democracy is not exclusively Western and that non-Western civilizations are no more naturally inclined to ethnic nationalism. From the resurgence of the "new right" in European politics to chronic racism in America, ethnic nationalism remains a permanent presence in Europe and North America. Conversely, Huntington's contention that "Latin American civilization" is more authoritarian than European civilization echoes 1970s scholarship that has been discredited by the democratization of every major Latin American country.

Similarly, the assertion that Asian values are inherently authoritarian depends on overlooking democratic governments in India, Japan, South Korea, the Philippines, and Taiwan. Other cases demonstrating the importance of democracy in Asia include the prospects for further democratization in Thailand, the popularity of Martin Lee and the Democratic Party in Hong Kong, enormous strides toward democracy in Indonesia, and a hardy if not yet successful democracy movement in Burma. Efforts by Lee Kuan Yew, the Chinese leadership, and various other Asian authoritarians to claim that their oppressive rule corresponds to local values are patently self-serving.[25]

There are many examples of societies that once seemed to acquiesce to authoritarian rulership but that were later revealed to have been waiting and hoping for change. Passivity is not equivalent to consent. James Scott persuasively argues that the normal human response to extreme domination is to avoid confrontation with overwhelming force while exploiting every available opportunity for maximum advantage.[26] To cite one obvious example, Vaclav Havel, now president of the Czech Republic, was once widely understood as an isolated intellectual whose views had little support among the Czech people. Passivity can be understood as a rational response to repression rather than a cultural predisposition. While Taiwanese were once understood to lack a cultural foundation for democracy, the current success of democracy in Taiwan suggests that passivity was a response to the KMT's violent suppression of peaceful demonstrators in February 1947 and subsequent acts of oppression rather than an innate predisposition.

Nationalism and the pursuit of profit may seem to have derailed political reform on the mainland, but accounts of public opinion and intellectual currents in mainland China that fail to consider the impact of censorship, repression, temporary traumas, and fear will make the current system seem more stable than it is. While it is unpleasant, embarrassing, and even dangerous for Chinese to speak about such matters too clearly, most Chinese are consciously and unconsciously aware of the risks and limits imposed by their authoritarian system. As James Scott would predict, most avoid direct confrontation with the state while seeking personal advantage wherever possible. The pursuit of profit in China's booming economy offers both material benefits and personal autonomy. Similarly, nationalism seems to offer a desperately needed quick and safe route to personal dignity.

The present moment marks a low ebb in China's democracy movement, but it is much too soon to declare that movement finished for all time. China's oppressive political system carries a high cost. It not only imposes a burden on China in international politics and economics, but also delegitimates the state with ordinary citizens. While China's authoritarian political system provides massive material benefits to a relatively narrow elite, it also burdens the elite with the necessity of remaining eternally vigilant. Leaders and citizens both understand that the status quo cannot be sustained without constant supervision of public opinion, extensive censorship, careful monitoring of social organization, an expensive and corrupt patronage system, and a large coercive apparatus of informants, police, and prisons. This system is an economic and political liability. While the fear of a general breakdown and the elite's short-term interests in the status quo may stifle political reform initiatives, they cannot solve the long-term problems.

Both Chinese intellectuals and leaders have a demonstrated commitment to democracy. Democracy has had intellectual supporters throughout the history of the twentieth century.[27] A current of thought that could not be extirpated by the Japanese invasion, the Anti-Rightist Campaign, and the Cultural Revolution is likely to persist through the growth of markets and prosperity. Moreover, this current of thought is not confined to intellectuals. The general idea that good government requires an energetic press, competitive elections, and rule of law is an established part of the party's political theory and has been advocated by leaders such as Peng Zhen, Qiao Shi, and at times even Jiang Zemin.

The experience of other formerly socialist countries tells us that democratization in China could well be a protracted and difficult process. Decades of repression and corruption leave any Chinese government a difficult legacy. But the costs of maintaining the existing system of post-totalitarian government are high and the pressures for change are enormous. Democracy is not inevitable, but it is possible.

What Difference Would Democracy Make?

Democratization in China would facilitate better relations between China and the United States. Chinese and American leaders do have some conflicting international interests. Some of these would not be affected by institutional change in either country. But domestic political processes may have a decisive impact on how national interests are perceived and pursued. As David Lake states, "Regime type matters in international relations."[28] As "democratic peace" theory claims, "national interests" cannot be discerned by purely objective processes and are not carved in stone. Rather, different types of regimes define and pursue national interests in different ways. A democratic China might well see its national interests in different ways from an authoritarian China, and might be more willing to enter into collaborative relationships with international partners. This difference could be critically important to the future of U.S.-PRC relations.

To make this argument, I must first digress to consider the nature of China's existing government. Most commentators agree that China now has an "authoritarian" government. Inasmuch as this term calls attention to significant improvements that have occurred since the death of Mao, it is a good term to use. The Chinese state no longer has the ambition or the ability to dominate as much of Chinese society or to penetrate society as thoroughly as it once did. Large portions of the economy and even popular culture are no longer directly controlled by the state. Local governments have considerable autonomy. There have also been significant if limited attempts to create a legal system and representative institutions. Ideology is not at all as important as it once was.

The Chinese state, though, remains among the most repressive in Asia. The Chinese government's penetration and control of civil society is matched only by Vietnam and North Korea, and to the best of our knowledge, these two countries have avoided large-scale massacres such as occurred on June 4, 1989. In this regard, the Chinese government also resembles Burma's violent junta. Even before Suharto's fall Indonesia's press was far more critical than China's, and the Indonesian opposition enjoyed more, if nonetheless limited, legal legitimacy. The Indonesian government's struggle to suppress Timorese resistance may well have reached genocidal proportions not matched by China in Xinjiang or Tibet, but this is more a result of the Timorese's more violent opposition than a sign of relative tolerance on the part of China's leaders.

The Chinese government is also extremely corrupt. Transparency International's 1996 compilation of ten international surveys ranking fifty-four countries for corruption ranked China fiftieth. In subsequent years China has received a more favorable ranking, partly because more countries were included.[29] Corruption nonetheless remains enormously important in Chinese politics, influencing politics and business at all levels of government. China's leaders have declared corruption to be a grave threat to political stability on many occasions.

Repression and corruption are expedient short-term tactics for maintaining the stability of a government with weak legitimacy, not a cultural predilection. Repression—including media censorship, tight restrictions on autonomous organizations, and harassing and detaining activists—prevents public discussion of many issues that the party leaders find difficult and embarrassing and slants all political discourse to favor the party's interests. The party has yet to allow a full accounting of the tragic history of the People's Republic, and would be sorely tested by an open discussion of events like the Great Leap Forward or Cultural Revolution. Public discussion of contemporary issues such as crime, unemployment, corruption, pollution, the lives of leaders, and relations between local residents and migrants from other provinces are also restricted and channeled in ways that protect the interests of power holders.

Recovering legitimacy looks to be at best a long-term project. Economic growth has built popular support for the party's economic reforms, but this is only a limited form of legitimacy. First, the success of the reforms has undermined most of traditional ideology's social theory. Once central ideas like class struggle, collectivism, and command planning are now embarrassing reminders of how badly the party misunderstood the world. Moreover, the traditional ideology set standards of equality and probity that are now hopelessly beyond the party's reach. Meanwhile, the benefits of economic reform have not been equally distributed and losers such as workers and peasants—the heroes of traditional ideology—are increasingly restive. Finally, should economic growth falter, the party will be in difficult straits.

In these circumstances, the party has turned to nationalism to bolster its flagging legitimacy.[30] The form of nationalism the party favors, as noted above, conflates the party's authoritarian rule with China's political stability and economic prosperity. Those who would argue that China could have both prosperity and stability without authoritarian government are construed as enemies or traitors. The party spokespeople have even asserted that the traditionalistic religious exercise movement, Falun Gong, is a foreign-inspired attempt to undermine the patriotic government.[31] The party construes exercising harsh control over Tibet and Xinjiang, gaining control over Hong Kong and Taiwan, and even claims to the distant Spratly Islands as important means by which it protects the rights of the Chinese people.

Of course, these are not the only means by which the party could or does seek to restore its legitimacy. Since the beginning of reforms the party has also been committed—to different degrees at different times—to political and legal reforms that could lead toward democratization.[32] At least on paper, China now has a legal system. People's congresses at all levels of government are more active than at any time in history. The success of competitive elections for village leaders is leading the way to similar elections for township leaders. For much of 1997 and 1998 the media were increasingly open and, in particular, were encouraged to expose corruption.

Unfortunately, in the waning months of 1998, Jiang Zemin seemed to have chosen repression over democratization. 1999 was a difficult year. Besides intensifying the repression of traditional dissidents, such as the leaders of the China Democracy Party, the regime has repressed workers upset by layoffs and unpaid wages and pensions in state-owned enterprises and farmers outraged by corrupt local leaders. The troubled state of the East Asian regional economy coupled with problems in China's domestic economy such as unprofitable state-owned enterprises and overextended banks may result in difficult economic times. Unemployment will increase and add to the already significant numbers of strikes and protests. Jiang Zemin, evidently agreeing that an economic slowdown will leave the party in a difficult position, has responded by tightening controls over the media and cracking down on dissidence.[33]

Remaining oppressive and authoritarian places the Chinese government at odds with significant portions of the international community. The smaller part of the problem is directly linked to the institutions of authoritarian rule. Local governments, military units, and the sons and daughters of ranking cadres have important stakes in enterprises that export arms to controversial states, violate intellectual property rights, profit from import barriers, and are accustomed to using their power and position to gain advantages over international businesses. When foreigners complain and urge the authorities to deal with such problems, leaders have to make difficult choices. While the Chinese state undoubtedly has the capacity to crack down on individual abuses, the patronage system as a whole remains a critical tool for maintaining ties among elites.

A larger problem, as noted above, is that the ethos of Chinese authoritarianism runs contrary to the current logic of the world economy. It is not easy to maintain a state with a legacy of secrecy, repression, and hierarchy in a world economy that rewards the free flow of capital, goods, and information and favors the development of lateral networks. Inasmuch as few foreign leaders take their claim to be socialist seriously, the Chinese leaders' claim that the hostility they face is a result of their commitment to socialism is without foundation. But inasmuch as remaining Leninist political institutions are profoundly at odds with the existing international system, the claim nonetheless has some merit. The conflict between the norms of this system and the needs of this type of state creates a permanent danger that some Chinese leaders will respond to international criticism with rhetoric and policies that they and some Chinese citizens will understand to be defensive but which neighbors, trading partners, and American leaders may understand as aggressive.

A still larger problem concerns the type of nationalism that authoritarian politics is likely to foster. There are two general themes to official nationalism that are linked to authoritarian politics. The first of these is a defensive reaction to international criticisms of authoritarian abuses that takes the form of asserting maximal notions of Westphalian sovereignty. The second is a propensity to deflect attention from domestic failures by focusing on international issues, not least territorial issues linked to questions of sovereignty. Both of these claims can be couched in terms of the myth of national humiliation, such as defending China from more depredations like the Opium War or the Japanese invasion. They will be understood by many Chinese citizens as calling for a reasonable defense of legitimate national interests.

Chinese nationalism can exacerbate international conflicts even if, as Suisheng Zhao argues,[34] its origins are domestic rather than international, and even if, as Jianwei Wang argues,[35] Chinese understand it to be defensive rather than aggressive. Nationalist rhetoric has a propensity to become increasingly vehement, and Chinese leaders, like leaders everywhere, find it difficult to back away from rhetoric that pleases domestic audiences even if it does have grave international consequences. Most of the world's most dangerous nationalisms, including, for example, Serbian claims against Islamic groups, Hutu claims against Tutsis, Israeli claims against Palestinians, Afrikaner claims against Blacks, and Ulster Protestant claims against Irish Catholics, all understand themselves as defensive reactions to others' aggression. China's Southeast Asian neighbors, Japanese, South Koreans, and Americans all have their own security concerns and are all attentive audiences trying to discern the intentions of a secretive Chinese leadership. These audiences are unlikely to accept arguments that official Chinese nationalism is either exclusively defensive or primarily for a domestic consumption, but are instead likely to respond with their own nationalist rhetoric and to increase military spending as well. It is sadly easy to foresee a spiral of nationalisms leading toward unintended conflicts in the Taiwan Straits, the South China Sea, or the Diaoyutai/Senkaku Islands.

Democratization is unlikely to result in Chinese suddenly abandoning nationalist rhetoric. Unfortunately, attempts to portray Europeans and North Americans as resentful of China's rise and eager to sabotage China's return to power and prosperity seem all too reasonable to all too many Chinese. As Harvey Nelsen's chapter in this volume argues, the myth of China's national humiliation has a factual foundation and, more important, is well rehearsed. Some of the Chinese government's most controversial policies—demands for reunification with Taiwan, for sovereignty over the Diaoyutai/Senkaku Islands, and the suppression of ethnic dissent in Tibet and Xinjiang—are evidently warmly welcomed by many Chinese citizens. Many Chinese understand American policy toward China as a form of aggression rather than a defense of international norms and standards, and as such support their government's resistance.[36]

Democratization may even increase opportunities for nationalist politics. There is every reason to expect that a fledgling Chinese democracy would be plagued by figures like Vladimir Zhirinovsky. Aggressive nationalists and other unscrupulous politicians will work to prevent any quick or lasting solutions to conflicts over Taiwan, Tibet, Xinjiang, or the Spratly or Diaoyutai/Senkaku Islands. Chinese will continue to debate the virtues of international culture for the foreseeable future, and some will find it immoral and polluting.

While many have argued for a sharp distinction between a "civic nationalism" fostered by democracy and a more dangerous "ethnic nationalism," the distinction is not tenable. Eric Hobsbawm, for example, defines "civic nationalism" as inclusive, participatory, and inwardly oriented and "ethnic nationalism" as maintaining the exclusive purity of an ethnic group, and usually portraying the ethnic group in question as locked in a zero-sum conflict with other groups.[37]

However, as Bernard Yack counters, the attempt to excavate and celebrate the civic aspects of nationalism is commendable, but leads in unfortunate directions. Yack argues that "civic nationalism" often seems to imply that Anglo-Saxon nationalism is good nationalism while other nationalisms are bad. As such this term obscures the important role that chauvinism such as British *resentiment* of the French and American attitudes toward the Old World played in shaping Anglo-Saxon identities.[38] Moreover, linking democracy with Anglo-Saxon nationalism may also make it seem as if democracy itself is an Anglo-Saxon ideal unsuitable or unlikely elsewhere. Finally, what Hobsbawm calls "ethnic nationalism" is present in most human communities most of the time. Ethnic nationalism is present in the United States not only in the racism of fringe groups but also in the rhetoric of prominent politicians like Pat Buchanan and Jesse Helms.

However, Hobsbawm's dichotomy works to the extent that it calls attention to the possibility that civic virtues—or democracy—can moderate the extent and impact of nationalist chauvinism. This argument resembles Russett's explanation of the "democratic peace." He argues that the reason democracies do not go to war with each other is because democratic institutions foster a common culture of negotiation and compromise that generates some degree of mutual trust and respect.[39] Guiseppe Di Palma similarly argues that democratic institutions produce democrats rather than vice versa.[40] Both argue that institutions shape behavior—regardless of culture. This does not necessarily mean that democracies produce better policy than dictatorships. Rational choice studies of collective action dilemmas and free rider problems have offered cogent explanations of the myriad of ways in which democracies produce less than optimal policy. The United States's inconsistent, ill-timed, and often ill-considered policy toward China has certainly exemplified the pathologies of democratic politics. But democracy may nonetheless offer the best hope of restraining nationalist chauvinism.

China's present political institutions, on the other hand, make nationalism seem far more reasonable and promising than democracy. The party officially encourages citizen participation in forms of civic politics such as elections to people's congresses, suing officials for their misconduct, official unions, and Lei Feng–style campaigns for public morality. But while they welcome these as steps in the right direction, most people still believe that individual leaders hold most of the power, are more or less immune to criticisms from below, and make important decisions with minimal regard for popular sentiment. For better or worse, the regime has conclusively demonstrated that civic politics of the sort that dominated the 1989 democracy movement is both futile and dangerous. With only a few exceptions, activists who have subsequently dared to mount public campaigns for democracy have been harassed, deported, arrested, and/or tortured. Civil society initiatives for less ambitious goals such as promoting environmental awareness or supporting battered women face continual surveillance and recurring troubles with administrative authorities.

Censorship and ideological leadership have combined to present distorted information to the Chinese public. Central leaders have taken steps to encourage nationalism ranging from explicit guidelines to newspaper and periodical editors to grant money for academics. Information that might stimulate concern about human rights problems is either absent from the media or presented in oblique and limited ways. The Chinese press, for example, offered extensive coverage of the terrible impact of NATO bombs on Yugoslav citizens, but only limited coverage of Yugoslav efforts to expel Albanians from Kosovo. While Chinese citizens who protested the American bombing of China's Belgrade embassy were understandably upset by suggestions that they had been manipulated by their government, Vice Premier Li Lanqing took a different view, stating that:

> Our teachers and students have demonstrated intense patriotic emotion, acute political awareness and a heightened sense of the law in their protests against the United States-led Nato's barbaric bombing of our embassy in Belgrade. . . . This has fully demonstrated the importance of party construction and political ideological work on campus and their effect.[41]

The media are structured in ways that favor nationalism and make it difficult for democrats to publicly state their case. The present government's attitude is demonstrated in the different treatment accorded the two different journals, *Orient* (Dongfang) and *Strategy and Management* (Zhanlüe yu guanli). Both could make a serious claim to be unofficial magazines operating in the guise of official magazines. *Orient* was widely understood as a platform for liberal intellectuals while *Strategy and Management* advocates neoauthoritarianism and nationalism. *Orient* was required to cease publication in late 1996 while *Strategy and Management* persists. Similarly, in the fall of 1997 many liberal intellectuals saw the ambiguous treatment accorded to the polemical nationalist book, *The China That Can Say No*, as evidence of the authorities' tacit support for nationalism. While this book was officially criticized, the official sanction was only to halt publication of more copies, not to block further distribution. Long after this sanction was decreed the book was still widely available even in state-run bookshops. Moreover, the commercial success of this book stimulated an explosion of similar titles.

The argument that democracy would help to moderate Chinese foreign policy is contingent and probabilistic. There is no absolute correlation between types of political systems and foreign policy. Democratically elected leaders can and do make bad choices and dictators can and do make good choices. On the whole, though, the logic of the democratic peace argument holds. The habits of negotiation and compromise that democracy demands facilitate making better foreign policy. Authoritarian hierarchy, secrecy, and repression are contrary to the demands of the contemporary international system. Authoritarian leaders are likely to perceive the outside world as hostile and threatening and are likely to encourage their citizens to hold similar views. Aggressively asserting national sovereignty serves the interests of dictators. Authoritarianism does not make conflict between China and the United States inevitable, but it does significantly increase its likelihood.

Conclusion

As long as the United States wishes to retain its preeminent position in world politics and its status as an East Asian power, it must take a leading role in negotiating China's entry into the international system and China's status in the East Asian region. Unfortunately, even if the United States carefully seeks consensus and understanding with other concerned governments, this will place the United States in situations where it will appear in Beijing as the People's Republic of China's leading adversary. There is, however, no other country or coalition that can play this role.

China's post-totalitarian government will face incessant temptations to become more authoritarian and nationalistic. Chinese leaders—and the rest of the world—can hope that the Chinese economy will continue to grow. However, even in the best of circumstances weak ideological and procedural legitimacy will provide a powerful temptation to leaders trying to find a popular base of legitimacy to promote increasingly virulent nationalism. If the economy falters, the temptation will be even stronger. It is possible that nationalist rhetoric and forceful foreign policy will lead to a conflict that neither China's leaders nor American leaders really want, and which would have horrific consequences for the people of both nations.

But what are China's real national interests? I believe that the United States, the world community, the region, and the Chinese people all have a critical interest in fostering a climate of compromise and negotiation. Conversely, if China's entry into the world further weakens the world's already weak human rights regime, undercuts arms proliferation controls, or demonstrates the advantages of violent solutions to terri-

326 • WHAT IF CHINA DOESN'T DEMOCRATIZE?

torial disputes, all the world will be worse off. These goals are so important that China's leadership may recognize them and work toward them even without democratization, but democracy remains the best hope for peace.

Notes

1. Michael W. Doyle, *Ways of War and Peace* (New York: W.W. Norton & Company, 1997); Bruce Russett, with W. Antholis, C. Ember, M. Ember, and Z. Maoz, *Grasping the Democratic Peace: Principles for a Post-Cold War World* (Princeton, NJ: Princeton University Press, 1993); and John M. Owen IV, *Liberal Peace Liberal War: American Politics and International Security* (Ithaca, NY: Cornell University Press, 1997).

2. Russett, *Grasping the Democratic Peace.*

3. Ibid., pp. 12–15.

4. This accounts for the apparent anomaly of war between the NATO countries and Yugoslavia, for while Milosevic is an elected leader, at this writing Yugoslavia is not a liberal democracy.

5. R.J. Rummel suggests this comparison in his book *Power Kills: Democracy as a Method of Nonviolence* (New Brunswick, NJ: Transaction Publishers, 1997).

6. Hannah Arendt, *On Revolution* (New York: Penguin Books, 1965).

7. Samuel P. Huntington, *Political Order in Changing Societies* (New Haven, CT: Yale University Press, 1968).

8. See Edward Friedman, "Immanuel Kant's Relevance To An Enduring Asia-Pacific Peace" in this volume.

9. Edward D. Mansfield and Jack Snyder, "Democratization and War," *Foreign Affairs*, 74(3) (May/June 1995), pp.79–97.

10. As Edward Friedman's paper in this volume points out, their finding may only mean that autocracies often intervene to reverse democratization in their neighbors.

11. For a business perspective on China, see William H. Overholt, *The Rise of China: How Economic Reform is Creating a New Superpower* (New York: W.W. Norton & Company, 1993). See also Jim Rohwer, *Asia Rising: Why America Will Prosper as Asia's Economies Boom* (New York: Simon and Schuster, 1995).

12. David Murphy, "Milosevic Hailed for Battling 'Hitler' Clinton," *South China Morning Post*, April 5, 1999 [www.scmp.com].

13. See, for example, Joseph S. Nye, Jr. "The Case for Deep Engagement," *Foreign Affairs* 74 (4) (July/August 1995), pp. 90–102.

14. Jim Mann, "A Confident China No Longer Wants America's Military Muscle in Asia," *Los Angeles Times*, August 7, 1995.

15. Richard Bernstein and Ross H. Munro, *The Coming Conflict with China* (New York: Alfred A. Knopf, 1997), p. 21.

16. For an example, see James Shinn (ed.), *Weaving the Net: Conditional Engagement with China* (New York: Council on Foreign Relations, 1996).

17. "Beijing Issues Strong Response to Controversial Book," *China News Digest*, March 13, 1997.

18. "Guangming Ribao Article Sees Self-Interest Behind U.S. Talk of 'China Threat,'" *Guangming Ribao*, Beijing, July 1, 1995, p.3. Translated in *BBC Monitoring Service: Asia-Pacific*, July 14, 1995.

19. Samuel P. Huntington, *The Clash of Civilizations: The Remaking of World Order* (New York: Simon and Schuster, 1996).

20. Samuel P. Huntington, "The Clash of Civilizations?," *Foreign Affairs* 72 (3) (Summer 1993), pp. 23–49.

21. See, for example, "Xinhua Article Castigates U.S. Human Rights Record," Xinhua News Agency, March 10, 1996. Translated in *BBC Monitoring Service: Asia-Pacific*, March 12, 1996.

22. "The Sphere of Human Rights Calls for Cooperation, Not Confrontation," *Ta Kung Pao*, March 18, 1997, p. A2. Translated in "Editorial Calls for Cooperation in Human Rights," FBIS-CHI-97–077, March 18, 1997.

23. For a persuasive argument to the contrary, see Ann Kent, *Between Freedom and Subsistence: China and Human Rights* (Hong Kong: Oxford University Press, 1993). See also Michael J. Sullivan, "Development and Political Repression: China's Human Rights Policy since 1989," *Bulletin of Concerned Asian Scholars* 27 (4) (October/December 1995).

24. See, for example, State Council Information Office, "Progress in China's Human Rights Cause in 1996," Beijing Xinhua Domestic Service. Translated in "White Paper on Human Rights," FBIS-CHI-97–062, March 31, 1997.

25. This point is admirably made in Mark T. Berger, "Yellow Mythologies: The East Asian 'Miracle' and Post-Cold War Capitalism," *Positions* 4 (1) (1996), pp. 24–39.

26. James C. Scott, *Weapons of the Weak: Everyday Forms of Peasant Resistance* (New Haven, CT: Yale University Press, 1985) and *Domination and the Arts of Resistance: Hidden Transcripts* (New Haven, CT: Yale University Press, 1990).

27. See, for example, Marina Svensson, *The Chinese Conception of Human Rights: The Debate on Human Rights in China, 1898–1949* (Lund, Sweden: Department of East Asian Languages, 1996); Merle Goldman, *Literary Dissent in Communist China* (New York: Atheneum, 1971); and idem, *Sowing the Seeds of Democracy in China: Political Reform in the Deng Xiaoping Era* (Cambridge, MA: Harvard University Press, 1994).

28. David Lake, "Powerful Pacifists: Democratic States and War," *American Political Science Review* 86:1 (March 1992), pp. 24–37.

29. These rankings can be found at http://www.gwdg.de/~uwvw/.

30. Suisheng Zhao's contribution to this volume describes this in greater detail than is possible here.

31. Jacques deLisle, "Who's Afraid of Falun Gong?" *Foreign Policy Research Institute E-Notes,* August 5, 1999 (fpri@aol.com).

32. For an optimistic assessment of these reforms, see Minxin Pei's contribution to this volume.

33. Liu Binyan, "Climbing a Tree to Look for Fish," *China Focus* 7 (1) (January 1, 1999), pp. 1, 7. For a more detailed consideration of Jiang Zemin's choices, see Su and Sullivan's contribution to this volume.

34. See Suisheng Zhao's contribution to this volume.

35. See Jianwei Wang's contribution to this volume.

36. The bestselling book, *The China That Can Say No*, has often been cited as evidence of the popularity of nationalism in China. In the fall of 1997, this author was part of an investigation of bookstores, book distribution, and publishing, in Beijing and Shanghai that found books with similar themes to be ubiquitous.

37. E.J. Hobsbawm, *Nations and Nationalism Since 1780: Programme, Myth, Reality* (Cambridge, UK: Cambridge University Press, 1990).

38. Bernard Yack, "Reconciling Liberalism and Nationalism," *Political Theory* 23 (1) (February 1995), pp.166–182; and idem, "The Myth of the Civic Nation," *Critical Review* 10 (2) (Spring 1996), pp.193–211. I thank Edward Friedman for alerting me to this argument.

39. Dixon offers more evidence for Russett's argument. See William J. Dixon, "Democracy and the Peaceful Settlement of International Conflict," *American Political Science Review* 88 (1) (March 1994), pp.14–32.

40. Guiseppe Di Palma, *To Craft Democracies: An Essay on Democratic Transitions* (Berkeley: University of California Press, 1990).

41. "Students Lauded for Nato Protests," *South China Morning Post*, June 21, 1999 [www.scmp.com].

Conclusion: Points of Agreement and Disagreement and a Few Thoughts on U.S.-Chinese Relations

Barrett L. McCormick

This volume was written in response to a number of recent books that have argued that conflict between the United States and China is unavoidable. These arguments use cultural determinism to claim that democracy is a Western concept that will not take root in China. This suggests that the fundamental values of Chinese and Americans are and will remain in stark conflict. Given China's steadily growing economy, this value conflict might well lead to armed conflict. The preceding chapters all argue that this is dangerously wrong. It is wrong because democracy is possible in China and wrong because conflict between the United States and China can be avoided. It is dangerous because the thinking and policies that follow from this argument could become a self-fulfilling prophecy leading to an otherwise avoidable but tragically destructive conflict between China and the United States.

This volume, however, contains as much if not more debate than consensus. As usual—and desirably—answering some questions only raises more. These chapters put forward radically different images of contemporary China. How well has the Chinese political system adapted to the new situation created by economic reform? Some of the chapters in this volume see substantial progress toward a democratic political system and an effective leadership which is capable of maintaining a steady rate of reform. Others see a troubling array of political, social, and economic problems and a weak and desperate leadership likely to seek foreign scapegoats for domestic problems. Some chapters argue that China is now well on its way toward integration into the international system and that China's present leaders have only limited international ambitions. Others argue that China's leaders pose a fundamental challenge to the existing international system. Some chapters argue that democratization would diminish the chance for conflict between the Chinese and other states while others argue that at least in the short term, democratization might even exacerbate the potential for conflict.

Issues on Which We Agree

All of the chapters in this book agree that U.S.-Chinese relations are encumbered by a series of vexing issues. Different authors use different conceptual frameworks to categorize these issues and rank their importance differently, but the overall list of issues remains much the same from chapter to chapter. Many issues will cross the boundaries of the categories I will use. First, there are a series of territorial conflicts which China's leaders' view as involving threats to China's sovereignty. On the other hand, some U.S. and regional leaders see the Chinese leaders' claims as potentially destabilizing. These issues include Taiwan, the South China Sea island disputes, and the Diaoyutai/Senkaku dispute. The growth of China's military expenditures and the transparency of military operations are closely related issues.

Second, there are diverse issues related to Chinese leaders' adherence or nonadherence to various international regimes. These include China's admission to the World Trade Organization (WTO), observance of intellectual property rights agreements, and observance of weapons nonproliferation agreements. The Chinese government sometimes argues that these agreements are structured to favor the interest of the strong and the wealthy who have not been willing to make reasonable concessions to China's legitimate interests. Many American leaders fear that these claims mask an unwillingness to be bound by international agreements.

Third, there is a series of conflicts related to human rights issues. Chinese leaders protest that Westerners have no right to impose Western concepts of human rights on China or to interfere in China's administration of territories such as Tibet, Xinjiang, or Hong Kong. Human rights advocates argue that they are only attempting to maintain minimum international standards of human decency.

Fourth, there are conflicts over trade. These include China's trade surplus with the United States, demands for increased access to Chinese markets, protection of intellectual property rights, strengthening legal procedures, and the standardization and transparency of accounting and administrative procedures. These issues involve both sides' desires to protect domestic constituents from international competition while creating opportunities to exploit foreign markets.

Fifth, there is a range of issues that David Bachman labels "new age issues." These include China's contribution to global warming, China's production of acid rain that falls on neighboring countries, and various other social and economic problems such as illegal immigration and illegal trade in drugs.

The length of this list leads to ambiguous conclusions. On one hand, the length and complexity of this list suggests that the relationship between the United States and China will remain troubled for some time. On the other, the wide range of conflicts indicates that China now has a broad, deep, and complex relationship with the rest of the world. Many sectors of both societies are involved in this relationship and both countries' leaders face conflicting demands from different constituents. In the United States this is amply dramatized in the give and take of a pluralist politics that all too often results in inconsistent and ambiguous policy. Leaders in Beijing strive to maintain the appearance of unanimity, but the realities they face are no less complex than those faced by Washington. Nationalist self-assertion may seem a unifying solution to several of Beijing's problems, but it is a double-edged sword. As Sam Kim points out, however much Beijing may wish to resist being woven into multilateral commitments, China can ill-afford to give up its status as the biggest beneficiary of multilateral lending institutions. Taking a tough line toward Taiwan may appeal to Beijing's hawks, but Taiwanese investment is critical to the coastal provinces that provide most of China's economic growth. Nationalism may provide a rebuttal to U.S. human rights charges, but alienating the United States might imperil trade and investment. Nationalism in general may provide a means of criticizing the government regarding its own deep involvement with the Japanese.

There are times when international relations analysis is well served by treating states as unitary rational actors. But when as many diverse

domestic interests are engaged as come into play in U.S.-China relations, it is necessary to consider "two level games" in both countries.
Both U.S. and Chinese elites are simultaneously engaged in domestic
and international politics and must often sacrifice an advantage in one
arena to gain an advantage in the other. It is particularly ironic that
President Clinton, who criticized President Bush for being "soft on
China," is now the target of similar charges from congressional leaders. The authors in this book are agreed that analysis driven by the
exigencies of U.S. domestic politics is prone to simplification. China
is not—as some who seek to protect American workers from cheap
imports would argue—a large prison camp whose inmates toil to produce the products now found in America's discount stores. But nor is
China—as some of those whose sole concern is to gain access to Chinese markets—just another third world country with "normal" third
world human rights problems.

One of the most important misperceptions found in American politics concerns the strength and potential strength of the Chinese military
forces. June Teufel Dreyer argues that the People's Liberation Army is
unlikely to be able to dominate East Asia for a long time to come. Friedman holds that the Chinese military's actual strength may be a moot
point if leaders in other countries perceive it as being strong and doubt
American willingness to come to their aid. But we nonetheless agree
that it will take many years for Chinese military technology to reach
international standards, that Beijing will not be able to project power far
beyond its own shores for some time to come, and that corruption and
the pursuit of profit have a deleterious impact on Chinese military discipline. China is a nuclear power, but no useful purpose is served by exag-
gerating China's conventional military capacity.

During the deliberations that preceded this book the authors agreed
that the least we can do to capture the complexity of Chinese politics is
to distinguish between "the Beijing government" and "the Chinese
people." The chapters found in this volume, as will be noted below,
disagree about how much democratization has occurred in China and
what the present rate of democratization may be. They agree, though,
that at present the Chinese government's claim to speak on behalf of the
Chinese people deserves a skeptical response. Rational actor analysis
that treats the public or private statements of a few leaders in Beijing as
a clear guide to China's national ambitions all too easily assumes the
worst. Even when political elites and intellectuals appear united, as many

analyses of Chinese nationalism argue, the reality may be far more complex. Suisheng Zhao's article in this volume points out that while intellectuals and party leaders may superficially seem to agree, they arrived at nationalist conclusions from different directions and use nationalism for different ends. Chinese citizens have often used nationalism to discredit their governments, and may well do so again.

Most of the chapters in this book agree that the sources of Chinese nationalism (whose importance they contest) are primarily domestic. Some, such as my chapter, see official nationalism as the attempt of a weak regime to regain legitimacy. Others, such as Jianwei Wang, see real problems in "nation building" that Chinese must overcome. Chinese leaders, like American leaders, make statements intended primarily for domestic audiences that end up having serious international repercussions.

Drawing a distinction between the Beijing government and the Chinese people allows the authors in this volume to believe that democracy is possible. They disagree, as will be noted below, about how much progress has been made so far, how soon a transition could occur, what the transition to democracy might look like, and what the immediate impact of democracy might be on U.S.-China relations. The argument that China's present state is the embodiment of Chinese tradition—which has been made by Chinese as well as Westerners—runs counter to too many facts. Democratic Taiwan is not the fifty-first American state as one recent Chinese book claimed, but a genuinely Chinese form of government which—in the limited and clumsy way of all democracies—responds to the will of the people of Taiwan.

The primary obstacle to democracy in China is not Chinese tradition or any special characteristics of the Chinese people. The primary obstacle to democracy in mainland China is the Beijing government whose post-Mao leaders have resisted political reforms while implementing economic reforms. Su and Sullivan's chapter focuses most directly on this point, arguing that Jiang Zemin has at least temporarily chosen to maintain this strategy, but nonetheless has the option of changing strategies. This is not to say that even this government has not made significant progress toward democracy. While some authors find his analysis overly optimistic, all would agree that the reforms discussed in Minxin Pei's article point to real changes that have already significantly improved the lives of Chinese citizens.

The authors in this volume thus agree that the long list of U.S.-China conflicts is not a symptom of deeply rooted conflict between two irreconcilable civilizations. They find instead that conflicts between China and the United States stem from the normal rough and tumble of international relations. Some are typical of north-south conflicts. Others stem from the adjustments that must be made when the existing balance of power shifts in favor of a newly rising power. Still others stem from China's long and difficult process of modernization, a process that has lasted through a hundred years of invasion, anarchy, and civil war and which has called into question several succeeding generations' most cherished beliefs. The United States is intimately involved in this process not because American values are especially contrary to Chinese values, but because the United States is the primary guarantor of the existing security system in East Asia, and because of the critical role of the United States in the world economy.

This leads to the critical conclusion that conflict between the United States and China can be avoided. We strongly believe that compromises can be found that will respect the fundamental values and interests of both sides. Indeed, each side has much to offer the other. China's rapid economic growth has been facilitated by access to international capital, markets, and technology and these chapters agree that most Chinese want to expand this access. The American business community is no less keen to expand its own stake in China's phenomenal economic growth. Similarly, while the Beijing and Washington governments are in conflict on a wide range of security issues, any violent conflict would be tragically costly to both sides.

These authors, then, readily recommend a policy of engagement with China. Neither isolation nor "containment" will serve fundamental U.S. interests. We would strongly encourage American leaders to consider the U.S.-China relationship as so intrinsically important that it must be treated as an end in itself and not as a means of gaining advantage in domestic politics. Americans do need to be carefully cognizant of the very real problems raised by China's growing power, but we must not be lured into self-fulfilling prophecies of unavoidable conflict.

Issues on Which We Disagree

Unfortunately, while the authors in this book are agreed that "engagement" is desirable, this is not a clear guide to policy. All authors support an open-ended dialogue between the U.S. and Chinese governments. All authors see considerable potential for finding mutually satisfactory means of managing relations between the United States and China. However, there are different estimates of how difficult it may be to find such means. Some of the chapters argue that the current Chinese leaders could become adversaries. Others see the current Chinese government as less ambitious and more amenable to compromise.

To begin with the most critical point of disagreement, both Edward Friedman and I argue that there is a chance for a violent conflict between China and the United States or between China and Japan. Neither believes that either Washington or Beijing wants war, but we do argue that official Chinese nationalism may lead to an unintended conflict. Friedman argues that the Chinese government's nationalism is so pervasive that it is unable to understand how others could see it as threatening. In Beijing's eyes, for example, the missile tests conducted prior to Taiwan's presidential elections were entirely justified and were a matter of no concern to outsiders. From their perspective, it is incomprehensible that the Japanese could feel threatened by China, and therefore actions taken by Japan to ward off any such threat will be understood as aggressive in Beijing. Friedman argues that this may well lead to a conflict that neither side actually wants.

Other articles do not see any prospect for war. First, the logic of economic development demands a peaceful environment and the fabulous success of the post-Mao reforms has amply demonstrated the power of this logic. China has received massive amounts of foreign investment and has developed hugely successful export industries. China's leaders well understand that any military adventure would profoundly disrupt the flow of goods and capital with enormous consequences to follow for China's political stability. In other words, China already is inextricably woven into the world capitalist system. If countries with McDonald's seldom go to war with each other—a proposition that is challenged by NATO's war in Yugoslavia—then we can take comfort from the many McDonald's in China's major cities.

Second, the balance of forces is such that China would be likely to lose. As noted above, all of the authors agree that the People's Liberation Army is technologically inferior to U.S., Japanese, and Taiwan forces and has a limited ability to operate at any distance beyond China's borders. In any large-scale conflict, China would be likely to suffer enormous losses. Those who argue that war is unlikely or impossible argue that China's leaders are aware of these imbalances and are unlikely to court disaster in the manner of Saddam Hussein.

Third, Harvey Nelsen and June Teufel Dreyer do not see as much conflict between China and neighboring states as Friedman. In part, they hold that the above economic logic holds sway in the region. Much of the capital invested in China, after all, originates with Chinese living in Taiwan and Southeast Asia. They are also inclined to see ASEAN (Association of Southeast Asian Nations) leaders as not fearing China. Friedman instead argues that ASEAN leaders, believing that American power and will are fading as China rises, have decided that it is prudent not to anger Beijing.

There are subtler shades of difference with policy implications among those who see little prospect for war. Jianwei Wang argues that the Chinese government poses little challenge to the international system. He sees that the policies others view as a challenge to the existing order are merely intended to reestablish China's territorial integrity and national sovereignty, tasks which were accomplished long ago in Japan and the West, but which remain pressing items on China's national agenda. From his perspective, China poses little threat to anyone and the prospects for a policy of engagement to reach mutually beneficial results are very good. On the other hand, June Teufel Dreyer sees more prospects for conflict between China and others in the region.

Wang views Chinese nationalism as much less of a threat than any of the above authors. All of the authors in this volume agree that official Chinese nationalism is a response to the collapse of Marxist-Leninist ideology. But Wang, like Suisheng Zhao, sees nationalism as answering to domestic dynamics rather than international affairs. Both Wang and Zhao point to what Nelsen calls the "myth of national humiliation" (his intention in using the word "myth" is not to deny the reality of imperialist aggression against China but rather to call attention to the frequent invocation of this history as a means of justifying policies and attitudes) as justification for their claims that Chinese nationalism is defensive in character. Wang and Zhao emphasize that Chinese nationalism responds to real political and cultural needs and suggest that as long as the United States and other major powers are not overly sensitive, it can be isolated from the conduct of foreign affairs.

The articles by Edward Friedman and me see more danger in Chinese nationalism. I agree with some of Jianwei Wang's argument that China is in the "primary stage of nationalism." The difference is that while Wang sees the "primary stage of nation building" as an ordinary part of most nations' history, I view ethnic nationalism's preoccupation with territorial issues and its racist tendencies as dangerously destabilizing. I argue that the combination of this form of nationalism, the Beijing government's many complaints about the existing world order, and China's rising power might be explosive. Like Friedman, I argue that it is not necessary for governments to want war to get war, only to misunderstand and misjudge the intentions of their rivals.

How much room the United States has for maneuver also depends on how quickly the Chinese government may be changing. These articles are also in deep disagreement about the status and trajectory of political reform in China. The most optimistic author, Minxin Pei, catalogues an impressive list of democratic reforms including the increasing use of competitive elections for village officials, the increasingly important and autonomous role of national and local people's congresses, and the strengthening of the legal system, to argue that Western observers have fundamentally underestimated the degree of political change in post-Mao China. Pei's argument leads to the conclusion that something like "peaceful evolution" is already well underway in China and that the United States would therefore do well to avoid adopting harsh policies that might result in a disruptive nationalist backlash.

Other authors, however, dispute both Pei's characterization of the current situation and the direction of change. My article, for example, agrees that the reforms Pei cites are significant, but points out that the Beijing government remains one of the most despotic in Asia and one of the most corrupt in the world. Su and Sullivan—who do support Pei's argument for tolerant American policies—argue that the Jiang Zemin government has been tightening controls. Friedman also disputes Pei's optimistic view of the current situation.

The articles by Nelsen, Dreyer, and Bachman question the premise that China's democratization will improve relations between the United States and China. Bachman's argument makes two critical claims. First, he argues that most of the issues underlying the various conflicts between the United States and China have little to do with political institutions but relate to national interests and popular demands. Bachman and Nelsen argue that the nationalism that fuels territorial claims ranging from the Spratlys to the Diaoyutai/Senkaku Islands—and including Taiwan—are overwhelmingly popular with the Chinese people and likely would be popular with voters in a democratic China. Bachman also points out that trade disputes are driven by fundamental economic interests that will not change just because political institutions change. Second,

Bachman notes that the "democratic peace" literature has been challenged by articles presenting evidence that newly established democracies are likely to be more aggressive than established authoritarian regimes. He points out that in most scenarios by which democracy might come to China, the result, at least initially, would be a weak democracy that might not be willing or able to impose unpopular policies on voters whose sentiments would likely remain nationalist. Bachman does allow that the rise of democracy in China would most likely put human rights issues to rest and also agrees that it would provide a fresh start and offers better prospects over the longer run.

My article does not contest important aspects of Bachman's argument, and yet nonetheless reaches different conclusions. Much of the difference between us lies in the difference between the problems that concern us. Bachman does not think that war is a real possibility and consequently is primarily concerned with whether or not the long list of problems cited earlier in this conclusion can be resolved by the democratization of the Chinese government. His conclusion—which I accept as sound—is that many of these issues would remain and that U.S.-Chinese relations would continue to be difficult. Where I depart from Bachman is in imagining that it is possible that state-sponsored ethnic nationalism could lead Chinese foreign policy in directions that would be far more challenging to the United States than the present list of troubles, and that two profoundly self-centered governments could blunder into an armed conflict that neither wanted. It is this last scenario that leads Friedman to reconsider Kant's hope for a world peace based on democratic republics. Friedman rescues Kant from the simplistic interpretation he is often given, arguing that Kant did not claim that democracies never go to war with each other, only that democracy provides the best hope of avoiding war.

Some Concluding Thoughts

Some readers, especially those who are looking for answers to the many concrete foreign policy problems that plague U.S.-China relations, may not find this book particularly helpful. The book offers little explicit advice on the issues of the day. There is scant discussion, for example, of what U.S. diplomats should be telling their Chinese and Taiwan counterparts regarding the United States's willingness to go to war to defend Taiwan, little discussion of what can or cannot be conceded or demanded in negotiations over China's admission to the WTO, and not even much advice about how to handle human rights questions. Perhaps, then, this is just another academic book written by scholars for use within universities. I regret to say that readers who have endured until these last pages hoping that at last they would find such recommendations will be disappointed.

This book nonetheless establishes a fairly clear set of principles by which policy can be made, and these principles might be more enduring than any specific recommendations on the issues of the day. The first and most important of these points is that we must avoid assuming that there is any fundamental conflict between the Chinese people and Chinese culture and Western people and Western culture. There is a subtle but critical distinction between being sensitive to cultural differences and arguing that people in different cultures do not share fundamental values. Of course people who live in different cultures use different languages, symbols, and codes of behavior. The failure to appreciate such differences leads to mutual misunderstanding and recrimination.

It is, however, a huge leap from recognizing these sorts of differences to arguing that other cultures do not equally value human life or human rights. In this volume, it may well be Sam Kim who speaks most eloquently to this point. The international human rights debate, he argues, is not so much a debate between the north and the south as it is a debate between southern governments and southern nongovernmental organizations. There may or may not be such a thing as "Asian values," but there is no consensus in Asia that supports arbitrary, coercive, opaque, corrupt, or even authoritarian government.

Thus the writers in this book debate how and when democracy may come to China and what the consequences of democracy in China might be for the United States, but we all believe that democracy is possible in China. We debate the speed and extent of political reform in the People's Republic, but we all agree that China has already taken important steps toward democracy.

The contrary argument that the Chinese people and Chinese culture are enemies to democracy leads to the conclusion the United States and China will remain locked in conflict for decades to come. The argument that democracy and human rights are the exclusive province of Americans or Westerners is a form of nationalism that encourages others to act in equally nationalist ways. Unfortunately, the confrontational policies that these arguments recommend will fuel Chinese nationalism in a manner likely to create the very China that they claim to guard against.

The authors in this book argue that the U.S. government should approach the Chinese government with the hope and expectation that conflicts can be resolved to mutual satisfaction. They disagree, however, about how much Chinese leaders may resist further integration into the existing international order. Some see the existing Chinese government as preoccupied with domestic problems and unlikely to pose a threat to any foreign powers. Others take a more skeptical view. The following issues are the critical issues that divide these two viewpoints in this book:

- Is Chinese nationalism a benign force whose role is to build a strong and stable China? Or does Chinese nationalism pose a threat to regional stability?
- How serious are Beijing's disputes with other governments in the region? Is war in East Asia possible? Are leaders in ASEAN trying to make the best of a bad situation or genuinely assured of Beijing's good intentions? How serious is the rivalry between Tokyo and Beijing?
- What sort of government is the Beijing government? Is this a government that has committed itself to a gradual process of institutional reform that will eventually lead to democratization? Or is this an increasingly illegitimate authoritarian government that might be tempted to undertake risky adventures in foreign policy to solve domestic problems?
- If China does democratize, how will this affect U.S.-China relations? Are the conflicts between China and the United States matters of national interest, the result of conflicting values, or the divergent aspirations of the two peoples? Or are they linked to different institutional frameworks?

American policy makers should be skeptical of their own ability to influence China's future. Despite the Chinese leaders' concerns about China's sovereignty, there is little evidence that Washington, Tokyo, or any other foreign capital has the ability to shape events in Beijing. China's leaders do want foreign capital and technology, access to foreign markets, security, and prestige, and thus foreign leaders have some amount of leverage. But China remains a large country whose leaders remain well insulated from domestic constituents, let alone from foreign leaders. Moreover, the array of domestic problems faced by the Chinese leaders is substantially more complex than those they face in the international arena.

In the absence of international consensus, the U.S. government will be only one prominent voice among many. The lure of China's emerging market complicates any U.S. attempt to influence Chinese policy. Various European countries, the Japanese, and the Russians as well as the Americans all have important economic interests in China. The Chinese leaders have skillfully exploited this to weaken concerted efforts to change Chinese policies. American policies that are not supported by other countries will have at best a limited impact.

Despite these limits, the United States has a critical interest in facilitating China's integration into the existing international system. The Chinese economy is an increasingly important part of the East Asian economy, which is in turn critical to the U.S. economy. China will have increasing weight in East Asian security issues. As long as the United States remains the major power in East Asia—and there are no alternatives in sight—China's intentions will be a critical factor in U.S. security policy.

This book thus ends with significant questions identified and debated but as yet unresolved. If U.S. leaders allow China policy to be driven by the exigencies of domestic politics, and particularly if they give in to the temptation to view China as an alien culture that does not share basic human values, American policy could have catastrophic results. On the other hand, even the wisest American policies will face great uncertainty and have at best limited leverage. This just might, however, be enough to manage a mutually beneficial relationship.

The Editors and Contributors

The Editors

Edward Friedman, the Hawkins Chair Professor of Political Science at the University of Wisconsin, Madison, served as a China specialist on the U.S. House of Representatives Committee on Foreign Affairs in 1981, 1982, and 1983. His most recent book was *National Identity and Democratic Prospects in Socialist China.* His next book will be *Revolution, Resistance, and Reform in Village China*, which is a sequel to the prize-winning book, *Chinese Village, Socialist State.*

Barrett L. McCormick received his Ph.D. in political science from the University of Wisconsin in 1985. Since then he has been in the Political Science Department at Marquette University, but he has also worked at the Australian National University. He writes about political reform in contemporary China with a special interest in the prospects for democracy. His current project is a study of the impact of media markets on China's public sphere.

The Contributors

David Bachman is Chair of the China Studies Program at the University of Washington and Associate Professor at the university's Henry M.

Jackson School of International Studies. In addition to research and teaching at the University of Washington, Bachman is Vice President of the Washington State China Relations Council, a member of the editorial boards of *Asian Survey* and *The American Asian Review.* He is the author of several books and more than three dozen essays on aspects of Chinese politics.

June Teufel Dreyer is Professor of Political Science at the University of Miami, Florida. She previously served as Senior Far East Specialist at the Library of Congress and Asia Adviser to the Chief of Naval Operations. Her latest book is *China's Political System: Modernization and Tradition*, 3rd edition.

Samuel S. Kim is Adjunct Professor of Political Science and Senior Research Associate at the East Asian Institute, Columbia University. He is the author or editor of fifteen books including most recently *Korea's Globalization* (ed., 2000).

Andrew Nathan is Professor of Political Science at Columbia University, co-author with Robert S. Ross of *The Great Wall and the Empty Fortress: China's Search for Security* (1997), and author of *China's Transition* (1997).

Harvey Nelsen is a Professor in the Department of Government and International Affairs, University of South Florida, Tampa. He is the author of two books and numerous articles and book chapters on China, the most recent of which is "The Future of the Chinese State," in David Shambaugh, ed., *The Modern Chinese State* (2000).

Minxin Pei is a Senior Associate at the Carnegie Endowment for International Peace in Washington DC. He received his Ph.D. in political science from Harvard University in 1991 and was an Assistant Professor of Politics at Princeton University from 1992 to 1998. His main interest is the development of democratic political systems, the politics of economic reform, the growth of civil society, and legal institutions. He is the author of *From Reform to Revolution: The Demise of Communism in China and the Soviet Union* (1994). He is the recipient of a National Fellowship at Hoover Institution, the Robert McNamara Fellowship of the World Bank, 1994–95, and the Olin Faculty Fellowship.

Su Shaozhi was Director of the Institute of Marxism-Leninism and Mao Zedong Thought in Beijing from 1982–1987 and remained as a Research

Professor at that institute until 1989. Following a brief period as a Professor in the Graduate Institute of the Chinese Academy of Social Sciences, he was as a Visiting Professor at Marquette University, the University of Minnesota, and Harvard University until 1994, when he accepted an appointment to the Princeton China Initiative. He is now the President of the Princeton China Initiative.

Michael J. Sullivan is an independent scholar and international business consultant. He received his Ph.D. from the University of Wisconsin-Madison, and has published articles on political change, development, and human rights in China. His current research focuses on business development and social responsibility in Asia.

Jianwei Wang, is an Associate Professor of Political Science, University of Wisconsin-Stevens Point. He received his B.A. and M.A. from Fudan University in Shanghai and Ph.D. from the University of Michigan. He has held positions as Senior Fellow at the Atlantic Council of the United States in Washington DC, Research Fellow at the East-West Center in Hawaii, and Research Fellow at the United Nations Institute for Disarmament Research in Geneva. His research focuses on Chinese foreign policy, Sino-American relations, and East Asian security affairs. He is the author of *Limited Adversaries, Post-Cold War Sino-American Mutual Images* (2000).

Suisheng Zhao is 1999–2000 Campbell National Fellow at Hoover Institution of Stanford University and Associate Professor of Government/ East Asian Politics at Colby College. He is also founder and editor of the *Journal of Contemporary China* published by Carfax Publishing, Ltd. in England. He received a Ph.D. degree in political science from the University of California-San Diego, a M.A. degree in sociology from the University of Missouri and a M.A. degree in economics from Peking University. Formerly a research fellow at the Economic Research Center of the State Council in China, his most recent book is titled *China and Democracy: Reconsidering the Prospect for a Democratic China* (2000). He has published widely on Chinese politics and foreign policy and East Asian international relations.

Index

Acadera, Arnulfo, 173
Administrative Litigation Law (ALL), 84–85
Affirmative nationalism, 40, 47n.62
Aggression
  domestic/foreign policy linkage, 50, 51–52, 54
  nationalism and, 40, 43, 47n.62
Annan Doctrine, 151
Anti-Rightist Movement (1957–58), 93
Aquino, Corazon, 184
Asian regional conference (1993), 143–45
Asian Regional Forum (ARF), 176, 230, 236, 240, 270–71
Asia That Can Say No, The, 39
Assertive nationalism, 40, 43, 47n.62
Association of Southeast Asian Nations (ASEAN), 176–77, 178, 181–82
  Asian Regional Forum (ARF), 176, 230, 236, 240, 270–71
  democratic peace, 230–31, 232–33, 236
  antidemocratic campaign, 240–41
  democratization possibility, 249–50, 252–53
  democratization future, 183–86, 249–50, 252–53, 270–71
  See also Regional relations; Territorial disputes
Aung San Suu Ki, 165, 171, 180
Australia, 179
  Olympics (2000), 165, 187n.5
  territorial disputes, 175–76
Authoritarianism
  democratic peace and, 230, 231

Authoritarianism *(continued)*
  antidemocratic campaign, 241
  culture, 314–15
  democratization impact, 318, 320–21
  democratization possibility, 243, 315–17
  democratization future, 243, 261–62, 265–68, 282n.15
  government corruption, 263–64, 276
  nationalism and, 22–23, 38
  neoauthoritarianism, 31, 32–33
  nation building and
    domestic/foreign policy linkage, 50, 51–52, 55, 56–57, 66–68
  U.S. perspective, 49, 50–52, 69
  U.S./China relations
    Chinese domestic policy, 285, 290–93, 295–97
    Chinese foreign policy, 285, 297
  See also Soft authoritarianism
Authority, 203–5

Bangkok Declaration, 144–45, 146
Bharatiya Janata Party (BJP), 171
Brunei, 166
Bureaucracy
  democratization impact, 206–7
  democratization transition, 218
Burma
  alliance system, 179, 180
  ASEAN admission, 176
  State Law/Order Restoration Commission, 165, 171, 180

Central Bank Law, 83
Chaos theory, 137, 146, 155, 156
Chiang Kai-shek, 101–2, 103, 111, 185
Chi Haotian, 173, 181–82
Chile, 227, 228
China Society for Human Rights Studies,
    129, 145–46
China That Can Say No, The, 3, 22, 36, 39,
    67, 114, 324, 327n.36
Chinese Communist Party (CCP)
    Central Propaganda Department, 27–28, 29,
        30
    domestic/foreign policy linkage, 50, 51,
        52–53, 56
    nationalism and, 26, 27–28, 29, 37, 38, 41,
        42
    patriotism education, 27–28, 29, 30
    soft authoritarianism
        educational qualifications, 79, 80–81,
            97n.13
        elections, 79–80, 92–93
        impact on, 93–95
        leadership norms, 79–81
        leadership purges, 79
        legal reforms, 84, 87
        mandatory retirement, 79, 80,
            96n.9
        National People's Congress (NPC), 81–
            82, 83
        village elections, 87, 88–89
    See also Authoritarianism; Soft authoritarian-
        ism; State government
Civil society
    democratization future, 260, 261
    soft authoritarianism
        civic organizations, 89–90
        danwei/unit system, 90
        institutional pluralism, 89–91
        leisure time, 91
*Clash of Civilization and the Remaking of
    World Order, The* (Huntington), 137,
    138–39, 144, 182, 224–25, 279, 281, 286–
    90, 313–15
Communist ideology
    nationalism, 21, 23, 25, 30
        intellectuals and, 31, 32, 33–34, 36,
            37
    nation building
        domestic/foreign policy linkage, 50, 51,
            52–54, 56–57, 71n.9
        U.S. perspective, 50–51
Communist Youth League of China Central
    Committee, 28
Comprehensive Test Ban Treaty
    China, 178–79
    India, 65–66

Confident nationalism, 40
Confucianism
    nationalism and
        government support of, 30
        intellectual support of, 32–33, 34–35
    regional relations and, 182–83
Containment policy, 57, 285
    cultural determinism, 286–90
    democratization future, 249, 250,
        251
Convention Against Torture and Other Cruel,
    Inhuman or Degrading Treatment or
    Punishment, 142, 154
Cultural determinism
    civilization clash theory, 137, 138–39, 144,
        182, 224–25, 279, 281, 286–90, 313–
        15
    democratic peace and, 305, 306, 308, 313–
        15, 329
        antidemocratic campaign, 241–42
        authoritarianism, 314–15
        democratization possibility, 243–45
        economic affairs, 314
        human rights, 314
        international system, 315
        nationalism, 313–14
    democratization future, 243–45, 259, 272
        religion, 276–78
    human rights and
        Asian values theory, 136–37
        chaos theory, 137, 146, 155, 156
        cultural clash theory, 137, 138–39, 144
        state sovereignty, 133–34, 135, 137,
            142, 144, 146, 148–49, 151–52,
            152–53, 155
        vs. universality, 131, 132, 133, 134,
            143, 144, 145, 146, 147, 152–53,
            158n.9
    nationalism and
        democratic peace, 313–14
        government support of, 24, 29–30, 37
        intellectual support of, 31–32, 34–37,
            38–39
        patriotism, 24, 29–30
    U.S./China policy and, 286–90
Cultural Revolution, 53, 54
    mandatory retirement and, 80, 97n.10
Currency crisis, 179

Danwei/unit system, 90
Defensive nationalism, 42–43
Democratic peace, 224–25, 227–36
    antidemocratic campaign, 225–26, 236–43
        ASEAN, 240–41
        authoritarianism and, 241
        culture and, 241–42

Democratic peace, antidemocratic campaign
(continued)
economic affairs, 237
human rights and, 225–26, 236–41,
242–43
India, 238, 240
Japan, 239–40
military affairs, 236–37
power implications, 237–38
Taiwan, 240
United States, 238–39
Association of Southeast Nations
(ASEAN), 230–31, 232–33, 236
antidemocratic campaign, 240–41
democratization possibility, 249–50,
252–53
authoritarianism and, 230, 231
antidemocratic campaign, 241
democratization possibility, 243
constitutional republic requirement, 230,
231–32, 233, 234
containment policy, 249, 250, 251
culture and
antidemocratic campaign, 241–42
democratization possibility, 243–45
democratization possibility, 243–53
ASEAN, 249–50, 252–53
authoritarianism and, 243
containment policy, 249, 250, 251
culture and, 243–45
democracy dysfunction, 246
democracy movement, 246–48
economic affairs, 226–27, 245–46
engagement policy, 248–50
human rights and, 243
technology and, 245
United States, 250–51
economic affairs, 229–30, 232
antidemocratic campaign, 237
democratization possibility, 226–27,
245–46
engagement policy, 248–50
European Union, 228, 230
human rights and
antidemocratic campaign, 225–26, 236–
41, 242–43
democratization possibility, 243
India
antidemocratic campaign, 238, 240
Pakistan and, 227, 228
Sri Lanka and, 227
island regions, 228
Japan, 228, 229, 234–36, 254n.15
antidemocratic campaign, 239–40
land borders, 228, 229
military affairs, 235–36

Democratic peace, military affairs *(continued)*
antidemocratic campaign, 236–37
mutual interests, 232–33, 253n.13
national interests, 228, 231, 232–33
nationalism, 233
power implications, 237–38
rule of law, 231
Taiwan, 240
technology and, 229, 245
See also United States-China relations,
democratic peace
Democratization, future prospects
ASEAN, 183–86, 249–50, 252–53, 270–71
authoritarianism and, 243, 261–62, 265–68,
282n.15
government corruption, 263–64, 276
civil society, 260, 261
containment policy, 249, 250, 251
culture and, 243–45, 259, 272
religion, 276–78
democracy dysfunction, 246
democracy movement, 246–48
economic affairs, 226–27, 245–46, 266–67,
281
income distribution, 259, 262–63,
282n.14
rapid growth, 262
trade relations, 260–61, 273–75, 276
engagement policy, 248–50
government corruption, 263–64, 276
Hong Kong, 268–69, 279
human rights, 267, 276–77
Japan, 271–73, 280
military affairs, 267–68, 270, 280–81
nuclear armament, 274, 275–76
nationalism, 262, 264–65, 268, 272, 279–
80
National People's Congress (NPC), 260
neo-liberal institutionalism, 260–61
religion and, 276–78
Taiwan, 268, 269–70, 281
technology and, 245
United States, 250–51, 273–78, 279, 280, 281
China perspective, 275–78
Taiwan and, 269–70
U.S. perspective, 273–75
village elections, 260
Deng Liqun, 27–28
Deng Xiaoping
Five Principles of Peaceful Coexistence, 54
human rights, 130–131, 137
Japan-China relations, 102
nationalism, 26, 28
regional relations, 163–64
soft authoritarianism
leadership norms, 79–81

Deng Xiaoping, soft authoritarianism *(continued)*
   leisure time, 91
   political repression, 75–78, 92
   U.S./China policy, 285, 290–92, 295, 297
Diaoyu Islands, 22
   democratization impact, 65, 66
   nation building and, 60–61, 65, 66
   power implications, 60–61
   territorial disputes, 60–61, 65, 66, 166
      Japan, 167, 169–71, 184
      U.S./China relations, 198
Ding Guangeng, 27–28

Economic affairs
   democratic peace, 229–30, 232
      antidemocratic campaign and, 237
      culture and, 314
      democratization impact, 319, 320
      democratization possibility, 226–27,
        245–46
      realpolitik and, 309, 310–11
   democratization future, 226–27, 245–46,
      266–67, 281
      income distribution, 259, 262–63,
        282n.14
      rapid growth, 262
      trade relations, 260–61, 273–75, 276
   nationalism
      government and, 26, 28
      intellectuals and, 32, 35
   nation building
      democratization impact, 63, 68
      domestic/foreign policy linkage, 55–56
      power implications, 58
      U.S. perspective, 49, 50–51, 56, 70
   regional relations, 163–64
      currency crisis, 179
   trade relations
      democratic peace and, 309, 310–11
      democratization future, 260–61, 273–
        75, 276
      democratization impact, 210–11
      democratization transition, 218
      scholarly debate, 8, 331, 337
      U.S. perspective, 197, 199–200
   U.S./China relations
      Chinese domestic policy, 284, 290–91,
        292, 293, 296, 298–99
      democratization impact, 205, 210–11
      U.S. perspective, 49, 50–51, 56, 70,
        197, 199–200
Education
   Communist Party qualifications, 79, 80–81,
      97n.13
   for patriotism, 27–28, 29, 30
Education Law, 83

Elections
   soft authoritarianism and, 79–80, 87–89,
      92–93
   village
      Chinese domestic policy, 294, 296
      democratization future, 260
      soft authoritarianism and, 87–89
Encyclopedia on Human Rights in China,
   129, 150
Engagement policy, 285–86
   democratization future, 248–50
   Japan and, 124
Enterprise Bankruptcy Law, 82–83
Environment, 197
Ethnic nationalism, 41–42, 322–23

Fall, Ibrahima, 146
Falun Gong, 4–5
Fernandes, George, 171
Five Power Defense Arrangement, 179
Five Principles of Peaceful Coexistence, 54, 71n.7

Gang of Four, 53
Government. *See* Authoritarianism; Chinese
   Communist Party (CCP); Soft
   authoritarianism; State government
Great Leap Forward Famine, 93
Great Wall, 30
Guatemala, 177–78, 227, 228
   UN peacekeeping mission, 166

Haiti, 166
   territorial disputes, 177
Han Chinese, 41–42
Hashimoto, Ryutaro, 170, 175–76, 184
Hegemony
   Japan-China relations, 107, 108, 113, 114,
      115, 116–17, 118–19, 121, 123, 286
   regional relations, 167–68, 183
He Xin
   nationalism, 31, 67
   neoconservatism, 33
Hong Kong
   nation building
      power implications, 60, 62–63
      U.S. perspective, 60, 206
   territorial disputes, 60, 62–63
Hosokawa, Morihiro, 104
Human rights
   Annan Doctrine, 151
   Asian regional conference (1993), 143–45
   Asian values theory, 136–37
   Bangkok Declaration, 144–45, 146
   chaos theory, 137, 146, 155, 156
   China Society for Human Rights Studies,
      129, 145–46

Human rights *(continued)*
Convention Against Torture and Other Cruel,
Inhuman or Degrading Treatment or
Punishment, 142, 154
criminal procedure law, 154
cultural relativism
Asian values theory, 136–37
chaos theory, 137, 146, 155, 156
cultural clash theory, 137, 138–39, 144
democratic peace and, 314
state sovereignty and, 133–34, 135,
137, 142, 144, 146, 148–49,
151–52, 152–53, 155
vs. universality, 131–34, 143–47,
152–53, 158n.9
democratic peace and
antidemocratic campaign, 225–26,
236–41, 242–43
culture, 314
democratization possibility, 243
realpolitik, 309, 311, 312
democratization and, 130, 137–38, 152–57
criminal procedure law, 154
future of, 267, 276–77
globalization and, 154–55
International Bill of Rights, 152,
153–54
social protests, 155
divide/conquer strategy, 145–46, 147, 149,
150, 152–53
globalization and, 129–30, 131, 132, 139,
140, 141, 142, 143
International Covenant on Civil and
Political Rights (ICCPR), 129–30,
139, 140, 150, 154, 267
International Covenant on Economic,
Social and Cultural Rights (ICESCR),
129–30, 135–36, 139, 140, 154, 267
International Criminal Tribunal for Rwanda
(ICTR), 153
International Criminal Tribunal for the
Former Yugoslavia (ICTY), 153–54
international human rights regime, 139–52
Annan Doctrine, 151
Asian regional conference (1993),
143–45
Bangkok Declaration, 144–45, 146
divide/conquer strategy, 145–46, 147,
149, 150, 152–53
International Bill of Rights, 139, 140,
152, 153–54
International Criminal Court (ICC),
148–49
international peace and, 142
UN General Assembly, 140, 143, 147,
148

Human rights, international human rights
regime *(continued)*
UN High Commissioner for Human
Rights, 147, 150
UN Human Rights Commission, 140,
147–48, 149–50, 151
Universal Declaration of Human Rights
(UDHR), 130, 131, 133, 139, 140,
141, 147
UN Security Council, 140, 148, 152,
153–54
U.S. relations, 142–43, 150, 151
Vienna Conference on Human Rights
(1993), 143, 145–47, 150, 161n.44
publications, 129, 150
white papers (1991), 129, 133, 142,
143, 154
scholarly debate, 7, 8, 330–31, 338
state sovereignty and, 133–34, 135, 137,
142, 144, 146, 148–49, 151–52,
152–53, 155
Tibet, 135
U.S./China relations
Chinese domestic policy, 293–94
democratization impact, 209–10
democratization transition, 218, 219
U.S. perspective, 197, 198–99
Vienna Conference on Human Rights
(1993), 143, 145–47, 150, 161n.44
achievements of, 146
weaknesses of, 147
Huntington, Samuel P., 7–8, 23, 34–35, 57,
137, 138–39, 144, 182, 224–25, 279,
286–90, 313–15
Hu Yaobang
Japan-China relations, 102–3
removal of, 79

Ibrahim, Anwar, 179
Income distribution, 259, 262–63,
282n.14
India, 163
democratic peace
antidemocratic campaign, 238, 240
Pakistan and, 227, 228
Sri Lanka and, 227
territorial disputes, 171–72, 175, 188n.29
nation building and, 65–66
Indonesia, 181
Natuna Islands and, 167, 174–75
Institutional pluralism, 81–91
civil society emergence, 89–91
civic organizations, 89–90
danwei/unit system, 90
leisure time, 91
wealth accumulation, 91

Institutional pluralism *(continued)*
  legal reforms, 84–87
    administrative litigation, 84–85, 86*t*
    Administrative Litigation Law (ALL),
      84–85
    commercial litigation, 84, 85*t*
    Communist Party and, 84, 87
    National People's Congress (NPC),
      84–85
    professional growth, 85–87
  National People's Congress (NPC), 81–84,
    97n.17
    Communist Party and, 81–82, 83
    composition of, 82
    legal reforms, 84–85
    legislation of, 82–83
    mandatory retirement, 80
    as public forum, 83–84
    senior leadership and, 83
  village elections, 87–89
    Communist Party and, 87, 88–89
Intellectuals, nationalism support, 22, 23,
  30–37
  anti-American sentiment, 31, 32, 35–36,
    38–39
  capitalism and, 34
  communist ideology and, 31, 32, 33–34,
    36, 37
  Confucianism and, 32–33, 34–35
  culture and, 31–32, 34–37, 38–39
  economic reform and, 32, 35
  globalization, 35
  Islamic culture, 34–35
  leadership of, 30–31
  Marxism-Leninism, 33
  modernization and, 31–32, 34, 35–36, 38
  nativism, 36–37
  neoauthoritarianism, 31, 32–33
  neoconservatism, 33, 46n.41
  objectives of, 31
  social order and, 31, 32, 34
  state-led nationalism, 37
International Bill of Rights, 139, 140, 152,
  153–54
International Covenant on Civil and Political
  Rights (ICCPR), 129–30, 139, 140, 150,
  154, 267
International Covenant on Economic, Social
  and Cultural Rights (ICESCR), 129–30,
  135–36, 139, 140, 154, 267
International Criminal Court (ICC), 148–49
International Criminal Tribunal for Rwanda
  (ICTR), 153
International Criminal Tribunal for the
  Former Yugoslavia (ICTY),
  153–54

International human rights regime, 139–52
  Annan Doctrine, 151
  Asian regional conference (1993), 143–45
  Bangkok Declaration, 144–45, 146
  divide/conquer strategy, 145–46, 147, 149,
    150, 152–53
  international peace and, 142
  UN General Assembly, 140, 143, 147, 148
  UN High Commissioner for Human Rights,
    147, 150
  UN Human Rights Commission, 140,
    147–48, 149–50, 151
  Universal Declaration of Human Rights
    (UDHR), 130, 131, 133, 139, 140,
    141, 147
  UN Security Council, 140, 148, 152,
    153–54
  U.S. relations, 142–43, 150, 151
  Vienna Conference on Human Rights
    (1993), 143, 145–47, 150, 161n.44
  white paper publication (1991), 129, 133,
    142, 143, 154
International system
  democratic peace and, 305–6
    culture, 315
    democratization impact, 320–21,
      324–25
    realpolitik, 309, 310, 311, 312
  regional relations, 165, 166, 171, 180
  scholarly debate, 8–9, 330, 336
Iran, 179, 180
Ishihara, Shintaro, 171
Islamic culture, 34–35

Japan-China relations
  Chinese leadership, 106
  Chinese nationalism, 39, 67, 102–3
    war threat and, 107–9, 112, 114–15,
      118, 119, 120, 123
  democratic peace, 228, 229, 234–36,
    254n.15
    antidemocratic campaign, 239–40
  democratization future, 271–73, 280
  Japanese militarism, 106, 115
    nuclear armament, 100–101
  Manchuria invasion (1931–45), 102, 103,
    106
  Mao era, 100, 101–2, 103, 104
  Marco Polo Bridge incident (1937), 103, 185
  Marxism-Leninism, 100, 106, 122
  Nanjing massacre, 103
  Shimoneseki Treaty, 101–102, 113–14
  Taiwan, 163–64, 184–85
    cooperation, 181
    war threat, 104–5, 111, 112–13,
      119–20, 122, 123–24

Japan-China relations *(continued)*
  territorial disputes, 175–76
    Diaoyu Islands, 167, 169–71, 184
    grant suspension, 171
    Senkaku Islands, 166, 167, 169–71, 184
  United States and
    Japan alliance, 116, 120
    Japan security treaty, 100–101
    military response, 121–22
    perspective of, 99, 104, 110, 111
    Ryukyus Islands, 101
    Senkaku Islands, 101
  war threat
    Chinese democratization, 105–6, 109,
      112, 113, 114, 115, 117–18, 119,
      121, 124
    Chinese expansionism, 108–11, 120
    Chinese hegemony, 107, 108, 113, 114,
      115, 116–17, 118–19, 121, 123
    Chinese nationalism, 107–9, 112,
      114–15, 118, 119, 120, 123
    conservative chauvinism, 106, 107–8,
      109–10, 113, 118, 120, 122, 123,
      124
    economic affairs, 107, 117, 127n.56
    nuclear armament, 100–101, 119
    Taiwan and, 104–5, 111, 112–13,
      119–20, 122, 123–24
Japan That Can Say No, The, 39
Japan Youth Federation, 170
Jiang Zemin
  Japan-China relations, 119
  nationalism, 26, 27, 42–43, 67
  U.S./China policy, 285, 292–300

Kant, Immanuel, 5–6, 224, 225, 227, 229–36
Kato, Koichi, 115–16
Kim Dae Jung, 113, 155
Kissinger, Henry, 7, 101

Le Duan, 101
Lee Kuan Yew, 110
Lee Teng-hui, 4, 60, 65, 109, 123, 269–70
Legal reforms
  administrative litigation, 84–85, 86t
  Administrative Litigation Law (ALL),
    84–85
  commercial litigation, 84, 85t
  Communist Party and, 84, 87
  democratization impact, 319–20
  institutional pluralism, 84–87
  National People's Congress (NPC), 84–85
  professional growth, 85–87
Leisure time, 91
Li Hongzhi, 4–5
Li Lanqing, 180

Lilley, James, 23
Lin Biao, 53
Li Peng, 285
Li Ruihuan, 29
Li Tenghui, 4–5
Liu Kang, 36
Li Xiguang, 36
Lumput, Kuala, 182

Malaysia, 179
  territorial disputes, 175
    Spratly Islands, 166, 182
Manchuria invasion (1931–45), 102, 103, 106
Mao Zedong
  Japan-China relations, 100, 101–2, 103,
    104
  leisure time, 91
  nationalism, 26
  political repression, 76–78, 92
  regional relations, 163, 164
  revolutionary policy, 53
Marco Polo Bridge incident (1937), 103, 185
Marxism-Leninism
  Japan-China relations, 100, 106, 122
  nationalism and, 25, 26, 28–29, 33
  patriotism and, 28–29
May Fourth Movement (1919), 22, 31
Michnik, Adam, 7
Military affairs
  democratic peace and, 235–36, 308–9,
    310–11, 312
    antidemocratic campaign, 236–37
    war threat, 306–7
  democratization future, 267–68, 270,
    280–81
  nuclear armament, 274, 275–76
  Japan-China relations
    Chinese chauvinism, 106, 107–8, 109–
      10, 113, 118, 120, 122, 123, 124
    Chinese democratization, 105–6, 109,
      112, 113, 114, 115, 117–18, 119,
      121, 124
    Chinese expansionism, 108–11, 120
    Chinese hegemony, 107, 108, 113, 114,
      115, 116–17, 118–19, 121, 123
    Chinese nationalism, 107–9, 112,
      114–15, 118, 119, 120, 123
    economic affairs, 107, 117, 127n.56
    nuclear armament, 100–101, 119
    Taiwan and, 104–5, 111, 112–13,
      119–20, 122, 123–24
  nation building
    democratization impact, 63, 64, 68,
      73n.36, 73n.44
    power implications, 59, 61–62, 72n.22
    U.S. perspective, 49, 50, 51, 56, 70

Military affairs *(continued)*
nuclear armament
Comprehensive Test Ban Treaty, 65–66,
178–79
democratic peace and, 310–11
democratization future, 274, 275–76
India, 65–66
Japan-China relations, 100–101, 119
Nuclear Nonproliferation Treaty, 65–66
regional relations, 166, 171–72, 178–79
regional relations
budget, 164
expenditures, 164
nuclear armament, 166, 171–72, 178–79
weapon development, 165
weapon purchases, 164–65
U.S./China relations
Chinese foreign policy, 284, 285, 298,
299–300
democratization impact, 208–9
democratization transition, 218
U.S. foreign policy, 288, 301
U.S. perspective, 49, 50, 51, 56, 70,
197–98
weapon development, 165, 202
Milosevic, Slobodan, 5, 8, 9–10, 153–54
Ministry of Broadcast, Film, and Television,
28
Ministry of Culture, 28
Mischief Reef
nation building and, 61
Philippines, 166–67, 172–73, 179
Miyako Island, 171
Modernization, nationalism and, 40, 41
intellectuals and, 31–32, 34, 35–36, 38
Mongolia, 65

Nanjing massacre, 103
National essence, 30
National interests, 228, 231, 232–33, 305,
306
democratization impact, 317–18
Nationalism
affirmative nationalism, 40, 47n.62
aggressive nationalism, 40, 43, 47n.62
anti-American sentiment
government and, 22, 23, 28, 37, 38–39,
42–43
intellectuals and, 31, 32, 35–36, 38–39
anti-Japanese sentiment, 39, 67, 102–3
assertive nationalism, 40, 43, 47n.62
authoritarianism and, 22–23, 38
neoauthoritarianism, 31, 32–33
Chinese embassy bombing (Yugoslavia), 3–
4, 8–10, 17n.3, 22, 67, 99, 106, 151–
52, 186, 262, 324
communist ideology, 21, 23, 25, 30

Nationalism, communist ideology *(continued)*
intellectuals and, 31, 32, 33–34, 36, 37
Communist Party, 26, 27–28, 29, 37, 38,
41, 42
confident nationalism, 40
Confucianism
government support of, 30
intellectual support of, 32–33, 34–35
culture and
government support of, 24, 29–30, 37
intellectual support of, 31–32, 34–37,
38–39
patriotism and, 24, 29–30
defensive nationalism, 42–43
democratic peace and, 306, 307–8
culture, 313–14
democratization impact, 319, 321–24,
327n.36
democratization possibility, 316
democratization future, 262, 264–65, 268,
272, 279–80
economic reform
government and, 26, 28
intellectuals and, 32, 35
emergence of, 24–25
culture, 24
foreign imperialism, 25
internal crisis, 25, 41
ethnic nationalism, 41–42, 322–23
government support, 22, 24–30
anti-American sentiment, 22, 23, 28, 37,
38–39, 42–43
Communist Party, 26, 27–28, 29, 37,
38, 41, 42
Confucianism and, 30
culture and, 24, 29–30, 37, 38–39
economic reform and, 26, 28
Maoism, 26
Marxism-Leninism, 25, 26
nationalism emergence, 24–25
nationalism ideology, 21, 23–24, 26–27
patriotism, 26, 27–30, 37
patriotism education, 27–30, 37
social order and, 23, 25, 30
state-led nationalism, 27
ideology of, 21, 23–24, 26–27
intellectual support, 22, 23, 30–37
anti-American sentiment, 31, 32, 35–36,
38–39
capitalism and, 34
communist ideology and, 31, 32, 33–34,
36, 37
Confucianism and, 32–33, 34–35
culture and, 31–32, 34–37, 38–39
economic reform and, 32, 35
globalization, 35
Islamic culture, 34–35

Nationalism, intellectual support *(continued)*
  leadership of, 30–31
  Marxism-Leninism, 33
  modernization and, 31–32, 34, 35–36,
    38
  nativism, 36–37
  neoauthoritarianism, 31, 32–33
  neoconservatism, 33, 46n.41
  objectives of, 31
  social order and, 31, 32, 34
  state-led nationalism, 37
  inward/outward directed, 40–43
  affirmative nationalism, 40, 47n.62
  aggressive nationalism, 40, 43, 47n.62
  assertive nationalism, 40, 43, 47n.62
  confident nationalism, 40
  defensive nationalism, 42–43
  ethnic nationalism, 41–42, 322–23
  inward directed, 25, 41, 42, 43
  nationalistic universalism, 40
  state nationalism, 40, 322–23
  Japan-China relations, 39, 67, 102–3
  war threat and, 107–9, 112, 114–15,
    118, 119, 120, 123
  Marxism-Leninism and, 25, 26, 28–29, 33
  modernization and, 40, 41
  intellectuals and, 31–32, 34, 35–36, 38
  neoauthoritarianism, 31, 32–33
  neoconservatism, 33, 46n.41
  as patriotism, 21–24
  culture and, 24, 29–30
  education for, 27–30, 37
  government support of, 26, 27–30, 37
  national essence, 30
  vs. Marxism, 28–29
  pragmatic concerns, 38
  regional relations and, 164, 183–86
  social Darwinism and, 39
  social order
  government and, 23, 25, 30
  intellectuals and, 31, 32, 34
  state-led
  government and, 27
  intellectuals and, 37
  state nationalism, 40, 322–23
  Tiananmen Square incident, 22, 23, 25, 26,
    31, 33, 37
  U.S./China relations, 195–96, 205
National People's Congress (NPC)
  democratization future, 260
  soft authoritarianism
  Communist Party and, 81–82, 83
  composition of, 82
  emergence of, 81–84, 97n.17
  legal reforms, 84–85
  legislation of, 82–83
  mandatory retirement, 80

National People's Congress (NPC) *(continued)*
  as public forum, 83–84
  senior leadership and, 83
  territorial disputes, 166, 169
Nation building
  authoritarianism and
  domestic/foreign policy linkage, 50,
    51–52, 55, 56–57, 66–68
  U.S. perspective, 49, 50–52, 69
  communist ideology and
  domestic/foreign policy linkage, 50, 51,
    52–54, 56–57, 71n.9
  U.S. perspective, 50–51
  democratization impact, 63–69
  Diaoyu Islands, 65, 66
  economic affairs, 63, 68
  India, 65–66
  military affairs, 63, 64, 68, 73n.36,
    73n.44
  nationalism, 66–67
  peace, 63–64
  Philippines, 66
  positive effects, 68–70
  Taiwan, 64–65, 69, 73n.46
  territorial disputes, 64–66, 69, 70
  transition period, 63–64
  U.S. perspective, 68–69
Diaoyu Islands
  democratization impact, 65, 66
  power implications, 60–61
domestic/foreign policy linkage
  aggression, 50, 51–52, 54
  authoritarianism, 50, 51–52, 55, 56–57,
    66–68
  communist ideology, 50, 51, 52–54, 56–
    57, 71n.9
  Communist Party, 50, 51, 52–53, 56
  domestic behavior, 52
  economic affairs, 55–56
  Five Principles of Peaceful Coexistence,
    54, 71n.7
  ideological domination, 50, 51, 52–54,
    71n.9
  leadership control, 52
  revolutionary policy, 53, 71n.6
  Tiananmen Square incident, 55, 56
economic affairs
  democratization impact, 63, 68
  domestic/foreign policy linkage, 55–56
  power implications, 58
  U.S. perspective, 49, 50–51, 56, 70
Hong Kong, 60, 62–63
military affairs
  democratization impact, 63, 64, 68,
    73n.36, 73n.44
  power implications, 59, 61–62, 72n.22
  U.S. perspective, 49, 50, 51, 56, 70

Nation building *(continued)*
  power implications, 56–63
    Chinese glory, 56
    Diaoyu Islands, 60–61
    economic affairs, 58
    Hong Kong, 60, 62–63
    military affairs, 59, 61–62, 72n.22
    Mischief Reef, 61
    political affairs, 58–59
    Spratly Islands, 60–61
    state sovereignty, 62, 72n.30
    Taiwan, 60, 61–63, 72n.24
    territorial disputes, 57–58, 60–63, 71n.17
  state sovereignty, 62, 72n.30
  Taiwan
    democratization impact, 64–65, 69,
      73n.46
    power implications, 60, 61–63, 72n.24
    U.S. perspective, 60
  territorial disputes
    democratization impact, 64–66, 69, 70
    Diaoyu Islands, 60–61, 65, 66
    Hong Kong, 60, 62–63
    India, 65–66
    Mischief Reef, 61
    Philippines, 66
    power implications, 57–58, 60–63, 71n.17
    Spratly Islands, 60–61
    Taiwan, 60, 61–63, 64–65, 69, 72n.24,
      73n.46
  U.S. perspective
    authoritarianism, 49, 50–52, 69
    communist ideology, 50–51
    containment, 57
    democratization, 63, 68–69, 72n.32
    economic affairs, 49, 50–51, 56, 70
    Hong Kong, 60
    military affairs, 49, 50, 51, 56, 70
    Taiwan, 60
Nativism, 36–37
Natuna Islands, 167, 174–75
Neoauthoritarianism, 31, 32–33
Neoconservatism, 33, 46n.41
Neo-liberal institutionalism, 260–61
New world order
  democratization impact, 213
  democratization transition, 218–19
  U.S. perspective, 197, 202–3
Nicaragua, 227, 228
Nixon, Richard, 7, 101
Nobuske, Kishi, 100
Nuclear armament
  Comprehensive Test Ban Treaty, 65–66,
    178–79
  democratic peace and, 310–11
  democratization future, 274, 275–76

Nuclear armament *(continued)*
  India, 65–66
  Japan-China relations, 100–101, 119
  Nuclear Nonproliferation Treaty, 65–66
  regional relations, 166, 171–72, 178–79

Oil exploration, 166, 167, 172
Olympics (2000), 165, 187n.5
Opium War (1840–42), 25
Organic Law of the Village Committees of
  the PRC (1987), 87
Outlaw behavior
  democratization impact, 213
  democratization transition, 218
  U.S. perspective, 197, 202

Paracel Islands, 166, 172
Patriotism, 21–24
  culture and, 24, 29–30
  education for, 27–30, 37
  government support of, 26, 27–30, 37
  national essence, 30
  vs. Marxism, 28–29
  See also Nationalism
Peng Zhen
  National People's Congress (NPC), 82
  village elections, 87
People's Liberation Army (PLA)
  Tiananmen Square incident, 22
  weapon development, 165
Pham Van Dong, 101
Philippines, 176
  Mischief Reef, 166–67, 172–73, 179
  nation building and, 66
  Spratly Islands, 166–67, 172–74, 182, 184
Political Consultative Conference (PCC), 80
Political reform
  Chinese domestic policy, 291–97, 298–99
  scholarly debate, 3, 337
  See also Soft authoritarianism
Political repression
  Chinese domestic policy, 285, 290–95
  democratic peace and, 318–19, 320
  soft authoritarianism, 75–79, 92
    conservative backlash, 75–76
    counter-revolutionary incarceration, 75–
      78, 96n.3
    counter-revolutionary prosecution, 75–
      78, 96n.3
    Deng era, 75–78, 92
    Mao era, 76–78, 92
Power implications
  democratic peace, 237–38
  nation building, 56–63
    Chinese glory, 56
    Diaoyu Islands, 60–61

Power implications *(continued)*
  economic affairs, 58
  Hong Kong, 60, 62–63
  military affairs, 59, 61–62, 72n.22
  Mischief Reef, 61
  political affairs, 58–59
  Spratly Islands, 60–61
  state sovereignty, 62, 72n.30
  Taiwan, 60, 61–63, 72n.24
  territorial disputes, 57–58, 60–63,
    71n.17
  U.S./China relations
    democratization impact, 203–4, 211–13
  U.S. perspective, 197, 201
Preval, René, 166

Qiao Shi, 82, 285

Rabe, John, 103
Racism, 212
Rafsanjani, Hashemi, 180
Ramos, Fidel, 172–73, 184
Realpolitik, 305, 306, 308–13
  Chinese power, 312
  economic affairs, 309, 310–11
  human rights, 309, 311, 312
  international system, 309, 310, 311, 312
  military affairs, 308–9, 310–11, 312
  nuclear armament, 310–11
  state sovereignty, 309, 312
  trade relations, 309, 310–11
Regional relations
  alliance system, 179–80
    Burma, 179, 180
    Iran, 179, 180
    Russia, 179–80
    tensions in, 181–83
  Asian currency crisis, 179
  Australia, 179
  Olympics (2000), 165, 187n.5
  Burma
    alliance system, 179, 180
    ASEAN admission, 176
    State Law and Order Restoration
      Commission, 165, 171, 180
  Chinese hegemony and, 167–68, 183
  Confucianism and, 182–83
  cooperation
    Indonesia, 181
    Japan, 181
    Taiwan, 181
    United States, 181
    Vietnam, 180–81
  democratization and, 164, 183–86,
    191n.107
  economic affairs, 163–64

Regional relations *(continued)*
  future of, 183–86
  Guatemala, 166, 177–78
  Haiti, 166
  India, 163
  Indonesia, 181
  international assertion
    Guatemala peacekeeping mission, 166
    Haiti peacekeeping mission, 166
    Nuclear Non-Proliferation Treaty, 166
    Olympics (2000), 165
    State Law/Order Restoration Commission
      (Burma), 165, 171, 180
  Iran, 179, 180
  Korea, 163
  leadership and
    Deng era, 163–64
    Mao era, 163, 164
  Malaysia, 179
  military modernization
    budget, 164
    expenditures, 164
    weapon development, 165
    weapon purchases, 164–65
  nationalism and, 164, 183–86
  nuclear armament, 166, 171–72, 178–79
  provinces, 185
  Russia, 179–80, 182
  Soviet Union, 163, 164
    weapon purchases, 164–65
  Taiwan, 163
    cooperation, 181
  Thailand, 181–82
  Tibet, 163
  United States, 163
    cooperation, 181
    weapon development, 165
  Vietnam, 163
    ASEAN admission, 176
    cooperation, 180–81
  See also Association of Southeast Asian
    Nations (ASEAN); Japan-China
    relations; *specific countries*;
    Territorial disputes
Rising power. *See* Power implications
Robinson, Mary, 150
Rule of law, 204–5, 231
Russia, 179–80, 182
  democratic peace, 228
Ryukyus Islands, 101

Senkaku Islands, 101
  Japan and, 166, 167, 169–71, 184
Sheng Hong, 39
Shimoneseki Treaty, 101–102, 113–14
Siazon, Domingo, 182

Social order
government and, 23, 25, 30
intellectuals and, 31, 32, 34
Soft authoritarianism
civil society emergence
civic organizations, 89–90
danwei/unit system, 90
institutional pluralism, 89–91
leisure time, 91
wealth accumulation, 91
Communist Party and
educational qualifications, 79, 80–81,
97n.13
elections, 79–80, 92–93
impact on, 93–95
leadership norms, 79–81
leadership purges, 79
legal reforms, 84, 87
mandatory retirement, 79, 80, 96n.9
National People's Congress (NPC), 81–
82, 83
village elections, 87, 88–89
Deng era
leadership norms, 79–81
leisure time, 91
political repression, 75–78, 92
elections, 79–80, 92–93
village, 87–89
implications of, 91–95
institutional norms, 79–81
educational qualifications, 79, 80–81,
97n.13
elections, 79–80, 92–93
leadership purges, 79
mandatory retirement, 79, 80, 96n.9
National People's Congress (NPC), 80
Political Consultative Conference
(PCC), 80
institutional pluralism, 81–91
civil society emergence, 89–91
legal reforms, 84–87
National People's Congress (NPC), 81–
84, 97n.17
village elections, 87–89
legal reforms
administrative litigation, 84–85, 86*t*
Administrative Litigation Law (ALL),
84–85
commercial litigation, 84, 85*t*
Communist Party and, 84, 87
institutional pluralism, 84–87
National People's Congress (NPC), 84–
85
professional growth, 85–87
Mao era
leisure time, 91

Soft authoritarianism, Mao era *(continued)*
political repression, 76–78, 92
National People's Congress (NPC)
Communist Party and, 81–82, 83
composition of, 82
emergence of, 81–84, 97n.17
legal reforms, 84–85
legislation of, 82–83
mandatory retirement, 80
as public forum, 83–84
senior leadership and, 83
political repression decline, 75–79, 92
conservative backlash, 75–76
counter-revolutionary incarceration, 75–
78, 96n.3
counter-revolutionary prosecution, 75–
78, 96n.3
Deng era, 75–78, 92
Mao era, 76–78, 92
U.S. perspective, 74–75, 95
village elections
Communist Party and, 87, 88–89
institutional pluralism, 87–89
Sovereignty. *See* State sovereignty
Soviet Union, 163, 164
communist ideology, 50
Russia, 179–80, 182
democratic peace, 228
weapon purchases, 164–65
Spratly Islands, 60–61, 176, 177, 178
Brunei and, 166
Malaysia and, 166, 182
nation building and, 60–61
Philippines and, 166–67, 172–74, 182, 184
Taiwan and, 166
United States and, 166, 172
Vietnam and, 166, 172
State Education Commission, 28, 29
State government
bureaucracy
democratization impact, 206–7
democratization transition, 218
corruption in, 263–64, 276, 318
nationalism and
anti-American sentiment, 22, 23, 28, 37,
38–39, 42–43
Communist Party, 26, 27–28, 29, 37,
38, 41, 42
Confucianism, 30
culture, 24, 29–30, 37, 38–39
economic reform and, 26, 28
emergence of, 24–25
ideology of, 21, 23–24, 26–27
Maoism, 26
Marxism-Leninism, 25, 26
patriotism, 26, 27–30, 37

State government, nationalism and *(continued)*
  social order, 23, 25, 30
  state-led, 27, 37
  state nationalism, 40, 322–23
  support of, 22, 24–30
  See also Authoritarianism; Chinese
    Communist Party (CCP); Soft
    authoritarianism
State Law and Order Restoration Commission
  (Burma), 165, 171, 180
State Peace and Development Council
  (Burma), 165
State sovereignty
  democratic peace and, 305–6
  democratization impact, 321
  realpolitik, 309, 312
  human rights and, 133–34, 135, 137, 142,
    144, 146, 148–49, 151–52, 152–53, 155
  nation building, 62, 72n.30
Sun Yat-sen, 30

Taiwan
  democratization future and, 268, 269–70, 281
  Japan-China relations, 163–64, 184–85
    cooperation, 181
    war threat, 104–5, 111, 112–13, 119–
      20, 122, 123–24
  nation building
    democratization impact, 64–65, 69,
      73n.46
    power implications, 60, 61–63, 72n.24
    U.S. perspective, 60
  territorial disputes, 166, 167, 176
    nation building and, 60, 61–63, 64–65,
      69, 72n.24, 73n.46
    Spratly Islands, 166
  U.S./China relations, 176
    democratization impact, 206, 211
    U.S. perspective, 60, 197, 198, 200
Technology, 229, 245
Territorial disputes
  Asian Regional Forum (ARF), 176, 230,
    236, 240, 270–71
  Australia, 175–76
  Brunei/Spratly Islands, 166
  democratization and, 64–66, 69, 70
  Diaoyu Islands, 166
    Japan, 167, 169–71, 184
    nation building and, 60–61, 65, 66
  Haiti, 177
  Hong Kong, 60, 62–63
  India, 171–72, 175, 188n.29
    nation building and, 65–66
  Indonesia/Natuna Islands, 167, 174–75
  Malaysia, 175
    Spratly Islands, 166, 182

Territorial disputes *(continued)*
  Mischief Reef
    nation building and, 61
    Philippines, 166–67, 172–73, 179
  Miyako Island, 171
  National People's Congress (NPC), 166, 169
  nation building and
    democratization impact, 64–66, 69, 70
    Diaoyu Islands, 60–61, 65, 66
    Hong Kong, 60, 62–63
    India, 65–66
    Mischief Reef, 61
    Philippines, 66
    power implications, 57–58, 60–63,
      71n.17
    Spratly Islands, 60–61
    Taiwan, 60, 61–63, 64–65, 69, 72n.24,
      73n.46
  Natuna Islands/Indonesia, 167, 174–75
  oil exploration, 166, 167, 172
  Paracel Islands, 166
    Vietnam, 166, 172
  Philippines, 176
    Mischief Reef, 166–67, 172–73, 179
    nation building and, 66
    Spratly Islands, 166–67, 172–74, 182,
      184
  reactions to
    accommodation, 167–68
    complaints, 168
    countermeasures, 168–69
  Senkaku Islands/Japan, 166, 167, 169–71, 184
  Spratly Islands, 176, 177, 178
    Brunei, 166
    Malaysia, 166, 182
    nation building and, 60–61
    Philippines, 166–67, 172–74, 182, 184
    Taiwan, 166
    United States, 166, 172
    Vietnam, 166, 172
  Taiwan, 166, 167, 176
    nation building and, 60, 61–63, 64–65,
      69, 72n.24, 73n.46
    Spratly Islands, 166
  United States, 175–76
    Spratly Islands, 166, 172
  Vietnam
    Paracel Islands, 166, 172
    Spratly Islands, 166, 172
  See also Japan-China relations; Regional
    relations; *specific countries*
Thailand, 181–82
Tiananmen Square incident (1989)
  domestic/foreign policy linkage, 55, 56
  nationalism and, 22, 23, 25, 26, 31, 33, 37
Tibet, 135, 163

Trade relations
  democratic peace and, 309, 310–11
  democratization future, 260–61, 273–75,
    276
  democratization impact, 210–11
  democratization transition, 218
  scholarly debate, 8, 331, 337
  U.S. perspective, 197, 199–200
Treaty of Nanking (1842), 23

Union to Protect the Diaoyu Islands, 22
United Nations
  High Commissioner for Human Rights,
    147, 150
  Human Rights Commission, 140, 147–48,
    149–50, 151
  Security Council, 140, 148, 152, 153–54
  Universal Declaration of Human Rights
    (UDHR), 130, 131, 133, 139, 140,
    141, 147
United States-China relations
  anti-American sentiment
    Chinese government and, 22, 23, 28,
      37, 38–39, 42–43
    democratic peace, 306, 308, 310
    intellectuals and, 31, 32, 35–36, 38–39
    scholarly debate, 10–11
  authority, 203–5
  bureaucracy
    democratization impact, 206–7
    democratization transition, 218
  conflict reduction, 195–97
  democratization future, 250–51, 273–78,
    279, 280, 281
    China perspective, 275–78
    Taiwan, 269–70
    U.S. perspective, 273–75
  democratization impact
    authority, 203–5
    bureaucracy, 206–7
    conflict reduction, 195–97
    economic affairs, 205, 210–11
    human rights, 209–10
    nationalism, 195–96, 205
    new world order, 213
    ·utlaw behavior, 213
    ⁻view, 195–97, 219–21
    ˑl system, 205–6
    ˑplications, 203–4, 211–13
    ˑ
         ˑ4–5
          ⁷–8

              ˑ1
               ˑ–69, 72n.32

          ₁96–97

United States-China relations, democratization
  transition *(continued)*
    bureaucracy, 218
    fiscal/political federalism, 217, 219
    gradual/above, 216, 219
    gradual/below, 214–15, 219
    human rights, 218, 219
    impact of, 218–19
    military affairs, 218
    new world order, 218–19
    outlaw behavior, 218
    political system, 218–19
    radical/above, 216–17, 218–19
    rapid/below, 215, 218–19
    trade relations, 218
    war threat, 219
  Diaoyu Islands, 198
  economic affairs
    democratization impact, 205, 210–11
    U.S. perspective, 49, 50–51, 56, 70,
      197, 199–200
  environment, 197
  Hong Kong, 60, 206
  human rights
    democratization impact, 209–10
    democratization transition, 218, 219
    U.S. perspective, 197, 198–99
  Japan-China relations
    Japan alliance, 116, 120
    Japan security treaty, 100–101
    military response, 121–22
    Ryukyus Islands, 101
    Senkaku Islands, 101
    U.S. perspective of, 99, 104, 110, 111
  Korea, 175–76, 198
  military affairs
    democratization transition, 218
    U.S. perspective, 49, 50, 51, 56, 70
    weapon development, 165, 202
  nationalism, 195–96, 205
  new world order
    democratization impact, 213
    democratization transition, 218–19
    U.S. perspective, 197, 202–3
  outlaw behavior
    democratization impact, 213
    democratization transition, 218
    U.S. perspective, 197, 202
  political system
    democratization impact, 205–6
    democratization transition, 218–19
  power implications
    democratization impact, 203–4, 211–13
    U.S. perspective, 197, 201
  racism, 212
  regional relations, 163
    cooperation, 181

United States-China relations, regional
relations *(continued)*
    weapon development, 165
rule of law, 204–5
Senkaku Islands, 198
social order, 207–8
soft authoritarianism and, 74–75, 95
Spratly Islands, 166, 172, 176
Taiwan, 176
    democratization impact, 206, 211
    U.S. perspective, 60, 197, 198, 200
trade relations
    democratization impact, 210–11
    democratization transition, 218
    U.S. perspective, 197, 199–200
U.S. perspective
    authoritarianism, 49, 50–52, 69
    communist ideology, 50–51
    democratization future, 273–75
    democratization impact, 63, 68–69,
        72n.32
    economic affairs, 49, 50–51, 56, 70,
        197, 199–200
    environment, 197
    Hong Kong, 60
    human rights, 197, 198–99
    military affairs, 49, 50, 51, 56, 70
    new world order, 197, 202–3
    outlaw behavior, 197, 202
    power implications, 197, 201
    Taiwan, 60, 197, 198, 200
    trade relations, 197, 199–200
    war threat, 197–98
war threat
    democratization impact, 208–9
    democratization transition, 219
    U.S. perspective, 197–98
United States-China relations, democratic
peace
anti-American sentiment, 306, 308, 310
antidemocratic campaign, 238–39
authoritarianism and
    culture, 314–15
    democratization impact, 318, 320–21
    democratization possibility, 315–17
Chile, 227, 228
Chinese power, 312
culture and, 305, 306, 308, 313–15, 329
    authoritarianism, 314–15
    economic affairs, 314
    human rights, 314
    international system, 315
    nationalism, 313–14
democratization impact, 317–25
    authoritarianism, 318, 320–21
    economic affairs, 319, 320
    government corruption, 318

United States-China relations, democratic
peace, democratization impact *(continued)*
    international system, 320–21, 324–25
    legal reform, 319–20
    national interests, 317–18
    nationalism, 319, 321–24, 327n.36
    political repression, 318–19, 320
    state sovereignty, 321
democratization possibility, 250–51, 315–17
    authoritarianism, 315–17
    nationalism, 316
economic affairs
    culture and, 314
    democratization impact, 319, 320
    realpolitik and, 309, 310–11
government corruption and, 318
Guatemala, 227, 228
human rights
    culture and, 314
    realpolitik and, 309, 311, 312
international system, 305–6
    culture and, 315
    democratization impact, 320–21, 324–25
    realpolitik and, 309, 310, 311, 312
legal reform, 319–20
military affairs, 308–9, 310–11, 312
national interests, 305, 306
    democratization impact, 317–18
nationalism, 306, 307–8
    culture and, 313–14
    democratization impact, 319, 321–24,
        327n.36
    democratization possibility, 316
Nicaragua, 227, 228
nuclear armament, 310–11
political repression
    democratization impact, 318–19, 320
realpolitik and, 305, 306, 308–13
    Chinese power, 312
    economic affairs, 309, 310–11
    human rights, 309, 311, 312
    international system, 309, 310, 311, 312
    military affairs, 308–9, 310–11, 312
    nuclear armament, 310–11
    state sovereignty, 309, 312
    trade relations, 309, 310–11
Russia, 228
state sovereignty, 305–6
    democratization impact, 321
    realpolitik and, 309, 312
trade relations, 309, 310–11
war threat, 306–7
United States-China relations, policy and
Chinese domestic/foreign policy linkage
    aggression, 50, 51–52, 54
    authoritarianism, 50, 51–52, 55, 56–5ʳ
        66–68

United States-China relations, policy and
(continued)
   communist ideology, 50, 51, 52–54, 56–
      57, 71n.9
   Communist Party, 50, 51, 52–53, 56
   domestic behavior, 52
   economic affairs, 55–56
   Five Principles of Peaceful Coexistence,
      54, 71n.7
   ideological domination, 50, 51, 52–54,
      71n.9
   leadership control, 52
   revolutionary policy, 53, 71n.6
   Tiananmen Square incident, 55, 56
Chinese domestic policy
   authoritarianism, 285, 290–93, 295–97
   economic affairs, 284, 290–91, 292,
      293, 296, 298–99
   human rights, 293–94
   nationalism, 299
   political reform, 291–97, 298–99
   political repression, 285, 290–95
   village elections, 294, 296
Chinese foreign policy
   authoritarianism and, 285, 297
   military affairs, 284, 285, 298, 299–300
   political repression and, 285
   U.S. hegemony and, 286
Chinese leadership
   Deng Xiaoping, 285, 290–92, 295, 297
   Jiang Zemin, 285, 292–300
relationship flux, 284
U.S. containment, 57, 285
   cultural theory and, 286–90
   democratic peace and, 249, 250, 251
U.S. domestic policy, 287, 288
U.S. engagement, 285–86
   democratic peace and, 248–50
   Japan and, 124
U.S. foreign policy, 300–302
   cooperation, 287–88
   military affairs, 288, 301
United States-China relations, scholarly
   debate
   ʾgreement on, 330–34
      conflict avoidance, 334
      ʾvironmental compliance, 331
      ʾn rights, 330–31
         ʾional relations analysis, 331–34
         ʾal system, 330
            ʾirs, 332
            ʾ1, 332–33
               ʾdations, 334
               ʾ330

                  10–11

United States-China relations, scholarly
   debate *(continued)*
   ASEAN, 336
   conflict avoidance, 3, 334, 335–36, 338
   democratic peace, 5–13, 337–38
   disagreement on, 334–38
      ASEAN, 336
      conflict avoidance, 335–36, 338
      democratic peace, 5–13, 337–38
      human rights, 338
      international system, 336
      nationalism, 335, 336–38
      policy recommendations, 334–35
      political reform, 337
      territorial disputes, 337
      trade relations, 337
   environmental compliance, 331
   human rights, 7, 8, 330–31, 338
   international relations analysis, 5, 331–34
   international system, 8–9, 330, 336
   military affairs, 4, 332
   nationalism, 3, 331, 332–33, 335, 336–38
   overview, 329–30, 338–41
   policy recommendations, 334–35
   political reform, 3, 337
   realism vs. idealism, 7–8
   territorial disputes, 330, 337
   trade relations, 8, 331, 337
   U.S. soft policy, 4, 11–13
Universality theory, 131–34, 143–47, 152–
   53, 158n.9

Vienna Conference on Human Rights (1993),
   143, 145–47, 150, 161n.44
   achievements of, 146
   weaknesses of, 147
Vietnam, 163
   ASEAN admission, 176
   cooperation, 180–81
   Paracel Islands, 166, 172
   Spratly Islands, 166, 172
Villa, Renato de, 173
Village elections
   Chinese domestic policy, 294, 296
   democratization future, 260
   soft authoritarianism
      Communist Party and, 87, 88–89
      institutional pluralism, 87–89

Wang Dan, 76
Wang Huning, 33
Wang Jingwei, 117
Wang Jisi, 35
Wang Xiaodong, 35, 37
Wan Li, 82
War threat. *See* Military affairs

Wealth accumulation, 91
Wei Jingsheng, 76
World Trade Organization (WTO), 10, 12–13,
    274–75, 276

Xiao Gongqin
    nationalism, 31, 33–34
    neoauthoritarianism, 33

Ye Jianying, 82
Yellow Emperor, 29–30
Yeltsin, Boris, 179
Yi Baoyun, 34

Yuan Hongbin, 31
Yugoslavia, Chinese embassy bombing, 3–4,
    8–10, 17n.3, 22, 67, 99, 106, 151–52,
    186, 262, 324

Zhang Zoulin, 106
Zhao Ziyang
    dismissal of, 79
    neoauthoritarianism, 33
Zhou Enlai
    Five Principles of Peaceful Coexistence, 54
    Japan-China relations, 101
    revolutionary policy, 53